720,47

WLM
160
CHE

Architects, city planners, and other design professionals have used theory
and research from psychology and other behavioral sciences to make their
work more responsive to the needs of people who use the buildings, parks,
and city streets the designers help to shape. *Applications of Environment–
Behavior Research* describes and analyzes 13 projects for which the final
plans were informed by social-scientific research. Using a common conceptual framework, author Paul Cherulnik considers a variety of settings,
including treatment facilities, public housing, offices, parks, neighborhoods, and city centers. Some of the cases utilize basic behavioral theory
or research, including classic studies in psychology and other disciplines,
whereas in other cases applied research was conducted specifically for the
purposes of the project in question.

0521337704

APPLICATIONS OF ENVIRONMENT–BEHAVIOR RESEARCH

Cambridge Series in Environment and Behavior

General Editors

Daniel Stokols
University of California, Irvine

Irwin Altman
University of Utah

APPLICATIONS OF ENVIRONMENT– BEHAVIOR RESEARCH

Case studies and analysis

PAUL D. CHERULNIK
University of Science and Arts of Oklahoma

CAMBRIDGE
UNIVERSITY PRESS

Published by the Press Syndicate of the University of Cambridge
The Pitt Building, Trumpington Street, Cambridge CB2 1RP
40 West 20th Street, New York, NY 10011-4211, USA
10 Stamford Road, Oakleigh, Melbourne 3166, Australia

First published 1993

Printed in the United States of America

Library of Congress Cataloging-in-Publication Data

Cherulnik, Paul D., 1941–
    Applications of environment-behavior research : case studies and
analysis / Paul D. Cherulnik.
        p.   cm. – (Cambridge series in environment and behavior)
    Includes index.
    ISBN 0-521-33189-7 (hc) – ISBN 0521-33770-4 (pbk.)
    1. Architecture—Environmental aspects—United States—Case
studies.   2. Environmental engineering—United States—Case studies.
    I. Title.   II. Series.
    NA2542.35.C74   1993
    720'.47–dc20   93-2760
                                                              CIP

A catalog record for this book is available from the British Library

ISBN 0-521-33189-7   hardback
ISBN 0-521-33770-4   paperback

To Donald Appleyard, whose work inspired me to study environmental–design research and whose untimely death left a void in the field that may never be filled.

CONTENTS

SERIES FOREWORD

In recent decades the relationship between human behavior and the physical environment has attracted researchers from the social sciences – psychology, sociology, geography, and anthropology – and from the environmental-design disciplines – architecture, urban and regional planning, and interior design. What is in many respects a new and exciting field of study has developed rapidly. Its multidisciplinary character has led to stimulation and cross-fertilization, on the one hand, and to confusion and difficulty in communication, on the other. Those involved have diverse intellectual styles and goals. Some are concerned with basic and theoretical issues; some, with applied real-world problems of environmental design.

This series offers a common meeting ground. It consists of short books on different topics of interest to all those who analyze environment–behavior links. We hope that the series will provide a useful introduction to the field for students, researchers, and practitioners alike and will facilitate its evolutionary growth as well.

Our goals are as follows: (1) to represent problems the study of which is relatively well established, with a reasonably substantial body of research and knowledge generated; (2) to recruit authors from a variety of disciplines with a variety of perspectives; (3) to ensure that they not only summarize work on their topics but also set forth a "point of view," if not a theoretical orientation – we want the books not only to serve as texts but also to advance the field intellectually – and (4) to produce books useful to a broad range of students and other readers from different disciplines and with different levels of formal professional training. Course instructors will be able to select different combinations of books to meet their particular curricular needs.

Irwin Altman
Daniel Stokols

PREFACE

My interest in environment–behavior studies began quite by accident. Roger Stough, a colleague at the College of Charleston, introduced me to a visiting friend, Ralph Taylor. We talked in Roger's office about applying social psychology to important problems and testing its theories in the real world. Not long afterward, in 1980, Roger and Abe Wandersman, of the University of South Carolina, coordinated the 11th annual conference of the Environmental Design Research Association (EDRA 11) in Charleston and gave me an opportunity to participate in the conference. I have been hooked ever since.

For quite some time, my involvement in the field was limited to teaching environmental psychology and dabbling in research on environmental perception using traditional social-psychological methods. It was that teaching assignment more than anything else that convinced me that applications such as those described in this volume deserve more recognition than they have received, to the credit of both environmental-design research (EDR) and the science on which it is based. It seemed to me that students were missing the excitement of seeing successful applications of the research and theory they were studying and the theory and research were not being accorded the ultimate validation warranted by their successful application.

Almost 10 years ago I decided that a collection such as the case studies presented here could make a useful contribution toward correcting that oversight. That decision was shaped by my exposure to Rich Wener's NEA-sponsored exhibit of EDR "success stories" at an EDRA conference and the further information about those cases he so kindly provided afterward. It was also shaped by my participation in a National Endowment for the Humanities (NEH) summer seminar at Columbia University in 1983, where the brilliant urban historian Ken Jackson showed me the exciting possibilities of taking scholarship to a wider audience.

Any success I may have achieved in this effort is due in large part to those who have helped me along the way. Irv Altman and Dan Stokols, the editors of this series of books, helped me to reshape the entire project gradually into something far more interesting and useful than that which I first proposed to them, and they were patient enough to wait for me to catch on. Intramural research grants from Susquehanna University and Southeast Missouri State University made it possible for me to travel to the sites of many of the projects I have written about, and to others I was not able to include. The libraries at those schools, as well as the libraries I visited at Andrews University (the location of the invaluable collection of the Environmental Action Group [TEAG] and the sponsor of recent book exhibits at EDRA conferences),the State University of New York at Buffalo, the University of Michigan, and Columbia University, and the authors and publishers of the many reference works listed in chapter 16 made it possible for me to study many of the documents on which this book is based.

Of course, all of the environmental-design researchers who created this body of cases were the principal sources of inspiration and information for this book. Many of them and their institutions also gave generous assistance and encouragement throughout the project. Rich Wener supplied copies of his postoccupancy evaluations (POEs) for the federal Metropolitan Correctional Centers, Pat Kaya of Kaplan McLaughlin Diaz sent copies of drawings, Craig Zimring sent a copy of his follow-up POE report, and Administrative Officer Les Glenn arranged for me to tour the Contra Costa County Main Detention Facility. Jan Carpman allowed me a lengthy interview over lunch in Ann Arbor and provided copies of many documents, and Toni Sheers of the Public Relations Office took me on a tour of the new University of Michigan Hospital. William Weitzer of the University of Massachusetts provided a rare copy of the Belchertown State School report, and Jerome Feldstein, the director of psychology, took me on a tour of Belchertown State School. Sam Sloan sent me important documents and spent valuable time on the telephone, and Walter Kleeman sent documents and a helpful letter about the Seattle Federal Aviation Administration building project.

Officials at Trinity College provided useful information about the Jones Dormitory redesign there. Michael Bakos of the firm Architecture-Research-Construction (ARC) in Cleveland provided many documents and helpful letters about ARC's work on Ward 8 of Cleveland State Hospital. Margaret Lundin of Project for Public Spaces helped me to acquire documents describing that firm's research and the Exxon Minipark redesign work. Architect Jeff Oberdorfer of Santa Cruz, California, gave generous help with my research on Donald Appleyard's "livable streets" work (although I was able to give Jeff's important work only a brief mention in the final writing). Oscar Newman responded thoughtfully to my inquiry about his defensible-space research and design work. Joe Valadez supplied documents and spent a good part of a day in Cambridge helping me to do justice to his work in Macul. Ken Craik took me on a tour of the Environmental Simulation Laboratory at Berkeley (on a trip financed by a grant from the Southern Regional Education Board), and Laurie Glass, the publications officer of the Institute of Urban and Regional Development at Berkeley, helped me to obtain the documents I needed for the chapter on the development of San Francisco's high-rise zoning regulations. Rick Chenoweth helped me with the chapter on the Wisconsin State Riverway project with documents and a lengthy interview in his office in Madison.

Drafts of several chapters benefited from the comments of those whose work was being described. I owe a great debt to Rich Wener, Jan Carpman, Sam

Sloan, Andy Baum, Michael Bakos, Bob Sommer, Skip Holahan, and Rick Chenoweth for their thoughtful advice.

The quality of the entire manuscript was improved greatly through the assistance of those at Cambridge University Press: editor Julia Hough and production editor Andrée Lockwood.

Last, but not least, my wife Beverly put up with numerous "vacations" planned around visits to sites of EDR projects and endless "conversations" about "the book." I hope that her forbearance and support and the help of all those who were named earlier, as well as those whose names were inadvertently omitted, are justified by what I was finally able to accomplish. The limitations of the final product are my responsibility alone.

PART I
INTRODUCTION

1
AN APPROACH TO
ENVIRONMENTAL DESIGN

Environmental-design research

The subject of this volume is a particular approach to environmental design and planning, the decision-making processes that shape the physical forms of our rooms, buildings, communities, and nations by influencing what people build and how they act in the physical environment. In all its various forms, this approach is distinguished by the explicit consideration it gives to the needs and preferences of the people who are destined to use those physical settings.

For a very long time, people have relied on the good judgment or good taste of trained professionals who are delegated the authority to make design and planning decisions for them. Those designers and planners differ widely in the attention they give to the needs of everyday users of the physical environment. Some fulfill their professional obligations by concentrating on the use of the technical expertise they have acquired, including their knowledge of materials, structural stresses, and traditional devices for solving the problems left to them. According to the well-known architect Philip Johnson, for example, "the job of the architect is to create beautiful buildings; that's all" (Sommer, 1976, p. 4).

Such an approach may be sufficient to please the designer's or planner's clients, especially if they defer to a great reputation such as Johnson's, but it seems to give little consideration to the needs of the building's users, especially if those needs go beyond aesthetics to such concerns as finding their way around the building, having enough privacy at their workstations, or being comfortable in their surroundings. Fortunately, some design and planning professionals do recognize and attempt to serve the needs of users. Another noted architect, Mies van der Rohe, designed a headquarters building for the Seagram Corporation in New York City in 1958. In front of that building, he designed a small public plaza consisting primarily of two rectangular pools bordered by low, broad, flat-topped stone walls. Those walls became such a popular place for office workers and passersby to sit, watching people and eating their lunches, that they provided William H. Whyte with the inspiration and the initial opportunity to study systematically the determinants of the use of such public spaces, leading to an eventual decision to revise the city's zoning laws to require developers to construct public plazas that people would be likely to use and enjoy (see chapter 9).

3

Over the past several decades, environmental-design researchers have gradually introduced what seems a surer method of taking user needs and preferences into account in design and planning decisions. It *requires* decision makers to raise questions about the needs and preferences of prospective users, to seek verifiable answers to those questions, to incorporate features based on those answers into the final design or plan, and then to evaluate the resulting physical setting for the degree to which the targeted user needs and preferences are actually satisfied.

This new approach to environmental design and planning has been characterized in many ways by practitioners and analysts. Holahan and Wandersman (1987), stressing the role of physical settings in helping people to reach specific goals, have used the phrase "proactive intervention" to describe the process of user-needs-based design. Moore (1987) has suggested that design be defined "in the broadest sense, [as] the application of knowledge [gained through research] to the solution of real-world problems in the everyday physical environment" (p. 1,383). Sommer (1974) has described an evolutionary design process in which, instead of building, for example, all the needed classrooms or prison cells at one time, a small number will be built, and then evaluated, and the results of the evaluation will be incorporated into the design for the next batch, and so on. And, finally, Osmond (1970) has suggested as a model for environmental design and planning the airplane designer's motto: "Draw 'em, build 'em, test 'em, fly 'em, scrap 'em."

Whatever definition or analogy or combination one chooses, the important point is the contrast between environmental-design research and the traditional authoritative approach to design and planning that it seeks to replace. First, the behavioral needs of users are made explicit, their dependence on the physical setting is determined objectively, the eventual design or plan incorporates physical or policy elements that are identified in the course of that determination, and the efficiency of the design or plan is evaluated systematically, with the results being fed forward into subsequent design or planning decisions. It is the purpose of this volume to describe and evaluate the past accomplishments, present status, and future prospects of environmental-design research through detailed examination of specific design and planning projects in which it has played a prominent role.

The case-study approach

The original goal of this book, simply put, was to publicize the contributions that environmental-design research has made to environmental design and planning. In teaching environmental psychology, I was struck by the lack of emphasis in textbooks on actual applications of the theories, research results, and research techniques that had been documented in such great detail. Long chapters on theories and research findings either contained brief mentions of relevant applications or ended with separate brief sections describing examples of applications. That presentation was in stark contrast to my own view that those applications constituted the most exciting aspects of the field, because of their actual impact on places and on people's lives (evident even in the brief descriptions provided), and because of their value as the ultimate tests of the validity of generic theories and research findings. For both those reasons, they seemed to deserve much more attention than they had received.

None of this is intended to deny the value of gaining knowledge for its own sake. Basic research and theory have made significant contributions to our understanding of environment–behavior relationships and will continue to do so. Some would go so far as to argue that basic research and theory ultimately have made possible applications such as those described in this volume. On the other hand, it seems just as clear that basic research and theory cannot simply be transposed onto specific environmental settings by designers or planners. Therefore, the importance of applications seemed to warrant separate and detailed consideration.

The plan for accomplishing that goal was to present detailed case studies of actual applications or projects. That approach was chosen for several reasons. The first was the belief that the application of knowledge about environment–behavior relationships in environmental-design research is a process in which the local context or the setting for which design or planning decisions are being made must be taken into account. Whereas theories or research findings might be applicable to a variety of settings and might be used as the basis for generic guidelines for classrooms, college dormitories, or jails, a successful design or plan must also take into account the specific history, climate, and population of the setting in which it is to be implemented. Detailed case studies of environmental-design research (EDR) applications for specific settings are more likely to make that point clear than are less detailed reviews of EDR applications for categories of settings, if that is in fact the case.

Historically, there has been a well-known division of opinion on this issue. In a series of articles published in the *Personality and Social Psychology Bulletin,* Irwin Altman (1976a,b) argued for the development of general theories of environment–behavior relationships, and Harold Proshansky (1976) maintained that theory-building research, particularly when carried out in context-free laboratory settings and with a truncated temporal perspective, may produce generalizations about environment–behavior relationships that fail to take into account influential sociohistorical characteristics of the specific settings to which practitioners may wish to apply them. In agreement with Proshansky's view, Schneekloth (1987) has made a strong argument for the uniqueness of each application or intervention based on environment–behavior theory or research. A designer, she also pointed out that each project takes place in a specific context, subject to the operation of diverse constraints on users' behaviors, including their personal characteristics and those of environmental decision makers, sociohistorical factors, and organizational policies.

Again, I do not wish in any way to deny the possibility of developing generalizable theories or empirical relationships that could inform design or planning decisions. Yet it still seems important to consider EDR projects on a case-by-case basis so that the role of the local context can be evaluated. And in the collection of cases presented here, project-specific research was a far more common source of environment–behavior knowledge than was general theory or research.

A related reason for adopting the case-study approach concerns the value of applications to specific settings in the process of building and evaluating theories of environment–behavior relationships. Although analyses of the EDR process typically focus on the flow of information from theory and research to application (design or planning), the relationship between the two areas is actually reciprocal. Although some argue that setting-specific analyses can hinder the development of generic data-based (scientific) theories, the argument can also be made that applications can add invaluable data to the theory-building process. Given the methodological problems inherent in all behavioral research (cf. Campbell & Stanley, 1966), where trade-offs between realism and freedom from artifact often leave disturbing residual questions about both, the fact that applications of theory and data can be shown to be successful in operation through empirical evaluation, under conditions where methodological artifacts are unlikely and relevant context is restored, should add greatly to one's confidence in the generalizations that underlay the design or plan in question.

An excellent example of the reciprocal relationships among research, theory, and application is provided by the work of Newman (see chapter 11). It began with an interest in the environmental determinants of crime in New York City public housing. The bare empirical relationships discovered in that specific setting provided the basis for a limited version of the theory of "defensible space" that was applied successfully in the redesign of the Clason Point Gardens housing project (chapter 11). At the same time, the theory was elaborated and extended, partly through the use of new data from private neighborhoods in St. Louis. The more elaborate theory provided the basis for design and planning decisions in varied types of settings, both residential and nonresidential, as well as for a large body of empirical research designed to test the theory itself.

A further reason for choosing case studies over reviews of categories of cases was to enhance the impact on the reader in order to further the original goal of this volume, namely, proselytization. Brief descriptions of applications, such as those found in most environmental-psychology textbooks, are not able to convey to the reader the importance of the problem being addressed, the ingenuity with which data and theory are brought to bear on that problem, or the importance of the final design or planning solution to the lives of those who use the setting in which it is implemented. A chapter-length case study, on the other hand, permits an adequate description of the setting, the problem, the programming and design process (including the use and/or generation of useful behavior theory or research), and the results of any evaluation of the subsequent use of the setting, to make the aforementioned points clear to the reader.

Many analyses of the status of environmental-design research have pointed to a gap between environment–behavior research, on the one hand, and design and planning practice, on the other, that is blamed for inhibiting applications of knowledge about environment and behavior from reaching their true potential. The magnitude of that gap is evident from the fact that most environmental-design activities taking place today do not benefit noticeably from available or obtainable knowledge about environment–behavior relationships. In my correspondence with Michael Bakos about the work of his firm Architecture-Research-Construction (ARC), I was fortunate to obtain his eloquent summary of the current state of environmental-design research (M. Bakos, personal communication, February 20, 1989):

It is too simplistic to say that designers/architects work with pictures and researchers work with words. Over and again . . . I have seen architects skip over the theory and insight of an architectural program to go straight to the square footage listing – "how big do you want the room" is the concrete level at which they are comfortable. There is of course "informal" design happening today, but all too rarely. If the field of environment–behavior research can be said to have failed, it would be in the lack of impact on so much of what is designed today. Whether it be daycare centers, the office environment, schools, playgrounds, hospitals, prisons or the workplace, too much is designed with conventional wisdom and without the benefit of research or evaluation.

One means that has been suggested for closing that gap is greater exposure of successful applications, to convince all of the parties concerned of the potential value of utilizing environment–behavior research and theory to inform design and planning decisions. In a special issue of *Environment and Behavior* devoted to assessing the contributions of environmental and behavioral research to design (Kantrowitz & Seidel, 1985), several authors stressed the importance of increasing people's knowledge of successful applications (Kantrowitz, 1985), of *more effective* dissemination of environment–behavior theories and research (Seidel, 1985), and of providing *evidence* of the benefits of using environmental-design research (Shibley, 1985). As if to add emphasis to the point, one author (Seidel, 1985) reported that as far as he knew, "no attempts at fully instrumental [directed to a specific project] research use have been tried" (p. 52). The need for greater communication of the potential of environmental-design research was also stressed in an earlier report on the status of the field published under the auspices of the American Institute of Architects (Dudik & McClure, 1978).

A selection of case studies may not indicate the overall extent to which environment–behavior theory and research have been applied to planning and design, but these cases do emphasize the degree to which such applications have influenced specific design and planning projects and, in some cases, the benefits that have accrued to clients and users. There is reason to believe that this is a more effective approach to communicating the potential of environmental-design research. Psychological research in the area of human judgment processes indicates that people's judgments about causal relationships, such as the impact of environment–behavior knowledge on the quality of design and planning decisions, may be influenced more by memorable details of specific cases, such as those described in this volume, than by statistical evidence of a relationship that might emerge from a review of the entire body of such cases (Hamill, Wilson, & Nisbett, 1980).

The selection of cases

When this project began, prospective cases were to be evaluated against the following stringent set of criteria, not unlike those proposed by Wener (1982):

1. The goals for the design or plan placed significant emphasis on users' needs.
2. The relationships between design or plan features and users' needs were evaluated on the basis of behavioral research or theory.
3. Recommendations based on that research or theory were incorporated explicitly in the final design or plan.
4. The completed project included those recommended design or plan features.
5. The impact of those features on users of the affected setting could be estimated from an empirical evaluation of user behavior.

The first three criteria were used throughout the selection process, with the minor exception that the definition of behavioral research was broadened to include any form of empirical evaluation of the likely impact of design or planning decisions on users of the setting (e.g., in chapter 14, research on the shadowing effects of different locations or designs for high-rise buildings in San Francisco was used to formulate recommendations for zoning controls, on the assumption that the predictable shadowing of public spaces would influence pedestrian comfort and the likelihood of use of the affected space).

The last two criteria were revised substantially along the way. It became clear in the course of investigating prospective cases that the process by which behavior-based recommendations were incorporated into the final design or plan for a project, following negotiation with other interests (financial, aesthetic, etc.), was an important phase of environmental-design research that could be illuminated as well by cases where behavioral needs were among the losers in such negotiations as by cases where they were among the winners. For example, the results of the study comparing the legibility of alternative floor-numbering systems for a new hospital building had only limited impact, because a contract had already been signed to purchase elevators with electronic displays of floor numbers that would not accommodate the designations found to be the most legible (see chapter 4).

Finally, several projects were included despite the fact that no formal evaluation of their success in supporting targeted user behaviors had been carried out. One of those projects was too recent to have been evaluated, and the others accurately reflected the overall low frequency of such evaluations.

The decision to alter some of the selection criteria en route was influenced by the need to add further criteria whose importance became evident during the selection process. After reviewing the documentation for many prospective cases, it was decided that if the collection was to fairly represent successful cases of environmental-design research, it was important to include projects in a variety of setting types (e.g., interior spaces, buildings, communities, scenic areas), projects that utilized a variety of sources of environment–behavior knowledge (e.g., mainstream theories and research findings, project-specific surveys of potential users, comparisons of simulated design alternatives), and projects that provided historical perspective on the field (in addition to providing opportunities to evaluate long-term impacts) and displayed the contributions of key figures in its history (e.g., Robert Sommer, Donald Appleyard, Oscar Newman).

In brief, the initial goal of the selection process was to assemble a collection of ideal cases. That goal was changed to the presentation of cases that were successful on their own terms and that provided a basis for understanding the process of environmental-design research through their representation of the existing variety of settings, behavioral needs, and research approaches, as well as the problems that competent, even exemplary, practitioners are likely to encounter. It was decided, finally, that the development of the field would be furthered more by a realistic picture than by an idealistic portrayal of the current state of the art. This direction is also consistent with the view that this volume is not primarily a source of facts that can be used in research or planning or design, but rather a source of process that can be applied to the combination of research and planning and design that is environmental-design research.

The selection process was also influenced by a variety of practical considerations. As has been pointed out by some of those who have cited the need for greater publicity for successful EDR projects, documentation of such work can be difficult to obtain. For example, in editing a special issue of *Environment and Behavior* on applications of environment–behavior research, Kantrowitz and Seidel (1985) intended to devote the entire issue to case studies, but failed in their attempt to assemble a collection of cases. Although some cases have been described in academic journals such as *Environment and Behavior* and the *Journal of Architectural and Planning Research,* and others in professional periodicals such as *Progressive Architecture* and *Landscape Architecture* (usually brief descriptions in "awards" issues), detailed reports are more difficult to obtain. They are often considered proprietary information. That is, the reports are written for environmental-design researchers' or designers' clients, and they are not published because the client who has paid for the work feels entitled to be the exclusive beneficiary of the results of it, or even because the researcher or designer is pressed to concentrate his or her efforts on activities that can be billed to a client. This is not as likely when the client is in the public sector (e.g., a government agency), but even in those cases such reports often are not published, but are made available only to a small circle of colleagues known to the authors. It has been my experience that practitioners differ greatly in their willingness to share such information with academicians or others with an "interest" in it. Some are eager to help and/or to have their work publicized, whereas others seem unwilling to respond no matter how earnestly or how often they are asked.

Thus, the collection of cases in this volume is to some extent what social-science researchers call an opportunity sample. There are other cases that meet the criteria for inclusion and would have been valuable additions to the collection, but they have proved to be inaccessible. There may be others that remain completely unknown.

Description and analysis

At the outset, this volume was intended to present cases of successful environmental-design research in a purely descriptive fashion. To a large extent, that plan was predicated on the assumption that such a mode of presentation would make the material more accessible to the broad audience for which the book was intended. Although some design practitioners and other interested parties are trained in the behavioral or social sciences and understand (even relish) the methodological and statistical technicalities of research in those fields, others are trained principally in the design professions, where such matters may appear arcane or even obfuscatory.

In discussing this project with Irv Altman and Dan Stokols, the editors of this series of books, I became convinced that by avoiding analysis I would do an injustice to the field to which I was so committed and to the readers with whom I was so concerned. Around the same time, reading John Zeisel's *Inquiry by Design* (1981) convinced me that my own training as a social scientist had left me ignorant of the importance of analyzing the design process as well as the research methods for each case.

For these reasons, the plan for presenting the cases was changed from that of pure description to that of description and analysis. To accommodate the needs of readers whose backgrounds had not acquainted them with the basic principles of both social-science research and the design and planning processes, it was decided to include an introductory chapter (chapter 2) that would describe briefly the underlying principles of each form of analysis (research methods and design processes) and thus provide the reader with a conceptual model of the analyses to be found at the end of each case presentation.

Contribution to the field

The ultimate goal for this volume remains the same as it has been from the first, despite the numerous changes in format that have been made along the way. It seems clearer now than ever that both the potential and the actual contributions of environmental-design research to design and planning have been greatly underestimated and understated, even by those who are intimately involved in the work and strongly committed to its success. It is gratifying to be able to state with confidence today, after several years of reading about these projects, discussing them with participants and clients, and visiting the sites of many around the country, that the field of environmental-design research has already influenced in a positive way the lives of millions of people around the world and that the work that has been done already provides a firm foundation for even greater progress in the future. It is to be hoped that telling the story of some of these accomplishments will add in some small way to that progress.

References

Altman, I. (1976a). Environmental psychology and social psychology. *Personality and Social Psychology Bulletin, 2*, 96–113.

Altman, I. (1976b). A response to Epstein, Proshansky and Stokols. *Personality and Social Psychology Bulletin, 2*, 364–370.

Campbell, D. T., & Stanley, J. F. (1966). *Experimental and quasi-experimental designs for research*. Chicago: Rand McNally.

Dudik, E. M., & McClure, P. K. (1978). *Environmental design research: Problems and needs*. Washington, DC: AIA Research Corporation.

Hamill, R., Wilson, T. D., & Nisbett, R. E. (1980). Insensitivity to sample bias: Generalizing from atypical cases. *Journal of Personality and Social Psychology, 39*, 578–579.

Holahan, C. J., & Wandersman, A. (1987). The community psychology perspective in environmental psychology. In D. Stokols & I. Altman (Eds.), *Handbook of environmental psychology* (Vol. 1, pp. 827–861). New York: Wiley.

Kantrowitz, M., & Seidel, A. D. (Eds.). (1985). Applications of E&B research. *Environment and Behavior, 17* (Whole No. 1).

Moore, G. T. (1987). Environment and behavior research in North America: History, developments, and unresolved issues. In D. Stokols & I. Altman (Eds.), *Handbook of environmental psychology* (Vol. 2, pp. 1359–1410). New York: Wiley.

Osmond, H. (1970). Function as the basis of psychiatric ward design. In H. M. Proshansky, W. H. Ittleson, & L. G. Rivlin (Eds.), *Man and his physical setting* (pp. 560–569). New York: Holt, Rinehart & Winston.

Proshansky, H. M. (1976). Comment on "Environmental psychology and social psychology." *Personality and Social Psychology Bulletin, 2,* 359–363.

Schneekloth, L. H. (1987). Advances in practice in environment, behavior, and design. In E. H. Zube & G. T. Moore (Eds.), *Advances in environment, behavior, and design* (Vol. 1, pp. 307–334). New York: Plenum.

Seidel, A. D. (1985). What is success in E&B research utilization? *Environment and Behavior, 17,* 47–70.

Shibley, R. G. (1985). Building evaluation in the main stream. *Environment and Behavior, 17,* 7–24.

Sommer, R. (1974). *Tight spaces: Hard architecture and how to humanize it.* Englewood Cliffs, NJ: Prentice-Hall.

Sommer, R. (1976). *Social design: Creating buildings with people in mind.* Englewood Cliffs, NJ: Prentice-Hall.

Wener, R. E. (1982). Environment-behavior research "success stories." New York: Polytechnic Institute.

Zeisel, J. (1981). *Inquiry by design.* Monterey, CA: Brooks/Cole.

2

A MODEL OF ENVIRONMENTAL-DESIGN/ PLANNING RESEARCH AND A FRAMEWORK FOR ANALYZING CASES

Cases in which environment–behavior research and theory have been applied to the design or planning of environmental settings document dramatically the great promise of the relatively new field of applied social science known as environmental-design research. A major purpose of this book is to bring to light the impressive number and scope of such applications, as illustrated by 13 case studies. It is hoped that an enhanced awareness of the ultimate practical value of environment–behavior research and theory will serve to stimulate the efforts of researchers, whet the appetites of designers and planners for the knowledge that researchers produce, enhance cooperation between those two groups, and even foster the integration of their disciplines.

At the same time, it would be shortsighted to take these cases at face value, no matter how promising they seem. If the usefulness of environment–behavior research and theory is to be accepted, and if that acceptance is to be justified, the cases in which the theory has been applied need to be analyzed thoroughly and critically. These cases constitute a potentially invaluable source of evidence of the validity of the research and theory on which this new field is being built, as well as a basis for developing guidelines for making environment–behavior research and theory even more valuable in the future.

Analysis of these cases is complicated by the fact that they combine research with design. Systematic analysis of the validity of social-science research is well established. But that analysis, perhaps exemplified best by the seminal work of Campbell and Stanley (1966), has been concerned primarily with discovering the causes of human action and has paid little attention to the question of how such knowledge can be applied. It is clear that the usefulness of environment–behavior knowledge to designers and planners depends on much more than the validity of causal inferences or even their generality. On the other hand, attempts to address the issue of how social-science research can be applied to design problems, represented most prominently in the field of environmental design by the work of Zeisel (1981), have focused primarily on analysis of the design process, while treating much more lightly the question of the validity of design-relevant research.

In order to evaluate the cases we will be considering, these two approaches need to be combined and supplemented. Both the validity of the underlying environment–behavior research and theory and their utilization in the design process will need to be evaluated for each case.

To that end, a framework has been developed that incorporates Campbell and Stanley's analysis of the threats to the validity of research findings and Zeisel's analysis of the environmental-design process, as well as other issues whose importance has become clear in the course of examining many cases of environmental-design research, including those that are described in detail in this volume. That framework will be described here and then later applied to each of the cases to be presented, insofar as that is possible. The framework depicts an idealized sequence of stages, not all of which are represented in every environmental-design research (EDR) project. The varied natures of the cases that will be considered will require some variability in the questions to be posed and in the emphasis to be placed on each one.

It should be pointed out that in order to conserve space and to enhance clarity, the analyses by Campbell and Stanley and by Zeisel have been extensively adapted to the present purpose. The goal is to introduce the reader to the major issues they raise, as well as to expand the discussion to the more general problem of evaluating environmental-design research. The reader who desires a truer and more complete representation of their original analyses is encouraged to consult the original sources.

The framework: an overview

Table 2.1 summarizes the framework on which evaluations of the cases will be based. The sequence of stages into which the EDR process is divided, for the sake of clarity, is adapted from Zeisel's (1981) analysis of the environmental-design process, based on an examination of the cases reported in this volume and many others. We first identify the major goals toward which the effort of an EDR project team is directed in each stage. Then we identify the principal criteria by which the success of that effort can be judged. The following discussion will attempt to clarify and further specify each of these elements.

Stage 1: Understanding the setting

Environmental-design research often incorporates generalizations about environment–behavior relationships, either from statistical summaries of the results of research studies or from theories that integrate the results of many studies. However, those generalizations must be adapted to the requirements

Table 2.1. *A framework for analyzing cases of environmental-design research*

Stage	Goals	Criteria
1. Background analysis of setting	Identifying prospective users, important activities, and relevant sociohistorical context for the setting in question	Clarity, importance, and impact of background information
2. Behavioral goals for design plan	Specifying the behaviors to be supported or facilitated in the setting	Clarity of behavioral goals and importance relative to other goals for design/plan
3. Relevant environment–behavior (E–B) relationships	Adducing E–B research and/or theory that suggests environmental features likely to further the specified behavioral goals	Amount, type, and quality of E–B knowledge used
4. Specific design/plan elements	Creating E–B-based design/plan elements appropriate to the specific requirements of the setting	Identifiability and appropriateness of E–B-based elements in design/plan
5. Design/plan	Incorporating the E–B-based elements into an overall design/plan	Extent and specific role of E–B-based elements in overall design/plan
6. Postoccupancy evaluation (POE)	Evaluating systematically the degree to which the behavioral goals for the design/plan were achieved	Amount and quality of data collected, and degree of success indicated
7. Impact on future design/planning and E–B knowledge	Using knowledge gained from the design/planning process to enhance future designs/plans for related settings	Extent and type of impact of project on design/planning guidelines and/or other projects, and on the E–B knowledge system

of a specific setting. Such a setting consists of a physical site where an aggregation of users will pursue an array of activities.

The character of the physical site itself is defined by elements from both the present and the past. In the present, such characteristics as climate and location (e.g., transportation links) may be important considerations. As we will see in chapter 14, for example, high-rise development around public open spaces in San Francisco, with its cool, damp summer weather, poses different problems than it would in the hot, dry environment of Phoenix.

Environmental settings also need to be understood in their historical context. The plan for high-rise zoning in San Francisco discussed in chapter 14 reflects that city's history as well. San Franciscans are proud of their city's unusual low-rise character, and they have a long history of resistance to pressures for high-rise development, or "Manhattanization," as some of them term it.

Besides the physical site itself, environmental-design researchers need to identify the individuals who are likely to use the setting and the specific activities in which they will be engaged. This is especially important when the user groups are likely to have special characteristics, as when they are not representative of the community as a whole in regard to age, ethnicity, or gender, and when there is a limited range of behaviors or activities to which most of their attention and effort will be devoted while in the setting, as in an office or factory.

An evaluation of the background analysis of the setting should begin with a judgment about the clarity with which the current character and past character of the site, the prospective users, and the important activities have been identified. Of course, this judgment will need to take into account the ease with which access can be gained to that information. For example, the office building whose interior design and layout are described in chapter 6 was planned for a specific group of employees who were working together in a nearby building that was to be replaced. However, some settings must be designed for less predictable user groups and less certain activities.

In addition, it is necessary to evaluate the importance of background information for the development of an adequate design or plan. Almost anyone seated on a park bench in San Francisco's cool, damp summer air could be expected to prefer sunlight over shadow; so knowledge of user characteristics might not be very important in that case. But Latin-Americans and Anglo-Americans might have very different preferences for the degree of privacy in their neighborhoods (see chapter 12), making an understanding of the needs of the particular group of prospective users critical to the success of such a project.

Finally, the actual impact of the background analysis on the quality of the eventual design or plan can be evaluated.

Stage 2: Setting behavioral goals for the EDR project

In Zeisel's analysis, the first stage in the environmental-design process is "programming." It consists of two subsidiary stages, the first of which is labeled "imaging." At this stage, the designer (or planner) must identify the important behavioral issues to be addressed by the design (or plan). In most cases, as Zeisel has pointed out, this involves a specification of the more general goals of maximizing the comfort and efficacy of the users in the target settings.

To do this requires, first of all, a broad familiarity with the theoretical and empirical literature in the field of environment–behavior studies. Such familiarity will make possible the optimization of concepts such as privacy in the design of institutional residential settings, territoriality in high-density housing, or passive social contact in new or transient communities. Together with background information about the setting, such concepts can then provide the basis for setting more specific goals for the design or plan, the ultimate goal at this stage. For example, college dormitories might be designed to provide residents with greater control over their encounters with others (chapter 7), public-housing projects can be designed to make it easier for residents to distinguish between neighbors and strangers (chapter 11), and new suburban communities can be laid out so as to encourage greater contact among neighbors (chapter 12).

The ways in which behavioral issues are framed or imaged and specific behavioral goals are set can be evaluated in two ways. First, it is possible to evaluate the clarity with which inferences are drawn from the relevant environment–behavior research or theory in identifying specific behavioral goals for the design or plan. Second, it is possible to estimate the importance of goals regarding the behavior of the setting users relative to other goals for the design or plan, such as aesthetic appeal, cost, and political support.

Stage 3: Adducing relevant information concerning environment–behavior relationships

According to Zeisel's analysis, architectural programming begins with the process of imaging, followed by the process of presentation, in which alternative designs are developed to address established behavioral goals. In progressing from imaging to presentation, it is important to ascertain more specific empirical or theoretical relationships between the behaviors in question and environmental features. The goal at this intermediate stage of programming is to identify specific features that can be incorporated into the design or plan that will be capable of supporting or facilitating the behaviors already targeted as outcomes of the imaging process.

Information about environment–behavior relationships from which such specific design or plan elements can be inferred can be obtained either from theory or from research. Although some approaches would prescribe that theory be grounded firmly in research data, some influential theories have originated in much more speculative form. In the chapters to follow, examples of both types of theory – that which summarizes data and that which anticipates data – will be encountered.

The research on which these kinds of inferences about design or plan features may be based can also take two forms. First, there exists an extensive literature of research studies that document relationships between the features of environmental settings and behaviors. Generic research findings from that literature can be used as a basis for selecting environmental features whose inclusion in the design or plan can be expected to promote achievement of the behavioral goals that have been established. Alternatively, new research can be undertaken to address those goals more directly. Such research, dedicated to the specific problems posed by the design or planning project in question, may be based on more abstract representations of relevant environment–behavior relationships investigated in a laboratory setting, or it can be based on more realistic simulations in the actual context of the design or plan or one very similar to it.

The use of knowledge of environment–behavior relationships to suggest functional elements for a design or plan can be evaluated for its impact on the development of that design or plan. In cases where inferences are based on theory, evaluation will focus on the degree to which the theory is grounded in data and on the apparent reasonableness of the inferences drawn. In cases where research-based knowledge is utilized, well-established criteria exist for evaluating the equality of the methods used in that research and the consequent trustworthiness of the resulting findings. One of the most respected and most systematic approaches to understanding those methodological questions has been provided by Campbell and Stanley (1966). Despite the fact that this seminal work is far less complex than subsequent elaborations of their approach, limitations on space and limitations imposed by the disparate backgrounds of those in the EDR community suggest the value of a simplification of these issues, such as that to be attempted here.

In its most basic form, research into environment–behavior relationships consists of comparing some target behavior across variations in some feature of an environmental setting, either among different groups of users or potential users exposed to those variations or over time as that feature varies for a single group. The results generally take the form of a quantitative estimate of the effect of environment on behavior in the form of the statistical reliability of differences among group means. Examples include findings of greater sociability among residents of suite-design college dormitories than among residents of corridor-design dormitories, greater crime rates in high-rise public-housing projects than in low-rise (different groups compared), and the finding that psychiatric patients engaged in social interaction more often after their quarters were modified to provide more settings conducive to interacting than they had before (the same group at different times).

In either case, the findings need to be evaluated, based on an examination of the methods by which they were produced, for two important qualities that determine the degree of trust that can be placed in them as a basis for creating elements of a design or plan that will be effective in achieving the behavioral goals set for it.

The findings need to be evaluated for the confidence with which variations observed in behavior can be attributed to associated variations in the environmental features whose effects were studied. Research methods that rule out plausible alternative explanations, or rival hypotheses, for those observed differences produce findings that permit causal inferences to be made with confidence. Such findings are said to be high in internal validity.

The findings also need to be evaluated for the confidence with which they can be generalized from the specific context in which the effect of environmental variations on the target behavior was observed to the context or setting in which they are to be applied. Findings that can be generalized more safely are said to be high in external validity.

Of the threats to internal validity that may compromise research findings, four seem especially important for environment–behavior research. First, there is the threat that differences among the environmental variations being compared other than those being studied may be responsible for observed differences in behavior. For example, dormitories with different internal layouts may also differ in terms of location on campus, so that street noise could actually be responsible for lower satisfaction that had erroneously been attributed to lack of privacy. Or an improvement in worker performance in a new office might be the result of coincidental changes in management policies or personnel, rather than the new design whose effects are being evaluated. To prevent such *extraneous events* from obscuring the effects of the environmental features being studied, the researcher must exert preventive control over all aspects of the settings other than the one whose variations are of interest. Traditionally, this has meant conducting research in laboratory settings where greatly simplified analogues of the settings and behaviors of interest could be studied. An alternative approach is to assess as many of the extraneous conditions as possible and evaluate their effects, in order to rule out statistically the rival hypotheses. The latter procedure suffers from the weakness that important conditions may escape the notice of the researcher, but it has important advantages for external validity that will be considered later.

A second threat to internal validity is that the individuals who are observed under different environmental conditions are not equivalent. These groups may differ in demographic or personal characteristics that could influence their responses to the conditions to which they are exposed. Thus, differences in their behaviors could be attributed incorrectly to the environmental variations under study rather than to the differences in *group composition* actually responsible for them. For example, residents in different types of housing in an institution for the developmentally disabled may differ in the severity of their disabilities.

In laboratory research, this problem can be avoided by randomly assigning individuals from the pool of available research subjects to various environmental variations. In natural settings, such as schools, offices, or hospitals, that approach may not be possible. In those cases, background information about the participants can be used to assure that there are no preexisting differences or to control for their effects statistically, although, again, some doubt always remains that all important factors have been assessed. In addition, individuals who are alike at the beginning of a study may change at different rates during the study. Differences in age or intelligence may influence learning rates, so that two groups equal at the outset may become progressively more unequal as the study continues. Only random assignment can ensure equivalence among the groups. Other procedures can increase confidence in comparability among groups only up to a point.

A third threat to internal validity is that the behavior being studied may be changing independent of any effects of the environmental conditions being evaluated. This problem of confusing *coincidental cyclical changes in behavior* and the effects of differences in environmental conditions is especially acute in studies that evaluate the effects of changes in a single setting over time. For example, the redesign of a public-housing project may be implemented at the same time as a cyclical low point in crime rates and thus be credited with an improvement in crime prevention for which it was not responsible. Even in studies comparing different settings, interpretation of observations that are made over long periods of time may suffer from this sort of confusion if different cycles operate in different settings (e.g., crime-rate changes in different communities). The only solution to these problems is to collect closely spaced measures of the behavior in question over periods that are long enough to reveal cycles that are separate from the effects of the environmental changes or variations being evaluated. Statistical analyses of these "time series" of measures can permit those separate effects to be differentiated, if the series are detailed enough and long enough and if the appropriate analysis is employed.

Finally, the internal validity of research findings may be threatened by the application of *biased measurement procedures* that result in behaviors under different environmental conditions being assessed by different criteria. For example, crime rates may be estimated differently in different neighborhoods. In a neighborhood where a new crime-prevention program is being tested, one that may incorporate findings from environmental-design research, the authorities may categorize an incident differently than they would elsewhere. This problem can be minimized by having the behavior in question evaluated independently by someone who is trained to make the judgment consistently and who is unaware of the source of the observation to be judged. This "blind" judge can even be presented with observations whose temporal order has been disguised to further avoid bias caused by his or her expectations for the outcome of the study.

In practice, studies of environment–behavior relationships cannot avoid all of these (and other) threats to internal validity. This is particularly true of dedicated research, which is conducted most often in natural settings, where experimental research methods based on random assignment of subjects and precise controls in laboratory settings cannot be utilized. However, there are, fortunately, some reasons for optimism about the value of such research. First, it is not necessary to rule out all possible rival hypotheses, only those that would provide *plausible* alternative explanations for any observed behavioral differences. The corps of workers in an office may change over the period of months during which a new office layout is being designed and built, but if the personnel changes that take place do not alter the group of workers in a way that will affect their overall productivity, then observed changes in productivity still can be attributed safely to the design change. In addition, there are alternative quasi-experimental methods that substitute statistical controls of the type described earlier in ways that will produce findings with acceptably high levels of internal validity.

Even more important, these methods are far superior to an absence of any empirical evidence at all in suggesting environmental conditions that might make possible the achievement of the behavioral goals for a particular setting. The findings they produce can be discounted by a knowledgeable user for whatever limitations the research methods might contain, and yet still be of great value to environmental-design researchers.

In addition to the problems with the internal validity of research findings that can jeopardize causal inferences about the research results, there may be serious questions whether or not those results can be generalized beyond the specific context in which the research was conducted. This is especially true in cases where findings from the existing research literature are utilized. These generic findings, in contrast to dedicated research conducted in connection with a particular EDR project, often will have been produced in studies conducted in laboratories or in settings far removed from the setting whose design is being considered. In these cases, in particular, there are two important reasons to be concerned about whether or not one should try to generalize the findings to the project setting; that is, there are two main threats to the external validity of the findings.

First, there is the possibility that the relationship between environmental features and behavior that is observed in the specific context of subjects, tasks, and broader setting characteristics employed in the research will take a different form in the context of the setting in which the eventual design or plan is to be implemented. This is one reason that a comprehensive background analysis of the setting is important, so that researchers will have a clear picture of the nature of the users, activities, and important sociohistorical contextual factors that need to be represented in the research. Still, some social-science researchers show little reluctance to take findings from trivial laboratory tasks performed by college students, for example, and extrapolate them to meaningful jobs being done by experienced and committed workers.

One problem that is characteristic of both dedicated research and generic research concerns the duration of environmental effects on behavior. Both types of research tend to be limited in their duration because of practical concerns to produce findings quickly. Yet environmental effects can change dramatically during realistically long periods of time, in large part because of the phenomenon of sensory habituation that causes the effects of changes in environmental conditions to dissipate over time. Another problem is that generic research studies, particularly those conducted under laboratory conditions, often deal with the potential threats to internal validity posed by contextual factors by eliminating as much of the context as possible. As a result, the observed environment–behavior relationship may be different from that which will obtain in the rich natural context of the design or planning project, where such influential contextual factors will be restored. Finally, many environment–behavior studies utilize simulations of the settings of interest. These vary from sample drawings or photographs to elaborate dynamic video tours through scale models. Anyone who has walked through a heavily treed residential neighborhood with a still camera, trying to take photographs that would accurately convey the feeling of being there, is aware of the limitations of static simulations, and yet a good deal of research is based on them.

The second threat to the generalizability of research findings is restricted to generic studies conducted in laboratories or other settings where subjects are aware that their behaviors are under the scrutiny of the researchers. Under such conditions, which methodologists label "reactive," subjects may respond differently than they otherwise would to the environmental conditions to which they are exposed. Whether they attempt to act as they believe that the researchers expect them to, or attempt to avoid embarrassing themselves, their behaviors may prove a poor guide to the responses of similar individuals going about their normal business in similar but natural settings. Unobtrusive measures of subjects' behaviors may be more effective in such circumstances than would questionnaires or interviews that would make strategic self-presentation easier (e.g., time-lapse photography to assess preferences for public open space by frequency of use), but conducting research in natural settings where subjects are unaware of being studied is the only sure way to avoid nonrepresentative findings due to reactivity.

As is true of the internal-validity issue, it is not necessary to discard automatically any findings produced outside the actual setting being designed or planned simply for their presumed failure to satisfy requirements of external validity. Well-established research findings, even from laboratory research, have proved quite useful in environmental-design research, as we shall see in several of the examples to follow. But it does seem prudent to be cautious about using findings from settings that differ clearly in context, or findings from studies involving high levels of reactivity, particularly where more representative or less reactive alternatives are available.

Stage 4: Creating specific design/plan elements

In this stage of the EDR process, the one labeled *presentation* by Zeisel, research findings are translated into specific physical features or policies to be included in the design or plan, respectively. In most cases, these specifics must be inferred from the findings of antecedent environment–behavior research or theory. Such inferences vary considerably in the degree to which they follow directly from research or theory. Research showing that dormitory corridors shared by larger numbers of students were associated with greater perceived crowding led quite directly to a renovation design that divided one long corridor into two shorter corridors (chapter 7). On the other hand, findings about the role of high-rise design elements as architectural correlates of crime rates in public housing were first used in the development of a general theory, from which the elements of a new design for the configuration of outdoor spaces in a low-rise project were later inferred (chapter 11).

At this stage the EDR process can be evaluated for the clarity with which the design or plan elements selected have reflected the environment–behavior knowledge from which they were inferred and for the directness with which those elements have been incorporated into the eventual design or plan. The latter outcome reflects not only the quality of both the knowledge and the inferences drawn from it but also the degree to which such efforts later prove influential in competition with other forces (cost, aesthetics, etc.) that operate simultaneously to shape the design or plan.

Stage 5: Assembling the overall design/plan

Following the process of comparing and choosing among alternative designs or plans, labeled *design/plan review* by Zeisel, a final design or plan is accepted that incorporates elements resulting from the EDR process that address behavioral goals for the project, as well as elements addressed to different goals. In some projects, design review is accomplished through dedicated environment–behavior research (i.e., two stages earlier in the process). In those cases, realistic simulations of designs that provide alternative means of achieving the behavioral goals for the project are compared directly. One example would be an assessment of the perceptual effects of alternative designs for building structures such as highways or bridges in scenic areas. Realistic simulations of alternative designs may be compared for their effects on scenic resources on the basis of respondents' judgments of them, with the least damaging one being chosen as the final design. Another example is the use of full-scale mock-ups of rooms that present alternative means of fulfilling behavioral goals. In such a case, the room design in which the best behavioral outcomes are observed will be incorporated into the final design.

Success at this stage can be evaluated in terms of the extent and specific role of environment–behavior-based elements in the overall design or plan. Though admittedly a subjective judgment, such analysis provides an important opportunity to view the EDR process in the context of the overall design or planning process. In particular, it may reveal the extent to which environment–behavior-based recommendations are not implemented because of competition from other goals and their proponents.

Stage 6: Evaluating the achievement of behavioral goals

Once the design or plan has been implemented, it is possible to assess the extent to which the behavioral goals for the project have been achieved. Known commonly as postoccupancy evaluation (POE), this process is distinguished by its systematic and objective or scientific character, in contrast to the casual judgments or selective testimonials so common in design and planning, as well as other fields. In other words, it takes the form of a social-science research study and can be judged on the same methodological criteria as other research. A POE study can be evaluated for the extent to which relevant data were collected and the degree to which those data form the basis for trustworthy causal inferences about the utility of environment–behavior-based design elements incorporated as a result of the prior stages of the EDR process. Because the POE study is of necessity conducted in the actual setting for which the design or plan was developed, the representativeness of the research context is unlikely to be an issue. However, reactivity may well be. More difficult, however, is ruling out alternative explanations for observed changes in behavior over time (e.g., predesign to postdesign) or across settings (e.g., new design versus traditional design). Experimental research designs requiring random assessment of subjects (users) are very unlikely to be appropriate for POE studies, but the use of appropriate quasi-experimental designs can greatly enhance the value of such studies.

Finally, the findings of the POE can be evaluated, in light of appropriate reservations about threats to their validity, for the degree to which the results indicate that the design or plan has achieved its behavioral goals.

Stage 7: Influencing future design/planning and contributing to environment–behavior knowledge

The impact of a completed EDR project may be felt long after the design or plan has been implemented and far from its original setting. Knowledge gained from the project can enhance future design or planning projects in a variety of ways. Reviews of research and theory can be used to facilitate imaging in other projects. New design elements can be copied or adapted to new settings. And overall project results can serve as a basis for the development of formal guidelines for similar projects in the future. In addition, knowledge gained from the project can contribute to what Zeisel has called the environment–behavior knowledge system. Dedicated research and POE research can add to the existing empirical research literature and influence subsequent theory development.

The continuing impact of an EDR project can thus be evaluated for the degree to which subsequent projects are influenced, either directly by the incorporation of innovative elements or through the application of general guidelines, as well as for the empirical and theoretical contributions made to the environment–behavior knowledge system.

In the chapters to follow, each of the EDR projects to be described will be analyzed and evaluated on the basis of the framework described in this chapter, including the specified criteria. However, the variations among the cases will necessitate different points of emphasis, highlighting the unique contributions and problems in each case.

References

Campbell, D. T., & Stanley, J. F. (1966). *Experimental and quasi-experimental designs for research*. Chicago: Rand McNally.

Zeisel, J. (1981). *Inquiry by design*. Monterey, CA: Brooks/Cole.

PART II
BUILDING DESIGN

What to look for

Part II presents six case studies that describe and analyze EDR projects whose scope was limited to all or part of a single building. As was discussed in detail in chapter 1, these cases compose an opportunity sample, chosen for their variety from a limited group for which sufficient documentation was available to support such detailed presentations.

A number of salient comparisons might be made by way of understanding how these cases exemplify the wide variety of ways in which environmental-design research may proceed. One such comparison is based on the scale of the project. The Contra Costa County Main Detention Facility (chapter 3) is a $25 million project, shaped almost entirely by environmental-design research, that serves the needs of several hundred inmates at a time and many thousands each year, as well as hundreds of corrections-department staff. The University of Michigan Medical Center (chapter 4) is a $285 million building whose design was influenced in hundreds of significant details by environmental-design research. It serves tens of thousands of patients each year, in addition to their family members and the medical, nursing, and other staff. In each of these cases, the user population contains many vulnerable individuals whose safety and health depend heavily on the appropriateness of the design of the facility.

Both the Federal Aviation Administration (FAA) Seattle building (chapter 6) and the sociopetal-space projects (chapter 8) were undertaken on a somewhat smaller scale. They were limited to interior-design decisions. Their users numbered from tens to hundreds of individuals whose well-being depended somewhat less on the adequacy of those decisions. Finally, the Belchertown State School (chapter 5) and Jones Dormitory (chapter 7) projects involved even more limited design decisions affecting fewer users for shorter periods of time.

The cases in part II also differ in terms of the relative importance in each case of social-science concerns (e.g., the theoretical importance of research and the methodological adequacy of research design) and design concerns, giving precedence to practical considerations over underlying environment–behavior relationships. The Jones Dormitory renovation project (chapter 7) and the Sommer and Ross sociopetal-space project (chapter 8) were as much research studies concerned with understanding the basic environment–behavior processes of crowding and sociopetal space as they were design projects. Toward the other end of the continuum, the Contra Costa County jail project (chapter 3) arose primarily out of design concepts that reflected the experience and needs of corrections professionals. The University of Michigan Hospital (chapter 4), the Belchertown State School (chapter 5), the Seattle FAA building (chapter 6), and the sociopetal-space projects (chapter 8) represent more of a balance between social-science concerns and design concerns.

Finally, for the purposes of this discussion (see chapter 16 for further analysis), the projects in part II differ clearly in the extent to which they have been influential beyond their own boundaries. Both the Belchertown State School (chapter 5) and the Jones Dormitory (chapter 7) renovation projects were entirely self-contained. There is no record of those designs being applied in or adapted to other institutions for the developmentally disabled or college dormitories, or even related settings where privacy in institutional housing is an important concern. The designs for the University of Michigan Hospital (chapter 4) and, to a lesser extent, the Seattle FAA building (chapter 6) have been circulated more widely as recommended guides for the attainment of similar behavioral goals in other hospitals and open-plan offices. Finally, the designs for sociopetal-space arrangements (chapter 8) and especially the modular direct-supervision design for the Contra Costa County Main Detention Facility (chapter 3) have influenced designs for numerous other hospitals and jails and provided well-known models and guidelines for the design of those types of facilities, addressing behavioral goals that are likely to be important in most such cases.

It is hoped that readers will find other areas in which to draw useful comparisons among these cases. However, even without such higher-order analysis, each of these cases can provide important positive and negative lessons for designers and researchers who need to consider similar behavioral issues in similar settings. Whether it be a key explanatory concept, an innovative design alternative, a method for evaluating the effectiveness of a design in use, or a model for the entire process of environmental-design research, the work of these social scientists and designers provides a useful basis from which future work can proceed.

3
CONTRA COSTA COUNTY
MAIN DETENTION FACILITY

Location: Martinez, California
Participants: Kaplan McLaughlin Diaz, San Francisco (architects);
Richard Wener, Polytechnic University, Brooklyn, New
York (background research); Frederick W. Frazier,
Contra Costa County Sheriff's Department
(postoccupancy evaluation)

One visit to the Contra Costa County Main Detention Facility (CCCMDF) in
Martinez, California, was enough to convince this observer that, in general,
there is precious little good that can be said for being in jail. As one enters the
building and makes one's way toward the receptionist's desk, one passes
through a lounge where families wait to be admitted to visit their loved ones
who are inmates in this county jail. Beyond the double set of locked doors, the
smell reveals that there are people confined in this place, probably too many
in too little space. Walking through the various modules, or self-contained
units, where groups of men eat, sleep, exercise, see visitors, and generally
spend the rest of their time, it is clear that the inmates are mostly the poor, the
disappointed, the lost in our society.

Somehow, though, despite the pall of despair that hangs over the place, this
facility seems to work. As my guide, a Contra Costa County deputy sheriff
who rotates through tours of duty at the jail along with his fellow deputies, put
it, most of the inmates and guards, who circulate together freely on the open
modules, have "bought the program" at CCCMDF. That program is a complex combination of architecture and management policies known as a podu-
lar (or modular) direct-supervision jail.

The Contra Costa County jail (Figure 3.1) came into existence following a
series of earlier jails that had been designed to meet a set of functional goals
established by the U.S. Bureau of Prisons for federal detention centers that
were built in the early 1970s in New York, Chicago, and San Diego. The
goals set by the Bureau of Prisons for these Metropolitan Correctional Centers
(MCCs) were to protect the inmates from the physical and psychological risks
that existed in traditional facilities and to impose the fewest restrictions on the
inmates' freedom of action consistent with maintaining security (keeping
inmates in and others out).

To a large extent, those goals reflected the need to build what Frazier (1985)
has called a "constitutional jail." At the time this program was being devel-

Figure 3.1. CCCMDF in Martinez, California. Photo by author.

oped for the federal MCCs there was a mounting list of court rulings suggesting that corrections officials might be held liable for the loss of constitutionally protected freedoms suffered by inmates, in the form of violence (especially sexual assault), substandard living conditions (crowding, in particular), isolation from family visitors and legal counsel, and more. These concerns were particularly acute in the case of detainees who had never been convicted of a crime. In fact, the great majority of the intended inmate population for the MCCs would be individuals being held for trial because they could not arrange for bail (or were still trying) or because their requests for bail had not been granted. Other detention inmates (as distinguished from, for example, prison inmates) would be held following their convictions while sentencing decisions were being made (some would ultimately be placed on probation). Others would be held on judicial writs pending court hearings. Still others would be serving brief sentences for minor violations.

The modular/direct-supervision design for the MCCs was developed by facilities planners at the Bureau of Prisons and local architectural firms hired by the bureau (Gruzen and Partners in New York, Harry Weese in Chicago, and Thomas Tucker in San Diego). They developed site-specific designs for the federal MCCs in New York City, Chicago, and San Diego that were later carefully evaluated by Wener (in particular, the New York and Chicago facili-

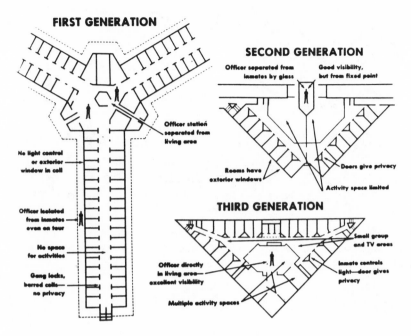

Figure 3.2. Diagrams of linear (first generation), remote-supervision (second generation), and direct-supervision (third generation) jail designs. Source: Wener, Frazier, and Farbstein (1987, p. 48); reproduced with permission of New American Magazines, publisher.

ties). Their designs and the results of the evaluations provided the groundwork for the design of the Contra Costa facility.

The generic design that was developed for the MCCs is referred to as a modular design because the inmates in each facility are divided into small groups (typically 40 to 50) that are housed in self-contained modules (sometimes called podules or functional units), where they sleep, eat, and spend most of their free time (Figures 3.2–3.4). This contrasts with the traditional linear design, in which inmates are housed in large cell blocks, where they sleep and spend long hours locked in their cells and must be moved periodically to centralized facilities for dining, exercise, and other organized activities. In the decentralized modular design, inmates have much more freedom of movement and choice of activities for most of the day (they may be locked in their rooms at night, for the convenience of staff during cleaning and meal preparation, and once per shift for very brief periods to be counted). The most obvious exception in the design of the federal MCCs was the provision of a large-scale outdoor recreation area for sports activities, beyond the scale of the individual unit, typically on the roof of the building.

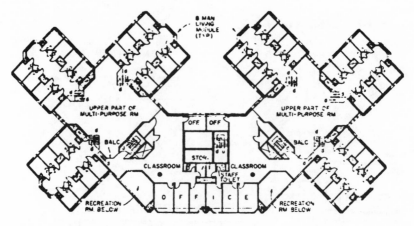

Figure 3.3. An example of a direct-supervision design – a diagram of two modules (one two-story level) of the New York MCC. Source: Wener and Olsen (1980, p. 483); reproduced with permission of Sage Publications.

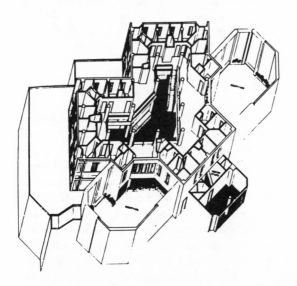

Figure 3.4. A perspective drawing of a two-story direct-supervision module design. Source: Wener, Frazier, and Farbstein (1985, p. 85); reproduced with permission of Sage Publications.

The federal MCCs were to be located in the heart of urban areas to provide easy access for attorneys, law-enforcement officials, and the inmates' families. This meant that their behavioral goals would have to be met on cramped urban building sites, in high-rise structures without secure outdoor space at ground level.

The design is referred to as "direct-supervision" because corrections officers spend their working hours locked in the module, unarmed, without any physical barriers between themselves and the inmates. This arrangement is in contrast to the traditional remote-supervision (or surveillance) design, where officers observe inmates from secure control rooms or corridors, either continuously or on intermittent patrols. With remote supervision, the officer is physically separated from the inmates, entering the inmates' space only when required to transport inmates or deal with emergency situations.

New York and Chicago MCCs: the first generation

The particular modular/direct-supervision design for the CCCMDF facility evolved from earlier versions built as MCCs in Chicago and New York, and particularly from the results of the postoccupancy evaluation (POE) studies of the Chicago facility (Wener & Clark, 1976; Wener & Olsen, 1977). These facilities were designed differently, to fit different sites. That turned out to be a fortuitous development because it made possible some comparisons between the two that provided useful information for the subsequent design of the Contra Costa facility. However, the Chicago and New York MCCs shared several common design elements that addressed the central goals of the behavioral program for the MCCs.

Both the Chicago and New York designs eliminated many of the traditional physical features of correctional facilities. Painted walls replaced bars. Floors were carpeted. Furniture was of conventional design, with fabric upholstery. Public areas were visually interesting spaces, with multilevel design, abundant natural light, and brightly colored graphics on the walls. The designers' intention was to replace the symbols associated with incarceration, despair, and violence with symbols associated with home and normal social interaction.

The New York MCC was designed as an 11-story building in the government complex in lower Manhattan. Residents were housed on nine floors of the building, with two two-story 48-place podules, or functional units, on four pairs of floors and two short-term dormitory units on the top floor. Each housing floor was served by one common lobby and elevator area between the two units. The remaining floors accommodated administrative functions, including receiving and discharge, medical facilities, food preparation, and office space. There was a large screen-enclosed recreation area on the roof.

In each functional unit of the New York MCC there were six eight-room tiers, located one-half flight up or down from the main level. In addition to its eight private rooms equipped with sink and toilet, bed, chest of drawers, desk with desk lamp, and an outside window, each tier had its own pay telephone and shower room, as well as a table and chairs in the hallway. The other areas of the units consisted of two-story multipurpose areas with tables and chairs (used for meals), balcony areas outside the tiers, corner areas for television viewing, large windows for natural lighting that provided panoramic views of the city, a kitchenette where meals could be heated in microwave ovens, a solarium area containing exercise equipment, and staff offices.

The Chicago MCC was designed for a 25-story triangular building that could accommodate only one functional unit in each two-story level. Each unit followed the shape of the building: a right triangle. The center of the unit housed a two-story general-purpose area containing dining tables, Ping-Pong and pool tables, a kitchenette, and large windows. Each of the two acute angles contained a wing of 11 private rooms on each floor, 44 in all. The rooms were equipped similarly to those in the New York facility. At the entrance to each wing was a small lounge with a television set and two couches. The right angle contained office space, an exercise room, and a bank of pay telephones. As in New York, outdoor recreation space was located on the roof of the building.

One of the key elements in the design for both facilities was the provision of spaces that provided varied types of privacy, thereby increasing inmates' control over their interactions with others. In both facilities, inmates were to have private rooms, a place to be alone (official jail policy prohibits visitors in rooms). Inmates could join small groups in the tier hallways, on balconies, in the television-viewing areas, or in the exercise room or solarium, where weight-training equipment was provided. In the larger multipurpose areas, inmates could mingle more freely, around tables for cards or conversation, or at mealtimes, around Ping-Pong and pool tables, or just walking about.

In addition to the choices among different degrees of privacy, an effort was made to provide ample amounts of scarce activities resources – games, exercise equipment, television sets, telephones, showers, and the like. It was the intention of the designers to avoid conflicts created by competition for those resources and to permit conflicts to be defused by retreat to a private room or to the company of a small group of friends. This could reduce the standing level of tension, which might also make conflicts less likely to arise.

However important the design of the facility and the individual modules and their elements, the importance of the complementary role of the corrections officer in the module cannot be overemphasized. Unlike the situation in traditional facilities, where officers act after incidents (whose causes they can only guess) to clean up the damage and punish the offenders, in the direct-supervision facility the officer's role is proactive. He or she is in constant contact with 40 to 50 inmates. That makes it possible for the officer to learn about inmates' personal problems and relationships, to become sensitive to early signs of trouble, and to use interpersonal skills to head off problems. It also personalizes the control system for inmates, permitting communication about such issues before they become aggravated. Rules may be perceived as less arbitrary and less far outside inmates' control under these circumstances than when a remote-surveillance model is used.

These New York and Chicago MCCs underwent extensive POEs conducted by Rich Wener of New York's Polytechnic University and his colleagues (Wener & Clark, 1976; Wener & Olsen, 1977, 1978). Interviews were conducted with the designers, as well as with inmates and staff members; observers mapped and categorized the behaviors of inmates and staff; and institutional records were used to determine how well each facility lived up to the behavioral goals for which it had been designed. Paralleling the designs, there were similarities and differences in the functioning of the two facilities.

Both of the first-generation MCCs appeared to be very successful in meeting the major behavioral goals of the designers. There were very high levels of satisfaction with the degree of privacy afforded by the design: the opportunity for isolation in an inmate's private room, small-group interaction in the tier hallway or on the balcony in the New York design, groups sharing the same interests in the television-viewing areas or solarium, mingling with larger numbers of inmates in the multipurpose spaces in both designs.

There also was a very favorable response to the "soft" or noninstitutional design in both facilities. The levels of attractiveness, comfort, and visual interest of the spaces – an overall sense of design normalcy, quality, and concern for the feelings of the residents – were noted frequently and appreciatively. In addition, the rooms and furnishings were kept clean and were treated respectfully by the inmates, with very little evidence of careless damage or vandalism.

Officers expressed high levels of satisfaction in both facilities. A good deal of the officers' enthusiasm for the designs stemmed from their perceived success in minimizing behavioral problems among the inmates. There were relatively few of the individual problems or interpersonal conflicts typical of traditional facilities. However, the officers themselves attributed the low levels of stress and conflict to the character of the space itself. First, they credited the normalized design concept. They also noted that the design permitted good surveillance of all inmates in all parts of the unit as the officers were able to circulate freely through it.

Behavioral observations corroborated the interview data. There were almost no instances of problem behavior, and inmates made extensive use of the isolation afforded by their private rooms, perhaps withdrawing from potential conflicts with their fellow inmates that way. However, the finding that inmates spent most of their time alone was also consistent with the most negative finding from interviews with inmates and staff. The self-contained units in which the inmates were housed provided too few opportunities for inmates to engage in pursuits more active than sleeping, reading, or attending to their personal hygiene needs by themselves or watching television or playing cards with other inmates. The facilities available for group activities, like games and exercise, were inadequate for the numbers of inmates in the units, and the use of the rooftop exercise areas was limited by space and weather conditions. In addition to the lack of adequate space and variety of facilities, the self-contained nature of the MCC designs meant that inmates very rarely left their units. Only exercise periods on the roof, court appearances, and medical treatment provided inmates with opportunities to break the monotony of life in the unit. Sleeping, eating, educational programs, family and lawyer visits, and recreation all took place in that same self-contained module. The design of the unit itself was exemplary, but the unit was a very small world for inmates and officers alike.

In addition to monotony or boredom, dissatisfaction was expressed with the lack of control over ventilation. The amount and temperature of the air being circulated were controlled centrally. Inmates' exterior windows could not be opened, and vents in their rooms could not be adjusted. Another problem was overcrowding. Almost from the time the facilities were opened, the units were occupied by more inmates than the number for which they had been designed. Private rooms became doubles, hallways and balconies were occupied by extra beds, access to television sets and telephones was limited, and meals and other mass activities were delayed and disrupted. Finally, officers at high-rise facilities were frustrated by inadequate elevator service. Movements to and from the units were painfully slow.

Although the designs of the New York and Chicago facilities were similar in many ways, and they functioned similarly for the most part, there were some differences in design (as listed earlier) and performance. The New York MCC provided more space per inmate and a greater variety of spaces in the tier hallways and balconies, reducing the feeling of confinement somewhat. In the New York facility there was a view from the windows in the multipurpose area, and there was a larger rooftop exercise area (because the footprint of the building was larger, with two modules per floor, as opposed to one in Chicago), both advantages over the Chicago design. In the Chicago MCC, the four minilounges on each unit provided greater access to television and fostered the development of cohesive groups of inmates, and the exercise equipment was housed in a separate room, rather than competing with other uses as in the solarium in New York. Perhaps more important, the Chicago facility contained a separate unit for inmates who had created problems on the open modules. This made it possible to maintain an inmate population on the open housing modules that was compatible with the freedom of movement they afforded.

The Second Generation: the Contra Costa County Main Detention Facility

The Contra Costa County Main Detention Facility (CCCMDF) was built in Martinez, California, for the Contra Costa County Sheriff's Department to replace a badly outdated jail. The design process, including strong accompanying political and economic components, took 17 years (see Frazier, 1985, for an excellent history). On January 16, 1981, the 386-bed facility, designed by Kaplan McLaughlin Diaz, a San Francisco architectural firm, built at a final cost of $25.5 million, was opened. It was the first local jail built on the modular/direct-supervision model, and the choice of that design was based directly on the evidence of the success of the federal MCC program provided by the Chicago POE carried out by Wener and his colleagues. Two separate visits to the Chicago MCC provided the final touch in convincing the planning group, including Contra Costa County officials and a citizens' advisory committee, that an adaptation of the generic MCC design would give them what they wanted – protection of inmates' rights and the safety for inmates and staff that lay at the heart of the MCC program.

As with the federal MCCs, the design for the CCCMDF was tailored to the local site. Martinez is a small city of 16,000 in a semirural area 30 miles northeast of San Francisco. Despite its proximity to the large population centers of the San Francisco Bay area, it has none of the trappings of an urban area. The jail was planned for a site in a complex of Contra Costa County government buildings (the civic center) a block or two west of the approximately four-square-block "central business district" of Martinez. It adjoins a residential neighborhood of modest middle-class homes on a hill to its west.

The residents of the neighborhood above the county government complex had a view of downtown Martinez and beyond that had to be protected. As a result, the height of the CCCMDF building was limited to four stories. The irregularly shaped building contained nine modules, or housing units, along with an intake area and administrative offices, arranged around a central courtyard that provided a large outdoor recreation area comparable to those located on the roofs in designs for urban areas. Following the finding in the Chicago MCC that a segregation unit for inmates who failed to adapt to the direct-supervision system seemed to improve the functioning of the facility, the modules in the CCCMDF were designed to separate identifiable groups of inmates even further. There were three units for unsentenced (detained) and one for sentenced (serving a sentence) males, one for newly arrived inmates (the intake module), one for females, one for inmate workers (trustees), and one each for inmates who were segregated for medical and administrative problems. Further, all new inmates were interviewed and examined extensively during their 72-hour stay on the intake module. Those whose demeanor or medical or psychological condition raised serious doubts about their suitability for the normal housing modules were assigned to medical or administrative segregation.

Unlike the federal MCC designs, there was no single module size or design. Modules were designed to house 30 to 54 inmates each. The normal housing modules were designed with individual rooms arranged in two tiers along one side of a two-story central multipurpose area. Each room was provided with an outside window, toilet and sink, bed, desk and chair, and storage space. The central area was supplied with tables for dining and cards, a television lounge area, telephones, kitchen facilities, and a desk for the officer stationed on the module.

As in the case of the federal MCCs, the modules at CCCMDF were designed with "soft" interiors. Furniture was movable and of noninstitutional design, with attractive fabric upholstery. Floors were covered with commercial-grade carpet, except for the food-preparation areas. Walls were painted in warm, attractive colors. Inmates' rooms had Sheetrock walls and solid doors with small windows.

Like those in the federal MCCs, also, the modules at CCCMDF were designed with a variety of interior spaces affording several different levels of privacy. Inmates' rooms were private. The balconies outside the rooms on the upper tier were widened in three or four places to provide "activity alcoves" where television sets, game tables, and weight-training equipment could be installed. Along with furniture groupings around television sets and dining tables in the multipurpose area, these provided a large number of areas for interaction in small groups with common interests. The public space in the multipurpose area was augmented by an outdoor recreation area adjoining each module, where large-scale body-building equipment was located. This feature was included in the design because of the finding that limited access to the outdoors was a major deficiency in the Chicago and New York MCCs.

In short, the design for the CCCMDF was based on the same behavioral goals as those set originally for the federal MCCs. It elaborated on the basic modular/direct-supervision design that had been proved successful in the Chicago and New York MCCs evaluated by Wener and his colleagues. The private rooms and noninstitutional interior design found in both federal MCCs and evaluated very positively there were incorporated in the design for CCCMDF. Two of the features of the Chicago MCC design that proved successful were adopted for use at CCCMDF. An administrative-segregation module was included, where troublesome inmates would be housed in a more traditional design (locked in their cells most of the time) where they would be segregated from one another and supervised from a remote location. And a wider variety of small-group areas and public activity areas was provided. Greater access to outdoor recreation was provided, consistent with the mild northern California climate, in the form of separate outdoor spaces for each of the standard living modules.

Figure 3.5. The CCCMDF building is so close to a nearby street that security (preventing unauthorized contact with prisoners) is compromised, as indicated by this sign, which is clearly visible to passersby. Photo by author.

Two of the recommendations made by Wener and his colleagues on the basis of their POEs for the Chicago and New York MCCs were, however, ignored: Individual controls were not provided for ventilation in inmates' rooms, and outside windows were located close enough to adjoining streets to create security problems (Figure 3.5).

William Frazier, who was serving at the time as director of inmate services for the Contra Costa County Sheriff's Department, conducted the evaluation of CCCMDF as part of the research for his doctoral degree at Golden Gate University in San Francisco (Frazier, 1985). His study documented the functioning of the facility three years after it had opened. He distributed questionnaires used by Wener in the Chicago and New York MCC POEs to staff and inmates, and he interviewed designers, staff members, and inmates. In all, 160 inmates (of the 269 housed in normal modules at the time) and 109 staff members (of 180 at the time) participated in the evaluation study. He also conducted taped interviews with 50 designers and staff members.

Staff members reported that the appearance of the facility, the privacy for inmates, and the lack of behavioral problems were important positive features. They saw lack of control over temperature and ventilation, lack of adequate staff facilities (lockers, gym facilities, and private dining space), security around the building, and overcrowding as the principal negative features. At the time of Frazier's study, the population of the facility was approximately 500, exceeding the number for which it had been designed by over 25%.

Inmates rated most positively the privacy, appearance, spaciousness, and safety of the facility. They cited lack of temperature control and inability to have their own radios as the greatest problems.

Both staff and inmates' responses were characterized most conspicuously by an absence of traditional complaints – inadequate space, recreational facilities, and privacy, and the dangers posed by conflict among inmates and between inmates and staff. Frazier drew the following conclusions from his findings: "Conspicuous by their absence are the horror stories that one associates with jails. Inmates are not being physically abused or sexually attacked. There is a high level of staff pride in the facility and in the jobs they do. Almost all the staff recognize that it is easy to work in this facility. Many are frankly surprised that the program and design have worked so well" (Frazier, 1985, p. 235).

A follow-up POE

CCCMDF has been subjected to an unusually thorough evaluation. Approximately eight years after the facility first opened, Dr. Craig Zimring of the Georgia Institute of Technology completed a second POE study in November 1989. In a comprehensive evaluation based on interviews, questionnaires, observations, institutional records, and other studies, Zimring found that the original design, incorporating direct supervision, soft furnishings, and plentiful activity spaces and amenities and supported by a well-trained and motivated staff and a sympathetic management, was still functioning successfully. Despite being operated at over twice its capacity, there was still evidence of enthusiastic endorsement by management, deputies, and inmates, a high degree of security for the community, staff, and inmates, and very low levels of vandalism and repair costs, even with the use of vulnerable furnishings and materials. Compared with other recently built jails and prisons being evaluated in a study for the American Corrections Association by Farbstein and Wener, CCCMDF is functioning better even though only one of the others is being operated above capacity (and that one at 40% above, compared with 120% or more at CCCMDF). There is some evidence that the system at CCCMDF is being stretched to its limits by overcrowding. There is growing concern about the quality of interactions among inmates and between inmates and staff, although little or no evidence thus far of actual problems having developed. Nonetheless, it certainly seems that the Contra Costa facility deserves its acclaim as a model jail.

The fourth generation: West County

In 1990, Contra Costa County opened its second direct-supervision jail. The West County Detention Facility was built to house inmates on a 25-acre site in a remote area of Richmond, California, among light industry and farms. It was designed to implement two important recommendations made by those who had evaluated CCCMDF and the federal MCCs. First, it provides much greater variation in inmates' daily routines, including many varied activities and greater freedom of movement among more varied settings. This was recommended in Wener and Olsen's evaluation of the MCCs and Frazier's POE of CCCMDF, although it was not raised as an issue by Zimring in his follow-up POE of CCCMDF. Five housing modules, including one for females, are located in separate two-story buildings. They share a large outdoor area and a number of activity buildings housing medical services, educational programs, visiting facilities, and the like. Except for nighttime hours, inmates are free to move in and out of their housing modules, and they are responsible for scheduling and finding their own way to the activities of their choice. Dangerous inmates are screened out of the West County population, and men and women are allowed to mix freely, eliminating the need for separation among the modules. The entire compound is surrounded by a security fence with a sophisticated electronic alarm system.

Within the housing modules themselves, the inmates are housed in "dry cells," with the toilets and other plumbing facilities located outside the inmates' rooms, off the central dayroom. Inmates are able to leave their rooms at all hours. Building materials include more normal items, such as Sheetrock walls and china sinks and commodes. This design lowers construction costs and adds to the inmates' freedom of movement and privacy and was recommended in both of the CCCMDF POEs.

West County incorporates the interior design features that have proved successful in the third-generation jails – interesting two-story spaces, warm colors, soft furnishings, private rooms, and so on. It will also relieve some of the overcrowding at CCCMDF, although the inmate population there will be somewhat tougher than it is today as more problematic inmates are concentrated there. Inmates who pose the least threat will continue to be sent to the county's farm facility. It will be important to determine how well the even freer and softer version of direct supervision works at West County, even with a less dangerous inmate population.

Evaluation

Stage 1: Background analysis

A jail is a more self-contained and constrained setting than most. There is far less free interchange with those outside and far less freedom of choice or action afforded those inside. As a result, background analysis would not seem to be a critical issue in jail design. Nonetheless, there are some interesting points to be made with respect to the Contra Costa County facility.

The shape of the building itself was responsive to the nature of the surrounding community. Its location at the base of a hill covered with private houses dictated a height limit of four stories to avoid interference with neighborhood residents' views of the waterfront just beyond downtown Martinez, as well as exterior design and landscaping to minimize the conflict of scale between the 180,000-square-foot jail/courthouse building and surrounding structures. Input from the citizens' advisory committee helped the architects to avoid conflicts with neighbors and others in the surrounding community.

The suitability of the design for the user population was assured through controls over the nature of the inmate population as much as by the design itself. Direct-supervision housing modules are not appropriate for inmates who are stubbornly committed to antisocial behavior or for those who are unable by virtue of psychological problems to get along with fellow inmates in a freely interactive setting. The provision of a 72-hour intake module gave skilled corrections, nursing, and mental-health professionals the opportunity to weed out most problem inmates. Those individuals were housed on a separate, higher-security administrative-segregation module, along with others who were transferred out of the open housing modules later at the request of module deputies. This was especially important in light of the fact that this was the first time a modular/direct-supervision design was used outside of the federal MCC program, although the segregation concept had been introduced originally at the Chicago MCC.

Analysis of jail activities suggests that boredom is a serious problem at most facilities. At CCCMDF, inmates were provided with unrestricted communication, including family visits (although the facility is not centrally located in Contra Costa County), telephone, television, and movement within the module, along with a variety of games, exercise equipment, and an outdoor courtyard connected to each module.

Stage 2: Behavioral goals

The principal goals for the behavior of users of the CCCMDF were extremely clear, if somewhat general, from the outset – the prevention of violence and brutalization of the inmate population, as well as the safety of the professional staff. These goals were adopted directly from the federal MCC program. While the jail inmates may have differed from federal detainees in their socioeconomic backgrounds and in the offenses with which they were charged, they were similar in that most had not been convicted of any crime prior to their incarceration. At the time of Frazier's POE study, in 1985, 50% of all those booked into the Contra Costa facility were released within 16 hours, and half of the others within 72 hours of being admitted. The purpose of the facility for most inmates was clearly detention rather than punishment.

Stage 3: Environment–behavior relationships

The modular/direct-supervision design can be analyzed through the use of well-established theoretical concepts such as privacy and control. However, its roots lie more in practical considerations, illuminated through experience in corrections, than in theories of environment–behavior relationships. Environment–behavior theories are usually raised after the fact by social scientists, as an "overlay" (R. Wener, personal communication, 1991).

The knowledge about environmental conditions related to inmate and staff comfort and safety that was utilized in the design of CCCMDF came primarily from Wener's POE study of the Chicago MCC. Despite the obvious differences from the Contra Costa County project – urban location, high-rise design, and inmate population in particular – the finding at the "Chicago Triangle" facility that a modular/direct-supervision design with noninstitutional furnishings and decor was associated with high levels of safety and satisfaction for inmates and staff provided a clear design image for CCCMDF.

Like most POE studies, Wener's evaluation of the Chicago MCC was focused almost exclusively on that one facility. No attempt was made to conduct a formal quasi-experimental comparison with an MCC of a different design, either the previous facility in Chicago or a federal MCC built on a different design elsewhere. This makes it difficult to rule out alternative explanations for the favorable results. New administrative policies or improved staff training (extraneous events), different criteria for inmate selection (group composition), or coincidental cyclical changes in patterns of crime or in the judicial system could have contributed to that outcome.

However, given the high levels of violence and dissatisfaction throughout the correctional system, it seems implausible that any combination of those potential threats to internal validity could account for the findings. Moreover, because one could argue that modular/direct-supervision design is inextricably bound up with related administrative, staffing, and inmate selection policies, it is not clear that any effort needed to be made to determine which aspects of the total "package" of design and implementation produced the desired effects.

Stage 4: Design elements

The Chicago MCC POE study provided a number of clearly identifiable and feasible design elements to be incorporated into the design for the Contra Costa County jail. These included a number of elements found to be successful in the Chicago facility, principally the modular/direct-supervision layout, the use of soft, or noninstitutional, interior design elements, and the provision of variegated spaces affording different levels of privacy. They also included elements suggested by observed shortcomings in the Chicago facility, such as accessible outdoor exercise areas for each module (made more feasible by the nonurban location and California climate) and a separate internal circulation system to permit visitors to reach the modules more easily and safely.

In addition to elements of the physical structure, some of the associated operating procedures utilized in the successful Chicago MCC were adopted by administrators at CCCMDF. These included intake screening and segregation of potential problem inmates and relatively free access to communication with family and legal counsel.

Stage 5: Overall design

The final design prepared by Kaplan McLaughlin Diaz, after receiving extensive input from community members and local government officials, was shaped primarily by the inclusion of the elements borrowed and inferred from the successful Chicago Triangle design. The most important criterion for the choice of design features seems clearly to have been their probable contribution to the achievement of the basic behavioral goals set for the facility. In this case, environment–behavior-based design elements played a pervasive role in the presentation of a final design solution. One indication of the extent of that influence is that the need for staff facilities (for meetings, meals, and exercise) was overlooked because it fell outside the central focus on inmate–staff interaction inside the housing modules fostered by the modular/direct-supervision concept.

Stage 6: POE

The extent to which the behavioral goals for the CCCMDF design were achieved was documented much more fully than is typically the case. The strong concern for systematic and objective evaluation of the efficacy of the design is reflected in the fact that two large-scale POE studies were conducted, the first by Frazier (1985) four years after the facility first opened, and the second by Zimring (1989), a follow-up study four years after that.

These studies are fairly typical of POEs in their emphasis on assessing the functioning of the target facility, rather than on establishing causal relationships with specific design features through systematic comparisons with other designs, or on generalizing to different contexts. However, Frazier (1985) pointed out that the questionnaire and interview data he collected did provide implicit comparisons with traditional facilities, because 83% of the CCCMDF inmates he sampled reported having served time in other jails. And Zimring (1989) did compare the levels of safety and satisfaction at CCCMDF with the levels at other, fairly similar county jails.

Nonetheless, the reports by inmates and staff and the archival records on which these POEs were based reflect, again, the combined influence of the architectural and interior design elements described earlier and the administrative policies in the facility. The jail administrators followed up on the progressive approach to the design process itself with close attention to providing training for the staff and supportive programs for inmates (library services, legal assistance, volunteer services, and more). Besides the additive operation of design and administration, it has been argued (Frazier, 1985) that the demands of the direct-supervision design cause module deputies to adopt a more professional or "corrections" orientation to their jobs. Finally, the results are based on observations made in just one combination of contextual factors (location, inmate population, staff characteristics, etc.).

No matter the resolution of those methodological issues, however, it is abundantly clear that the design for CCCMDF was extremely successful in achieving its behavioral goals. Even though by the time of Zimring's (1989) POE the inmate population had reached more than double the level intended, safety and satisfaction remained extremely high, in comparison with other facilities. Despite the fact that overcrowding might have been expected to override many of the design features addressed to the behavioral goals for CCCMDF (private rooms are no longer private, activity alcoves are taken up by inmate beds, extensive activity spaces and equipment are overwhelmed by excessive demand, and so on), the design continued to work. Because architectural design and administrative policy are necessarily related and will inevitably exert influences on one another, the importance of this finding is not diminished by doubts about causal inference or generalizability.

The results of Wener's and Zimring's POE studies are also corroborated in the widespread acclaim that the CCCMDF has received from corrections professionals. It has been designated a training facility by the National Institute of Corrections. It is the only county jail in California to be accredited by the American Corrections Association, and one of only six in the United States. It has been designated as a model of design process and facility design by the California Board of Corrections. According to Frazier (1985), hundreds of corrections professionals have toured the jail, and most have admitted being converted from extreme skepticism about the radical new design concept to strong support for its performance. In fact, Frazier reports that one such visitor at first believed that the inmates he was observing on an open housing module were drugged, because their behavior was so calm and so normal in a free setting compared with his expectations based on long experience in traditional jails.

Combined with the results of Wener's POE studies of the Chicago and New York MCCs, it also seems clear that the effectiveness of the modular/direct-supervision jail design is fairly general across geographic, climatic, and user population differences in context. Although all POEs are somewhat reactive in nature, relying heavily on self-reports of inmates and staff, the convergence in these studies between reactive and nonreactive measures and the consistent findings regarding problems in the facilities evaluated argue against excessive concern about the validity of the POE findings on those grounds.

Stage 7: Future impact

Together with the results of POE studies of the federal MCCs, the documented success of the Contra Costa County facility has had a widespread influence on jail design. There have been published articles about the advantages of the modular/direct-supervision design (Wener, Frazier, & Farbstein, 1985, 1987), as well as design guidelines and regulations incorporating elements of that general design, such as those of the American Corrections Association and the California Board of Corrections. The generic modular/direct-supervision concept has been adapted to the renovation of the Manhattan House of Detention (the infamous "Tombs," closed by court order in 1974), to a 1,000-bed facility in Dade County, Florida, and to the Multnomak County Jail in Portland, Oregon. In 1985, Frazier estimated that 30 other corrections facilities utilizing variations of this design were being planned or built around the country. And there might be many more if not for the reluctance of corrections officials to advocate such a "soft," nonpunitive approach to housing jail inmates (Frazier, 1985).

Although the POE results have entered the environment–behavior research literature, ties to theory have continued to be implicit and weak for the most part. Although some have pointed out the relevance of concepts like privacy, control, and architectural symbolism, the interest in modular/direct-supervision jail design has been overwhelmingly practical in nature.

References

Frazier, F. W. (1985). *A postoccupancy evaluation of Contra Costa County's Main Detention Facility: An analysis of the first new-generation, modular, direct supervision county jail.* Unpublished doctoral dissertation, Golden Gate University, San Francisco.

Wener, R. E., et al. (1990). Can E&B bring about the end of punishment? A workshop on the role of person–environment relationships in the evolution of prison and jail design. In *Coming of Age: Proceedings of the 1990 Conference of the Environmental Design Research Association* (p. 348). Oklahoma City: EDRA.

Wener, R. E., & Clark, N. (1976). *A user-based assessment of the Chicago Metropolitan Correctional Center.* Report to the U.S. Bureau of Prisons.

Wener, R., Frazier, W., & Farbstein, J. (1985). Three generations of evaluation and design of correctional facilities. *Environment and Behavior, 17,* 71–95.

Wener, R., Frazier, W., & Farbstein, J. (1987, June). Building better jails. *Psychology Today,* pp. 40–44, 48–49.

Wener, R. E., & Olsen, R. (1977). *A user-based assessment of the New York Metropolitan Correctional Center.* Report to the U.S. Bureau of Prisons.

Wener, R. E., & Olsen, R. (1978). *User-based assessment of the federal Metropolitan Correctional Centers: Final report.* New York: Polytechnic University, Report to U.S. Bureau of Prisons.

Wener, R. E., & Olsen, R. (1980). Innovative correctional environments: A user assessment. *Environment and Behavior, 12,* 478–493.

Zimring, C. (1989). *Post occupancy evaluation: Contra Costa County Main Detention Facility.* Atlanta: Environment/Behavior Inquiry.

4

THE PATIENT AND VISITOR PARTICIPATION PROJECT, UNIVERSITY OF MICHIGAN REPLACEMENT HOSPITAL PROGRAM

Location: Ann Arbor, Michigan
Participants: Janet Reizenstein Carpman, Myron A. Grant, and
           colleagues (background research)

In 1979, planning was begun for a large new hospital complex at the University of Michigan in Ann Arbor. Known as the Replacement Hospital Program (RHP), the planning process would culminate in 1985 with the opening of the new Adult General Hospital, a building containing over 1 million square feet of floor space that cost approximately $285 million, making it the largest single public construction project in the history of the state of Michigan (Figure 4.1). It was to be the centerpiece of a larger project that now includes a new outpatient treatment facility and that is continuing today with additional phases not included in the original plan. The Adult General Hospital alone contains 586 patient beds, and during 1988 it served over 31,000 patients who stayed an average of eight to nine days each. During that same year, the hospital complex also accommodated over 600,000 outpatient visits.

    Almost by accident, this gargantuan architectural undertaking included a comparably extensive program of behavioral research that helped to shape hundreds of specific aspects of the final design, from the security system in the parking garage to the location of visitors' rest rooms, from the design of the storage wardrobes in patients' rooms to the numbering of the floors in the buildings, and from the seating used in the outdoor courtyard to the design of patients' hospital gowns. This research program, which was known as the Patient and Visitor Participation (PVP) Project, was begun through the efforts of a graduate student in architecture and sociology at the University of Michigan, Janet Reizenstein (now Carpman), who had a strong interest in the relationship between behavior and environmental design. She was able to convince the then executive director of the University of Michigan Hospital, Dr. Jeptha Dalston, whom she met in a graduate seminar, that the design for the new hospital should take into account the needs and preferences of the

Figure 4.1. A view of the new University of Michigan Hospitals. Photo by author.

patients and visitors who would use it, in addition to those of the professional and administrative staffs who had formal roles in the design process. After the writing of a formal proposal, the creation of a slide show, and approval by several hospital committees, the PVP Project was born. It was intended to serve as an advocate for patients and visitors in the design decision-making process.

Over a period of four to five years, under Carpman's direction, the PVP Project staff conducted over 30 original research studies and made hundreds of separate recommendations for specific design solutions based on the results of their research, as well as other research and theory bearing on patients' and visitors' needs. Presenting even a brief summary of their work is beyond the scope of this report, so we will focus on just four studies that came out of the PVP Program. All of them were addressed to one of the major patient and visitor needs identified by Carpman and her colleagues: finding one's way around a large, complex, and intimidating hospital. These studies were among a somewhat larger group devoted to wayfinding problems and research-based solutions that are described in a report titled *No More Mazes* (Carpman, Grant, & Simmons, 1984).

Wayfinding was considered a serious issue by the PVP Program staff and became a major focus of their research for a number of reasons. First, it was clear that the hospital would be a very large and complex structure, posing difficulties in wayfinding for all of those using it. Second, most of the users, patients and visitors, would be infrequent users and thus not very familiar with the structure. Third, many users would be forced to decode unfamiliar terminology as they sought specific departments or diagnostic or treatment facilities within the hospital. Finally, many of them would be unwell and/or feeling the stress of their own illness or that of a loved one and thus poorly equipped to tolerate the wasted time and effort of being lost in the hospital. These studies exemplify the focus on patient and visitor needs that characterized the PVP Program, illustrate the variety of research methods utilized in it, and provide insight into the role of environmental-design research (EDR) in the overall design decision-making process.

Study 1: Making signs and design-based visual cues work together in helping patients and visitors follow directions to the parking garage

The early plans for the new main hospital building included a 1,000-space parking garage to be located adjacent to the hospital's main entrance. An access road was to pass by in front of both the main entrance and the parking garage. From that road, a semicircular driveway was to provide access to the hospital entrance. Some of those driving to the hospital would want to drop off patients or visitors at the main entrance; then some would leave, and others would drive to the parking garage to leave their cars and return. Other drivers, especially visitors, would want to proceed directly to the parking garage. These different scenarios led to a proposal to locate one entrance, a north entrance, to the parking garage off the semicircular drive, past the point where passengers would be dropped off at the hospital entrance, with a second entrance, a west entrance, directly from the access road into the parking structure. Opponents of this design argued that even with signs placed before the drop-off circle that would indicate that those who intended to park their cars directly ought to proceed along the access road past the drop-off circle, some drivers would be led by the sight of the north entrance to the parking garage to disregard the sign and enter the drop-off circle. This would unnecessarily increase congestion at the main entrance to the hospital and would inconvenience all concerned.

The PVP Project staff designed a research study to evaluate that argument and seek to resolve the issue. They used a video simulation method similar to that developed at the Berkeley Environmental Simulation Laboratory (see chapter 14). Two small-scale models of the hospital entrance and parking garage were constructed, one with a north entrance (drop-off circle) and a west entrance, and one with two entrances from the access road on the west side of the parking garage, both past the drop-off circle. See Figure 4.2 for diagrams of the alternative designs. Then a miniature video camera was put through the models, creating a videotape that simulated the experience of a driver approaching the hospital, passing the signs that indicated the circle

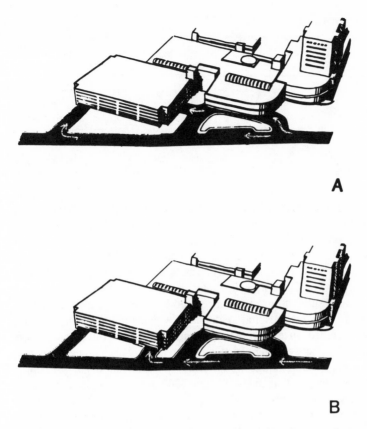

Figure 4.2. The alternate designs considered for the entrances to the parking structure. Diagram A includes the north (drop-off circle) entrance; diagram B shows both entrances on the main road. Source: Carpman, Grant and Simmons (1986, 30); reproduced with permission of American Hospital Publishing, Inc.

where passengers could be let off at the hospital entrance and the route to be followed by those who wished to proceed directly to the parking garage. A north entrance to the parking garage was visible in one tape, but not in the other. To clarify the issue further, two versions of each tape were made, one that simulated a crowded drop-off circle, and one an uncrowded scene.

The resulting simulation videotapes were viewed by 100 visitors to the existing (old) hospital who were approached in public areas and agreed to volunteer. They were told to imagine that they were driving alone to the hospital to visit a patient and were asked to indicate by pointing to the screen of the television monitor where they would turn off from the access road to park. Information was also collected about each subject's age, gender, and education level during an individual 10-minute testing session.

Table 4.1. *Percentages of respondents*

| | Simulated design | | | |
| | North entrance visible | | No north entrance | |
Condition	Turn into circle	Turn past circle	Turn into circle	Turn past circle
Crowded version	38	62	15	85
Uncrowded version	36	64	6	94

The results of this study indicated to a statistical certainty that visitors who intended to park their cars directly, but saw an entrance to the parking garage from the drop-off circle, would be less likely to obey the signs directing them to drive past the circle than would those who saw no north entrance as they approached. This was true regardless of whether the area was crowded with traffic or uncrowded. The complete results are shown in Table 4.1.

Based on the results of this study, it seemed clear that whatever advantage in convenience for some hospital visitors and patients might result from the design that included an entrance to the parking garage from the drop-off circle, the conflict between the visual cues provided by such an entrance and the signs for the parking garage would lead to a significant degree of confusion among drivers, so that many of them (20–30% of thousands per day) would enter the drop-off circle unnecessarily, adding to traffic congestion and inconveniencing themselves and others. This conclusion, along with information about the study, was presented at a meeting of key design decision makers for whom a long debate on the issue had been scheduled. After a very brief discussion, it was decided that the design alternative that provided both entrances to the parking garage off the access road (none on the drop-off circle) should be adopted. Figure 4.3 shows the final design in the context of the entire hospital complex, and Figure 4.4 shows the sign that directs patients and visitors to the drop-off and parking entrances.

Study 2: Choosing understandable designations for the two hospital floors below the level of the main hospital entrance

The new main hospital building was to be built on a hillside site. The 11-story building was to have two floors below grade. Patients and visitors who entered the building at its main entrance and might need to find a specific location on any of its 11 floors would need to be aware that two of those floors were located below the level where they had entered. It was important to number or designate those floors in such a way as to make clear their location

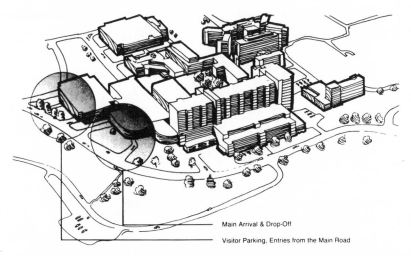

Main Arrival & Drop-Off

Visitor Parking, Entries from the Main Road

Figure 4.3. A drawing of the University of Michigan Hospital's campus showing the final design for the parking-structure entrances. Source: Carpman, Grant, and Simmons (1986, p. 32); reproduced with permission of American Hospital Publishing, Inc.

Figure 4.4. The main entrance to the hospital, on the drop-off circle, with a sign directing visitors to the parking structure beyond. Photo by author.

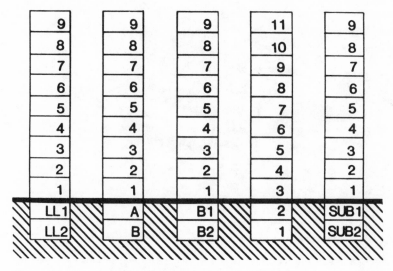

Figure 4.5. The alternative floor-numbering schemes evaluated in the PVP Project research. Source: Carpman, Grant, and Simmons (1986, p. 64); reproduced with permission of American Hospital Publishing, Inc.

and their relationship to the nine floors above grade. It was also desirable that these floors be identified in such a way that their designations would fit on the buttons of the hospital's elevators, which were limited to four characters.

The PVP Project staff generated five floor-numbering options to be evaluated. These are shown in Figure 4.5. They were presented to patients, visitors, and hospital staff members, who were asked to compare them for legibility and desirability, two factors that turned out not to be altogether consistent in this study.

Interviews lasting approximately 20 minutes each were conducted with patients and visitors. Four different responses were obtained from samples of 15 each of inpatients, outpatients, inpatient visitors, and outpatient companions.

Patients and visitors were shown a blank diagram of the first seven floors of the hospital in a format similar to that shown in Figure 4.5. They were asked to locate a floor in that diagram using each of the designations being evaluated. For example, they might be asked, "If you were told your appointment was on floor B1, where on the drawing would you expect to find it?"

The designations Sub1 and Sub2 were located correctly more frequently than any of the others. B1 and B2 and LL1 and LL2 were somewhat less clear, showing a greater tendency to be reversed. Numbers 1 and 2 were even less clear, with 1 being interpreted as the main or entry level by almost half of

Table 4.2. *Floor-numbering survey results*

Floor-numbering option	Clarity (% correct)	Preference (average rating on 5-point scale)	Best option (%)	Worst option (%)
LL1-LL2	30–44	2.65	22.6	37.1
A-B	3–10	2.53	3.2	29.9
B1-B2	37–38	3.48	29.0	3.2
2-1	19–30	2.90	28.5	22.6
Sub1-Sub2	53	3.27	19.4	8.1

those asked. Finally, A and B were by far the least likely to be located below grade.

A second question in the interview asked for respondents' preferences among the five options, based on a diagram similar to Figure 4.5 showing what each would look like when matched with the correct floors. Options B1-B2 and Sub1-Sub2 were rated highest, the same two that had been found to be clearest, although in the reverse order. Options 2-1, LL1-LL2, and A-B were rated considerably lower, in descending order.

A third question assessed preferences by asking respondents to indicate which option they felt was the best and which they felt was the worst. The results for this question were less clear-cut, although B1-B2 seems to have been preferred most, and A-B least. Sub1-Sub2 was chosen as the best option by a smaller percentage than any other except for A-B, but as worst by the second-smallest percentage. Options 2-1 and LL1-LL2 were chosen fairly frequently as best, but frequently as worst also.

The final question in the patient and visitor interview asked for suggestions for a designation for the entry level. The most frequent response was main floor (50%), with many fewer respondents suggesting ground floor (19%), lobby (11%), and floor 3 (6.5%). Several other alternatives were suggested by very small numbers.

The results of these interviews indicated that the designations Sub1 and Sub2 probably were best suited to the needs of patients and visitors, if one gives clarity precedence over preference (see Table 4.2 for a summary).

A survey form was printed in a hospital newsletter to assess the reactions of staff members to the alternative numbering schemes, yielding a total of 350 responses. Ratings of preferences on a five-point scale showed that 2-1 was liked best, along with LL1-LL2, while Sub1-Sub2, B1-B2, and A-B were rated lower, in that descending order. Staff members also indicated which options they felt were best and worst. The percentages choosing each option as best followed the same order as the scale ratings. B1-B2 was identified as the worst option least frequently, A-B most frequently, and the remaining three (2-1, LL1-LL2, and Sub1-Sub2) by intermediate numbers of respondents.

Interestingly, the inconsistency between patients' and visitors' responses to the floor-numbering options and those of staff members was interpreted as reflecting an aversion on the part of staff to designations that characterized the floors below grade as part of the building's basement. Staff members felt that such a designation would demean the people working on those floors and the work they did, independent of how easily the floors could be found. Patients and visitors presumably responded only on the basis of clarity, especially when asked to go from designation to location on a blank diagram of the hospital's floors.

The interview and survey data were interpreted by the PVP Program staff as support for using the Sub1-Sub2 designations for the first and second floors below grade, respectively. That recommendation was accepted by the design staff, but never implemented. The hospital had already contracted for an elevator model that used an electronic display to indicate floor numbers. Unexpectedly, it turned out that the display was limited to two characters, making it necessary to use what had been identified from the research data as the second-best option, B1-B2. The elevator manufacturer refused to alter the elevators' specifications to accommodate the Sub1-Sub2 designation for the floors below grade.

Study 3: Naming hospital buildings

The new hospital building was to be one structure in a whole complex, or campus. Patients, visitors, and others who had not had the opportunity to learn the layout of the entire complex would have to depend to a large extent on signs to find their way around. There was a serious concern on the part of the PVP Project staff that the terms that might be used to designate buildings in the complex that would be familiar to staff by virtue of long-term usage or because they made use of professional jargon would not be understood by patients and visitors.

The research to determine which terms would communicate clearly the functions of buildings, to assist patients and visitors who would need to follow directions on signs to find the buildings they needed, proceeded in two phases. For the first phase, 125 randomly sampled patients and visitors were given "generic descriptions" of five structures and asked to suggest a name for each one. The parking structure was described as a "building where people park their cars." The main hospital building was described as a "place where the sick or injured are given medical or surgical care." The ambulatory care facility was described as a "place where people make appointments, are treated and do not have to stay overnight." The entire medical complex was described as "the whole group of different facilities that provide care to patients here at the University of Michigan." Finally, the pedestrian bridge linking hospital buildings above ground level was described as "an enclosed area above the ground that lets people walk from one building to another."

In the second phase of the research, the terms suggested in the first phase, along with suggestions from committees involved in the hospital design process, were given to 105 randomly selected visitors, who were asked to identify what they thought were the best and worst in each list. Based on their responses, the PVP Project staff were able to make recommendations for terms to be used in the wayfinding system. The research subjects had shown consistent preferences for certain simple terms – Parking Garage, General Hospital, Outpatient Clinic, University of Michigan Hospitals, and Walkway – indicating that these would be the easiest to understand for those needing help in finding their way. These terms were recommended by the PVP Project staff, but their recommendations had only limited impact on the final decisions. Recommendations from design-review committees, reflecting the preferences of professional staff, carried a good deal of weight. The designation "University of Michigan Hospitals" was already in use for the entire medical complex. "Parking" was chosen instead of "Parking Garage." "Health Care Center" was chosen rather than "Outpatient Clinic," although the term "Outpatient Services" was added on signs. "Medical Center" was adopted in preference to "General Hospital."

Study 4: Terminology for departments and services

Once within a hospital building, patients and visitors are faced with the task of finding their way among dozens of departments, offices, clinics, laboratories, and the like. And these destinations are known within the medical profession by highly technical and unfamiliar names. For a population of visitors that will include many people with modest educational backgrounds, as well as many with limited visual and auditory capacities, the use of terminology such as "otorhinolaryngology" may prove less than helpful. Thus, the PVP Project staff sought to identify simpler, less technical, more descriptive terms that would contribute to an effective wayfinding system.

The research was conducted with a random sample of 240 individuals, including inpatients, outpatients, inpatient visitors, and outpatient companions. Altogether, 67 terms were tested for comprehension. Each subject was presented with each term on the list. For half the terms, the subject was presented with the technical term both in print and pronounced aloud by the interviewer. The subject was first asked if he or she knew the meaning of the term (yes or no), then for a definition of the term, which was later coded as correct or incorrect. For the other half of the terms, the subject was presented with a lay definition (e.g., "the department that treats diseases of the heart") and asked for the word that is used to represent it. Both formats were used to test each term, each with one-half the subjects.

The findings of this study showed that patients' and visitors' comprehension of technical medical terminology varied greatly with the specific terms. Some terms were well understood. For example, 68.9% of those tested defined "dermatology" correctly, and 65.6% cited it as a label for the lay definition. "Pediatrics" was also defined correctly by 68.9% of those tested and was given in response to the lay definition by 60.9%. "Cardiology" was defined correctly by 91.9%, although only 24.1% gave it as a label themselves (most used "heart disease" or some similar term).

Other technical terms were understood by very few of the respondents. "Endocrine" and "metabolism" could be defined by 11.3% and were offered spontaneously by only two individuals. "Otorhinolaryngology" was defined correctly by 10.9% and was never given as a response to the lay definition (92.6% gave "ear, nose and throat" as their response). "Ambulatory care" was defined correctly by only 4.8%, and 71% used the term "outpatient" in their response to the definition. Interestingly, people who did not understand the meanings of such terms often thought they did. As many as 60% of those who claimed to understand a term subsequently gave an incorrect definition.

The results of this study supported the use of nontechnical terms in those cases where technical terms would be poorly understood by the patients and visitors who needed to use them to reach their destinations in the hospital. But the recommendation by the PVP Project staff to use simple terms was never implemented. The medical professionals on the decision-making board felt that the hospital would lose prestige in the eyes of the medical profession if lay terms were used in preference to the "correct" medical terminology. This happened even though the research found that 50% of the patients and visitors tested said that if they had a choice, they would choose a hospital that used understandable lay terms, and only 12.7% said that they would choose one that used technical terms.

Evaluation

Stage 1: Background analysis

The spaces, people, and activities that constitute what Barker (1968) would have referred to as the behavior setting of a hospital are fairly predictable from the size and generic type of hospital in question. They are largely predetermined by standards of medical practice and developments in medical technology. These fairly strict constraints on what a hospital may be make the analysis of sociohistorical context less important than in more variable and fluid settings. The extensive investigations of the PVP Project were limited for the most part to behaviorally relevant elements such as signage and furnishings, within a structure whose overall design (size, layout, etc.) was chosen on the basis of considerations apart from patient and visitor comfort.

Even so, the likelihood that background considerations would jeopardize the outcome of the EDR process was minimized by the fact that the research for the design of the new hospital was conducted next door to the construction site, in the old hospital, with many of the same people and activities that would be housed in the new building. And the fact that the project was carried out using a "fast-track" construction process lessened the likelihood that historical changes would prove problematic.

Stage 2: Behavioral goals

The four studies described in this chapter were undertaken to further separate objectives, but all were addressed to the goal of making it easier for patients and visitors to find their way around the new hospital. Ease of wayfinding was an important example of the many goals of the PVP Project as a whole, all of which were concerned with patient and visitor comfort and satisfaction. Of course, the goals addressed by the PVP Project research were included among many others dealing with issues other than user behavior or satisfaction, as is clear from the final disposition of the PVP Project staff recommendations described earlier.

Stage 3: Environment–behavior relationships

In this case, evidence of environmental features contributing to ease of wayfinding was produced by the PVP Project staff in original research dedicated to use in the University of Michigan RHP. The four studies described here provided clear and sufficient evidence of the success of particular environmental arrangements in the specific wayfinding tasks examined.

A variety of research methods was used in the various studies. In the study to situate the parking-garage entrances, comparable samples of those driving to the hospital were exposed to simulations of contrasting design alternatives in an experimental design with no obvious internal-validity weakness. In the study of floor-numbering designation, a single group of individuals responded to alternative designations, in a different type of experimental comparison with comparable internal-validity advantages. The studies of building and departmental terminology were more like survey research, where frequencies of responses, whether labels, definitions, or preferences, were established. In those studies, causal inference (internal validity) was not an important issue.

There seems little doubt that the stimuli to which the subjects in these studies responded were faithful representations of the design elements that would be encountered at the new hospital building, especially in the case of the video simulations used in the study of the parking-garage entrances. The research was conducted using interviews and individual testing sessions in which trained research assistants could maximize the accuracy of responses. Although one can never be absolutely certain in a case like this that the responses in the research context will mirror exactly the responses in the actual hospital setting, great pains were taken in these studies to maximize external validity. The studies were based on large samples of subjects who were clearly comparable to the prospective users of the setting to be created, representing all concerned user groups: inpatients, visitors, outpatients, and companions escorting outpatients. And although the reactive research arrangements suggest that subjects very likely were aware of the purposes of the research, it seems quite implausible that they would intentionally have misrepresented their true reactions or opinions.

Stage 4: Design elements

The fact that these research studies were planned for direct application to this project facilitated the clear-cut inference of useful design elements from their findings (a feature of "dedicated" research). These included the unambiguous locations for the entrances to the new parking garage and the understandable symbols to identify the floors below grade in the new building, the various buildings in the new hospital complex, and the many departments and services in the new main hospital.

Stage 5: Overall design

The PVP Project research was clearly successful in identifying environmental correlates of wayfinding ease for a variety of wayfinding tasks. It did so in a way that suggested very specific design elements that could be incorporated fairly easily into the new hospital building. However, not all of those elements were actually utilized in the final design for the hospital. The fate of the findings of these four studies illustrates the important point that behavioral goals for a design, especially in a large, complex project such as the University of Michigan RHP, must compete with other goals in the design decision-making process. In this case, a preexisting contract with an elevator manufacturer made it impossible to use the floor-numbering system that promised to be most understandable to prospective hospital visitors and patients. And norms regarding appropriate nomenclature among medical professionals precluded the use of names for hospital buildings and departments that were found to be best suited to the needs of hospital users. Only the findings from the study of the parking-garage entrance location were accepted without alteration, presumably because they did not conflict with other goals.

Beyond these four studies and wayfinding issues, there were hundreds of recommendations resulting from PVP Project research that found their way into the final design for the hospital. Nonetheless, it is clear that these successes emerged from a decision-making process in which many other goals and their advocates were influential, and at times dominant.

The PVP Project had a rather unusual status in the University of Michigan RHP. Environmental-design researchers often act in a technical capacity to produce trustworthy answers to behavioral questions raised by a client's goals for a design. As many analysts of the EDR process have noted, however, the prospective users of a setting, such as hospital patients and visitors, often have little input into the establishment of goals, which are set by designers and the administrators who are their clients. In this case, the PVP Project staff undertook to represent those users' interests. Much of their research was based on their own analysis of users' needs, which might not otherwise be recognized by the various other groups participating in the design decision-making process (designers, health-care professionals, hospital administrators, etc.).

In this advocacy role, PVP Project staff were very sensitive to the political process in which they were engaged, and they sought to analyze and understand it along with the environment–behavior issues they were studying. First, they identified other examples, beyond the studies of wayfinding issues described in this chapter, where evidence suggesting effective ways of meeting users' needs failed to influence design decisions. Medical staff members argued successfully that hospital technicians should be provided with natural views of the outside from their laboratory windows, in preference to giving such window views to the patients across the hall, despite evidence in the environment–behavior research literature that the patients would benefit medically from having that natural view if space on the shared floor were arranged differently. Architects hid behind deadlines to avoid making changes in their designs that had been recommended by the PVP Project staff. Generous contributors to the hospital building fund influenced the design of some of the more monumental aspects of the building, including the main entrance and the large public spaces just inside it. And so on.

PVP Project staff also carefully analyzed their own points of leverage in the design decision-making process. They had strong support from the top level of hospital management because of genuine concern over the welfare of patients and visitors and because of concern that the hospital be perceived as user-friendly to gain the necessary share of health-care consumers in its service area. They also had allies among the professional staff with whom they worked in the design decision-making process, especially nursing staff, who shared a commitment to the welfare of patients and visitors. Finally, the PVP Project staff itself had outstanding professional expertise. This was true not only of their identification of user needs and related design issues, and their research supporting specific design solutions, but also of the political skill and perseverance they demonstrated in advocating the implementation of their recommendations.

The influence of the PVP Project on the final design of the hospital and the process by which it was effected were documented by Carpman (1983) in her doctoral dissertation research. For a period of 14 months during 1981 and 1982, she monitored the fate of 287 specific recommendations from 11 PVP Project research studies. Over 60% were eventually accepted, providing an estimate of the overall success of the project. The research also identified the factors that made the difference between success and failure. A basis in empirical research conducted at the hospital, support from other participants in the design decision-making process, a focus on issues peripheral to the core medical technology so important to the professional staff, and a focus on elements of the physical structure all contributed to the adoption of PVP Project recommendations.

Stage 6: POE

The work of the PVP Project ended before construction of the new hospital was completed. Although the staff members continued to develop the work in their own professional careers, their official ties to the University of Michigan Hospitals were severed. No provision was made for a formal empirical evaluation of hospital buildings, including the degree to which the design elements incorporated as a result of the PVP Project research contributed to ease of wayfinding or to the achievement of other specific behavioral goals for the design.

It would not be easy to conduct such POE research effectively. There would be few cases where comparisons could be made between user comfort and satisfaction in the old buildings and in the new. It would be difficult to arrange comparisons between the new buildings and comparable hospitals with different wayfinding or other arrangements. In some cases, comparisons might be made between users' responses to design elements consistent and inconsistent with research findings (e.g., signs with legible terms accepted by the medical professionals and those utilizing illegible terms because more legible alternatives were rejected as unprofessional). The quality of the PVP Project research and the clarity of its application, along with the many awards the work has received from the environment–behavior research and design communities, suggest that POE results likely would be quite favorable, but unfortunately no such evaluation data exist.

Stage 7: Future impact

In 1986, Janet Carpman, Myron Grant, and Deborah Simmons published *Design That Cares*, a book that summarizes the 33 separate research studies conducted during the PVP Project and describes the application of the research findings to the new hospital design. Through that book, separate articles published by the same individuals, and the widespread recognition of the work they describe, the PVP Project has had an important impact on hospital design, beyond its significant impact on the massive University of Michigan project itself. The PVP Project received a design award from the National Endowment for the Arts. *Design That Cares* won an applied-research award from *Progressive Architecture* and a best-of-category award from *Industrial Design*, in 1987, and was reviewed favorably in *Interiors, Industrial Design*, and the *Architectural Record*.

Design That Cares provides specific suggestions for improving the aspects of hospital design addressed directly by the PVP Project. In addition, and probably more important, it provides guidelines for incorporating concerns about patient and visitor comfort and satisfaction into the hospital design process (further augmented by the fine-grained analysis of the role of environmental-design research in the overall design process provided by Carpman's dissertation research). Their book is addressed to hospital administrators, who typically serve as the clients of hospital designers. It can help them to represent the interests of hospital patients and visitors in the design decision-making process, where otherwise the concerns of practitioners, benefactors, and others are likely to take precedence, particularly where EDR consultants such as the PVP Project staff cannot be employed. A recent article in *U.S. News and World Report* (Horn, 1991) cites this work as an outstanding example of a burgeoning movement to improve hospital care through patient-centered design.

References

Barker, R. G. (1968). *Ecological psychology*. Stanford, CA: Stanford University Press.

Carpman, J. R. (1983). *Influencing design decisions: an analysis of the impact of the Patient and Visitor Participation Project on the University of Michigan Replacement Hospital Program*. Unpublished doctoral dissertation, University of Michigan, Ann Arbor.

Carpman, J. R., Grant, M. A., & Simmons, D. A. (1984). *No more mazes*. Ann Arbor: Patient and Visitor Participation Project, Office of the Replacement Hospital Program, University of Michigan Hospitals.

Carpman, J. R., Grant, M. A., & Simmons, D. A. (1986). *Design that cares: planning health facilities for patients and visitors*. Chicago: American Hospital Publishing, Inc.

Horn, M. (1991). Hospitals fit for healing. *U.S. News and World Report*, July 22, 48–50.

5

THE EFFECTS OF THE LIVING ENVIRONMENT ON THE MENTALLY RETARDED (ELEMR) PROJECT

Location: Belchertown State School, Belchertown, Massachusetts
Participants: Arnold Friedmann and Harold L. Rausch (design);
Margaret J. Kent, R. Christopher Knight, Hollis
Wheeler, William H. Weitzer, and Craig M. Zimring
(evaluation research)

"Living in an institution" is an expression that carries strong negative connotations. It elicits oppressive mental images – dreary surroundings, hopeless people, white-coated attendants, disconcerting contrasts with large green lawns and beautifully landscaped grounds. These responses to the residential institutions that have been built to serve a variety of groups whose problems seem to prevent them from living independently in our communities may help to explain some of the recent movement toward deinstitutionalization. But the facts remain that many people continue to live in institutions and that many who have left them have been moved to settings that are not totally integrated into the community and that might be viewed simply as much smaller institutions than the more isolated ones they replaced.

Thus, even those who favor returning all institutionalized persons fully to the community must acknowledge the desirability of improving the way that institutions serve the needs of their residents, their staffs, and the treatment programs they house. The story of the Effects of the Living Environment on the Mentally Retarded (ELEMR) Project is the story of an attempt to do just that, through a rigorous evaluation of certain modifications of the living environment of the residents of Belchertown State School (BSS).

BSS was opened in the 1920s to serve people who at the time were known as the mentally retarded and today are called the developmentally disabled. By the 1960s it had grown to house about 1,500 males and females, mostly adults. Then, gradually, over the decade of the mid-1960s through the mid-1970s, the population of BSS was reduced to about half that number. This was one of many places where deinstitutionalization was taking place. Residential institutions for many different special populations were responding to the growing influence of the "normalization movement." There was increasing support for the belief that one could not expect people who were suffering from developmental disabilities or emotional problems, or any other behavioral problems, to behave normally while they were living in very non-normal institutionalized environments. The ultimate goal of the normalization movement was to return institutionalized people to the communities where the rest of us live. Then they would be left to contend with only their underlying organic problems, serious as those might be, free from the additional non-normalizing pressures of the institutional systems under which so many of them had been forced to live.

At any rate, by 1974, BSS had become (ironically, in part as a result of partial deinstitutionalization spurred by the normalization movement) the worst sort of "state school," worse than it had ever been. All of the elements of its old institutional system remained intact – the cold living arrangements lacking comfort or privacy, the oppressive daily routine lacking real treatment or warm human contact, and the sparse, underpaid, discouraged staff. The 700 or more residents who remained were those with the most serious problems, those whom the authorities had been unable to place outside the institution. Nestled in the beautiful hills of western Massachusetts, BSS was nonetheless not a pretty picture.

But the normalization movement was not finished with BSS. A group that called itself Friends of Belchertown State School, composed mostly of parents of the institution's residents, sued the Commonwealth of Massachusetts, claiming that the residents of the school were not receiving adequate care. The group's legal arguments emphasized the normalization principle. Whatever their disabilities, people could not be expected to reach their full potential while living under the institutional conditions at BSS. After inspecting the conditions at the school, Judge Joseph L. Tauro of the federal district court in Boston, Massachusetts, ruled in favor of the Friends of BSS, without even allowing the state's attorneys to present their case. He ordered changes to be made at BSS, including changes in the physical living environments of the residents, to be supported by an appropriation of $2.6 million by the state legislature.

The judge's ruling specified that, in accordance with the normalization principle, the living quarters of the residents of BSS be modified to be more homelike. At the time, the residents lived under conditions that provided virtually no privacy and that prevented any form of personalization. Most of them were housed in two-story buildings that were divided into six rooms, each approximately 30 by 40 feet in size (Figure 5.1). Three of the rooms were used as sleeping quarters. Fifteen to 20 residents slept in each of those rooms, in open-ward arrangements (Figure 5.2) – just their beds, some pushed together head-to-head, with no furniture or partitions to separate them and no personal belongings of any sort. Each morning, attendants brought them clothing and even items like hairbrushes from common storage places.

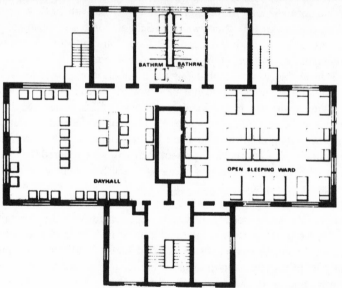

Figure 5.1. One of the buildings that underwent "experimental" renovation at BSS (photo by author); and floor plan of the prerenovation living environment. Source: Knight, Weitzer, and Zimring (1978, p. 46); reproduced with permission of the University of Massachusetts.

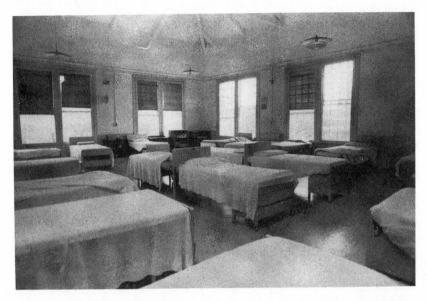

Figure 5.2. Photograph of an open sleeping ward (prerenovation design) at BSS. Source: Knight, Weitzer, and Zimring (1978, p. 47); reproduced with permission of the University of Massachusetts.

One of the remaining rooms served as a dayhall, sparsely furnished with waiting-room-type chairs lining the walls, and a large empty space in the middle. Another room was a dining hall, and the last was a bare multipurpose activity room. Throughout the buildings, floors were covered with asphalt tile, and many of the walls with ceramic tile; ceilings were of painted plaster, and the rooms were uniform, barren, and cold – in short, institutional.

The design of the existing living environment at BSS was the result of many factors. It was inexpensive to furnish and easy to keep clean. A small staff could easily keep track of the 45 to 55 residents of a single building. For those and other reasons of expediency, such arrangements probably made sense to administrators who felt that the institution's residents had little or no hope of overcoming their disabilities or of leaving the institution for more independent living arrangements where they might have learning opportunities that a place like BSS could never provide. The school provided a safe, clean place where they could be conveniently stored for the rest of their lives.

But to those who believed in normalization, and to those who simply wanted their sons and daughters and brothers and sisters to have a more pleasant place to live, those conditions were unacceptable. Their victory in court, along with the money awarded by Judge Tauro and a grant from the Department of Health, Education, and Welfare in Washington, made it possible for their view to carry the day. A process of change was begun at BSS that included an attempt to reshape the physical living environment of its residents in a way that might help them to achieve their full potential as human beings.

The renovations

One of the first outcomes of the court victory by Friends of BSS was a change in the administration of the school. The task of implementing the judge's order was put in the hands of an administration that was sympathetic to the goal of normalization. One of its first duties was to plan the physical changes that were to be made in campus buildings to create a more homelike living environment for the school's residents.

The design for the renovations to be made in the residence buildings at BSS involved a process that was rapid, complex, and somewhat mysterious. Despite the fact that voluminous reports were published documenting the evaluation of the project, the evolution of the design must be pieced together out of brief references and tenuous inferences.

Three renovation designs ultimately emerged out of that process. They eventually constituted (probably more than had been intended) a living laboratory in which to test basic concepts and theories from environment–behavior research and, at the same time, some basic assumptions underlying the normalization principle. After the fact, they were able to be ordered so that meaningful comparisons could be made among them. The fact that three alternative renovation designs were implemented made that possible. However, the multiplicity of renovation designs was the outgrowth of a complex combination of inputs into the design process: Variations among the existing buildings that needed to be renovated, as well as input from the school's administrators, the architects they hired to carry out the renovations, and a design team from the nearby University of Massachusetts, headed by Arnold Friedmann, professor of design, and Harold L. Raush, professor of psychology. Although one is tempted to suspect that Friedmann and Raush and their students, who had considerable knowledge of the existing research literature and theory concerning environment–behavior relationships, were largely responsible for the eventual array of designs that reflected such knowledge and made possible an evaluation that added a great deal to the designs, they have claimed to have had only minor input (Friedmann, 1976).

At any rate, the principal guidance for the physical renovations that were planned for BSS was the normalization principle. Following the judge's very specific ruling ordering the normalization of conditions at the school, the renovations were designed to make the living environment more homelike. For whatever reason (and to the great benefit of the eventual evaluation and of our knowledge about environment–behavior relationships), the three distinct forms of renovation that were carried out differed in the extent to which they

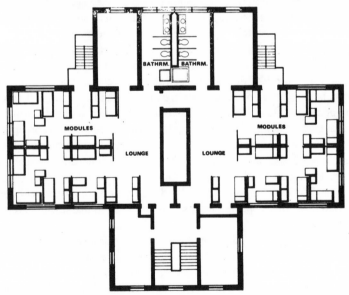

Figure 5.3. Photograph and floor plan of the modular form of renovation. Source: Knight, Weitzer, and Zimring (1978, pp. 48–49); reproduced with permission of the University of Massachusetts.

were homelike by virtue of their appearance (the element seemingly emphasized by proponents of the normalization principle) and in the extent to which
they provided the privacy and variety of spaces that distinguish homes from
institutional settings, the functional properties of "normal" homes that might
be expected on the basis of environment–behavior research and theory to
normalize residents' behaviors.

The first design provided minimal increases in both homelike appearance
and privacy over the prerenovation living environment. This modular-unit
design divided the open sleeping wards and dayrooms of a standard BSS
residential building into personal living spaces separated by partitions 4.5 feet
high (Figure 5.3). Each resident was provided with a bed, dresser, and desk
within his or her personal module. Thus, some privacy was afforded by
screening residents from the view of other residents and staff when they chose
to sit or lie on their beds, and the spaces in which they lived were personalized
to some degree by providing them with places for their personal belongings,
including clothing, rather than having all personal items shared communally
as they had been in the open sleeping wards. However, privacy was still very
limited. There was virtually no screening of sound. The barriers did little to
discourage residents or staff members from walking through modules whenever they wished. In fact, some modules were located such that they became
parts of paths through the large rooms that had been divided. Lights continued
to be controlled by central switches, restricting residents' freedom to control
their own activities. The furnishings were still quite institutional in appearance, and the overall effect of the renovation in each large room of the
building was more like that of an open-plan office than that of a home. The
contrast between the modular sleeping quarters and the public lounge and
dining areas outside was not great, a contrast between semipublic and public
spaces at best. In sum, this design provided something of a placebo or change-
only comparison for the evaluation of other renovation designs (a minimal
change at best). Despite the lack of firm evidence, one might suspect that it
was created in part for that purpose. Of course, it may have been a standard
institutional scheme that was known to the architects, or a relatively inexpensive alternative that appealed to cost-conscious administrators, among other
possibilities.

A second design provided a modest increase in privacy over the modular
design, but a great increase in homelike appearance. It was labeled the suite
design. The three sleeping wards and the dayroom in a standard BSS residential building were each converted into a suite of four rooms separated by
eight-foot-high partitions (Figure 5.4). Each of the suites contained three
bedrooms of different sizes, one for four residents, one for three, and one for
two. The fourth room in each suite was a lounge that was shared by the nine
suite residents (Figure 5.5). The homelike appearance of the suites derived, in
part, from the provision of semiprivate bedrooms and lounge, but even more
from the furnishings in those rooms. The furniture was noninstitutional and

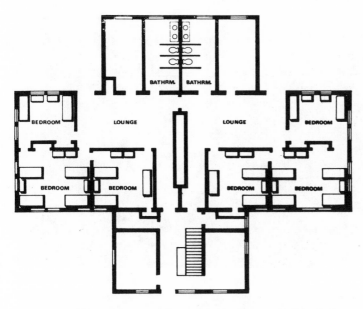

Figure 5.4. Floor plan of the suite renovation. Source: Knight, Weitzer, and Zimring (1978, p. 50); reproduced with permission of the University of Massachusetts.

complete, including beds and dressers, area rugs, lamps, draperies, and a television set in the lounge. In addition, residents and their families were able to add photographs, posters, and other personalized decorations. Of course, residents had their own clothing and toilet articles with them in their rooms. The privacy in these suites was increased by the separation of rooms with walls high enough to provide complete visual screening and the provision of doors to limit unwanted intrusions. Auditory screening was limited because of the incomplete walls, especially the sound of the television set in the lounge, and although residents controlled the artificial illumination in their own rooms, light did pass from room to room over the walls. Privacy was limited by the fact that bedrooms were shared with one to three other residents, and the sounds of conversation passed to adjacent rooms. Still, in regard to the levels of privacy in residents' bedrooms or personal spaces, the suite lounge, and the public areas of the dining and activity rooms, there was much greater variation in the suite design than there had been in the original configuration.

The third design seemed to reverse the proportions of privacy and homelike appearance found in the suites. Called the corridor design, it closely resembled one common design for a college dormitory (see chapter 7). Six single and six double bedrooms flanked a double-loaded corridor with a large lounge at one end (Figures 5.6 and 5.7). Two such corridor units replaced the large communal spaces in a BSS residential building that had been constructed in

Figure 5.5. Photographs of a suite bedroom (top), and suite living room (bottom). Source: Knight, Weitzer, and Zimring (1978, p. 51); reproduced with permission of the University of Massachusetts.

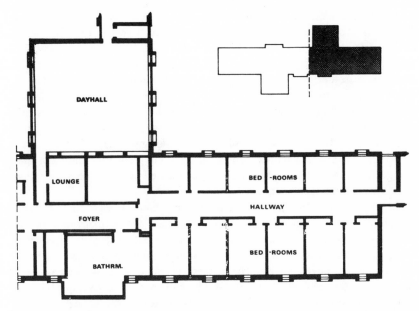

Figure 5.6. Floor plan of the corridor renovation. Source: Knight, Weitzer, and Zimring (1978, p. 53); reproduced with permission of the University of Massachusetts.

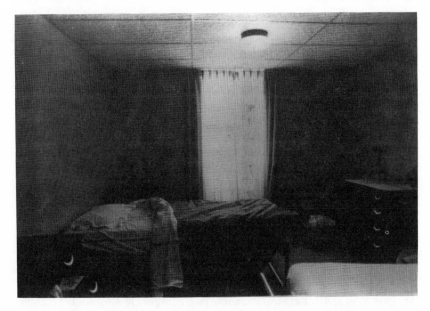

Figure 5.7. Photograph of a corridor bedroom. Source: Knight, Weitzer, and Zimring (1978, p. 54); reproduced with permission of the University of Massachusetts.

the 1960s, considerably later and according to a different design than the other residences at the school. The walls that separated rooms in this renovation extended from floor to ceiling. Bedroom doors that could be locked by the residents and controls for artificial lighting within the completely enclosed rooms increased privacy for residents and contributed to a broad continuum of available spaces in the corridor building, from the very private single bedroom (Figure 5.7), through the double bedroom shared with a roommate, to semi-public lounge and public dining and activity areas. Furnishings, on the other hand, were far less elaborate than in the suite design. This, plus the overall configuration in which rooms were lined up along a corridor and baths and lounges were located down the hall and were shared by 18 residents, resulted in a less homelike appearance than in the suite design.

Whether planned for that purpose or not, the choice of these three renovation designs made it possible to test the effects of the normalization of the residents' living environments in a particularly sensitive manner. If benefits could be shown for the modular units, it would seem that a minimal degree of normalization, or even any change or change per se, could make a measurable difference in the residents' lives. If the suite and corridor renovations brought equal benefits over the original living environment, it would seem that (1) increasing the homelike appearance and (2) increasing functional privacy and variety in living spaces would be equally effective ways of achieving normalization. If both suites and corridors proved more successful than the modular renovations, then a relationship between degree of environmental normalization and degree of behavioral normalization, and the need for more than change for the sake of change, would be demonstrated. And if either the suite or corridor design provided greater benefits than the other, and greater advantages over the original institutional living environment and/or over the modular renovations, then one or the other of the potential contributors to normalization – homelike appearance or privacy and variety – would be shown to be more important or even to be the key feature of normalized environments for the developmentally disabled.

Assessing the effects of the renovations: the ELEMR project

Although their involvement in planning the three renovation designs may have been minimal, environment–behavior researchers became heavily involved in the effort to evaluate the effects of those designs on the residents of BSS and on the system for caring for them at that institution. The work of the design team from the University of Massachusetts headed by Friedmann and Raush was carried on by a research team from the same institution, headed by designer Margaret J. Kent and including psychologists R. Christopher Knight, William H. Weitzer, and Craig M. Zimring and sociologist Hollis Wheeler. The evaluation study they planned and carried out, supported by a grant from the Developmental Disabilities Office of the U.S. Department of Health, Education, and Welfare, has been published (Knight, Weitzer, & Zimring, 1978).

The evaluation of the renovation designs was based on a conceptual analysis that encompassed two levels. On the first, the available environment–behavior research and theory were used to predict the effects of the renovations, and more importantly to provide a conceptual framework to guide an understanding of the results of the evaluation after it was completed. On the second level, the institutional system in which the residents' physical living environment was embedded was analyzed to plan the overall strategy for the evaluation study itself. In addition, the ELEMR team developed detailed plans for the observation and other data-gathering procedures to be used to carry out that strategy.

The effects of the renovations were predicted from an analysis that contrasted the view taken by proponents of the normalization principle with existing knowledge from environment–behavior research and theory. In statements of the normalization principle (e.g., Wolfensberger, 1973), physical settings are treated primarily in terms of the degree of normality of their appearance. Homelike settings, which are assumed to evoke more "normal" or adaptive behaviors, are assumed to be those that bear a strong physical resemblance to homes in the community. Colors, building materials, and furnishings typical of homes in the community are contrasted, in this view, with those found in an institutional setting.

But theories about environment–behavior relationships are based on research that fosters a functional view of the attributes of institutional and noninstitutional settings. For example, Sommer (1969) contrasted spatial arrangements that discouraged social interaction with those that encouraged interaction (see chapter 8), although the actual furnishings used in those "sociofugal" and "sociopetal" arrangements were identical. Similarly, Altman (1975) stressed the importance of privacy regulation in settings shared by groups over extended periods of time, with little consideration for the appearance of the materials out of which the settings were built.

These and other more general theories that stress the functional properties of environmental settings were used to develop a theoretical rationale for the ELEMR study. The general "behavioral hypothesis" that more nearly normal living environments would produce more nearly normal behaviors was recast into two more specific hypotheses based on the functional view of environment–behavior relationships. First, it was hypothesized that the residents of BSS, like everyone else, felt a need to be able to control the levels of stimulation in their living environments in order to maintain levels that matched their personal preferences and moods. Second, it was hypothesized that the residents of BSS, like the rest of us, needed to be able to control their interactions with others, to achieve whatever levels of privacy or contact with others were appropriate to their individual preferences or to the demands of the existing situation.

Thus, the designs that were developed for renovating the residents' living environments at BSS were viewed as a test between two contrasting positions. If the advocates of the normalization principle were correct, and homelike appearance of the living environment was the key, then the suite design should be superior to the others in bringing about normalization of the residents' behaviors. On the other hand, if the functional view of environment–behavior theory was correct, then the greater privacy and greater variety of settings afforded by the corridor design should cause it to emerge as the superior alternative.

The conceptual analysis on which the ELEMR study was based included a systems-theoretic analysis of the effects of residents' living environments on their behaviors. The plans for the evaluation study were based on the view that the "focal problem" of the effects of the physical living environment on residents' behaviors was embedded in a complex, interactive context that included all of the actors on the BSS campus, including residents, direct-care staff (attendants), professional staff (psychologists and physicians), and administrators, as well as actors outside the institution, including parents and other advocates for the residents, legislators, and state officials, plus the administrative policies for staffing the school, developing treatment programs for the residents, and specifying use of the facilities.

The scope of the ELEMR evaluation

The broad systems view of the role of the physical form of the residents' living environments widened the scope of the ELEMR study to include a variety of methods, measures, and targets.

A large part of the empirical evaluation of the effects of the three renovation designs, compared with the institutional prerenovation living environment, was based on direct observation of the residents and direct-care staff. Behavior checklists were constructed that allowed observers to categorize the actions that took place. The checklist for resident behaviors was designed to trace the relative frequencies of withdrawn/stereotypical and alert purposive behaviors, the degree to which residents made use of the personal spaces (beds, modules, or bedrooms) assigned to them, the frequency with which residents intruded into one another's personal spaces, and the frequency of occurrence of social interactions among residents, including special note of the occurrence of verbal interactions (those in which some form of vocalization occurred).

The checklist for staff behaviors focused on contacts between staff members and residents. Those contacts were broken down into two broad categories: the frequency of intrusions by staff into residents' personal spaces, and resident–staff interactions. The latter category was broken down, in turn, according to the source or initiator of the interaction (resident or staff member) and according to the nature of the interaction, distinguishing between formal interactions in which staff duties (such as caring for residents' personal needs or teaching specific tasks) were being carried out and social interactions that involved no formal duties.

The observations of residents' and attendants' behaviors were backed up with extensive information about the individuals in each of those groups. Information about residents came primarily from the school records, which contained background data such as the individual's age and the age at which he or she entered the institution, as well as information about the individual's history at the school. One key piece of information was the resident's tested IQ. The residents who were involved in the ELEMR study were in the groups commonly referred to as severely and profoundly retarded. These are the two lowest categories on the scale on which mental retardation is measured. The IQs of the severely retarded range roughly from 20 to 36, and those of the profoundly retarded fall below 20.

As adults, and all of the residents involved were adults, severely retarded individuals may be capable of taking care of their own basic needs, although their toilet, communication, and eating skills may leave a good deal to be desired, especially if they have physical handicaps. The severely retarded are sometimes successful at living and working in sheltered environments in the community, although the majority live in residential institutions like BSS. These individuals represent approximately 3.5% of the total population of the mentally retarded, or approximately 200,000 to 400,000 persons in the United States.

As adults, the profoundly retarded almost always have serious organic defects, often including brain abnormalities and observable physical handicaps, such as blindness, deafness, and cerebral palsy. Most are nonambulatory and are unable to contribute much to their own personal care. Except for those living with professional care in private homes, these individuals, about 1% of the total mentally retarded population, over 100,000 in the United States, are institutionalized. Of course, these "textbook" categorizations were developed in the context of a system of care that rarely provides normal physical or social environments for such individuals; in fact, these two groups were once referred to, together, as the "custodial mentally retarded." As might be expected, the intact residential groups that were studied at BSS during the ELEMR evaluation each tended to be homogeneous with respect to IQ and thus substantially different from one another in their capabilities and behavioral repertoires.

School records also contained information about the backgrounds and employment histories of staff members. Additional information about staff members was obtained from interviews, journals of their daily routines based on

participant observation, and extensive informal contact over the lengthy period of the evaluation study. This background information was helpful in
organizing and interpreting the quantitative results of the evaluation, as a part
of the "ethological" approach chosen by the research team. They believed that
the value of the objective empirical observations that were collected was
limited by the availability of information about contextual factors that tended
to preserve the complex interrelationships among all of the elements in the
unique institutional system that was BSS.

There was also extensive documentation of the actual physical changes that
were made in the course of the renovations. Photographs were the principal
means of recording those physical changes. In addition, however, precise
measurements were taken of one aspect of the physical environment that was
believed to be a crucial source of support for the normalization of residents'
individual and social behaviors. That was the acoustic environment for
speech. It was believed that high levels of background noise and highly
reverberant spaces in the prerenovation buildings were important causes of
residents' social withdrawal, which in turn was reflected in their individual
behaviors as a lack of alertness, as stereotypical repetitive actions, and as
deficiencies in social behaviors. These physical conditions, which were attributed to the large, open public spaces, the hard reflecting surfaces, and the
lack of sound-absorbing materials in the original buildings, were believed to
make speech more difficult, especially for those residents who already had the
most difficulty in speaking intelligibly and understanding speech, thus contributing to their tendency to withdraw into solitary, stereotypical patterns of
behavior. Measurements of noise levels were taken in prerenovation buildings
as well as in all three renovation designs. Those measurements were later used
in a laboratory experiment in which samples of both residents and staff members were tested for speech discrimination in simulated prerenovation and
postrenovation living environments.

A final element of the BSS institutional system was the professional and
administrative staff. These actors were not studied as individuals, as the
residents and staff were. Instead, their policies were evaluated in order to
understand some of the constraints under which resident and staff behaviors
were taking place. A good deal of information about administrative policies
was gained in the course of the researchers' extensive meetings with professionals and administrators, and during informal contacts with them during the
time the researchers spent inside the institution. In addition, a sociologist
member of the evaluation team carried out a participant-observation study in
the course of which she worked as an attendant for two weeks. Her study
provided a rich source of firsthand information about the experiences of
direct-care staff members and their perceptions of the policies under which
they worked – what an organizational theorist would call the organizational
climate of the institution.

In summary, elaborate means were devised to assess the key components of the system that the physical renovations were intended to help normalize. The individual, social, and spatial behaviors of the residents, the spatial and resident-directed behaviors of the direct-care staff members, the physical setting (with special emphasis on its acoustical properties), and the organizational climate or administrative policies that governed all the other elements were amenable to close examination in the course of the evaluation study.

The temporal plan and research design for ELEMR

Observations of resident and staff behaviors were carried out during six periods, each lasting six weeks, between July 1974 and February 1977. The plan was to establish baseline records, before renovations, for resident and staff behaviors in the original living environments at BSS. Comparison observations in the three renovation designs were to be made between six months and one year after the buildings were occupied by groups of residents and staff moved from unrenovated buildings. Because renovations were to be carried out in stages, building by building, it seemed that it would be possible to compare renovated and unrenovated buildings during the same time periods, when administrative policies and other contextual factors would be similar for both, in addition to the before-and-after comparisons for each of the three renovation designs. During the entire period, the interview, participant-observation, and laboratory-research components of the evaluation would also be carried out, to complete the picture of the institutional system within which the direct effects of the renovations were taking place.

The plans of the ELEMR team were as neat and logical – a very sophisticated quasi-experimental design, in fact – as one would expect of such highly trained researchers. But they met a fate that is not unusual when research is conducted inside an organization whose day-to-day operations are influenced by many powerful forces, all of which are beyond the control of the researchers. Although the extensive data-collection activities proceeded as planned, the evaluation team's painstaking plans for crucial comparisons to answer important practical and theoretical questions were eventually reduced to only a few discernible patterns that could be followed.

Changes in construction schedules and in administrative policies disrupted the timing of the observation periods, thereby reducing drastically the number of sequences of prerenovation and postrenovation observations that could be analyzed and the opportunities for concurrent comparisons of prerenovation and postrenovation settings. High rates of turnover within the resident and staff populations in the buildings chosen for observation frustrated the researchers' plans to carry out sensitive "within-subjects" comparisons that would track given individuals from one living environment to the next, in addition to the comparisons between different groups in comparable living

environments. Much of the turnover in the resident populations within specific buildings resulted from the ongoing process of deinstitutionalization that
was gradually reducing the total resident population at BSS. As the remaining
residents were consolidated in fewer buildings, new administrative policies
designed to respond to court-ordered normalization caused additional movement of residents between buildings. Turnover was chronically high among
the direct-care staff at BSS, especially among younger members, who often
were unprepared for the working conditions they found at the school.

The clash between the ELEMR team's logical plans for the evaluation study
and the realities of the institution left the researchers with only a limited basis
for testing their hypotheses. There were only three sequences of moves between the original prerenovation living environment and the three renovation
designs for which adequate prerenovation and postrenovation observations
were available. Even there, the picture was somewhat muddled: Not all the
moves were direct; far too few residents and staff made the moves together to
permit meaningful comparisons of the same individuals in different living
environments; one of the renovation designs was tailored to a building that
was newer and of a different design than the "standard" 50-year-old buildings
in which the other renovation designs were executed; the residents who were
observed in the three sequences differed markedly in the extent of their disabilities, despite the restricted variability of the resident population, from
which the better-functioning half had been removed to homes and
intermediate-care facilities in communities outside the institution by the time
the ELEMR Project got off the ground in 1974.

One comparison sequence consisted of a series of moves from an institutional living environment to the building that had undergone renovation to the
corridor design and finally to a building that had been renovated in the suite
configuration. At each stop along the way, a sample of the residents was
observed, 15 at the first and second stages, and 19 at the third. Only five
residents were present through all three phases of the sequence. As was true
throughout the ELEMR study, residents who were transferred out of the group
being studied were replaced by random selection from the other residents of
the building. One six-week observation period was conducted during each
phase of this sequence. The residents who were involved were among the
higher-functioning residents of BSS at the time. Those who were observed in
the original institutional setting had an average IQ of 17, those in the corridor-
design renovated building had an average IQ of 28, and those observed in
suites had an average IQ of 26. The second sequence permitted a comparison
between groups of residents and staff in a traditional institutional living environment and the same groups later on in the corridor-design renovated building (after the group in the sequence described earlier had moved on to their
final destination in suites). One six-week observation period was conducted in
each of the two settings, with 19 residents observed in the first period, and 18
in the second. In this case, only three residents were present in both settings.

The residents who were involved in this sequence were identified as lower-functioning individuals. The average IQ of those observed in the original institutional building was 13, and those who were observed later on in the corridor-design renovated building had an average IQ of 15.

The third sequence consisted of a move from the institutional living environment to a building renovated according to the modular design. Four observation periods were completed for this sequence, one in the prerenovation stage and three after the move into the modular renovation. Fifteen to 21 residents were observed during those four periods, and 10 were present throughout the sequence. These residents were described as moderate-functioning, with average IQ scores for the groups varying between 21 and 25 over the sequence.

In summary, the ELEMR staff were left with one opportunity each to observe the effects of the modular and suite renovations on resident and staff behaviors, and two opportunities to observe the effects of the corridor design. These opportunities were fewer than those originally planned, and much of the total volume of data collected during the study was rendered useless by changes in others' plans; also, it was possible to observe the effects of the suite renovation only after an intermediate move through the corridor-design renovated building, and the residents who were observed in the various renovation configurations were so different in their developmental capabilities and problems that comparisons had to be made across quite unlike circumstances. In view of all these difficulties, the presentation of the results of the evaluation by Knight, Weitzer, and Zimring (1978) is remarkably clear and coherent.

The results of the ELEMR evaluation

The results for each comparison sequence will first be presented separately, following the organization of the ELEMR report. For each sequence, the findings will be arranged in the same order, beginning with the effects on the residents' use of space, followed by the residents' solitary and social behaviors and staff interactions with residents. Then those results will be summarized over the three comparison sequences. Finally, the results of the analysis of administrative policies and of the experiment assessing the changes in acoustical environments will be presented and used to summarize the results again, briefly, in their broader context.

From institutional to corridor living environment

Residents were found to use their own personal spaces much more in the corridor-design renovated building than in the institutional living environment with which it was compared. In other words, the residents observed living in the corridor design spent much more of their time in their rooms than the residents observed earlier in a traditional building had spent in the area of their beds in the sleeping wards. Residents spent about 5% of the time during which they were observed in their own spaces in the original institutional setting, compared with 23% in the corridor building. In addition, there were fewer intrusions by residents into one another's personal spaces in the corridor building. In the original sleeping-ward arrangement, residents were in one another's personal spaces over 19% of the time they were observed. In the corridor building, intrusions occurred during only 6.4% of the observation periods, a little more than one-third of the earlier rate. These findings for spatial behavior were consistent enough across the two groups compared between the institutional and corridor settings to be combined into the overall means presented earlier, despite the large difference in IQ between those groups (an average IQ of 28.2 for the first group that would eventually move on to a suite building, compared with an average IQ of 15.1 for the second group to be observed in the corridor building).

The solitary and social behaviors of residents were also different in the corridor-design building. Residents were rated alert 62% of the time they were observed in the corridor setting, compared with 39.4% of the time in the original institutional building. Residents' behaviors appeared withdrawn only 2% of the time they were observed in the corridor building, compared with 22.3% in the institutional living environment. Interaction among residents was observed to occupy 10.9% of their time in the corridor building, compared with 4.7% in the institutional setting. Verbal interaction occupied 9.7% of residents' time in the corridor building, compared with 2.2% in the original, prerenovation setting. These solitary and social behaviors differed between the higher-functioning and lower-functioning groups compared between the corridor and institutional living environments, the former group being observed to be less withdrawn, more alert, and more sociable. However, the same pattern of differences between living environments was observed for both groups of residents, justifying a unified presentation of the findings.

Staff–resident interactions were far less frequent in the corridor-design building for both groups observed there, occurring in only 18% of the 15-second periods sampled, compared with 38% in the original institutional living environments. Both staff members and residents were less likely to initiate interactions with one another in the corridor-design building, each being observed to do so about one-third as often in that setting. Incidentally, resident–staff interactions were about 2.5 times as likely to be initiated by a staff member as by a resident in either setting.

From institutional to suite living environment

In general, the pattern of comparisons between the group that was observed first in a prerenovation institutional setting and later in a building renovated in the suite design (after a stop in the corridor-design building in between) resembles a weaker version of the comparisons between institutional and corridor living environments.

Residents of suites used their personal spaces almost twice as much as did the comparison groups in an institutional living environment: 9.6% of the time they were observed, compared with 4.9%. This increase fell far short of that observed in the corridor design, where the corresponding figure was 23%. In the case of residents' intrusions into one another's personal spaces, the suite design showed somewhat more of a reduction from the original institutional building than did the corridor design: 4.8% of the time for intrusions in suites, 6.4% in the corridor building, and 19.1% in the institutional living environment.

Residents were somewhat more alert while living in suites, as compared with their original institutional quarters, although less so than in the corridor building. Their behaviors were rated alert 55.2% of the time in suites, compared with 39.4% in the institutional setting (vs. 62% in the corridor building). They were rated withdrawn 17% of the time in suites, compared with 22.3% in the institutional setting (vs. only 2% in the corridor design).

Interactions between residents followed the same pattern: overall, 8.4% of the time in suites, compared with 4.7% in the original building (vs. 10.9% in the corridor building). Verbal interaction took up 6.7% of the residents' time in suites, compared with 2.2% in the original building (vs. 9.7% in the corridor design).

Residents' interactions with members of the direct-care staff were even more infrequent in the suite design (compared with the original setting) than they were in the corridor design. Staff members initiated interactions with residents during only 17.1% of the observation periods in suites, compared with 52.9% in the institutional setting (vs. 22.5% in the corridor design). Residents initiated interactions with staff members during 6.6% of the observation periods in suites, compared with 23% in the institutional setting (vs. 13.8% in the corridor design).

From institutional to modular living environment

Observations of residents showed that the modular renovation design had little impact overall, as compared with the baseline observations made in an institutional living environment. There was no increased use of personal spaces by residents, and residents' intrusions into one another's spaces actually increased. During the first postrenovation period, the proportion of the time during which residents were alert rose, and the proportion during which they were withdrawn fell. However, these gains were not maintained through the later observation periods. There was consistently less interaction among residents. Resident–staff interactions increased slightly, but the increase was entirely the result of more frequent initiation by staff members of interactions with the higher-functioning residents in the group. Overall, then, the modular design seemed to make little difference to the resident and staff behaviors that constituted the major focus of the evaluation study.

Administrative policies at BSS

A participant-observation study and interview study conducted by sociologist Hollis Wheeler documented the contribution of the administrative policies at the school to the pattern of behavioral effects described earlier. In combination with the informal observations of other ELEMR staff members, who had spent a great deal of time in the institution in contact with administrators and staff members at all levels, Wheeler helped to provide a picture of part of the context in which the resident and staff behaviors that were observed so painstakingly were taking place.

The information from these formal and informal sources showed a set of policies that resulted in the direct-care staff at the school being poorly trained and poorly motivated. The pay for direct-care staff, or attendants, was so low that no formal training for their work with the severely disabled residents could be required of new hires. The institution itself provided only a perfunctory training program for new staff members, and many newly hired staff never completed even that program. Nor did the direct-care staff receive support from the higher-level professional staff in dealing with their day-to-day work problems. The professionals set the policies that attendants were supposed to carry out, and then left the attendants to their own devices to deal with uncommunicative, physically disabled, and often uncooperative residents. In addition, the attendants had to undergo evaluation by the absentee professionals, whom they considered to be insensitive to the problems attendants faced.

New staff members had to rely on the cadre of older, experienced attendants, mostly local women who had worked at the school for many years to supplement their family incomes. These veteran attendants were quite different from the new hires, who often were young, idealistic graduates from nearby colleges. The advice they gave the new attendants had more to do with their personal survival – comfort, safety, and job security – than with their responsibilities to the residents.

The low pay for attendants not only affected the initial composition of the direct-care staff, through limitations on recruitment, but also combined with other institutional policies to produce low staff morale. Not only were direct-care staff members underskilled and undertrained for their difficult duties, but also they were faced with a staff "culture" that emphasized protecting their own skins, as well as supervisors˙who made difficult demands on the attendants and then stayed as far away as they could from the problems the attendants faced.

The poor skills and low morale of the staff were influential in shaping the patterns of behavior that were observed in all of the residential settings that were studied. They had impacts at several levels. The observation that staff–resident interactions were least frequent in suite and in corridor settings was attributable directly to the composition and motivation of the direct-care staff. When residents were provided with more private spaces of their own, staff members saw the opportunity to retreat from the battlefield of daily problems with residents to their own now-more-private spaces. In a different context, with a more competent and more highly motivated staff, the same suite and corridor designs might have afforded increased opportunities for staff members to engage in one-on-one helping and training of residents. In the climate that existed at BSS, that outcome was unlikely.

More specific effects of administrative policies also showed up in the pattern of behavioral observation. For example, during the last of the three postrenovation observation periods in the modular renovation, there was a large increase observed in residents' use of their personal spaces. This change in residents' spatial behavior might have been mistaken for a delayed positive effect of the modular design itself in the absence of information about the administrative context in which it occurred. In reality, it coincided with administrative directives to attendants to keep residents in their module areas, and out of the more public lounge and recreation areas, for a greater part of the day. Thus, residents used their modules more, not to take advantage of the minimal privacy they afforded but because they were herded into those spaces by the attendants, who had been ordered to do so.

In summary, the detailed picture of resident and staff behaviors in the variety of living environments created at BSS needs to be understood in the context of the administrative policies in which it developed, especially those that shaped the membership, motivation, and actions of the direct-care staff who played such an important part in shaping, in turn, residents' patterns of behavior.

The impact of the acoustical environment

A laboratory experiment was carried out by Gentry (cited in Knight, Weitzer, & Zimring, 1978) as part of the ELEMR evaluation study. Its purpose was to determine the extent to which changes in the acoustical properties of the residents' living environments contributed to the observed differences in behavior between the prerenovation and postrenovation periods.

The first step was to measure noise levels and reverberation times in the prerenovation institutional living environment and in the three renovation designs. On average, noise levels were found to be higher in the wide-open institutional buildings (72 dB) than in the more differentiated renovated settings (65 dB). Reverberation times were found to be longer in the barren, hard-surfaced institutional setting (1.77 seconds) than amid the more home-like spaces and furnishings of the renovated settings (0.79 second).

Twenty-five monosyllabic words (balanced for their phonemic content) were recorded in an anechoic chamber and then re-recorded with both 65 dB and 72 dB added background noise in dayhalls in both unrenovated (highly reverberant) and renovated buildings at BSS. Twelve staff members and 12 residents who had normal hearing and who were able to understand the words used and the directions for responding to them (these requirements forced the use of a sample of residents who were considerably higher in their levels of functioning, with an average IQ of 50.5, than any of the groups of residents observed in the behavioral comparisons between prerenovation and post-renovation settings) were tested on each of the four tapes created (high noise and long reverberation time, high noise and short reverberation time, low noise and long reverberation time, and low noise and short reverberation time). They heard the tapes through headphones in an insulated testing room.

Both the residents and staff members were able to discriminate the words they heard more accurately under low-noise conditions than under high-noise conditions and with the shorter reverberation time associated with the post-renovation recording venue. Residents' gains in accuracy of speech discrimination were greater than those of staff members between high- and low-noise conditions, but residents and staff benefited equally from the shorter reverberation times. A comparison between the two extreme conditions (tapes) revealed that the difference in accuracy between the low-noise/short-reverberation case and the high-noise/long-reverberation case was greater for the residents tested than for the staff members.

It seems, then, that some portions of the gains in alertness and verbal interaction among residents that were found for the suite and corridor renovation designs likely were attributable to the improvements in acoustical environment over the old institutional setting. It may be that residents, in their attempts to listen and to speak, were no longer frustrated by the masking effects of high levels of background noise and long reverberation times in large, open, tiled public rooms.

Evaluation

Stage 1: Background analysis

Although residential institutions for the developmentally disabled tend to follow a standard pattern because of their similarity in basic mission, the specific background of BSS, especially the events immediately leading up to the period under consideration here, had a clear and decisive impact on the course of the ELEMR Project. The arguments made in court by advocates for the BSS residents, based in large part on the normalization principle, formed the core of the judicial ruling mandating changes at the school, which in turn shaped the direction of the EDR process. The alternative designs that were compared in the ELEMR Project were created to provide a test of that principle, as well as an evaluation of alternative means of implementing it at BSS. This was due largely to the influence of outsiders advocating change at BSS, particularly Judge Tauro.

Stage 2: Behavioral goals

The behavioral goals that were set for the physical renovation of BSS, as it was envisioned at the outset of the ELEMR Project, could be considered almost universal for the treatment of severely and profoundly developmentally disabled adults. They amounted to increases in a variety of otherwise unremarkable purposive behaviors, such as alert observation of events, social interaction, and appropriate use of residents' living spaces and their contents. Such behaviors would be commonplace among other individuals of comparable age, but are all too rare among the developmentally disabled, particularly those living in institutional settings. The behaviors of the latter typically are dominated by stereotypical actions (rocking, repetitive vocalizations, etc.) unrelated to the people and activities surrounding them. Along with, and perhaps prerequisite to, caring for residents' physical needs and providing limited vocational training, the goals set for BSS would seem to be consistent with the basic mission of such an institution.

Stage 3: Environment–behavior relationships

Knowledge of the relationships between residence design and residents' behaviors on which to base a choice of the best design for encouraging alert functioning, social interaction, and privacy regulation was gained from dedicated studies conducted on the BSS campus comparing behaviors in full-scale mock-ups of the three contrasting renovation designs and the preexisting institutional environment. Comparisons were made between prerenovation living conditions and each of the new designs, as well as among the new designs themselves. These comparisons were based on comprehensive measures of resident and staff behaviors, as well as evaluations of the acoustical environment and organizational climate.

To permit unambiguous comparisons among the four types of residential settings, the ELEMR Project team planned a set of sophisticated quasi-experimental studies. Their plans included controls for the major threats to the internal validity of their findings. The influences of extraneous events (such as changes in administrative policy) and cyclical patterns (such as those associated with the seasons of the year) would be held constant by studying all three renovation designs during the same periods of time. Group-composition differences were to be ruled out by comparing the same residents across changes in residence. The use of objective behavior checklists, along with corroboration from other data, including school records, would assure comparable measures of the behaviors to be evaluated.

Unfortunately, changes in construction schedules and in the resident population of BSS that were beyond the control of the researchers made it impossible to carry out those research plans. It was only through astute use of the voluminous and varied data collected in just a few BSS residences, using information about residents' IQs, staff perceptions of administrative policies, and more, that meaningful conclusions could be drawn about the relative performances of the various residential-setting designs. Although those conclusions lacked the support of the more elegant and orthodox methodological controls originally planned, they did provide a clear and useful endorsement of the corridor design as the best choice for achieving the goals that had been set for normalizing residents' behaviors.

Given the nature of the ELEMR research, threats to external validity were relatively minor. The studies were carried out in the authentic context to which they were to be applied. The BSS residents themselves are unlikely to have responded to observers with self-protective or other deceptive strategies, although the direct-care staff probably were very sensitive to being observed, given their documented apprehension about being evaluated. However, the limitations imposed by schedule changes and selective reductions in the resident population made it difficult to estimate whether or not resident groups of differing capabilities would respond comparably to the different renovation designs. The limited evidence we have, from the comparison of two corridor-design residence groups, suggests that although there were clear differences in behavior between higher- and lower-IQ residents, the behaviors of the two groups were affected similarly by the environmental conditions being compared in that study.

Stage 4: Design elements

Based on the results of this research, one configuration of design elements, designated the corridor design, emerged as the best means for achieving the behavioral goals set for BSS residents: increases in alert purposive behavior, social interaction, and appropriate regulation of privacy. Had the direct-care staff at the school been better trained and more highly motivated, that might have encouraged more constructive resident–staff relationships as well. Of course, the methodological problems inherent in the evaluation studies limit somewhat the confidence one can place in a choice between the corridor and suite designs.

Stage 5: Overall design

Because the population of BSS was reduced so drastically, beginning during the period of the ELEMR Project, the planned renovation of the institution never took place. With only about one-fourth of its original population remaining, the residential buildings in which the three renovation designs were tested were no longer needed to house residents. With the removal of most of the higher-functioning residents, the range of behaviors open to facilitation by environmental or other means was reduced as well. In the end, most BSS residents were housed in one building, built more recently than the others on the campus, and with a layout similar to the corridor design tested in the ELEMR Project. Others were housed in small cottages, perhaps more like the suite design.

Stage 6: POE

Because none of the renovation designs was ever implemented beyond the test versions compared in ELEMR, no evaluation of their effects in actual practice was ever possible.

Stage 7: Future impact

The results of the ELEMR Project have been cited fairly widely in textbooks and review articles in environmental psychology and have been given some exposure in design publications (Friedmann, 1976). Still, perhaps because of the study's limited success and limited impact on BSS itself, in both cases largely due to the general upheaval at the institution caused in part by the same judicial mandate that engendered the ELEMR Project, its impact in both the environment–behavior and design fields has been limited. Had the research been able to proceed as planned, and had its findings provided the basis for a large-scale renovation of the school, followed by clear POE results, that impact would certainly have been far greater.

However, the results from such analysis as was carried out regarding the designs that were based implicitly on basic theoretical concepts such as normalization and privacy, thanks to the saving grace of the ethological, or systems, approach adopted by the researchers (a potential contribution to environmental-design research in itself), have some important implications for those same theoretical concepts. They provide some evidence favoring a functional (e.g., privacy) rather than a morphological (e.g., homelike room layout and furnishings) conceptualization of normalization in environmental design. Also, the ELEMR Project provides a valuable blueprint for comparing alternative residential settings, even if its great potential for improving life at BSS was never realized because of the uncontrollable external forces with which environmental-design researchers so often must contend.

References

Altman, I. (1975). *The environment and social behavior*. Belmont, CA: Wadsworth.

Friedmann, A. (1976, September). On politics and design. *Contract*, pp. 6, 10, 12.

Knight, R. C., Weitzer, W. H., & Zimring, C. M. (1978). *Opportunity for control and the built environment: The ELEMR Project*. Amherst, MA: Environment and Behavior Research Center, The Environmental Institute, University of Massachusetts.

Sommer, R. (1969). *Personal space*. Englewood Cliffs, NJ: Prentice-Hall.

Wolfensberger, W. (1973). *The principle of normalization in human services*. Toronto, Canada: National Institute on Mental Retardation.

6
FEDERAL AVIATION
ADMINISTRATION
NORTHWEST REGIONAL
HEADQUARTERS

Location: Boeing Field, Seattle, Washington
Participants: Sam Sloan/People Space Architecture (Spokane),
              Walter B. Kleeman, Jr., Robert Sommer, and Dennis
              Green (researchers and designers)

In 1973, more than 300 employees of the Federal Aviation Administration (FAA) moved into the new headquarters for its Northwest Region, at Boeing Field in Seattle. Whereas the building itself had been designed in a traditional manner, the plans for dividing up its large, open office areas into individual work stations and the choices of furnishings for those work stations were the results of a highly nontraditional design process. The former were based on extensive information about the individual needs and preferences of the workers who would occupy those office spaces, and the latter were left largely to the workers themselves (i.e., "user selection" of tools). Moreover, an energetic attempt was made to evaluate the presumed benefits of the alternative, behavior-based, participative approach to office design as compared with the predominantly aesthetic approach of the professional interior designer.

This project was initiated by Dennis Green, an administrator of the General Services Administration (GSA), the federal agency responsible for providing physical facilities, equipment, and supplies to all branches of the federal government. It was part of the GSA's Office Excellence Program, sponsored by GSA director Arthur Simpson and emphasizing the use of "experimentation" to improve the quality of the government's office space. Green has described the design of the Seattle FAA building as a project "in which the employees themselves guided the design of their new offices in contrast to the traditional design of offices as aesthetically pleasing machines" (Dickson, 1975, p. 297). Green took issue with the prevailing view of offices and other workplace designs that ignored the personal needs of workers in pursuit of efficiency. Green's concept of the workplace extended its functions, and the criteria by which it was to be designed, to include workers' interpersonal relationships, work motivation, and other "human needs." He termed this new

91

vision of the workplace the "social waterhole," based loosely on the gathering places where animals satisfy both their survival and social needs.

To carry out this worker-centered office-design project, Green convinced the GSA to budget funds for behavioral research and hired the Spokane architectural firm People Space Architecture to carry out the design work. Its principal, Sam A. Sloan, had spent two years in Australia on a Fulbright scholarship, testing methods for collecting the kind of information on which worker-centered office design might be based. His work there had been guided by Robert Sommer, a social psychologist with an extensive background in behavior-based environmental design, and Edward T. Hall, a noted anthropologist, merging their interests in a study of personality and space use. Sommer and Walter B. Kleeman, Jr., a consultant on office design, joined Sloan and Green to form a multidisciplinary team to devise a plan for designing and evaluating the office space in the new Seattle FAA headquarters building.

The team met in Seattle for five days during October 1972 to develop that plan, which was to be implemented in time for the building to be occupied the following summer. The plan that emerged can be outlined as follows:

First, a questionnaire was to be administered to the current work force, who were located in temporary quarters near the site of the new building, to determine their perceptions of existing problems with their offices.

A brochure was to be prepared to inform workers about the plan, the issues being considered, and their opportunities to participate in the design process.

An extensive questionnaire was to be prepared to assess individual workers' needs relative to their locations in the new office space and the design of their work stations. Issues raised by responses to the questionnaire were to be followed up in personal interviews with the workers and supplemented by direct observation of their behaviors in their old offices.

Based on the results of the questionnaire, interview, and observation, two documents were to be prepared to guide the design for the layout of office space. A "synthesis sheet" would summarize each individual worker's needs and preferences. A "group profile" would show how the needs of groups of workers, divisions, and departments coincided or diverged.

A rough design for the office layout would be prepared using "bubble diagrams" to establish worker adjacencies, and then compared carefully with the information in those summaries. Workers were to be left to arrange their workspaces themselves, with the advice of the design team if requested. Their decisions were then to be incorporated into the overall design.

Office furnishings would be chosen by the workers themselves in a mock-up of the new office space that was to be constructed in a nearby vacant airplane hangar.

Finally, the questionnaire used in the planning process was to be administered again one year after the new offices were occupied, to the Seattle workers and to the workers in a new FAA headquarters building that was being built at about the same time in suburban Los Angeles (Hawthorne, CA) and whose offices were being designed in a traditional professional manner. The results of this questionnaire, which was also administered to the Los Angeles workers while they were in their old offices, were to be used to evaluate the outcome of the design process used in Seattle.

With that background, a detailed description of the design process, the resulting office space, and the postoccupancy evaluation (POE) and comparison with traditionally designed offices is in order. First, the theoretical rationale will be examined. Then the implementation of the design process will be described. Finally, the outcome will be discussed.

The twin theoretical bases for the Seattle FAA office-design project: self-actualization and participation

Two major theoretical concepts underlay the plan that was devised for the design process. First, information was sought about the psychological and social needs of individual workers and the patterns of needs among groups of workers, so that the layout of individual work stations would satisfy workers' needs. Second, provision was made for direct worker participation in the design process, to maximize workers' contributions to the fit between the office environment and their needs and to maximize workers' sense of control over the office environment for the motivational benefits that a sense of empowerment might provide.

As an architect with a strong interest in designing offices that would meet the needs of those working in them, Sam Sloan turned to two experts in behavior-based design for guidance: Robert Sommer and Walter Kleeman. Based on their advice and on his reading, Sloan combined two elements. One was a widely used theory of worker motivation developed by Fred Herzberg from Abraham Maslow's theory of personality. Maslow postulated a universal hierarchy of needs, ranging from basic physiological or survival needs, like hunger and thirst, through needs for social relationships and self-esteem, to a need for self-actualization, or the satisfaction that one has realized one's full potential as a human being. Herzberg dichotomized that hierarchy and postulated different roles for the lower-level needs, or hygiene factors, and the higher-level needs, or motivators, in work settings. In the context of office work, the physical work setting provided for the worker would be a hygiene factor in the sense that its role was to make work less effortful and more efficient – a comfortable chair, office machines within easy reach, clean and temperate air, and the like. In the absence of a comfortable work environment, the worker would be expected to be dissatisfied with work and might try to leave for another job. However, a comfortable work environment, or a satisfactory level of hygiene, would hardly be noticed and would not motivate the worker to high levels of job performance or commitment. According to the Herzberg-Maslow formulation, that could result only from the presence of motivators. And the work environment could provide such satisfaction of higher-level needs only by such means as facilitating satisfying communication among workers, providing privacy or eliminating demeaning openness to others' observation, screening distractions that would interfere with intrinsically rewarding job performance, and involving the worker in important decisions about working conditions and work procedures in the office.

Sloan's reading of the social-psychological literature led him to focus on three higher-level needs whose satisfaction depends on favorable environmental conditions. He used the term "aggression" to denote a worker's need to compete with or outperform co-workers, or to pursue ambitious goals. "Sociability" was used to refer to the need for satisfying informal or personal interactions with co-workers. Finally, "territoriality" was conceived of as a need to mark the boundaries of one's own work area and to control others' access to it. Following Maslow's lead, Sloan postulated that office workers would differ in the degrees to which they experienced these three needs. It would be possible, then, to assess each worker's needs in these three dimensions and to create a pattern of work areas that would provide opportunities and constraints that would be compatible with the workers' needs. Borrowing again from Maslow, this would give each worker the opportunity for self-actualization, by lessening the effort needed to satisfy social and self-esteem needs. And this, following Herzberg's analysis, should provide motivators that would increase job satisfaction and, to the extent that the work itself provided opportunity for personal development (self-actualization), should result in increased productivity as well.

The second prong of the theoretical attack on the problem of designing offices for the Seattle FAA building dates back to the social psychologist and action researcher Kurt Lewin. Lewin believed and demonstrated empirically that people are more likely to accept and to function effectively under organizational policies to which they feel they have had an opportunity to contribute. Today, this concept is widely known by the label "participation."

Lewin and some colleagues who were committed to his approach did a series of field studies that established the credibility of this principle. During World War II, housewives were found to be more likely to accept new menus for their families that were compatible with the shortages imposed by the war effort if they were able to participate in discussions about those changes than if an expert simply lectured about them (Lewin, 1947). Young boys were found to be happier and more productive as members of social clubs if their adult leaders gave them a voice in planning and running the club's activities (Lewin, Lippitt, & White, 1939). It was found that workers in a pajama factory adjusted better to new work rules if given an opportunity to discuss and shape them, rather than having them imposed unilaterally by management (Coch & French, 1948).

Although these studies can be criticized on methodological grounds because increased participation may have been confounded with the friendliness of the leader who encouraged participation or the quality of the information produced with the benefit of participation, they continue to influence theory and practice to this day. And although there has been a great deal more research recently on the effects of participation, both generally and in environmental design and even more specifically in office design, and especially more systematic analysis of that work in recent years, Lewin's work provided Sloan and the rest of the Seattle FAA design team with a rationale for building worker participation into the design process.

Beyond theory: a pilot study

Sloan's development of the self-actualization approach to office design did not rest entirely on theoretical analysis. From 1969 to 1971 he conducted a preliminary test of his hypothesis in a bank office in Australia, with the advice and consultation of Robert Sommer. The needs of workers in that office regarding aggression, sociability, and territoriality were assessed using questionnaires and interviews. At the same time, their attitudes toward the existing office environment were measured to provide a baseline for evaluating the effects of the experiment.

The assessment of workers' needs was used to classify workers as high or low regarding each need – aggressiveness, sociability, and territoriality. A layout was then created for the office space that provided work areas with characteristics matched to those personality types. Work areas were provided with either "active" or "passive" locations, to fulfill the needs of sociable and unsociable workers, respectively. Active areas were located along circulation routes at the outer edges of work-area clusters, where workers would have frequent contacts with others. Passive areas were in interior locations, where such casual contacts would be infrequent. Work areas were also designed with open, controlled, or secluded entries to accommodate workers with varying degrees of aggressiveness. More aggressive workers would be assigned work areas to which others would have easier access – an open entry if they were high in sociability, or a controlled entry (intermediate in openness) if they were low in sociability. Less aggressive workers would be provided with secluded locations that would make access more difficult for others. Work areas with well-defined boundaries would be provided for workers with strong needs for territoriality, and areas that shared space without well-defined boundaries for those low in territoriality. In addition, workers' tolerances for cigarette smoke were assessed, in order to locate smokers as far as possible from those with the least tolerance for exposure to cigarette smoke.

Based on the information collected regarding workers' needs and the postulated relationship between those needs and specific office-layout features, or "translation from personal-characteristic-requirements to spatial-requirements" (Sloan, 1972, p. 14-5-8), a new office design was created to provide individual workers with work areas whose locations and accessibility would match their personalities. Furniture, partitions, and hanging fabric were used to divide the open office space to meet those spatial requirements.

In the original office space, in October 1969, 61% of the workers reported a desire to change the locations of their work areas. Shortly after the new design was implemented, in January 1970, only 24% expressed dissatisfaction with their new work areas. This rose to 31% during the following 12 months. In August 1971 the experiment was completed by returning the office to its original layout. Half the workers expressed dissatisfaction with their work areas at that point.

The goals of the participatory design process

Dennis Green (Kleeman, 1983) listed the following goals for user participation in the design process:

• relieving anxiety about the unknown
• satisfying needs for creativity
• incorporating workers' values in the physical design
• incorporating individual workers' points of view to improve the design process
• creating a climate of democracy and personal responsibility in the workplace
• educating participants about the design process
• expressing care for and belief in the self-worth of the employees
• creating a better fit between the artifacts used and workers' ergonomic needs
• encouraging a positive approach to conflict resolution
• structuring complementarity among workers' activities.

Together, these goals reflect Green's "social waterhole" theory of the office. He argues that the role of the office in our modern impersonal urban society needs to reach beyond a merely functional setting for job tasks, that it needs to assume the traditional role of the marketplace, church, and other settings or institutions that in earlier times brought the community together. Whereas some believe that the organization's goals should be limited solely to the efficiency of work (cf. Locke & Schweiger, 1979) and thus that attention to the satisfaction of workers' personal and interpersonal needs can be justified only if it will bring about increased work efficiency, Green argues that worker satisfaction with the work environment is a legitimate goal in its own right, even if its benefits are limited to the workers' psychological and social well-being.

The background research at Seattle FAA headquarters

The first step in the human-criteria programming approach adopted by the design team was an assessment of workers' satisfaction with their existing office spaces. This was accomplished using a questionnaire that would serve as a baseline for evaluating the effectiveness of the new office layout, as well as a basis for designing interview and observation protocols that, together with the questionnaire results, would provide the information about the workers' needs upon which the layout of the new office space would be based.

The initial questionnaire tapped five areas of concern about the existing workplace, with several items each covering acoustics, climatic comfort, lighting, space in the work area, and equipment, and 185 workers completed this questionnaire in Seattle. Their responses were summarized to provide general guidelines for the design issues to be explored in greater depth. The graphic summary prepared for the design team (Figure 6.1) reveals that the workers rated the office acoustics poor to bad, air temperature and comfort fair to poor, lighting good to fair, space and furnishings fair, and equipment or artifacts fair to poor.

Based on those results, and on discussions among the design-team members (the influence of Sloan's earlier work in Australia is evident), a much more extensive questionnaire was prepared. It covered 74 design issues or requirements in all, focusing on individual worker needs, compatibility among individuals, and requirements for group activities. These issues can be grouped into six categories, for each of which several examples are listed:

1. Privacy issues: auditory privacy, visual privacy, security of the work station, sensitivity to smoking by others nearby
2. Personal needs: social contact, brightness of colors, territorial control, movement, hierarchical differentiation, aggressiveness (competitiveness, ambition), living plants, support for physical disability, visual and auditory acuity, sensitivity to temperature changes, sensitivity to noise, sensitivity to distractions, satisfaction with furnishings and tools
3. Maintenance concerns: waste and dirt, interior and exterior traffic
4. Reuse preferences: special furnishings or tools from the existing office space
5. Group requirements: work and social spaces
6. Comfort issues: seating, work surfaces

These issues were followed up in individual interviews with the workers. The goal for these data was the development of a design for the new office space that would provide for the satisfaction of each individual's needs,

98   *Building design*

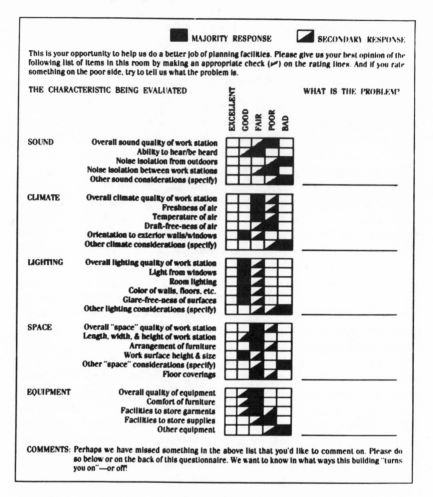

Figure 6.1. A summary of the results of the predesign survey of Seattle FAA office workers. Source: Kleeman (1983, p. 297); reproduced with permission of Van Nostrand Reinhold Co.

balanced against the needs of other individuals and of groups. As in the Australian office where Sloan had previously conducted a similar design exercise, the main issues were territory and traffic. The approach was summed up neatly by Kleeman (1983) in an example: Personable workers would serve as "fences" against unwanted traffic for their less personable colleagues; the latters' requirements for greater privacy would be served by placing their desks where invasion of their territories would be unlikely. An interesting example is a group of workers who, on a questionnaire, expressed an exceptionally strong preference for being located near outside windows.

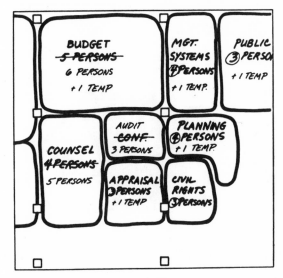

Figure 6.2. A sketch of the layout of group spaces for the Seattle FAA building. Source: Kleeman (1983, p. 299); reproduced with permission of Van Nostrand Reinhold Co.

Follow-up interviews with these individuals uncovered the fact that they were all pilots (remember, this is the FAA) who had developed a strong habit of following weather (flying) conditions closely. They felt a need to be able to see outdoors at all times, despite the fact that they were no longer flying on a regular basis.

The results of the survey and interviews were used to create two "design tools" that would guide the layout of the new office space. One was a "synthesis sheet" that summarized the needs of each individual, across the total of 74 design issues assessed. This represented an elaboration of the categorization process based on only the three personality variables of aggressiveness, sociability, and territoriality that had been used by Sloan in the Australian pilot study, expanded to include issues of ambient environment, work-station design, and others.

The second design tool constructed from the survey and interview results was the "group profile." The needs of workers who were to share a given space as members of a work group or department were considered together, to develop a consensual layout for that larger space that would make possible the greatest good for the greatest number in terms of satisfaction of the individual's personal and social needs, including those that were directly job-related, such as storage for work materials, and those that were not, such as sensitivity to cigarette smoke.

Each area of the office (Figure 6.2) was planned on the basis of the group

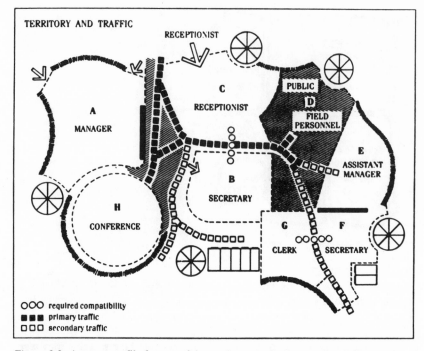

Figure 6.3. A group profile for one of the work groups in the new Seattle FAA offices. Source: Kleeman (1983, p. 299); reproduced with permission of Van Nostrand Reinhold Co.

profile for the individuals in the work group or department to be located there. Each worker's location was determined on the basis of proximity to traffic routes, windows, and smokers, as well as other factors related to the satisfaction of their individual needs (Figure 6.3). The locations of the workers' desks and of other office furniture, along with partitions or screens and other design elements, were combined to create a layout for the larger space. Then that rough layout was checked against each worker's synthesis sheet to make sure that the acute needs identified by the worker would be met as completely as possible by the design.

Full participation in choice of furnishings

The contribution of workers' questionnaire and interview responses to the final design for the office layout fell short of allowing workers to participate directly in the design process. It was closer to what has been called consultation (cf. Locke & Schweiger, 1979), a form of participation in which the role of the user is to provide design-relevant information that may influence the decisions made by the designer. However, the workers at the Seattle FAA offices were allowed an opportunity to engage in full participation (Locke &

Schweiger, 1979) or self-planning (Wandersman, 1979) in the design of their individual work stations.

Each worker was allowed to choose the furnishings for his or her work station from an array of the actual items available, shown by a member of the design team in an unused airplane hangar near the existing FAA office space at Boeing Field. A section of the hangar was used to create a mock-up of the new office space, with flooring and ceiling materials comparable to those being installed in the new building.

The items that were presented to each worker were chosen by the design team based on two sets of criteria. First, the preliminary and full-scale questionnaire and the interview results were used to identify problems with existing furnishings. That information was used by the design team in the selection of the array of office furniture from which workers could choose. Chairs were selected that would provide a wide range of adjustment for the comfort of workers of different sizes. Upholstery fabrics were selected that would provide thermal comfort as well as a wide range of color choices. The desks offered had work surfaces that would not cause glare from overhead lighting, and the desks would provide a variety of storage configurations from which workers could each choose one that would meet individual task requirements. In other words, the first criterion was that the array of furnishings meet the ergonomic needs expressed by the workers. In part, this was accomplished by providing a wide range of alternatives. In all, workers chose among 13 desks with varying drawer arrangements, sizes and shapes of work surfaces, and finishes, as well as 15 chairs, 6 credenzas, 16 fabric colors, a full range of telephone colors, and even six models of in/out baskets.

The workers' choices were limited, however, by the need to satisfy another criterion. The budget for office furnishings provided a maximum amount that could be spent for each worker, an amount that increased with the worker's position in the organization hierarchy (presumably based on the federal government's ubiquitous GS system). Thus, the array of furnishings offered to each worker was limited by that worker's job level and the total costs that were allowed for it. Given this restriction, along with that of the initial selection process (albeit based on the workers' own "consultation"), each worker chose the furnishings for his or her work station.

In addition, as noted earlier, workers participated fully in creating their own arrangements of the furnishings they chose, at the locations chosen for their workspaces by the design team. These arrangements were then documented by the design team.

Outcome of the Seattle FAA design "experiment"

One year after the Seattle FAA offices were occupied, a 14-page questionnaire was administered to the workers there, as well as those working in the new Los Angeles (Hawthorne, CA) headquarters building (Figures 6.4 and 6.5)

102   *Building design*

Figure 6.4. The Seattle FAA building, exterior view. Source: Sloan (undated); reproduced with permission of Sam Sloan.

Figure 6.5. The award-winning Hawthorne (Los Angeles) FAA building, exterior view. Source: Sloan (undated); reproduced with permission of Sam Sloan.

Table 6.1. *Degree of participation*

	Number of respondents	
Level of participation	Seattle	Los Angeles (Hawthorne)
Very active	60	12
Moderately active	77	32
Slightly active	39	64
None	69	303
Total[a]	250	436

[a]Not all respondents could be classified.

that had been occupied at about the same time with office space designed in the traditional manner, by design professionals based on their impressions of workers' needs. The purpose was to evaluate workers' satisfaction with their new offices, in the form of a nonequivalent-control-group quasi experiment (cf. Campbell & Stanley, 1966). The changes in levels of satisfaction among Seattle workers who had participated in the design of their new offices, through consultation and direct choice of office furnishings, could be compared with the changes among a similar group of workers in Los Angeles (performing the same jobs as a group, in the same organization) who moved into new offices at about the same time, but whose participation in the design process was minimal, if any. By comparing within each group, any preexisting differences in personnel, offices, or management presumably would be taken into account.

Approximately 80% of the workers in each facility returned completed questionnaires. In addition to their judgments of their offices, their responses documented the greater level of participation among the workers in Seattle. Over 50% of them reported that their participation had been moderate or greater. The comparable percentage for the Los Angeles FAA office staff was about 10%, and almost 70% of that group reported not participating at all in the design of their offices (Table 6.1). No statistical analysis was reported by the researchers (although Sloan has verified that it was carried out), but a comparison of participation rates using a χ^2 analysis reveals a highly significant difference between the two distributions ($\chi^2 = 172.81$, df $= 3$, $p <$ .001). The ϕ coefficient of the relationship between location (Seattle vs. Los Angeles) and participation, similar to a correlation, based on that χ^2 value, is .46.

The results of the follow-up questionnaire were analyzed by combining responses to evaluate 14 design issues. The issues are listed in Table 6.2, along with a summary of the results of these comparisons (see Kleeman,

Table 6.2. *Summary of Seattle FAA building research*

Design issue	Greater satisfaction		Change in satisfaction		Greater gain in satisfaction	Effect of participation[a]	
	Old bldg.	New bldg.	Seattle	L.A.		Seattle	L.A.
Building aesthetics	SE[b]	SE	+	+	LA	Strong	Strong
Sound/noise	SE	SE	0	−	SE	Strong	Strong
Climatic comfort	SE	SE	−	−	LA	Strong	Weak
Light adequacy	SE	SE	+	+	SE	Strong	Moderate
Space quality	SE	SE	+	+	LA/SE	Moderate	Moderate
Equipment	SE	SE	+	+	SE	Moderate	Moderate
Color/texture	SE	SE	+	+	LA	Moderate	None
Space arrangement	SE	SE	+	+	LA	Strong	Moderate
Communication	SE	LA/SE	0	+	LA	Moderate	Moderate
Privacy	SE	SE	−	−	LA	Strong	Strong
Personalization	SE	SE	−	−	LA/SE	Strong	Weak
Management policy	SE	SE	−	−	LA	Weak	None
Job performance	SE	SE	+	0	LA	None	Moderate
Building safety	SE	SE	+	−	SE	Strong	Moderate

	SE	LA
S	8	3
M	4	7
W	1	2
N	1	2

[a]Strong = all four gains in satisfaction ordered by level of participation
Moderate = greater gains in both of two highest levels of participation than in two lowest
Weak = greater gains in two highest levels combined
None = no greater gain associated with greater participation
[b]SE, Seattle; LA, Los Angeles (Hawthorne).

1983, for a more extensive description of the issues themselves). Whereas Seattle workers were more satisfied, overall, with their new offices than were the Los Angeles workers, they had also been more satisfied with their original offices (the old Los Angeles offices apparently had been located temporarily in World War II Quonset huts immediately prior to the move to the new building). However, there was also more positive change in satisfaction in Seattle. Workers there were more satisfied with the new offices on 8 of the 14 design issues, including their ratings of the contribution of the work setting to their job performance, as compared with 7 of the 14 in Los Angeles. More important, perhaps, the *gain* in satisfaction (whether to more positive or less negative) was greater among the Seattle work force than among the Los Angeles work force for only four of the issues, equal for two, and greater among the Los Angeles workers for eight. This may reflect the very low level of satisfaction in the old Los Angeles offices with which the new offices were being compared.

Finally, the gain in satisfaction was examined separately for workers at each level of participation (Table 6.1). For Seattle, the gain in satisfaction among workers was strongly related to their level of participation (greater gain in satisfaction with greater level of participation at every level) for 8 of the 14 design issues and moderately related for 4 of the remaining 6 design issues (greatest gain in the two highest levels of participation, in order). The remaining 2 issues showed weak correlation and no relationship. For the Los Angeles sample, there was a strong relationship for 3 issues, a moderate relationship for 7, a weak relationship for 2, and no relationship for 2.

In summary, there is mixed evidence that workers in Seattle were more satisfied with their new offices than were workers in Los Angeles, presumably validating their demonstrably greater level of participation (direct and indirect) in the design process. However, the great baseline difference between the two groups makes the meaning of these results difficult to interpret. There does seem to be evidence, however, that workers who participated more, in both locations (the low levels of participation in Los Angeles clouding the picture for those workers somewhat), experienced greater gains in satisfaction from their move to new offices.

Evaluation

Stage 1: Background analysis

This project was unusual for its use of empirical methods to take into account the social needs of individual users of the settings. Its use of such an individualized approach, together with survey data prioritizing the workers' consensual concerns about their office environment, as well as the prolonged close contact between members of the design team and the office staff, constituted an effective means of taking into account the specific people and activities that had to be accommodated in the new design.

Stage 2: Behavioral goals

There were two major goals for the office layout, both addressed to increasing workers' satisfaction with the office and with their jobs. The first was to maximize the fit between a worker's needs for achievement, social interaction, and territorial control and the location of his or her workspace in the layout of space for the entire work-group area. It was believed that the satisfaction of those needs would serve as a motivator, following Herzberg's theory (via Maslow) of the role of higher-order needs in worker satisfaction and productivity, and Green's broader conceptualization of the workplace as a "social waterhole."

The second goal was to enhance satisfaction with the workplace through workers' participation in the design decision-making process. In addition to providing information about the process, workers were to be consulted through questionnaires and interviews about the optimal locations for their workspaces and allowed to choose their own office furnishings and to decide how they would be arranged within the workspace.

Stage 3: Environment–behavior relationships

To a large extent, knowledge about the environmental antecedents of workplace and job satisfaction came from two prominent psychological theories. One was Herzberg's popular application to the workplace of Maslow's more general "needs hierarchy" theory of human motivation. The second was Lewin's analysis of the role of participation in the acceptance of social change, for which empirical evidence had been produced in a variety of settings, including the workplace.

The application of Herzberg's theory to office design was supported by Sloan's "case study" in an Australian bank. Although there may have been some question about generalizing across cultures and about the actual causes of increased worker satisfaction following the office rearrangement, because of the weak before–after research design (the change in layout may have coincided with other events that also increased satisfaction) and the reactive research arrangements (with the attendant possibility of an implicit demand that workers react positively to the change), the fact is that the same underlying theory has been applied in a wide variety of interventions to increase worker motivation with much less empirical support than was provided by this research.

The use of a participative approach to design, giving workers direct control over their furnishings and workspace layout, was supplemented by preliminary survey data indicating a strong concern among the workers with the ergonomic properties of their office furnishings. As a consequence of that survey, the design team limited the range of furnishings available to the workers to pieces that were suitably comfortable, adjustable, and otherwise functional.

Stage 4: Design elements

The layout of office areas for the various work groups at the Seattle FAA office followed directly from the questionnaire and interview data on the social needs of their individual members that were collected from the workers while they were still in their temporary quarters. Although the procedure was based on antecedent theory and research, there was no need to infer generic design elements in this personalized approach to office design. The location of each individual's workspace within the work-group area followed directly from knowledge of the worker's social needs vis-à-vis those of his or her co-workers.

Within the work-group layouts that resulted from that process, individual workspace designs were largely left up to the individuals who would occupy them. Within the constraints of budget limitations and the initial screening of furnishings for ergonomic design, workers chose their own office furnishings. Then, with the technical assistance of design-team members, they decided on configurations for those furnishings at the workspace locations assigned to them.

Stage 5: Overall design

The overall design for the office space in the new Seattle FAA building was constructed almost entirely out of the elements that came from the EDR process. Within whatever constraints may have been imposed by the design of the building itself (which was independent of the work of Sloan, Green, Kleeman, and Sommer), the choices of furnishings, arrangements of individual workspaces, and layouts of work-group areas were largely the results of the worker-needs-based, participative EDR process (although time and financial constraints made for a less direct application of those principles than in Sloan's Australian pilot study).

One way of gauging the impact of the EDR process on the overall design of the Seattle offices is by a visual comparison with the design at Hawthorne. The heterogeneous appearance of the Seattle offices, based on individual workers' needs and choices, contrasts clearly with the coordinated "designer" look of the Hawthorne offices (Figures 6.6 and 6.7). Kleeman (1983) has characterized as ironic the fact that the Hawthorne building won design awards, whereas the (more effective) Seattle design did not. However,

Figure 6.6. The Seattle FAA building, interior view. Source: Sloan (undated); reproduced with permission of Sam Sloan.

Figure 6.7. The Hawthorne FAA building, interior view. Source: Sloan (undated); reproduced with permission of Sam Sloan.

whereas Sloan (personal communication, 1991) has maintained that the Seattle offices were appreciated by the workers there for their homey appearance, there seems little doubt that they look less attractive in traditional terms, or, to the uninformed viewer, they look designed more for their function than for their photogenic appeal.

Stage 6: POE

The fact that the FAA was having another regional headquarters built outside of Los Angeles at about the same time as the Seattle project provided an opportunity to use a powerful quasi-experimental design (suggested by Sommer) to evaluate the success of the EDR process in fulfilling the behavioral goals for the Seattle FAA building. The same survey that was used to set goals for the Seattle project was administered to workers in Seattle and Hawthorne (Los Angeles) before their moves to new quarters. Then it was administered again to both groups after their moves. This "pre–post nonequivalent-control-group" design made it possible to take into account preexisting differences between the two groups of workers, the effects of merely moving to new offices, and other potential threats to internal validity. At the same time, its use in the natural context of workers and their jobs assured the external validity of the research findings.

Unfortunately, the analysis of the results of the research failed to exploit fully the strengths of the research design. The comparison of increases in postoccupancy satisfaction at the two new buildings shows less than a clear-cut advantage for Seattle. However, the much lower level of pre-move satisfaction at Hawthorne suggests that improvement may have been much easier to achieve there than in Seattle. It seems that a more sophisticated statistical analysis might have been able to account for that initial difference between the two workplaces, but no such analysis was reported. In fact, the most comprehensive account of this POE study, by Kleeman (1983), presents few data at all. The best source is a brochure prepared by Sloan (undated) that presents the data in tabular form without any summative statistical analysis.

The POE study was conducted mainly by the designers for their clients at the GSA and their colleagues. Sloan (personal communication, 1991) has pointed out that those in the design and construction fields mistrust the technical "hocus-pocus" of research design and statistical analysis so familiar and dear to social scientists. So, although Sommer and, to a lesser extent perhaps, Sloan might have felt comfortable with a more comprehensive statistical analysis that could have provided a clearer picture of the advantages of the EDR process used in Seattle over the traditional office-design process used at Hawthorne, their positions as members of an interdisciplinary team with designers and GSA and FAA officials may have inhibited their advocacy of such an approach.

Also, despite the relative robustness of the quasi-experimental approach, some threats to internal validity remain. Chris Walk, the FAA regional director in Seattle, was quite supportive of the experimental-design approach (Sloan, personal communication, 1991), suggesting the possibility that other management policies may have differed between Seattle and Los Angeles that could have affected worker satisfaction. And the possibility of other differences between the two offices (personnel, size, etc.) clouds the comparison in the POE study.

Despite the fact that there were no immediate problems with external validity in the POE study, changes in the work force, organizational policies, and other contextual factors over time may bring into question the generalizability of the observed effects of the EDR program at Seattle. Sloan's design team foresaw this problem and suggested a continuing storehouse of furnishings from which future employees could choose, as well as training for managers in using the "personality" approach to fitting those new workers into the existing office layout, in order to maintain the effects of the design program into the future. Unfortunately, Sloan (personal communication, 1991) has expressed little confidence that that will happen.

In summary, the results of the POE study suggest that the behavior-based design process used at the Seattle FAA was responsible for higher levels of satisfaction among workers there than at the Hawthorne facility. However, the extent of the differences and the measure of the relative increase in satisfaction over the level observed in the workers' previous offices are difficult to determine from the analysis of the data that has been reported.

One point on which there seems to be little dispute, however, is the impact of participation on the workers' satisfaction with their new offices. The results of that analysis were quite clear-cut. Workers who felt that they had participated more in the design of their new offices reported higher levels of satisfaction. The much higher level of participation at the Seattle FAA, evident both in the description of the design process and in workers' reports, provides strong support for accepting the POE findings of greater satisfaction among the Seattle workers than among the Hawthorne workers.

Stage 7: Future impact

The Seattle FAA project provides a rare model of the use of an integrated theoretical–empirical approach throughout the design process. Theory and some associated research literature were used to formulate behavioral goals, as well as to suggest design elements that might serve them. Research in a similar setting, a large open-plan office, was conducted to test the validity of that analysis. Then the instruments developed in that research were used to collect data on which to base the design of the Seattle FAA offices, as well as for an evaluation of the Seattle project in comparison with the contrasting design process used for the new Hawthorne FAA building.

Since the Seattle FAA project was completed, there has been increasing emphasis on the importance of designing offices to meet workers' needs and on the possible link between user-based office design and the productivity of office workers. For example, a national survey of office workers and their supervisors conducted on behalf of the Steelcase Company (office-furniture manufacturers) by Louis Harris & Associates (1980) revealed that majorities of both groups believed that office design was related to productivity and that office workers could make a positive contribution to design quality. Another large-scale survey, by BOSTI (1982), an environmental-design research and consulting firm, revealed that 70% of office workers felt that they had too little to say about the designs of their offices. Town (1982), using data from the BOSTI study, found that greater worker participation in the design of new office space was associated, for the most part, with greater worker satisfaction and motivation in the new offices.

It is likely that the Seattle FAA project played a role in bringing the issue of user participation in office design to the prominent place it occupies today. It has been widely publicized, both in scholarly books about workplace design (Sundstrom, 1986) and office design (Dickson, 1975; Kleeman, 1983) and in popular publications (Harris, 1977; Office of the '80's, 1980). Although the level of enthusiasm for the concept is not matched by the quality of empirical support provided by the Seattle FAA evaluation study (cf. Locke & Schweiger, 1979), even to the point where the benefits found in that study have been exaggerated, the growth of support for the idea and the role of the Seattle FAA project in that growth seem indisputable.

There are certainly good reasons for seeking greater productivity through congruence between office design and workers' needs. It has been estimated (Dickson, 1975) that 92% of the cost of office work is the cost of the personnel involved. Even a large increase in the cost of the physical facilities is justified by a small increase in worker productivity. Unfortunately, little is known about how to measure the productivity of office workers, and even less about how it might be influenced by office design. The Seattle FAA evaluation did show, however, that self-rated job performance increased slightly in the new Seattle FAA offices, but not at all in Los Angeles.

Thus, the impact in Seattle alone, where the annual payroll must reach into the tens of millions of dollars, and the safety of tens of thousands of airline passengers may hang in the balance, more than justifying the EDR program described in this chapter.

References

BOSTI (1982). *The impact of office environment on productivity and quality of working life.* Buffalo, NY: author.

Campbell, D. T., and Stanley, J. S. (1966). *Experimental and quasi-experimental designs for research.* Chicago: Rand McNally.

Coch, L., & French, J. R. P., Jr. (1948). Overcoming resistance to change. *Human Relations, 1*, 512–533.

Dickson, P. (1975). *The future of the workplace.* New York: Weybright & Talley.

Harris, L., & Associates, Inc. (1980). *The Steelcase national study of office environments. No. II: Comfort and productivity in the office of the 80s.* Grand Rapids, MI: Steelcase.

Harris, T. G. (1977). Psychology of the new work space. *New York, 10*(44), 51–54.

Kleeman, W. B., Jr. (1983). *The challenge of interior design.* New York: Van Nostrand Reinhold.

Lewin, K. (1947). Group decision and social change. In T. M. Newcomb & E. L. Hartley (Eds.), *Readings in social psychology.* New York: Holt.

Lewin, K., Lippitt, R., & White, R. K. (1939). Patterns of aggressive behavior in experimentally created "social climates." *Journal of Social Psychology, 10,* 271–299.

Locke, E. A., & Schweiger, D. M. (1979). Participation in decision-making: One more look. In B. M. Staw (Ed.), *Research in organizational behavior, Vol. 1.* Greenwich, CT: JAI Press.

Office of the '80's. (1980). *Fortune, 101,* June 2, pp. 29–30, 34, 38 (advertising section).

Sanoff, H. (1990). *Participatory Design: Theory and techniques.* Raleigh, NC: author.

Sloan, S. A. (1972). Translating psycho-social criteria into design determinants. In W. J. Mitchell (Ed.), *Environmental design: Research and practice, Vol. 1.* Los Angeles: University of California.

Sloan, S. A. (undated). *FAA tennant/GSA landlord/Maslow/love/participation/satisfaction/offices/personal space/work production/social needs/designers/users: Product process.* Unpublished pamphlet.

Sundstrom, E. (1986). *Work places.* Cambridge University Press.

Sundstrom, E. (1987). Work environments: Offices and factories. In D. L. Stokols & I. Altman (Eds.), *Handbook of environmental psychology* (Vol. 1, pp. 733–782). New York: Wiley.

Town, J. P. (1982). *Effects of participation in office design on satisfaction and productivity.* Unpublished doctoral dissertation, University of Tennessee.

Wandersman, A. (1979). User participation in planning environments: A conceptual framework. *Environment and Behavior, 11,* 465–482.

7

JONES DORMITORY REDESIGN, TRINITY COLLEGE

Location: Hartford, Connecticut
Participants: Andrew Baum, Stuart Valins, and Glenn E. Davis
(research, design, and evaluation)

Among all institutional residential settings, college dormitories must rank near the top in sheer numbers of residents and in the sheer madness of the residents' behaviors. Young men and women struggling to adjust to what is for many of them a threatening new way of life, many of them away from home and friends and supportive teachers for the first time in their lives, find themselves in a place that provides little privacy and little space or time for reflection, needing to marshal all their resources against the harsh academic and social demands being made on them.

The success with which young men and women adjust to dormitory life, and adjust to all of the demands of college life while living in a dormitory, depends on a large number of factors, including their own personal resources or traits and the support they receive from friends and family. But a series of studies by Andrew Baum, Stuart Valins, and their co-workers have shown that the architectural design of a dormitory can mediate college students' adjustment. And the results of those studies have been used as the basis for successful modification of an existing dormitory to improve the adjustment of its residents.

The theoretical rationale

Baum and Valins based their studies of dormitory design on previous environment–behavior research and theory on crowding. Not only has crowding been one of the most basic concerns in the field, but also it is a problem that has proved extremely elusive. Many researchers and theorists have tried to substantiate the assumption that an organism that is forced to live under conditions of high population density experiences stress, impairment of function, and severe coping demands that, if they are not met satisfactorily, may lead to physical breakdown and even death.

Studies of animal behaviors have been one source of information about this question. Calhoun (1962) studied rats whose numbers increased dramatically in an artificial habitat. He observed the disruption of instinctive patterns of mating and maternal behavior, in addition to aggressive and withdrawn behaviors uncharacteristic of the species under normal conditions. Christian, Flyger, and Davis (1960) reported a large-scale die-off among a herd of deer that had grown very large on an offshore island with limited space and resources. Autopsies showed extreme enlargement of the adrenal glands in the stricken animals, and that was interpreted as a sign that the animals had experienced extreme levels of stress.

The evidence that other mammalian species experience physical and behavioral abnormalities under conditions of "overcrowding" has led to attempts to link crowding and pathologic processes in humans. Studies comparing urban districts that vary greatly in population density for the physical and emotional health and social stability of their residents have found little association between density and behavior when socioeconomic and other background factors have been taken into account. These studies have been plagued by many methodological and conceptual difficulties, however. In particular, it has been difficult to establish meaningful measures of overcrowding, because very large numbers of people can live on an acre of city land in commodious, comfortable, luxury high-rise apartments. Even studies that have measured population density by the number of people per room or the number of dwelling units per building have failed to find strong associations with residents' behaviors that might be said to resemble the associations observed for nonhuman populations.

The failure to find similar effects in naturalistic studies of human populations may mean that the findings from studies of overcrowding among rats, deer, and other species cannot be generalized to humans. It may also mean that studies of humans in urban settings have failed to make crucial distinctions among the various forms of overcrowding – distinctions that would be necessary for accurate prediction of its effects. One distinction is between physical density and social density. Laboratory studies of human subjects, by Freedman and others, have shown that behavior is affected far more by a confrontation with large numbers of others (high social density) than by a comparable reduction in the amount of space available to the individual (high physical density) (Freedman, 1975). Having to cope with the demands of coordinating one's activities with or adjusting one's behavior toward many other people is more difficult, it seems, than is being confined to a very small space. Unfortunately, the evidence for this proposition comes from short-term studies of seemingly trivial activities performed by subjects who were well aware of the temporary and artificial nature of their circumstances.

A second distinction is between the objective condition of high density, whether it be physical or social, and the subjective condition of crowding. As Stokols (1987) and many others have pointed out, the affective and behavioral consequences of high density depend on many factors, including the nature of the person who is exposed and the activity in which the person is engaged. The same objective condition of density may be experienced as much more unpleasant and disruptive under some conditions than under others. Freedman (1975) has gone so far as to argue that extremely high social density can make pleasant experiences, such as attending an exciting rock concert or sporting event, more pleasant than they would be under conditions of lower density.

Despite the failure to apply these distinctions to the production of clear empirical findings on the consequences of overcrowding, several theorists have gained wide acceptance for similar analyses of the problem. The best known of these is Stanley Milgram (1970), who focused on density in urban environments. Milgram believed that the fundamental problem of the individual in the city, where social density is very high, is stimulus overload. There are too many events taking place in one's surroundings for one to attend to or respond to them all. Attempts to do so prove stressful, and one attempts to cope by responding selectively to only the events or people most directly relevant to one's personal concerns. Passersby and routine street activities are ignored. The individual's limited capacity to attend and to respond is reserved for family, friends, co-workers, personal needs, work, and so on. If successful screening or filtering mechanisms are developed, stress is reduced.

Out of this still unsettled tangle of empirical evidence and theory, Baum and Valins (1977) developed a theoretical rationale for their studies of dormitories. One of the most salient features of dormitory life is the high physical density. Compared with the comfortable middle-class homes from which most college dormitory residents come, there is far less space available, or far higher physical density. If a typical middle-class family of four shares 1,200 to 1,500 square feet of space in their home, the reduction in sheer amount of space that comes with a move to a dormitory is on the order of two-thirds to three-quarters. In addition, social density is higher in the dormitory. Many more individuals share the same spaces. Most dormitory residents share a bedroom with at least one roommate, and they typically share bath and lounge spaces with far larger numbers than they did at home.

There seems to exist, then, at least the potential for unpleasant feelings and disruption of behavior among dormitory residents. Under those conditions, it would seem reasonable to expect attempts to cope with such stress by selective attention and social withdrawal. Should such attempts to cope fail or be only partially successful, then anxiety, deficits in performance, and eventual physical and emotional breakdown can follow. Anyone who is aware of the "normal" rates of attrition, illness, and behavioral and emotional problems among college freshmen in dormitories probably will not find such a scenario farfetched.

The key point of Baum and Valins's analysis, however, was that students' experiences, coping efforts, and problems in dormitories would depend to some extent on the form of the architectural design that specified interior spaces and their functions. They reasoned that the fewer the students who had to share common living areas, especially areas outside their bedrooms that would have to be shared by large numbers, and the more control that residents could exert over their interactions with others, then the less crowding and the less resulting stress they would experience, the less extreme their coping responses (such as selective attention and withdrawal) would have to be, and the more successful their adjustment would be.

The research program

This rationale guided Baum and Valins's comparison of students' reactions to, and their behaviors in and beyond, two groups of dormitories on the campus of the State University of New York at Stony Brook, on Long Island, approximately 50 miles east of New York City. Both groups were composed of three-story buildings, housed about 34 students on each floor (one floor of one wing), and provided each student with approximately 150 square feet of living space, including his or her bedroom and closet, bathroom and lounge facilities on the floor, and circulation areas (hallways, lobbies, etc.) and public lounges throughout the building. They differed, however, in the way that the space on each residential floor was divided among the residents and their activities (Figure 7.1).

One set of seven dormitories, with a total capacity of 2,000 residents, followed a "corridor" design. The 34 residents were divided among 17 double bedrooms that opened off both sides of a double-loaded corridor. They all shared one common bathroom that was located near the midpoint of the corridor and one lounge that was located at one end. There were stairwell entrances at both ends of the corridor.

The second group of 15 dormitories, with 3,000 residents in all, followed a "suite" design. There were six suites on each floor, opening off a central corridor. Each suite had two or three double bedrooms plus its own bath and lounge. All of the freshmen who were studied in Baum and Valins's research lived in six-person suites.

Thus, the major difference between the corridor dormitories and suite dormitories lay in the social density within their residential units. In the corridor dormitories, each unit housed 34 students who shared the bathroom, lounge, and circulation areas on the floor as one large group. In the suite dormitories, the freshman residents were divided into groups of six, who shared a bathroom and lounge. Based on what they knew of the effects of high social density, Baum and Valins expected that the residents of corridor dormitories would feel more crowded, experience more stress as a result of having to accommodate their personal needs to those of so many other students, and show more signs of social withdrawal as a means of coping with that crowding stress – all by comparison with the residents of suite dormitories.

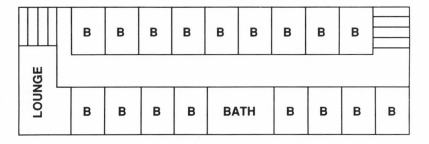

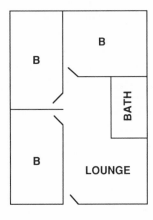

Figure 7.1. Diagrams of dormitory groupings at the State University of New York at Stony Brook. Above, a corridor floor, showing students' double bedrooms and the shared bathroom and lounge. Below, a dormitory suite (one of a cluster surrounding a circulation area on each floor), showing bedrooms, bathroom, and lounge. Source: Adapted from Baum and Valins (1977).

One can imagine – more easily, perhaps, if one actually lived in a dormitory as a college freshman – some of the problems a student living in a dormitory might have to contend with as a result of high social density: A student in his or her bedroom, trying to study or relax quietly or listen to music, hears the noise made by students in adjoining rooms, or especially in the hallway, including unwelcome greetings and glances from passersby through the typically open bedroom door. Some of these other students are acquaintances or even friends, but others are not, perhaps even strangers just passing through the floor, and it may be difficult to tell one from the other and to gauge one's responses. Or perhaps a student going to take a shower walks down the hallway, wearing only a towel, past many open bedroom doors and past other students using their only route to so many necessary services outside a student's bedroom, having to talk to friends, though in a hurry to get to the shower and uncomfortable without clothes or shoes. In these and so many other activities that can be disrupted when such a large group must share the same living space there is no easy way to develop rules or even informal norms that might ease the common discomfort of all the students on the floor, because there are so many individuals spread over so large an area. The student who lives in a suite, by comparison, has far fewer disruptions to contend with and has a small, close-knit group who share the same space and can develop norms to deal with those disruptions that do occur.

Following such a rationale, Baum and Valins carried out a series of studies over a period of three school years, between 1971 and 1975, to compare the effects of the corridor and suite dormitory arrangements on freshmen at Stony Brook. First, we will look at the varied comparisons they made, along with the results of each one. Then we will consider the ways in which they tried to bolster those comparisons with evidence that the students who lived in the two different types of dormitories, 70% of whom had some choice in where they would live on campus, were comparable in their backgrounds and in their predispositions to react to dormitory life before coming under the influence of the contrasting dormitory arrangements, followed by evidence that the results of their studies could be reproduced on another campus where similar phenomena occurred in a quite different context.

Between 1971 and 1975, five random samples of between 30 and 50 corridor and suite freshman residents were interviewed about their perceptions of the social environments in their dormitories. Each time, their responses showed the same expected pattern of differences. As compared with suite-dormitory freshmen, corridor-dormitory freshmen more often reported that they perceived their dormitories as more crowded, felt more strongly that there were too many people living in the dormitory to develop friendships easily, felt more strongly that there was too little privacy, reported more often that there seemed to be too much social interaction on the floor and that there were more people they wanted to avoid and more occasions on which they wanted to avoid interactions with other people on the floor, felt there was more unwanted interaction on the floor with both friends and strangers, and reported having fewer friends on the floor (despite the greater numbers of fellow students to whom they were exposed). In short, the perceptions and sentiments of the freshmen at Stony Brook were consistent with the hypothesis that the corridor arrangement would produce greater social density, greater crowding stress, and increased withdrawal from social contact, possibly in that causal order.

Early in the course of that research, observers visited both types of dormitories to determine the locations and natures of the residents' social and nonsocial behaviors. They found that on corridor floors, social interaction was concentrated in the hallways, with very little in lounges. On suite floors, the opposite pattern prevailed: interaction in the lounge, not in the hallways. Nonsocial behaviors such as studying were most frequent in bedrooms on corridor floors, but in lounges on suite floors. Corridor residents were found most often in their bedrooms, with about one-third in the hallways. Suite residents were found most often in their lounges, with about one-fourth in their bedrooms. Thus, it appears that the corridor arrangement promoted interaction in public areas, where it was difficult to predict or control, and, at the same time, avoidance of public areas whenever possible. The suite arrangement made it possible for small groups of students to use semiprivate lounge spaces, presumably aided by norms that regulated potentially disruptive behavior there. Suite residents interacted in locations of their own choosing, with suitemates or others they chose to invite or who invited them into the suite lounges, presumably under conditions acceptable to the parties involved. All of this is consistent with Baum and Valins's crowding-stress hypothesis, revealing both antecedents and consequences of high social density.

A third study in that series sought to assess the feelings of freshmen in corridor dormitories and suite dormitories about the numbers of people they lived with, by means of the model-room technique. Randomly selected samples from both groups of dormitories were tested alone in their own bedrooms. They were presented with models of three different rooms: a dormitory bedroom, a dormitory lounge, and a library reference room. Each model room was presented, in turn, with instructions being given to place miniature figures of people in the rooms until it seemed to the subject that the room would feel crowded. The floor of each model was made of cork, and from the bottom of each figure protruded a stickpin that could be pushed into the cork. Corridor-dormitory residents placed significantly fewer figures in the bedroom and lounge models, but significantly more in the reference-room model. This was interpreted as evidence that corridor residents were more sensitive to social density or had lower thresholds for crowding, by virtue of their exposure to crowded living conditions. Where interaction was more likely, in bedroom or lounge, they reached their limit of comfort regarding group size more quickly than did suite residents. Where interaction was unlikely, in a library, they showed the expectations for large numbers that had been developed on their crowded dormitory floors.

Another phase in the research program was designed to follow up on the earlier finding that corridor residents had fewer friends among their neighbors on their floors than did suite residents. Baum and Valins's evolving theoretical conception of the antecedents and consequences of crowding stress in dormitories was elaborated to include the differential formation of local friendship groups on dormitory floors as a mediator of crowding effects. They reasoned that the suite-dormitory design would facilitate the formation of such groups and, through them, more effective control of social interaction and greater comfort and sociability among the suite-dormitory residents.

Evidence that supports this argument was found through interviews. As compared with corridor-dormitory residents, suite residents more often reported that they agreed with their neighbors' attitudes and that they were more willing to disclose information about themselves to their neighbors. Further,

those corridor residents who reported relatively more inclusion in local friendship groups on their floors reported experiencing less crowding than did other
corridor residents.

In a follow-up survey of sophomores who had lived in corridor dormitories
as freshmen, it was found that those who stayed in corridor dormitories felt
more crowded than did those who switched to suite dormitories. And those
sophomore corridor residents who perceived those on their floors as less
cohesive were more likely to feel crowded.

Finally, in a study of discussion groups, each made up of suite residents or
corridor residents, it was found that consensus was more likely to emerge
among suitemates than among suite residents from different floors or among
corridor residents who were close neighbors or who lived on different floors.
Living close together appears to have led to the formation of cohesive groups
in the suite dormitories, but not in the corridor dormitories.

The final form of research in Baum and Valins's series of studies tested for
the possibility that the students' experiences in their dormitories, and the
feelings and coping mechanisms that developed from those experiences,
would influence their behaviors outside the dormitory. A series of studies was
conducted in which a general form was adapted to several variations. In each
of those studies, samples of corridor and suite freshman residents were recruited by telephone after being selected randomly from housing lists. If a
student was enrolled in a section of the introductory psychology course, he or
she was promised credit toward a course requirement for research participation. Otherwise, the student was offered money for participating.

In the first study, subjects arrived singly and were led to believe that they
were to be in a study of "simple motor performance" when the researcher was
ready for them. Each subject was shown to a waiting room, where another
subject who had arrived earlier (actually a same-sex confederate of the experi-
menter) sat one seat from the end of a row of seven attached chairs, and where
they could be observed through a one-way mirror. In this setting, corridor
residents showed signs of a generalized social withdrawal. They sat farther
from the confederate and looked at and spoke to him or her less, on the
average, than did suite residents. On a questionnaire administered after five
minutes of observation, corridor residents reported that they were less comfortable in the waiting room and that they found the confederate less attractive
than did the suite residents.

A second waiting-room study was similar except that subjects were asked
to report to the Stony Brook student health center, where they were led to
believe that they would be tested for their reactions to dental pain in a dental
office. Each subject waited alone or with an earlier-arriving subject (a confederate, again). For half of the subject, magazines were provided. Again, corridor residents sat farther from the confederate and looked and talked less.
Whereas suite residents were generally more comfortable if they were waiting

with the confederate than if waiting alone (according to their responses to a questionnaire), corridor residents reported feeling more comfortable with the confederate only if they had magazines available to screen themselves from any possible interaction with the confederate.

In a third waiting-room study, subjects expected to play the prisoner's-dilemma game under cooperative or competitive conditions. Corridor residents avoided interaction with the confederate and reported greater discomfort after waiting with the confederate, and those effects were greater under the cooperative condition than under the competitive condition.

In a fourth study, in a laboratory setting, each subject participated in a discussion with two confederates who either made a point of ignoring the subject or included the subject in the discussion. Ignored subjects were generally less comfortable and participated less, but corridor residents were less disturbed by being ignored than were suite residents.

In all of those waiting-room and laboratory studies, the behaviors of corridor residents indicated that they had developed a tendency to withdraw from opportunities for social interaction and that the tendency had been generalized to other social situations, presumably to cope with the higher social density and resulting crowding stress in their dormitories. They had become less friendly and probably less attractive people in the process of adapting to the unsatisfactory spatial arrangements on their dormitory floors. And still they continued to report greater social anxiety and discomfort in novel social situations. Such coping may have made their living arrangements more tolerable, but, despite its apparent costs in sociability, it had not erased the discomfort completely.

To demonstrate that their findings could be generalized beyond the students and dormitory designs at Stony Brook, Baum and Valins repeated several of their studies in a clearly different context, where the key contrast between dormitories of similar physical densities but different social densities or group sizes could also be studied. These new studies were conducted at Trinity College in Hartford, Connecticut, a much smaller and exclusively undergraduate institution whose students came from less urban and more affluent backgrounds than did those at Stony Brook.

The two dormitory types compared at Trinity College were both constructed following a corridor design, but they differed in the length of the corridors or floors and thus in social density. Each long corridor housed 38 students, in 8 single and 15 double bedrooms, with a bath at each end, but no lounge on the floor. Each short corridor housed 22 students, in four single and nine double bedrooms, with a single bathroom and a lounge on the floor. All Trinity freshmen (the source of subjects for Baum and Valins's studies) lived in double bedrooms in both types of dormitories.

A questionnaire survey of freshmen in long- and short-corridor dormitories found that long-corridor residents felt more crowded, were more likely to feel that they were unable to control their interactions on the floor, more often admitted that they avoided social contact with other students, and more often reported not belonging to a group of friends on the floor. Like their corridor colleagues at Stony Brook, the long-corridor residents showed a pattern of perceived crowding, discomfort, and social withdrawal compared with students whose dormitories created lower social densities.

A waiting-room study conducted at Trinity found that long-corridor residents avoided contact with an earlier-arriving "student" (the confederate) and reported greater discomfort after waiting with the confederate. In this study and a follow-up, Baum and Valins also tested the prediction than long-corridor (high-social-density) residents would display a pattern of learned helplessness, wherein they would make less assertive efforts on their own behalf as a consequence of their experience of failure at controlling the social environments in their dormitories. In the first waiting-room study, long-corridor residents displayed learned helplessness by less frequently exercising the prerogative to decide for themselves whether they would continue in the experiment alone or with other subjects. In a subsequent study, long-corridor residents more often adopted a helpless or withdrawal strategy in a version of the prisoner's-dilemma game when no interaction was permitted with the partner.

Thus, Baum and Valins were able to show that the general proposition that dormitory designs that resulted in higher social densities led to crowding stress, social withdrawal, and continuing discomfort in social situations inside and outside of the dormitory was supported empirically under a set of contextual conditions quite different from those that existed at Stony Brook, where it was first demonstrated. Even more exciting, they went on to show that these findings could be applied successfully in redesigning existing dormitory space to reduce social density and its unwelcome consequences.

The application

The application of Baum and Valins's research findings was described in a paper by Baum and Davis (1980). Based on the evidence that residential group size or social density was a key factor in freshman college students' adjustment to dormitory life, Baum and Davis planned and evaluated a reduction in group size in a dormitory built according to a long-corridor design, utilizing a simple architectural modification. The project was carried out in Jones Dormitory at Trinity College.

Jones Dormitory housed 43 students on each of its floors. There were 16 double bedrooms and 11 singles opening off both sides of a double-loaded corridor. Two bathrooms, one toward each end of the corridor, were shared by the residents of each floor. There was no lounge on the floor.

The modification consisted of converting the three bedrooms at the center of one floor, two singles and a double directly across the hall, into lounges, with doors installed on either side of this new lounge space. Beyond the new doors, there were two groups of residents. One group consisted of 18 residents housed in seven double bedrooms and four singles, sharing one bathroom. At the opposite end of the building was a group of 21, in eight double bedrooms and five singles, sharing the second of the original bathrooms. Thus, the original group of 43 residents, a number slightly larger than that associated with crowding stress and withdrawal on the long-corridor floors in Baum and Valins's earlier research at Trinity, was divided into two groups of 18 and 21, numbers similar to those on the short-corridor floors that had been associated with reduced stress and less withdrawal in the earlier Trinity studies. If the architectural modifications were successful, the residents on the modified floor would live in groups of 18 and 21, would experience reduced crowding stress, and would engage in less avoidance of social contact than would have been the case with the original floor design.

Baum and Davis's evaluation of the effects of the new design benefited greatly from extraordinary cooperation on the part of the Trinity College administration. The effects of reduced residential group size on the modified floor were assessed by comparing residents there with those on a similar but unmodified floor in the same dormitory, as well as with the residents of a floor in a different dormitory that followed a corridor design but housed only 22 residents, in nine double and four single bedrooms, sharing a common bathroom and lounge. With the cooperation of campus housing officials, freshmen were assigned to these three comparison floors (four if we count the two groups on the modified floor separately) at random to ensure that they would be comparable before being exposed to the different dormitory designs. In addition, all three (or four) spaces were refurbished and redecorated immediately before the freshman orientation period, when the study was begun, in order to avoid the possibility that the necessary recent renovations of the modified floor would set it apart as a more desirable residence because it would have been in better condition or because it would have received special attention.

Baum and Davis's evaluation of the attempt to reduce crowding stress by architectural modification to reduce residential group size on a long-corridor floor incorporated several of the same forms used in Baum and Valins's original research. Questionnaires were administered to random samples from each of the three types of settings to assess residents' perceptions and expectations. Observers visited each of the settings to determine the nature and locations of social and nonsocial behaviors on the dormitory floors, and a study was performed in a laboratory setting that made it possible to compare the four groups of freshmen for indications of social withdrawal and learned helplessness. All of the freshman students involved in these studies were women.

Questionnaires were administered to freshman students in their rooms on three occasions: at the beginning of the orientation period, after the fifth week of their first semester, and after the twelfth week. No differences among the groups were found at the time of the first administration, but their responses diverged after that on every question asked. The residents of the unmodified long-corridor floor felt more crowded, felt that they had less control over what happened on their floor, were more likely to characterize their floor as hectic, were more likely to attribute problems in the dormitory to the large number of people with whom they were living, were less sanguine about trying to structure their interactions with others or about trying to change things in the dormitory in general, and reported that formation of small groups of residents on their floor was less common and that fewer of their neighbors on the floor were friends. In every case, residents on the modified floor were equivalent to residents of the existing short-corridor floor in reporting fewer indications of crowding stress.

Observers visited the four dormitory locations three times per week during nine weeks in the middle of the students' first semester. They found increasing tendencies toward social withdrawal on the long-corridor floor over the course of the study. By week 8 there were fewer bedroom doors open on the long-corridor floor, and by week 10 there was less social interaction, as compared with the short-corridor and modified floors.

In a laboratory setting, students selected at random from each of the floors waited for five minutes with a same-sex confederate for a fictitious study of impression formation, completed a questionnaire about their moods, and then worked alone at a series of difficult anagram problems. Each anagram was presented with a 20-second time limit for completion, but subjects could request as many additional trials as they wished to attempt to solve those they had failed. Long-corridor residents sat farther from the confederate and looked at her less. They reported feeling greater discomfort after the waiting period and expected to have less control over the experimental session to follow. Then they attempted fewer additional anagram trials, independent of their success at solving the anagrams on the original 12 trials that all subjects were required to attempt.

In sum, there was considerable evidence, from subjects' own reports, from direct observation on the dormitory floors, and from subjects' behaviors in a standardized laboratory setting, that the architectural modification of the long-corridor floor had reduced crowding stress, social withdrawal, and signs of learned helplessness by effectively reducing residential group size to equal that in a short-corridor design. At the modest cost of 9% of the beds on the long-corridor floor, the installation of two doors, and the refurbishing of three bedrooms as lounges, the floor was transformed into a different design that provided greater support for residents' social needs, a design that was functionally equivalent to a short-corridor design or perhaps even a suite design.

Given the infrequent construction of new college dormitories today and the preponderance of the long-corridor design among existing dormitories, this is a finding of considerable practical significance.

Evaluation

Stage 1: Background analysis

This project was the work of social scientists whose primary interest lay in understanding the basic behavioral processes involved in the experience of crowding. Their involvement in design issues was largely a by-product of that interest and was limited to a simple intervention, a single design element that could be managed without much training in or sophistication about the design professions. As a result, this project was quite different in several respects from most of the others considered in this volume, in which designers played much more prominent roles. One facet of the approach taken in this case was the low level of interest in the particular persons, place, and time to which the resulting design solution was addressed. It is still more typical of social scientists to seek general laws of behavior (in this case, environment–behavior relationships) that hold across variations in sociohistorical context (merely error variance in this view), despite some methodologists' warnings about the danger of this practice (e.g., Gergen, 1973).

Stage 2: Behavioral goals

The behavioral goals for the renovation in Jones Dormitory were quite clear, set on the basis of Baum and Valins's conceptual analysis of conditions on an overcrowded dormitory floor. They included relief from the discomfort of crowding stress and a reduction in the resulting tendency toward social withdrawal, as well as more appropriate use of the variety of public and private living spaces available to dormitory residents. These behavioral improvements were to be expected, based on existing theory and research, to result from the increased privacy and control over social interaction that would be provided by smaller groupings of residents (in suites and on short corridors).

Stage 3: Environment–behavior relationships

The identification of design alternatives that would be likely to foster those behavioral goals was based on the original research carried out by Baum and Valins at Stony Brook (comparing corridor- and suite-design dorms) and at Trinity College (comparing long and short corridors). Those studies showed clear-cut advantages of the suite and short-corridor arrangements – those that created smaller groupings of residents having to share the bedroom, lounge, bath, and circulation spaces on their respective floors.

Those studies were conducted in the form of quasi experiments. All of the data, from questionnaires, observation on the dormitory floors, model-room projective tests, and observations made in the waiting-room laboratory setting, provided comparisons between two groups of subjects that existed in nature, perhaps in part by their own choice, rather than having been created by random assignment by the researchers. Therefore, the results of those comparisons must be interpreted in light of the possibility that there may have been systematic differences between the students who lived in corridor and suite dormitories, or on long- and short-corridor floors – in background, personality, academic skills, or some other characteristic that might account for the differences in perception, crowding threshold, and sociability that were observed in those studies. In other words, the contrasting groups (by housing type) of freshmen students may have been predisposed to respond differently to dormitory life even before they moved into their rooms at Stony Brook and Trinity.

Baum and Valins used two methods to try to rule out the possibility of such a selection bias and thus bolster confidence in the internal validity of their findings. The first, a more conventional and weaker method, was to use school records to show that the groups of students being compared were alike in many relevant respects; sizes of communities and high schools of origin, family size, ordinal position among siblings, family socioeconomic status, age, scholastic aptitude test (SAT) scores, personality, religion, interests, and more. Unfortunately, this approach can never rule out the possibility that the groups differed in some important way that the researchers failed to consider.

The second, a more original and more effective method, was used to establish the comparability of corridor and suite freshmen at Stony Brook. Baum and Valins repeated the model-room study of crowding thresholds – a key psychological component of the syndrome of crowding stress and coping responses they were trying to document – three times during one school year, with separate random samples of students. The first study was conducted during a summer orientation session, comparing prospective students who had indicated preferences for either a corridor or a suite dormitory and who eventually lived there. The second study was conducted during the first month of the school year, shortly after the freshmen had first moved into their dormitories. The third study compared corridor and suite residents the following March and April, after they had lived in their dormitories approximately six months. No differences were found between corridor and suite residents in responses to the model-room test in the summer or fall samples. However, in the spring the expected pattern of corridor residents placing fewer figures in rooms where social interaction was likely was found (no difference was found in the library reference-room model, in contrast to the original study). From this evidence, it seems unlikely that differences in behaviors between students in different dormitories were caused by preexisting differences in traits or predispositions, but rather that they emerged only after prolonged exposure to different living conditions. Thus, comparability (or lack of selection bias) was finally supported in a convincing manner.

Despite these impressive efforts, some minor threats to internal validity remained in these studies. In the Stony Brook studies, Baum and Valins reported that the suite dormitories were newer and were located in a more scenic, hilly, wooded area of the campus, as compared with the corridor dormitories. These extraneous factors, illustrative of the limitations of studying variations in nature, may have contributed to the more favorable responses and adjustments of suite dormitory residents.

In all, Baum and Valins's research program ranks as an outstanding example of the quasi-experimental approach. Threats to internal and external validity were reduced to the point that the consistent body of findings inspires an unusually high degree of confidence. The fact that they were able to reproduce virtually the entire range of their Stony Brook findings at Trinity College, where the design contrast was analogous to and yet different from that studied at Stony Brook and where there were striking differences in the size and composition of the student body, argues strongly for the external validity of their findings. It also suggests that the differences observed at Stony Brook were not artifacts of campus topography or any other such coincidental difference between the two dormitory types.

Stage 4: Design elements

Based on that research, and particularly the studies comparing long- and short-corridor dormitories at Trinity College, the division of a long corridor into two short ones was a direct, logical, and clear design choice for reducing crowding stress. The maintenance of separate bathrooms and the provision of new separate lounge facilities for each of the new short-corridor floors were details that merely followed from that choice.

Stage 5: Overall design

In this case, limited to the redesign of a single dormitory floor, those few elements inferred from the theoretical analysis of crowding stress and the dedicated research on its relationship to dormitory design constituted the totality of the design that was finally implemented in Jones Dormitory.

Stage 6: POE

The effects of the renovation that split one long-corridor floor in Jones Dormitory into two short ones were evaluated in a rare natural experiment. Comparisons were made among the two new short-corridor floors, a long-corridor floor in the same dormitory that was the equivalent of the floor that was divided in two for this experiment, and a short-corridor floor in another, assumedly comparable dormitory that had not been modified. The results showed clear-cut reductions in all signs of crowding stress in the new short-corridor floors, as compared with the unmodified long-corridor floor, making them comparable to the "natural" short-corridor floor.

Because Trinity College officials agreed to assign freshman women at random to the four floors compared in Baum and Davis's POE study, the four samples were equivalent, and there was no problem of selection bias. However, the research findings were still plagued by two plausible threats to internal validity. First, the two new, modified, short-corridor floors and the unmodified short-corridor floor they resembled so much all had on-floor lounge space for their residents, whereas the unmodified long-corridor floor, whose residents showed greater evidence of crowding stress, had none. Second, students living on the modified floors may have perceived a special interest on the part of the college administration, because no other floor in that dormitory had been altered from its original long-corridor design. Baum and Davis were able to arrange for all the floors compared in their study to be redecorated at the same time as the experimental modification was made, to minimize just such a special awareness, and the comparability between the two new short-corridor samples and the preexisting short-corridor sample suggests that they succeeded in doing so.

It is difficult to estimate whether or not the same effects would be observed in different students or on different campuses. All of the students involved in the implementation and evaluation of the long-corridor modification were freshman women at a small, exclusive liberal-arts college. It may be that more experienced students, especially if they had not lived in large groups as freshmen, or even students from less privileged backgrounds, might be less sensitive to the higher social densities on long-corridor floors. We do know that women dormitory residents may have a lower threshold for social density than men (Aiello, Baum, & Gormley, 1981). However, the fact that the findings of the prerenovation studies by Baum and Valins held up across several dormitories and two distinctly different campuses somewhat bolsters one's confidence in the generalizability of the success of Baum and Davis's implementation.

Finally, one is left to wonder if the negative effects of high social density created by "large-group" dormitory designs extend to what some educators consider the bottom line of campus life: academic achievement. None of the studies, either prerenovation or postrenovation, addressed that possible outcome of dormitory design, despite the apparent importance and feasibility of doing so.

Stage 7: Future impact

The contribution of Baum, Valins, and Davis's work to environmental design is much more modest in its actual implementation than in its potential. The renovation project in Jones dormitory was limited to one floor and involved fewer than 40 students (and was undone after less than a decade when the alteration was eliminated during a subsequent renovation of the entire building). But the project succeeded in demonstrating a promising approach to environmental-design research, one rooted firmly in the traditions of social science. It began with a sophisticated conceptual analysis bringing together several separate theories and extensive supporting research from such diverse traditions as ethology, laboratory experimentation, and naturalistic quasi experimentation. It continued with dedicated research in the context for which new design solutions were sought, research that was conducted using state-of-the-art methods. Finally, the design inferred from that research was evaluated with the assistance of careful arrangements that provided experimental comparisons in a natural setting.

Although their work has been circulated in traditional academic publications as a monograph (Baum & Valins, 1977) and a journal article (Baum & Davis, 1980), as well as in textbooks based on the mainstream research literature, it may be less familiar to design professionals. In part, its lack of accessibility to designers may be due to the limited scope of the application itself, the fact that it was not very impressive as a design project, and in part it may be due to the subtle, technical theoretical analyses and methodological solutions that were emphasized throughout.

It is still rare to see a true integration of design and social science in environmental-design research. Perhaps this work ought to be seen as a model for the first stages of EDR projects that would continue with large-scale implementation based on an evaluation of an experimental pilot design of the sort with which this project ended, following the model of "staged innovation" described by Campbell (1969). If the antecedent deep theoretical analysis and rigorous research demonstrated by Baum and his colleagues could be modeled more often in environmental-design research, the quality of consequent large-scale design projects might be improved considerably. Perhaps that is the biased view of a social scientist, but this project suggests that such an approach deserves to be tested more widely than it has been thus far.

References

Aiello, J. R., Baum, A., & Gormley, F. B. (1981). Social determinants of residential crowding stress. *Personality and Social Psychology Bulletin, 7,* 643–649.
Baum, A., & Davis, G. E. (1980). Reducing the stress of high-density living: An

architectural intervention. *Journal of Personality and Social Psychology, 38*, 471–481.

Baum, A., & Valins, S. (1977). *Architecture and social behavior.* Hillsdale, NJ: Erlbaum.

Calhoun, J. B. (1962). Population density and social pathology. *Scientific American, 206*, 139–148.

Campbell, D. T. (1969). Reforms as experiments. *American Psychologist, 24*, 409–429.

Christian, J. J., Flyger, V., & Davis, D. E. (1960). Factors in the mass mortality of a herd of Sika deer, *Cervus nippon. Chesapeake Science, 1*, 79–95.

Freedman, J. L. (1975). *Crowding and behavior.* San Francisco: Freeman.

Gergen, K. J. (1973). Social psychology as history. *Journal of Personality and Social Psychology, 26*, 309–320.

Milgram, S. (1970). The experience of living in cities. *Science, 167*, March 13, pp. 1461–1468.

Stokols, D. (1987). Conceptual strategies of environmental psychology. In D. Stokols & I. Altman (Eds.), *Handbook of environmental psychology* (Vol. 1, pp. 41–70). New York: Wiley.

8
SOCIOPETAL SPACE IN PSYCHIATRIC HOSPITALS

Locations: Saskatchewan Hospital, Weyburn, Saskatchewan,
Canada; Cleveland State Hospital, Cleveland, Ohio;
"Bridgehaven" Hospital
Participants: Humphry Osmond (theory); Robert Sommer (research
and design); Michael Bakos and David Chapin,
Architecture-Research-Construction (research and
design); Charles J. Holahan and Susan Saegert (research
and design)

Over 30 years ago, Humphry Osmond, then superintendent of Saskatchewan
Hospital, a mental hospital of approximately 1,500 beds in Weyburn, Saskatchewan, in western Canada, began to publicize his views about the importance of architecture to the therapeutic functions of such facilities. Shortly
thereafter, Robert Sommer, a new social psychology Ph.D. from the University of Kansas, took a job as a research psychologist at the hospital, joining an
unusual interdisciplinary team of researchers assembled by Osmond (Sommer, 1983), and helped to translate Osmond's views into a more precise and
useful framework for improving conditions at the hospital. Subsequently,
Sommer began a systematic program of laboratory and field research that
helped to establish a comprehensive theory of the way in which social interaction is influenced by the spatial arrangements in which it occurs. More recently, there have been further attempts to build theories about the effects of
spatial arrangements on social interaction and to improve the design of institutional facilities based on the work of Osmond and Sommer. Taken together,
all of this work provides an instructive example of the way in which theory,
research, and application can enrich one another through interchange among
social psychologists, mental-health practitioners, and designers.

Osmond's view of the therapeutic environment

Osmond's view of the role of the physical milieu in the treatment of the
mentally ill was based on prior work by ethologists Heini Hediger and Jacob
Von Vexkull and on his analysis of the behavioral deficit of mental patients
and the ways in which traditional hospital design served to aggravate patients'
problems of adaptation (Osmond, 1957, 1959, 1966). According to Osmond,

131

mental patients' behaviors showed disturbances in perception (such as hallucinations and delusions, characteristics of schizophrenia), mood (such as the instability of bipolar disorder), and thinking. At the same time, the settings in which mental patients were then housed (in the large "state hospitals" that are so much less common and less heavily populated today) were characterized by spaces of monumental size, with very large rooms, high ceilings, hard surfaces, and long corridors that made visual and auditory discriminations difficult. Large numbers of patients shared dormitory-style sleeping rooms and large, open dayrooms, making the management of interpersonal relationships difficult. Patients were denied access to spaces where they could not be observed and were denied possession of personal belongings, further impairing their fragile self-concepts. Osmond described an ornate wall frieze in one mental hospital that contained cleverly hidden grotesque figures whose eyes might suddenly be discovered staring out of their camouflage at an unsuspecting observer.

Out of this assortment of mismatches between design and patients' needs that might vary in intensity across patient groups, Osmond identified one particular behavioral problem that he believed to be common to all mental patients and to which the architecture of mental hospitals seemed to be especially relevant. In his words, all of the mentally ill are victims of a "rupture in interpersonal relationships resulting in alienation from the community culminating in expulsion or flight" (Sommer, 1969, p. 561). This fundamental problem of alienation, Osmond believed, was aggravated by the physical setting – large spaces, great distances, harsh echoes, depersonalization, and overconcentration. Thus, the physical setting actually made it more difficult to see and to hear others and to understand oneself, and it created the problem of sorting through large numbers of often difficult, disturbed people.

Thus, Osmond believed that the combination of patients' impairments and an unsuitable physical environment discouraged the formation of stable human relationships in mental hospitals, serving to aggravate the behavioral problems for which patients had been admitted in the first place. Osmond identified the characteristics of the physical environment that discouraged social interaction with the label "sociofugal space." He pointed out that such spaces are found elsewhere, as in hotels and railroad stations, and can even be desirable in some of those cases (although some disagree; see Sommer, 1974). Osmond also conceived of alternative physical arrangements – small rooms, appropriate privacy gradients, personalized and noninstitutional spaces, spatial arrangements that tend to draw people together – that might encourage social interaction. He gave such places the name "sociopetal spaces."

Although Osmond gave consideration to implications in the wider society, his primary concern was with the mental hospital and its residents. Striking a theme that has become much more common in subsequent years, Osmond pointed out that mental-hospital patients have particular difficulties in forming relationships because of the individual impairments in perception, mood, and thought that make it more difficult for them to understand and to be understood, and thus they are particularly vulnerable to the disruptive effects of sociofugal spaces on social relationships. In particular, sociofugal spaces discourage formation of the small groups in which most relationships develop. Osmond believed that such effects were common in mental hospitals and that they aggravated patients' problems. He wrote that "it is pleasanter not to guess how many patients have been irreparably damaged by unsuitable buildings and how many are presently being tortured by them" (Osmond, 1957).

Sommer's experimental redesign of a sociofugal dayroom

Shortly after his arrival at the Saskatchewan Hospital, Robert Sommer was consulted by a physician in charge of a women's geriatrics ward. Using a windfall of newly discovered pension funds owed its patients by the government of Canada, the hospital had recently completed extensive renovations that included the creation of a large dayroom on the women's geriatric ward, with new and luxurious furnishings, as compared with previous conditions and those typical of such institutions. Against this auspicious backdrop, the ward physician was struck by how little interaction he observed among the patients in the new dayroom.

The women's geriatrics ward housed 83 residents, whose average age was 74. Most of them suffered from atherosclerosis. Slightly fewer than one-third were diagnosed as schizophrenic or depressed. An indeterminate number might today be diagnosed as suffering from Alzheimer's disease, or dementia. Despite the fact that some of these elderly women were not mental patients, Sommer found Osmond's dual conceptualization of sociofugal and sociopetal spaces helpful in understanding the behavior described by the ward physician. The general notion that spatial arrangements could encourage or discourage social interaction, together with his informal observations of social behavior in a wide variety of public and private settings, guided Sommer's analysis of the situation in the dayroom.

Sommer hypothesized that the new dayroom furniture had been arranged in the beautiful new space in a way that discouraged social interaction among the 30 or so women who used it regularly. Although Sommer did not directly apply Osmond's ideas about the perceptual and cognitive effects of institutional spaces on the mentally ill – after all, most of the women on the geriatrics ward did not belong in the traditional diagnostic groups emphasized by Osmond – he did hypothesize that the dayroom space was sociofugal. Most of the 43 chairs and four couches in the room were placed shoulder-to-shoulder along the walls in facing rows spaced more than 20 feet apart. The rest of the seating was in clusters of short rows back-to-back with one another, or chairs placed around columns, all facing in different directions. The four card tables were set off by themselves, away from any of the seating. He reasoned that anyone would find it difficult to sustain social interaction under such conditions, but especially elderly women, who would be forced to turn 90 degrees in their chairs, or to see and speak across large distances, in order to converse with one another.

To test these hypotheses and, at the same time, intervene to improve conditions in the dayroom, Sommer and Ross (1958) carried out a six-week experiment to evaluate a change toward a more sociopetal spatial arrangement, as part of an interdisciplinary research team headed by Osmond and including psychologist Teddy Weckowitz and architects Kyo Izumi and Art Allen. During the first two weeks, social interaction in the dayroom was observed during 33 five-minute samples of time. An observer counted every interaction and differentiated between those that were brief and those that were sustained. Sustained interactions were required to be reciprocal and to last at least two minutes. Brief interactions could be remarks directed by one resident toward another. The number of residents involved in each interaction was also recorded.

After the two-week "baseline" period, Sommer directed a rearrangement of the furniture in the dayroom. Three of the four couches were removed, and five new tables were brought in. Most of the chairs were placed in groups of four around the 30-inch-square tables spaced throughout the room. Thus, the large space was broken up into nine "islands" of chair-and-table arrangements. Almost all of the shoulder-to-shoulder, back-to-back, and solitary seating arrangements were eliminated.

A two-week transition period was allowed to permit residents and staff to become accustomed to the new arrangements. Both constituencies showed considerable resistance, including repeated instances when pieces of furniture were moved back to their old locations. Sommer attributed much of this to the disruption of "institutional sanctity," the traditional or familiar structure of the institution. He also became aware of specific complaints from staff members about increased difficulties having to do with surveillance of residents (nurses), movement of carts through the room (food-service personnel), and cleaning (maintenance staff), as compared with the old arrangement of orderly rows of seating with broad "highways" in between them. During this transition period, flowers and magazines were placed on the tables to encourage residents to sit at them. Staff complaints abated as they were reassured by the researchers and by the behaviors of the residents.

During the following two-week period, observations of resident interactions were repeated – an additional 33 five-minute samples of behaviors. A comparison with the baseline period showed that the rates of both brief and sustained interactions in the dayroom had increased substantially. Tables 8.1 and 8.2 reproduce Sommer's original presentation of those findings. The study was rather modest in its methodological approach (Sommer justified the small number of observations and the use of a single observer as sufficient for the small number and clear-cut nature of the interactions that took place; he

Table 8.1. *Total number of subjects involved in verbal interactions during 33 five-minute observation periods*

Condition	Brief interactions	Sustained interactions
Old arrangement	47	36
New arrangement	73	61

Table 8.2. *Number of participants in each interaction*

	Old arrangement		New arrangement	
Number interacting	Brief	Sustained	Brief	Sustained
Two	24	16	40	30
Three	3	0	4	0
Four or more	0	0	0	0

began with two observers, but found that they agreed so well that only one was needed) and in the amount of data it produced (again, 33 five-minute periods seemed sufficient to Sommer) and the analysis of those data (no real statistical comparison was made). Still, it seemed to validate in a general way Osmond's conceptualization of the distinction between sociofugal and sociopetal spaces and Sommer's more specific hypotheses based on Osmond's analysis and his own elaborations and extensions of them. It also served to demonstrate the potential utility of those ideas for improving the design of institutional facilities for long-term geriatric care by simple, almost cost-free means such as rearranging furniture within an existing space. It suggested to Sommer the need to study further the relationship between physical setting and social interaction, and it suggested to him and to others the possibility of more and broader applications of such knowledge.

Ward 8: Cleveland State Hospital

More than a decade after Sommer's work in Saskatchewan, a behaviorally oriented architectural firm in Cleveland, Ohio, led by David Chapin and Michael Bakos, designed and implemented an imaginative application of Osmond's sociopetal space in a ward for chronic mental patients at Cleveland State Hospital (ARC, 1976). That firm, Architecture-Research-Construction (ARC), was hired to plan a large-scale redesign of the hospital, although this first phase was barely completed before a decision was made to close the hospital, in the spirit of the deinstitutionalization movement of the time (see chapter 5 for a fuller discussion), which terminated the project.

Ward 8 at Cleveland State Hospital was a locked ward housing almost 50 long-term, seriously disturbed male patients with diagnoses such as chronic schizophrenia and severe regression. Their behaviors, influenced strongly by the medications they were being given, were characterized by the anomaly of periods of listlessness and purposelessness punctuated with episodes of violence. The ward itself was of the classic mental-hospital design described by Osmond. There were large sleeping (dormitory-style in three rooms), dining, and "dayhall" rooms. Smaller rooms that might have housed activities for patients were locked during the day, along with the dormitories, to make it easier for staff to locate patients and maintain surveillance for outbreaks of violence. Ceilings were high, surfaces highly reflective, and lighting poor, all contributing to difficulty in maintaining purposeful activities, including conversation. There were virtually no planned activities or spaces arranged to promote purposeful activities, including social interaction.

The goals for ARC's redesign of Ward 8 were developed during a period of a few weeks when the professional research and design team spent considerable time on the ward among the patients and staff. During that time, described by the ARC team as a collaborative exploration of the problems and possibilities on Ward 8, lack of purposeful activity was identified as the principal target behavior to be addressed in the new design. At the same time, it was clear that the existing spaces were configured and furnished in ways that would reinforce, if not produce, those problematic behaviors or behavioral deficits. In Osmond's terms, they were sociofugal spaces. The promise that physical changes, toward more sociopetal arrangements, might help to remediate those deficits was raised during this "period of acquaintance" when one of the patients, presumably a man so disturbed for so long that efforts at therapy had mostly been abandoned in favor of chemical restraints and isolation, passed a written note to one of the ARC staff in which a group of patients asked the team to pursue an attempt to improve conditions on the ward.

The plan developed by ARC, with the help of the staff and patients of Ward 8, addressed both the needs of the physical setting and the need to evaluate the effects of physical changes on the target behaviors (i.e., the efficiency of the design in addressing the behavioral goals for the ward).

The physical changes were intended to create spaces that would foster social interaction among patients as well as, or in conjunction with, other activities, in addition to spaces that would provide for patients' needs for nonsocial activities, both in public areas with other patients and in solitary locations. Partitions were used to divide sleeping dormitories into two-bed modules, each with a "social space" containing table and chairs (Figures 8.1 and 8.2). In the dayroom, activity spaces were created by building raised platforms on which two to four curved three-seat clusters were used to create

Figure 8.1. Two views of the more private sleeping arrangements created for Ward 8. Source: ARC (1975a, p. 7); reproduced with permission of Michael Bakos, principal, ARC.

Figure 8.2. A diagram of the new sleeping modules. Source: ARC (1975a); reproduced with permission of Michael Bakos, principal, ARC.

Figure 8.3. Staff and researchers in one of the activity areas designed for Ward 8. Photo from Michael Bakos of ARC.

circular or semicircular arrangements (Figure 8.3). On some of these plat-forms, the seating surrounded activity centers such as television sets, washer and dryer machines, and cooking facilities. In some cases, counters were erected in front of the seating to encourage leaning forward, closer to those seated across, approximately six feet away. Partitions were used to further define these sociopetal arrangements, including in some cases low walls directly behind the seats where passersby could lean in on the activity taking place on the platform (Figure 8.4).

To provide patients with more choices among spaces, and more privacy in the sense of being able to control others' access to them, doors were kept open throughout the ward, and new doorways were built to facilitate movement among the rooms and to break up long corridors and large spaces, at least functionally. Sleeping modules provided a place for isolation and for the safe display of personal possessions. Sound baffles were built below the ceilings to reduce reflection and facilitate conversation. Lighting was improved to make activities easier, and bright colors and large signs were used to provide orien-tation aids and to improve the aesthetic appearance of the ward (Figure 8.4). The new decor was intended to enhance the patients' self-images by their indication of respect from those in charge of the institution and the patients'

Figure 8.4. One of the leaning surfaces used to foster interaction on Ward 8. Photo from Michael Bakos of ARC.

lives, as well as to facilitate higher levels of activity. This included the variety of new activity equipment: laundries, kitchenettes, television sets, and table games.

To evaluate the effects of the new design on the patients' behaviors, a three-phase study was planned. A technique known as behavioral mapping, developed by Ittelson, Rivlin, and Proshansky (1970) for research in mental hospitals, provided the empirical data (Figure 8.5). It makes use of floor plans on which patterns of patients' movements can be charted, as well as several sets of categories (Table 8.3) into which their behaviors can be classified (observers record the behaviors of individual patients at specified intervals during selected periods on designated days).

Behavioral mapping was carried out on three occasions. The first was a two-week baseline period in August 1972 before any changes had been made on the ward. An "interim mapping" was carried out in June 1973. At that point, the raised platforms had been built in the dayroom, but no seating or activity equipment or partitions had been installed. Ceiling acoustical baffles were in place, some table games had arrived, some new doorways had been cut, and three prototype two-bed sleeping modules had been constructed. The measures collected during that period were intended as a check on a "Hawthorne effect." That is, they would indicate whether or not attention by the

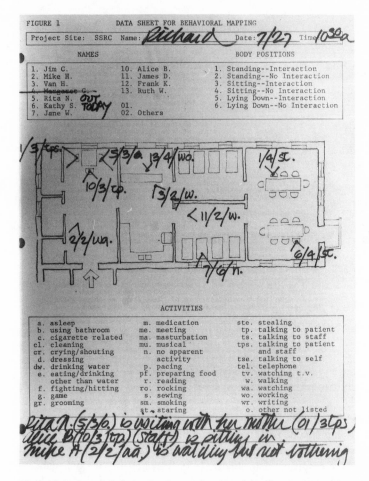

Figure 8.5. A sample behavioral-mapping data sheet used in the ARC evaluation of the Ward 8 redesign. Source: ARC (1975b, p. 15); reproduced with permission of Michael Bakos, principal, ARC.

ARC team and activity on the ward per se, without the creation of the spatial arrangements intended in the design, were sufficient to produce the behavioral changes intended to measure the effects of the design itself. A final evaluation mapping was carried out in December 1973, when the physical changes on the ward had been completed.

Comparisons among the three observation periods were made for 22 men who had been present on the ward in all three periods. During the 16-month period of the study, some of the other men had been moved out of the ward,

Table 8.3. *Behavioral mapping categories for Ward 8 study*

Category label	Observations
Isolated passive	Lying awake
	Sleeping
	Sitting alone
Isolated active	Writing
	Personal hygiene
	Reading
	Standing
	Pacing
Mixed active	Eating
	Housekeeping
	Phonograph-radio
	Arts and crafts
	TV
	Watching an activity
Socializing	Games
	Talking
Visiting	Talking to visitor
Traffic	Traffic

many to other locations in the hospital, and the ward census had shrunk to 33 men in all. No changes were observed in the amount of passive behavior or in the amount of social interaction between the baseline and interim mapping periods. However, between the baseline period and the final evaluation, the overall incidence of social interaction more than doubled, and the incidence of passive behavior or inactivity declined from 55.2% of all observations to 32.1% (despite the fact that dormitories were opened during the day, and thus more spaces were created where patients could be alone if they wished). Another indication of the changes in patients' behaviors and the social atmosphere of the ward was the need for observers to create a new category for the final mapping period: "watching an activity."

Thus, the effects of altering the spaces on Ward 8 to create a more sociopetal arrangement were similar to those observed by Sommer and Ross in the geriatrics-ward dayroom in Saskatchewan approximately 15 years earlier. Because the results of the interim mapping indicated that nonspecific attention to patients' problems and simple activity on their behalf had no observable effect on patterns of patient activity, the ARC team concluded that "the physical changes on Ward 8 seemed to be a major factor to which the ultimate increase in patient interaction might be attributed" (ARC, 1976, p. 29).

"Bridgehaven" Hospital

Shortly after the ARC project at Cleveland State Hospital was completed, Skip Holahan and Susan Saegert (Holahan & Saegert, 1973) undertook yet another application of Osmond's concept of sociopetal space, this time "in the psychiatric pavilion of a large municipal hospital, which we will call Bridgehaven" (Holahan, 1976, p. 154). One admissions ward was remodeled to fulfill a three-part behavioral program. First, the new space was intended to provide encouragement for social behaviors among patients and to prevent their social withdrawal. Second, it was intended to elicit a positive emotional state from patients, rather than depression and lethargy. Finally, it was intended to provide patients with more varied activities.

Although the goal of promoting social interaction among mental-hospital patients could have been justified on the basis of Osmond's theoretical analysis and Sommer and Ross's well-known application of it, Holahan and Saegert took the time to document its relevance to the particular ward on which they were working. They conducted interviews with patients and staff on the ward and made their own observations before setting the behavioral program. They came to agree with the ward staff that the patients' abilities to engage in successful social behaviors held the key to their being able to live outside the hospital. In fact, they learned that passive, withdrawn behavior on the part of any patient would serve as a contraindication to the professional hospital staff of the patient's readiness to be discharged.

The design changes for promoting social interaction were reminiscent of those used by Sommer and Ross and ARC for the same purpose. One of the two dayrooms on the ward was furnished with sociopetal groupings of tables and chairs (cf. Sommer & Ross, 1958). The large dormitory-style sleeping rooms were partitioned into two-bed sections, each with its own "conversation area" furnished with table and chairs (cf. ARC, 1976).

To promote a positive emotional state, the entire ward was repainted in bright, noninstitutional colors and provided with modern, comfortable furniture. Finally, opportunities were provided for more varied activities by equipping a second dayroom with television sets and table games.

Six months after the remodeling was complete, its effects on the behaviors of patients on the ward were evaluated through comparison with a second admissions ward. The comparison ward was selected for its similarity to the remodeled ward in physical environment (before remodeling), number, type, and morale of staff, and treatment approach. Because of the hospital's policy of randomly distributing newly admitted patients between the remodeled and unchanged wards (Ward R and Ward C, respectively), using a computerized admissions procedure, the evaluation of the effects of remodeling took the form of a powerful true experiment.

During a five-week period, observations were made of random samples of 25 patients admitted to each of the two comparison wards. Each patient was observed during his or her first week on the ward, during two 75-minute sessions, morning and afternoon, both on Tuesday and Thursday. Observations were made every five minutes, yielding 15 observations per session and 60 observations in all for each patient. The observations were made using the same type of floor plans and behavior-category system adapted from Ittelson et al. (1970) by ARC for the Cleveland State Hospital project.

In addition to the observations, 30-minute structured interviews were conducted with all patients in the study at the end of the week during which they had been observed. A rater blind to the patient's ward assignment listened to an audio tape of each interview and completed six rating scales to indicate the rater's impressions of the patient's attitude toward the physical environment (4 scales) and toward the social atmosphere on the ward (2 scales).

Multiple observers were used to collect data for assessing the reliability of measures of patients' locations and activities as well as the scaling of interviews. The results were highly acceptable levels of .94 for patient location, .98 for category assignment, and .82 for interview scoring. Patients' records were used to compare the samples observed on Wards R and C. They were highly similar in diagnosis, age, and gender, but the Ward C sample contained a greater proportion of African-Americans compared with caucasians and Chicanos.

Analysis of the location and behavior categorizations showed clear positive effects of the remodeling on Ward R. More social interaction was observed on Ward R, and less isolated, passive behavior. This was true of interactions with patients, staff, and visitors and was observed in all areas of the ward – dayrooms, dining rooms, bedrooms, and corridors – although the differences between the wards were especially pronounced in the dining rooms and corridors. There was no difference in the amounts of nonsocial active behavior observed on the two wards.

Analysis of the interview results showed that patients on Ward R expressed more positive attitudes toward the physical environment of their ward than did those on Ward C. Their responses were scored significantly higher on two of the four individual characteristics scaled, "stimulating" and "attractive," and overall (across all four scales). When the patient samples were broken down on the basis of relative levels of activity, it was found that on Ward R the most active patients expressed the greatest approval of the ward environment, while on Ward C the least active patients were most satisfied. This seems to indicate that patients perceived accurately and differentially the global purpose of each ward. There was no significant difference between the Ward R and Ward C samples in the attitudes expressed toward the ward social atmosphere during the interviews, on either scale (referring to relations with other patients and with staff) or overall.

Thus, the evaluation supported the efficacy of sociopetal-space modifications in achieving the behavioral goals of increased social interaction and decreased passive, isolated behavior.

Evaluation

Stage 1: Background analysis

Beginning with Osmond's analysis of the behavior patterns and deficits of mental-hospital patients, the original impetus for all three of these projects, all of this work on sociopetal space was shaped by an analysis of the particular people and activities that are found in traditional "state hospitals." In addition, in each of these projects, special efforts were made by the EDR teams to acquaint themselves with the local patient and staff populations their work was intended to serve. It cannot be seen easily how those background analyses influenced the course of the EDR projects that followed, but the individuality of the designs themselves suggests that some such influence may have been felt.

Stage 2: Behavioral goals

There seems to be little disagreement with Osmond's (1957, 1966) initial analysis that mental-hospital patients suffer foremost from an inability to form satisfying social relationships. Accordingly, the principal behavioral goal of each of these projects was to increase the amount of social interaction involving the ward residents. Secondarily, each was designed to encourage the substitution of purposive activities for the stereotypical, passive behaviors that typically occupy most of mental-hospital patients' waking hours. Finally, both the social and nonsocial behaviors that were to be supported by the new designs were believed to depend on environmental conditions that would facilitate normal, adaptive visual and auditory perceptions.

All of these goals followed fairly directly from Osmond's original conceptual distinction between sociofugal space and sociopetal space, which was bolstered later on by the evaluation of Sommer and Ross's experimental application of that analysis and additional research by Sommer and others on the effects of spatial arrangements on social behavior.

Stage 3: Environment–behavior relationships

Sommer and Ross's efforts to create sociopetal space at Weyburn were based on their interpretation and elaboration of Osmond's theoretical analysis. The POE study of the new spatial arrangements they created then served to inform the ARC and Holahan and Saegert projects. The general principles deduced from those sources were combined with background information about the conditions at the Cleveland and "Bridgehaven" hospitals to provide more specific guides to the spatial arrangements that would further the behavioral goals that were mostly common to all three projects.

The influential Sommer and Ross study was conducted using what methodologists would consider a relatively weak research design. Differences in the dayroom behaviors of ward residents between the prerenovation and postrenovation observation periods cannot be attributed unequivocally to the changes in spatial arrangements without ruling out alternative explanations, such as changes in administrative policies or staff behaviors. In the absence of a comparison with another ward that differed only in furniture arrangement, or analysis of a long series of measures that could reveal fluctuations in behaviors caused by factors other than spatial arrangements, such a level of confidence is probably unwarranted. It could be justified only by assuming that the geriatrics ward where Sommer and Ross's study was carried out was effectively insulated from the influence of factors other than those they manipulated. On the positive side, the comparison of separate samples of behavior from a single group of individuals eliminates any doubt about the equivalence of those individuals. Of course, this type of preexperimental (cf. Campbell & Stanley, 1966) arrangement is used very commonly in natural settings where comparison groups and long series of measures are so often impracticable. The subsequent success of the ARC and Holahan and Saegert projects, which were based on Sommer and Ross's results, provides some independent corroboration that possible threats to the internal validity of those findings did not in fact materialize. The combination of all three sociopetal-space projects in diverse venues also strongly supports the generalizability of Osmond's analysis and of the results of Sommer and Ross's application of it.

The degree to which Sommer and Ross's findings need to be discounted in light of the susceptibility of their research design to threats to internal validity is also reduced somewhat by a study done by Holahan (1972). In that study, Holahan carried out a virtual replication of Sommer and Ross's study in a laboratory setting. In a room set apart from the normal hospital routine, psychiatric patients were exposed randomly to shoulder-to-shoulder (sociofugal) or to around-the-table (sociopetal) furniture arrangements, as well as to other variations. In that true experimental design, Holahan reproduced the effects on social interaction observed by Sommer and Ross, free from the threats to internal validity that plagued their research design.

Stage 4: Design elements

Sommer and Ross's design for the women's geriatrics ward at Saskatchewan Hospital consisted of a rather simple rearrangement of the existing dayroom furniture and a modest number of additional pieces. This new arrangement followed quite directly Osmond's original concept of sociopetal space, bolstered by Sommer's more detailed analysis of the impact of spatial arrangements on social interaction that focused on the mediating exchange of visual and auditory information.

The ARC design for Ward 8 at Cleveland State Hospital extended Sommer and Ross's approach through their invention of new design elements that promised to strengthen the sociopetal attraction of furniture groupings and other interaction settings. Those activity areas and the customized furniture they contained, including the "leaning-in" walls that surrounded some of them, seemed to reflect the more sophisticated design expertise of the ARC team. The ARC renovation also went beyond the realm of social interaction in public spaces to include design changes in sleeping quarters and in ward circulation spaces, to spread sociopetal attraction throughout the ward and to provide greater privacy for purposive nonsocial activities.

The Holahan and Saegert redesign of an intake ward at "Bridgehaven" Hospital was intermediate between the Weyburn and Cleveland projects in its design complexity and comprehensiveness, but it was more similar to the ARC project in spreading sociopetal arrangements throughout the ward through a variety of design elements.

All three sociopetal-space projects, despite the differences in details, can be seen quite clearly to have been inspired primarily by Osmond's early ideas. The two later examples were encouraged by the evidence of Sommer and Ross's success, but that project provided little, if any, conceptual advance or design guidance. The designs evolved in those later projects still clearly reflected Osmond's analysis of sociofugal spatial interference with mental-hospital residents' functioning in both social and nonsocial spheres.

Stage 5: Overall design

In all three projects, the changes in spatial arrangements, including furniture arrangements (together with activity equipment in some cases), partitioning of space, and changes in the layout of ward areas, constituted the totality of the sociopetal designs that were implemented on the respective mental-hospital wards. They and the behavioral goals with which they were associated constituted the sole objective of each EDR project. There was no competition from other design goals or elements or their advocates.

Stage 6: POE

In each of the three projects the results were evaluated, and the evaluation was an integral component of the project. And in each case the results of the POE study confirmed the usefulness of the design that had been implemented on the ward in question. In each case, social interaction increased following renovation, justifying the claim that the design would create more sociopetal spatial arrangements. Other evidence suggested that nonsocial purposive behaviors also replaced some of the passive, solitary, stereotypical behavior patterns that had typified ward residents prior to the renovations.

Although the results of the three POE studies were fairly comparable, the methods or research designs employed in those studies differed considerably. In fact, a consideration of those differences reveals one of the most important lessons to be learned from this series of projects.

Sommer and Ross's preexperimental before–after comparison of behaviors in the women's geriatrics-ward dayroom at Saskatchewan Hospital left the interpretation of results open to conjecture about a host of possible coincidental changes, such as increased attention to patients by staff and even expectations-based changes in the criteria by which patients' behaviors were judged. All are rival hypotheses for the behavioral differences from before to after renovation. The design of the ARC evaluation study made some of those alternatives less plausible by adding a third observation period, scheduled after the institution was committed to the changes and the ward residents and staff had already become involved in planning them and were awaiting or expecting the outcome, but before the changes had actually been incorporated into the setting. This quasi-experimental approach (or close approximation thereof) strengthened the internal validity of the causal inference that linked observed changes in behavior to the new sociopetal arrangements themselves. Of course, both the Sommer and Ross and ARC POEs shared the advantage that premanipulation and postmanipulation data were obtained from the same patients, eliminating problems of group-composition differences.

Finally, the Holahan and Saegert study employed a powerful experimental design, including comparison with a second intake ward based on equivalent groups of patients assigned to the two wards at random. This approach to evaluation limited the threats to internal validity even further, although an experiment conducted in a setting as complex and fluid as a mental-hospital ward can never control or equate all possible influences on the behaviors being studied.

From the point of view of the assertion that sociopetal spatial arrangements can increase social interaction and other alert, purposive behaviors, the outcome seems quite clear. The fact that the results did not differ materially in cases where there were fewer threats to internal validity suggests very strongly that the results in cases with weaker research designs were not caused by coincidental or extraneous factors, but by the altered spatial arrangements to which they were attributed. This may give hope to environmental-design researchers working in organizations where institutional policies will not support the kind of manipulation and control that would make possible the use of powerful research designs to evaluate the outcome of their work. It may show others how arrangements can be made for evaluation studies whose results can be interpreted without concern for many troublesome alternative explanations.

Finally, the fact that sociopetal spatial arrangements were found to be successful in such different forms, in such different places, and with such a variety of patients, staffs, and therapeutic milieux, lends great credibility to the generality of their effects and confidence in their applicability over a broad spectrum of target settings. Confidence in external validity is bolstered further by the results of a study by Holahan (1976), following up on his and Saegert's POE at "Bridgehaven." That study showed that the experimental ward modification there had positive effects on patients in part through its effects on the ward staff. Staff roles in managing the ward changed as a result of their participation in Holahan and Saegert's project. For example, the nurses' greater responsibility for the day-to-day operation of the ward was recognized for the first time by the attending physicians. The competence they demonstrated during the course of planning the remodeling influenced judgments of the nurses' subsequent contributions to plans for therapy and administration on the ward. Thus, it appears that the creation of sociopetal spaces for patients may create "social-systems" changes in the institution that can mediate the beneficial effects of the new physical environment (although the level of staff participation in the planning of design changes in the Holahan and Saegert project may have induced a greater effect in the institution than in cases where the changes are imposed, as in the Sommer and Ross study). It seems that although institutions that carry out such changes may differ in their social systems, the fact that such changes are made may make them more alike as a result. Therefore, social-systems variables may not limit the effects of sociopetal spatial arrangements so much as they mediate them.

Stage 7: Future impact

The fact that the Sommer and Ross study was published originally in an obscure journal seems to have had little effect on its ultimate impact. Perhaps, as Sommer believes (R. Sommer, personal communication, 1991), the idea was so good and so useful that its spread through citations in secondary sources was inevitable. In any case, it and the two later projects helped to make Osmond's distinction between sociofugal space and sociopetal space one of the best-known theoretical formulations in the field of environment–behavior studies (Kleeman, 1981; Lang, 1987). It has also been widely circulated in the mental-health profession (Griffin, Mauritzen, & Kasmar, 1969). Descriptions for the yet-uninitiated are still appearing in the literature today, as in a recent paper in the *Canadian Journal of Psychiatry* (Minde, Haynes, & Rodenburg, 1990) describing the Sommer and Ross project, which was completed almost 35 years earlier.

The concept of sociopetal space, reinforced by the successful, if small-scale, applications described earlier and by historical analysis of psychiatric-hospital design, has also contributed to the design of psychiatric and other residential institutional facilities on a broader scale. Working with architect

Kyo Izumi, Osmond has developed generic sociopetal designs for psychiatric facilities (Osmond, 1966; Izumi, 1957). These designs for entire institutions have also been adapted for specific facilities such as Haverford State Hospital, built near Philadelphia in 1962. Osmond and others have publicized the use of the concept of sociopetal space in design widely in the psychiatric literature. As a result, it has been taken up by practitioners in other fields who are concerned about the effects of their residential facilities on the social behaviors of patients. A prominent example is M. Powell Lawton, who has applied the concept in his work at the Philadelphia Geriatric Center, as described by Holahan and Wandersman (1987). Sommer has written that "the principles of sociopetal and sociofugal space have been incorporated into design curricula and used as the basis for designing and renovating buildings, including psychiatric facilities in New Jersey and Yorkton, Saskatchewan" (1983, p. 435).

Besides the wide exposure given to Osmond's original formulation, his ideas have influenced the development of related or expanded theories. Sommer and Osmond (1962, 1984) have postulated a descriptive theory of the lack of social organization among psychiatric-hospital patients, even compared with captive residents of other institutions, such as prisons and jails. It refers to the psychiatric-hospital population as the "schizophrenic no-society." Although the latter analysis suggests, on the basis of observation of deinstitutionalized psychiatric patients in jails and community treatment settings (e.g., foster homes), that the lack of social organization in mental hospitals may be the result of patient rather than hospital characteristics (apparently ignoring carry-over effects and continued drug therapy), there seems a clear line of development from the concept of sociofugal and spatial arrangements to the concept of the no-society.

Osmond's theory has also been extended by Sommer to a broader analysis of the reasons for the lack of fit between architectural design and human needs. In his conceptualization of "hard architecture," Sommer (1974) elaborates on how security, maintenance, and other administrative needs take precedence over user needs in the design of many public spaces, as they have in the psychiatric hospital, where many of the features of sociofugal spaces evolved for those very reasons.

In addition, Osmond's theory has been extended recently to small-town planning. Miller (1989) has described the need for a balance between sociofugal and sociopetal spaces, fostering privacy and community development, respectively, on that larger scale. Although Valadez and Bellalta (see chapter 12) make no mention of Osmond or his concepts in their analysis of "Macul," it is not inconceivable that some influence could be traced back in that case as well.

Besides their influence on design, the research by Sommer and Ross, ARC, and Holahan and Saegert contributed to the development of observational techniques introduced by Ittelson et al. (1970) and, collectively, to a better understanding of the use of social-science research methods in POE research. In a more recent paper, Sommer (1983) described his work with Ross at the Saskatchewan Hospital, along with other research programs that were supported by Humphry Osmond there, including work in organization development, behavior modification, and "disculturation" (the isolation of patients from the larger society). He argued that the results of that work, both its contribution to treatment in that particular hospital and its later impact, gauged by citations in both the practitioner and research literatures, support the effectiveness of the action-research paradigm originally described by Kurt Lewin. Rather than use research as a tool for outsiders to conduct summative evaluations of programs, action research promotes collaboration between researchers and program providers and contributes formative data that can guide program development. Through Sommer's efforts, the Sommer and Ross work thus continues to have an impact on research methods.

It might seem more logical for extensive research on environment–behavior relationships to precede application rather than to follow it. In the case of Robert Sommer's work, however, the latter course seems to have been followed. Sommer and Ross's design of sociopetal space on the women's geriatrics ward at Weyburn was based on what was, at the time, a rather loose formulation by Humphry Osmond. After Sommer left the hospital a few years later to begin a long and distinguished academic career, he embarked on a long series of research studies in the laboratory and in a variety of field settings to investigate the behavioral mechanisms through which sociopetal and sociofugal spaces influence levels of social interaction (e.g., Sommer, 1967, 1969). In that research, Sommer discovered clear preferences for seating positions and interaction distances that mediate the effects of the physical setting and are based in individual characteristics, such as gender, as well as in characteristics of the relationship or transaction among interactants. Sommer's work in this area, which he labeled "small-group ecology," stimulated many further studies by other investigators. Taken together, that work shows how the use of gaze (eye contact), distancing, and other nonverbal behaviors to regulate social interaction is impaired by sociofugal spatial arrangements, and it implies that such impairment will be especially great among those who have more fragile sensory and motor capacities and social skills, such as schizophrenics and the elderly.

In addition to the impetus given specifically to the ARC and Holahan and Saegert projects and to Sommer's later work, it could also be argued that the Sommer and Ross project was a seminal work in the history of both environmental psychology and environmental-design research. It has been identified as such in recent reviews by Sommer (1983) and Moore (1987), and its breadth of exposure in both areas certainly seems to bear out those claims. As such, it is difficult to gauge how great the impact of Osmond's theory and the subsequent applications of it has been on the research and design fields. What we know may be only the proverbial tip of the iceberg.

References

ARC (1975a). *Personal area.* Cleveland, OH: ARC.

ARC (1975b). *Observing and evaluating.* Cleveland, OH: ARC.

ARC (1976, July). Behavioral change on Ward 8. *Journal of Architectural Education,* pp. 26–29.

Campbell, D. T., & Stanley, J. S. (1966). *Experimental and quasi-experimental designs for research.* Chicago: Rand McNally.

Griffin, W. V., Mauritzen, J. H., & Kasmar, J. V. (1969). The psychological aspects of the architectural environment: A review. *American Journal of Psychiatry, 125,* 1057–1062.

Holahan, C. J. (1972). Seating patterns and patient behavior in an experimental dayroom. *Journal of Abnormal Psychology, 80,* 115–124.

Holahan, C. J. (1976). Environmental change in a psychiatric setting: A social systems analysis. *Human Relations, 29,* 153–166.

Holahan, C. J., & Saegert, S. (1973). Behavioral and attitudinal effects of large-scale variation in the physical environment of psychiatric wards. *Journal of Abnormal Psychology, 82,* 454–462.

Holahan, C. J., & Wandersman, A. (1987). The community psychology perspective in environmental psychology. In D. Stokols & I. Altman (Eds.), *Handbook of environmental psychology* (Vol. 1, pp. 827–861). New York: Wiley.

Ittelson, W. H., Rivlin, L. G., & Proshansky, H. M. (1970). The use of behavioral maps in environmental psychology. In H. M. Proshansky, W. H. Ittelson, & L. G. Rivlin (Eds.), *Environmental psychology: Man and his physical setting* (pp. 658–668). New York: Holt, Rinehart & Winston.

Izumi, K. (1957). An analysis for the design of hospital quarters for the neuropsychiatric patient. *Mental Hospitals, 8,* 31–32.

Kleeman, W. B., Jr. (1981). *The challenge of interior design.* New York: Van Nostrand Reinhold.

Lang, J. (1987). *Creating architectural theory.* New York: Van Nostrand Reinhold.

Miller, D. I. (1989). The ecological psychology of the small town. *Psychology, 26*(2–3), 11–14.

Minde, R., Haynes, E., & Rodenburg, M. (1990). The ward milieu and its effect on the behavior of patients. *Canadian Journal of Psychiatry, 35,* 133–138.

Moore, G. T. (1987). Environment and behavior research in North America: History, development, and unresolved issues. In D. Stokols & I. Altman (Eds.), *Handbook of environmental psychology* (Vol. 2, pp. 1359–1410). New York: Wiley.

Osmond, H. (1957, April). Function as the basis of psychiatric ward design. *Mental Hospitals, 8,* 23–29.

152   *Building design*

Osmond, H. (1959). The relationship between architect and psychiatrist. In C. Goshen (Ed.), *Psychiatric architecture* (pp. 16–20). Washington, DC: American Psychiatric Association.

Osmond, H. (1966). Some psychiatric aspects of design. In L. B. Holland (Ed.), *Who designs America?* Garden City, NY: Anchor Books.

Sommer, R. (1967). Small group ecology. *Psychological Bulletin, 67,* 145–152.

Sommer, R. (1969). *Personal space.* Englewood Cliffs, NJ: Prentice-Hall.

Sommer, R. (1974). *Tight spaces: Hard architecture and how to humanize it.* Englewood Cliffs, NJ: Prentice-Hall.

Sommer, R. (1983). Action research is formative: Research at the Saskatchewan Hospital. *Journal of Applied Behavioral Science, 19,* 427–438.

Sommer, R. (1987). Dreams, reality, and the future of environmental psychology. In D. Stokols & I. Altman (Eds.), *Handbook of environmental psychology* (Vol. 2, pp. 1489–1511). New York: Wiley.

Sommer, R., & Osmond, H. (1962). The schizophrenic no-society. *Psychiatry, 25,* 244–255.

Sommer, R., & Osmond, H. (1984). The schizophrenic no-society revisited. *Psychiatry, 47,* 181–191.

Sommer, R., & Ross, H. (1958). Social interaction on a geriatrics ward. *International Journal of Social Psychiatry, 4,* 128–133.

PART III
COMMUNITY PLANNING

What to look for

The following four cases exemplify the application of behavioral theory, data, and research methods to the resolution of a variety of planning issues. Although, again, there is no claim that they are representative of this class of projects, they are diverse cases with regard to the settings in which they were carried out (from New York City to the suburbs of Santiago, Chile), the lessons they teach, and the problems they raise.

Although these cases vary somewhat in scale, each has influenced the lives of large numbers of people, from whole neighborhoods in Berkeley, California, and Macul (Santiago), Chile, where traffic-diversion and community-development efforts were undertaken (chapters 10 and 12, respectively), to the Clason Point Gardens housing project in New York City, where design modifications were made in an effort to reduce crime (chapter 11), and Exxon Minipark (chapter 9), which was modified to increase its attractiveness to midtown Manhattan's office workers, shoppers, and tourists.

The scale on which the influences of almost all of these projects have spread beyond their own boundaries to serve as models for similar planning efforts in other places is even more impressive. The successful redesign of Exxon Minipark (chapter 9) illustrates the application of principles from research and practice by William H. Whyte and his colleagues at Project for Public Spaces, Inc., in New York City, that have shaped other projects they have undertaken across the country, as well as zoning laws in New York City that make very specific and far-ranging demands on the developers of many large building projects in that city. Oscar Newman's work at Clason Point Gardens (chapter 11) with colleagues such as Karen Franck in his Institute for Community Design and Analysis in New York has had a similar, if not even greater, reach. The influence of their projects in a variety of setting types and locations, as well as similar work by other practitioners, along with the pervasive influence of "defensible space" as a concept, theory, and set of design and planning guidelines, has spread to numerous sites and uncountable users across the country.

Donald Appleyard's efforts to protect residential neighborhoods from the harmful effects of heavy traffic (chapter 10) have also been influential, with individual practitioners as well as through published guidelines, although to a somewhat lesser degree than Whyte's work or Newman's work. Only Valadez and Bellalta's attempt to encourage community development by drawing groups of neighbors in Macul into cooperative interaction (chapter 12) seems not to have had an influence much beyond that community, although the underlying research is well known, and other applications may have taken place without ever having been described as related interventions or evaluated as such.

These cases also differ in the degrees to which they rely upon and contribute to theoretical analyses of environment–behavior relationships. Whyte's influence on public-plaza design (chapter 9) and Appleyard's contribution to traffic control on residential streets (chapter 10) were both based on research conducted for the purposes of understanding a particular sample of settings. Neither sought, nor for practical purposes was apparently in any immediate need of, ties to established social-science theory. Perhaps not coincidentally, neither conducted a formal evaluation of any of the specific projects described in chapters 9 and 10.

Valadez and Bellalta's plan for encouraging community development in Macul (chapter 12) was, by contrast, deeply and firmly rooted in an extensive research literature on friendship formation among neighbors, as well as in established views of the value of participation in social change and the value of an experimental approach to social reform. Newman's design-and-planning-based approach to crime prevention (chapter 11) employed dedicated research to describe the features of settings in which the target crimes were more likely to take place, as well as an ambitious effort to build a comprehensive theoretical support structure for that description and for the interventions that were its ultimate goals. Both the Macul and Clason Point Gardens projects included empirical evaluations that documented their efficacy, evaluated the underlying theoretical analyses, and contributed to further theoretical development.

Each of these cases makes its own positive and negative contributions to the continuing evolution of environmental-design research. That will be the subject of further analysis in chapter 16, although one of the most important potential contributions of these cases to that endeavor, the inspiration they provide for those facing similar challenges, is perhaps best discovered in the more detailed descriptions in the four chapters that follow.

9

EXXON MINIPARK REDESIGN

Location: New York, New York
Participants: William H. Whyte and colleagues, Project for Public
          Spaces, Inc. (research, design, and evaluation)

New York City is a place known for its rapid pace and for its architecture. People rush past one another on crowded sidewalks while traffic alternately stalls and races precariously through the streets, all among many of the tallest, most beautiful, and most renowned buildings in the world.

The work of sociologist William H. Whyte and the designers and researchers at Project for Public Spaces, Inc., has been of service to the 7 million New Yorkers, the 632,000 people who commute to work in New York, and the city's 17 million annual visitors by helping them to escape temporarily from the crowded streets, sidewalks, and buildings through their influence on the city's architecture. By studying the city's public spaces – places where people could relax, enjoy the street life, talk, and eat their brown-bag lunches or food purchased from street vendors – Whyte and his colleagues were able to identify the architectural features that made public spaces popular and thus more useful to people. His findings were eventually incorporated into zoning laws that have influenced the forms of many public spaces that have been built by private developers throughout the city during the past decade, in addition to being incorporated into the design and improvement of specific public spaces.

The problem

The story begins in 1961, when a new generation of public spaces was spawned in New York City. A new zoning law was enacted in that year to encourage the developers of new high-rise buildings in midtown Manhattan to provide public spaces as parts of their projects. The existing zoning laws in New York City limited the size, in square feet of floor space, of the building that could be built on any given site in the city, but that limitation could be eased for developers who incorporated public spaces into their projects. A developer would be allowed to add 10 square feet of floor space to a proposed building for every square foot of public space that was provided at street level.

Developers were quick to take advantage of the new law, which was designed to be economically advantageous to them. Some even went to great lengths to build attractive public spaces, applying the same care to their design as they did to the design of the building itself. In time, small public spaces – open plazas, atriums at the ground level of buildings, enlarged lobby areas with exhibition space for sculpture, and passages that provided indoor connections between streets – began to spring up all over middle and lower Manhattan.

The success of the developers' efforts in aesthetic terms could be argued endlessly, and probably will be, but they seemed to Whyte less than successful in providing people in New York City with the refuges envisioned by the framers of the "floor-area-bonus" zoning regulations that were ultimately responsible for their creation. Encouraged by Donald Elliott, chairman of the New York City Planning Commission, Whyte and the members of his Street Life Project sought to determine with greater certainty how successful those spaces were and why. They undertook the job of evaluating the usefulness of public spaces in New York and charting the direction of their future development.

The research

The Street Life Project began to investigate the patterns of use of 18 small urban plazas in New York in 1971. The basic plan of that research was to observe the activities in the plazas and to relate the patterns in those activities – differences in amounts and types of activities among the plazas – to the characteristics of the plazas themselves, such as physical and architectural elements, location, and nearby facilities (Whyte, 1980).

The research made extensive use of time-lapse photography. Motion-picture cameras were mounted at strategic locations overlooking each of the 18 plazas. The cameras were set to take wide-angle pictures of the plazas every 10 seconds. A clock was placed in a corner of the field of view of each camera to provide a record of the time at which each picture was taken.

From the running record of human activities at each of the 18 plazas over time, it was possible to determine such summary facts as how many people used a plaza, what types of people they were, how usage varied with time of day and day of week, how long people stayed, what they did, which areas of a plaza were most popular, and more.

Whyte's interest was drawn to the first and perhaps the most basic of these observations. The greatest variability, he found, was in the degrees to which the plazas were used. For example, in the hour between 12:30 and 1:30 in the afternoon, the peak period of use for every plaza, the average number of users in good weather varied from fewer than 25 to more than 150 across the 18 plazas. Two of the most successful plazas, Paley Plaza and Greenacre Park, are shown in Figures 9.1 and 9.2.

The search for the factors that were associated with, and might explain, this variability in the degrees to which people used the plazas concentrated on the physical features of the plazas themselves. Perhaps the fact that Whyte and the other researchers had spent so much time looking at the plazas, directly or

Figure 9.1. Paley Plaza, one of the modern designs identified by Whyte. Above, the visual access from adjacent East 53rd Street, near Fifth Avenue; below, the amenities inside the plaza. Photos by author.

on film, led them to focus their attention on a plaza's form rather than on the characteristics of the surrounding area, such as the volume of pedestrian and vehicular traffic nearby, the uses of the adjoining building and other buildings in the area, and so on. Whatever the reason, their approach seems to have paid off. They found several strong physical correlates of the plazas' popularity that they used to fashion a general explanation for the success or failure of

Figure 9.2. The smaller, simpler Greenacre Park, Whyte's other model plaza, seen from the sidewalk along East 51st Street, between Second and Third Avenues. Photo by author.

small public urban spaces – an explanation that fit the facts well and that in time proved quite useful in improving the design of such spaces.

Many false leads were encountered in the search. Not the amount of sunlight, nor the aesthetic appearance of the space, nor its shape or size, nor the design of the adjacent buildings made much of a difference in how much a plaza was used. The first physical feature that was found to relate to the rates at which plazas were used seems so obvious with hindsight that one can only wonder why the search had to go on at all: The amount of "sittable space" available in a plaza was strongly correlated with the plaza's rate of use. Benches, wide steps, and low walls or ledges that served as boundaries for a plaza or for walkways in the plaza gave its users places where they could sit, to relax, talk, eat, or people-watch. The more places there were to sit, the more people used a plaza.

The way in which the boundaries of a plaza were designed and built was also an important determinant of its rate of use. Pedestrians were more likely to enter a plaza if they could easily tell from the sidewalk that the space was indeed a public plaza. If people outside the plaza could see the people and their activities inside, they would feel invited in to use the plaza themselves. Plazas that had narrow entrances, that were not readily visible from the street, and that were too far above or below street level were used less.

In addition to seating, several other amenities were associated with a plaza being a busy place. Plazas that provided more sunny places to sit were more popular, especially when the weather was cool. At the same time, protection from wind or drafts down the sides of tall buildings made plazas more comfortable and more popular. Whyte also found that the plazas that were most heavily used often had trees and pools or fountains.

A final, but very important, attraction in the plazas Whyte studied was food. Plazas where street vendors were allowed to sell food were more popular. Whyte attributed this, in part, to the increase in activity that passersby saw and visitors to the plaza found there. Photographs of activities in the plazas showed that people were more likely to begin conversation in the midst of a dense crowd of other plaza users than when off by themselves in a quiet corner of the plaza. People seemed to enjoy using a busy plaza more than an empty one. Plazas that were located in areas of heavy pedestrian flow, such as street corners, were used more, perhaps because busier places are actually more attractive, not just because more potential users are around.

A case study: Greenacre Park

In addition to the comparative study of successful and unsuccessful plazas, Whyte and his colleagues undertook an intensive case study of one of the most successful of that group, shown in Figure 9.2, Greenacre Park (Burden, 1977). Located on 51st Street, just east of Third Avenue in Manhattan, Greenacre Park was built not as part of the floor-area-bonus program but through the generosity of a single wealthy patron, at an initial cost of approximately $1 million. Although less than 1.7 acres in size, Greenacre ranked a strong second among all the plazas in Whyte's sample of 18 in terms of the average number of users during peak hours: at lunchtime in good weather.

The case study of Greenacre Park was based mainly on intensive use of the same observational techniques, including filmed records, that had been used in the comparative study of all 18 plazas. In addition, the researchers made greater use of interviews and on-site observation, and their prolonged stay in the park led to conversations initiated by regular park users, during which additional information was obtained. The analysis was qualitative, documented by quotations from park users, photographs, and verbal summaries of observations made in person and from the filmed records of people and their activities in the park. Its goal was to understand why the park was used as much as it was, how its design features were related to that use, and how future parks could be designed so as to be so successful as Greenacre. Nine features stood out as responsible for the park's popularity and as promising guidelines for the design of future parks.

Location

The neighborhood surrounding Greenacre Park is made up of residential buildings interspersed with stores and restaurants. Not far to the west begins the concentrated office-tower development of mid-Manhattan. Therefore, the park has a very diverse population of potential users. Elderly neighborhood residents use the park before office workers arrive for the day, after they leave, and on weekends. Other neighborhood residents and passersby visit the park throughout its open hours: 8:00 a.m. to about dark. Office workers visit mainly during their lunch hours. The result is a pattern of continuous use, throughout the day and week, as well as a diverse group of users and a wide variety of activities that make the park a lively and interesting place.

Levels

Greenacre is built on three different levels. The largest part is the middle level, which visitors enter directly from the steps leading up from the street. There is also a raised terrace to one side and a sunken level in the rear of the park. This design provides a variety of perspectives and moods and natural culs-de-sac that afford more privacy than the park's small size would otherwise allow. The design enables users to tailor the park to their own reasons for visiting, by choosing one of many locations in the park that provide different combinations of privacy, sunlight, opportunities to watch others, space for larger groupings, and so on.

Access

Although the main level of the park is elevated above the level of the adjoining sidewalk, it is not so far above street level that passersby cannot see into the park easily and be attracted by the amenities and activities within. An important balance has been struck between screening the park from the street and showing passersby the attractive place they might visit.

Waterfall

One of the identifying features of the park is a 25-foot waterfall on its rear boundary. The waterfall provides a visual focal point for visitors and an effective mask of "white noise" for the city noise outside and for conversations that visitors wish to keep private.

Seating

The available seating, a combination of light, movable wire chairs and ledges that serve as benches, provides a number of benefits to park users. The chairs can be rearranged to accommodate single visitors or large groups, to follow the sun over the course of the day, and to suit other needs of visitors. The benches handle the large number of visitors during peak hours without making the park seem any more crowded than it is at other times. In all, there is flexibility in seating both for individual users and for the varying numbers of users over the day and week.

Food

There is a permanent concession booth to one side of the park entrance. It faces into the park and is not visible from the street. Approximately half of the people who enter the park go directly to the booth, and other visitors use it during their stay. It seems clear that eating and drinking are among the most popular activities in the park and that they make relaxation, conversation, people-watching, and other activities more pleasurable.

Shelter

Visitors to the park can find shade from the summer sun under a stand of honey locust trees on the main level, and there is protection from sun and rain under a trellis roof on the raised terrace level of the park. There is also a heating system, although its use is limited by the cost of fuel and by the fact that the park is closed during January, the coldest month. The buildings that surround the park on three sides also shelter visitors from the sights and sounds of the city.

Plantings

Ivy covers several areas of the walls surrounding the plaza. Flowers are displayed in many large masonry planters throughout the plaza and are changed frequently. Many regular visitors mention the floral displays as a major attraction and source of pleasure in the park.

Management

Both regular and infrequent visitors perceive Greenacre Park to be a friendly, comfortable place. This is due in part to the staff, who keep the park clean, tend the plantings, and run the concession stand. Two guards are on duty at all times, and they are known to regular users for their friendly and helpful manner. Park regulars help to control the infrequent misbehavior that occurs. The cost of maintaining the park has been estimated at $100,000 per year and is paid out of an endowment left by the original benefactor.

The findings of the Greenacre Park study both support and supplement the findings of the more conventional comparative study. In the latter, seating, plantings, food, and access emerged as features that differentiated between successful and unsuccessful plazas. Those features were all found to be important to the success of Greenacre Park. In the case of Greenacre, however, several other features came into focus: the character of the surrounding neighborhood, the variety of levels and associated atmospheres, the striking waterfall, and conscientious and supportive management policies. These characteristics of Greenacre are difficult to quantify, but they do add significantly to the information available to designers of future urban plazas.

Design recommendations

The presentations of Whyte's research findings were always more descriptive than analytical. He arranged his sample of 18 plazas in order of use, listed their physical characteristics, and pointed to patterns of association between use and physical form. The patterns that emerged in the data were not tested statistically to verify their magnitude or reliability. Similarly, the conclusions drawn about Greenacre Park were impressionistic rather than statistical. However, the descriptions Whyte was able to produce from long-term photographic records of plaza use and detailed measurements of the physical features of the plazas themselves were so precise that they could be translated quite straightforwardly into specific recommendations for the design of new plazas in the city. His treatment of the seating accommodations in plazas, the strongest single correlate of plaza use, is a good case in point.

Whyte found that no step or ledge or wall, or any other structure in a plaza, was used regularly as a seat if its surface was less than one foot or more than three feet off the ground. He also found that no ledge or wall or bench served regularly as a double-sided seating accommodation – people sitting back-to-back, facing in opposite directions – unless it was at least 30 inches wide. Both of these findings provide clear suggestions for design standards for those who wish to utilize steps, walls, and ledges as that most important resource in public spaces – sittable space.

Whyte also discovered some useful facts about the optimal density of seating in public plazas. The amount of sitting space, whether intended for that purpose or not, in the most heavily used plazas in his sample varied between 6% and 10% of the total open space in the plaza, and there was a common ratio, for the most popular plazas, between the amount of seating accommodations, measured in linear feet, and the area of the entire site, including the adjoining building. Popular plazas provided approximately one linear foot of seating for every 30 square feet of area. These precise descriptions also provide a clear basis for recommendations about the design of new plazas.

Whyte also described precisely the features of successful plazas that provided a clear and easy transition for those entering from the adjoining street. Heavily used plazas were no more than three feet above or below the level of the adjoining street, and each made up the difference with steps leading up or down into the plaza that provided a gentle pitch, with treads at least 11 inches wide and risers no more than 7.5 inches high.

Coupled with qualitative recommendations about sunlight, trees, food sales, and water pools or fountains, among others, these quantitative descriptions made Whyte's *The Social Life of Small Urban Spaces* (1980) a useful manual for designers of public urban spaces. But Whyte's research was also useful in more direct ways than that.

The 1975 zoning amendments

Approximately five years before publication of *The Social Life of Small Urban Spaces,* on May 21, 1975, the New York City Board of Estimate enacted a series of amendments to the 1961 floor-area-bonus regulations. The 1961 law had required only that the space provided be accessible to the public at all times in order to qualify for the 10-for-1 building-size waiver. According to Whyte, "that, as it turned out, was about all they were" (1980, p. 112). The 1975 amendments, based directly on Whyte's research findings, required that new plazas, if they were to qualify for the bonus, "be *amenable* to the public as well, and laid down specific guidelines for insuring that they would be" (Whyte, 1980, p. 112). Some of those guidelines are presented next, in outline form, to illustrate both their link to Whyte's research and their specificity:

1. Seating
   (a) Amount: 1 linear foot per 30 square feet of plaza area (less if the street is not level or the plaza joins two streets)
   (b) Depth: minimum of 16 inches (14 with seat back); counts double if 30 or more inches deep, providing there is access to both sides
   (c) Height: minimum of 12 inches and maximum of 36 inches above level of adjacent surface
   (d) Chairs: count for 30 linear inches of seating each

2. Trees
   (a) Number: for area of 1,500 square feet or more, minimum of 4; for 5,000 square feet or more, 6; for 12,000 square feet or more, 1 per 2,000 square feet
   (b) Size: minimum 3.5 inches in diameter

3. Access and visibility

(a) Times: open to use by the public at all times

(b) Boundaries: direct access along at least 50% of street; frontage elevation no more than 3 feet above or below street level; walls no higher than 36 inches or 5 feet above curb level of adjoining street

4. Amenities

(a) Food: kiosks and cafés permitted, but limited to 150 square feet and 20% of open space in size, respectively

(b) Retail shops: at least 50% of total frontage of building walls fronting on plaza, exclusive of entrances, lobbies, etc.

(c) Lighting: minimum of 2 horizontal foot-candles, throughout hours of darkness

Other sections of the amendments dealt with access for the physically disabled, as well as maintenance and replacement of trees and chairs when necessary. Almost all of the amendments followed directly from Whyte's research findings, even to the point of incorporating the precise measurements he made of existing plazas that had been found to serve the public well. Although some real-estate developers tried to persuade the Board of Estimate not to constrain the designs of floor-area-bonus plazas in ways that would make them more costly, the board was persuaded by the documentation that Whyte's research provided. They were able to see that the existing plazas often were of little use to the public and that the means for remedying that situation were clear and at hand. Although some compromises were made to enlist the support of board members who were sympathetic to the developers' arguments, a comparison between Whyte's findings and the amendments that were finally passed by the board suggests that the Street Life Project carried the day.

A specific design application: Exxon Minipark

Several years after Whyte's initial study of the use of public plazas in New York City, the design consulting firm he founded, Project for Public Spaces, Inc. (PPS), was engaged by the Exxon Corporation to study the plaza at its corporate headquarters in Rockefeller Center in mid-Manhattan and recommend design changes. Exxon Minipark had been one of the plazas included in Whyte's original sample of 18, and from the results of that earlier study it seemed moderately successful. Despite its relatively small size and limited seating, it was at about the median for the 18 in rate of use. However, there were problems at Exxon Minipark that did not show up in those summary statistics. A good deal of its use was by people who bought and sold marijuana and hung around to smoke it and listen to loud stereo "boxes." Workers in the Exxon Building and other office buildings in the area found it an uncomfortable, even forbidding place for that reason. Exxon was understandably dissatisfied and turned to PPS for help.

Armed with the methods and knowledge developed during the earlier plaza studies, PPS took a closer look at Exxon Minipark. The researchers used direct observation, time-lapse and documentary film records, and information from conversations initiated by regular users of the park, including the drug dealers, who were understandably sensitive about the researchers' presence in the park. They also conducted interviews with park users, with users of other parks in the area who could have gone to Exxon, and with potential users in the Exxon Building and at Manhattan Community College across the street.

Exxon Minipark was identified by many of its users and potential users with the drug dealing and the associated hangers-on who frequented the place. Although the park appeared drab and uninviting to the designers and researchers at PPS, few people in the immediate area of the park seemed to respond strongly to its appearance. In fact, some reported that they were attracted to the park because it was quieter and less crowded than some of the others in the area. Some even said that they liked the atmosphere in Exxon. But many avoided going there because of its reputation for harboring an "undesirable element."

Based on their understanding of environment–behavior relationships in such public spaces, the PPS researchers identified a number of physical features of the park that they believed to be indirectly responsible for its negative image and lack of success in promoting the kind of use for which it had been built. They came to the conclusion that the park's design first had failed to attract the passersby and office workers for whom it had been intended, which then led to its being taken over by the drug trade, for whom it turned out to be much better suited.

Exxon Minipark is one of several plazas that connect adjacent streets in the Rockefeller Center area of mid-Manhattan. Each one is associated with a large corporate headquarters building and connects two adjacent streets, between Sixth and Seventh Avenues. Together, they provide a pedestrian walkway, although not a perfectly straight one, that parallels the avenues for four blocks. Consistent with this shortcut function, one side of the Exxon plaza consisted of a broad walkway. Along one edge of the walkway was a long row of benches in front of a high boundary wall. At one end of the walkway, on the opposite side from the benches, was a seasonal café with some associated tables. At the other end, the plaza broadened out to a rectangular area with a fountain at the far end, bordered by more immovable benches.

The walkway area was a poor place for recreational use from the start. The end-to-end arrangement of the benches, facing the busy walkway, was ill-suited to conversation or privacy. The heavy flow of pedestrians using the park as a shortcut during the peak early morning, lunchtime, and end-of-workday hours made sitting there uncomfortable. It was a difficult place to eat, even without the congestion, balancing food on one's knees or twisting sideways to use the bench surface. The benches around the fountain were only slightly less uncomfortable, being somewhat removed from the congestion along the walkway. The café never became very popular, trying to cater to well-to-do young executives (a clientele very different from the majority of the park's users), having little space, and eventually keeping irregular hours because of its limited success.

When the park proved to be less popular than some of the others around it, it became a more congenial place for people to buy and sell and smoke marijuana and to listen to loud music, and its design encouraged that alternate use. The congested walkway and the benches along it were well suited to the casual contacts, solitary pot smoking, and music boxes of its regular users. Later, the Exxon management felt it necessary to build gates at the ends of the walkway to make it possible to close the park after dark to prevent those undesirable users from creating a more dangerous situation late at night. The new gates proved to be convenient places for the drug dealers to service customers passing by on 49th and 50th streets outside the park and became their informal "offices."

The problems that plagued the park discouraged its corporate sponsor from doing much to maintain or beautify it, or to program exhibits, musical performances, or other forms of entertainment that were so popular at some of its neighbor plazas. Thus, the park's uninspired design was compounded both by the undesirable pattern of use and by the neglect to which that led. The PPS researchers and designers suggested a number of design and management changes that they believed could change the pattern of use and eventually displace the drug trade in the process, a problem the police found too trivial to deserve their attention (PPS, 1978).

Among the redesign recommendations (Figure 9.3) were more-inviting entrances, with better transitions to the surrounding streets. Upgrading the landscaping and plantings would improve the appearance and increase the comfort of the park. Users' comfort would be increased by replacing many of the benches with movable seating and by building seating walls around the different areas that were to be created. Tables were to be introduced, and shelters, including trees, were to extend the use of the plaza to times of uncomfortably hot or wet weather. New users were to be attracted by the creation of two new cafés, one to provide take-out food that could be carried throughout the park. The existing café was to be redesigned in a more permanent form, and its services, both hours and menu, were to be improved. Finally, the park's maintenance and management were to receive greater attention, including security personnel, gardening, and the programming of exhibits and performances coordinated with the Exxon Corporation and the neighboring community college.

If the park's new look and the new users who were expected to be attracted

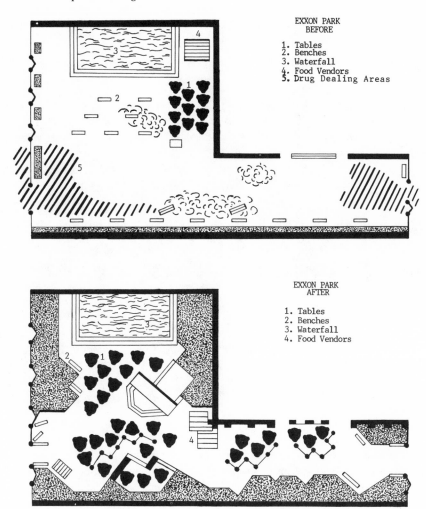

Figure 9.3. Diagram of the Exxon Plaza, before and after its redesign by PPS. Drawing by Lisa Hanks (after Levine, 1984, p. 61).

by it were not enough to encourage the drug dealers to leave, the park was also to be closed for several months while the alterations were being made, followed by a grand reopening, including a special program of activities. On the basis of their own comments, it seemed likely that during that period the dealers would find a more suitable place to conduct their activities. Then the new park would have a truly fresh start.

The PPS recommendations were passed along by the Exxon Corporation to an architectural firm engaged to plan and oversee construction of a new

Figure 9.4. Three views of Exxon Minipark in use, after the new design was implemented. Photos by author.

version of Exxon Minipark. To a large extent, estimated at 80–90% by a PPS staff member involved in the project (personal communication, 1985), those recommendations formed the basis for the architects' design and the eventual form of the rebuilt plaza.

The new plaza was built to create a variety of experiences, each section bordered by low walls suitable for use as seating during peak periods. Trees, shrubs, and flowers were planted to beautify the park and increase opportunities for privacy and shelter. Movable seating was introduced to replace many of the old benches, allowing park users more freedom to follow the sun, form groups, or choose their views. Tables were provided for eating and other activities, and new food concessions were established in permanent kiosks. Space was set aside for exhibits, and a stage was built for entertainment, with ongoing programs being developed to make use of it.

After the park was reopened, PPS conducted a POE study to determine the effects of the design changes that had been made. Overall use of the park was found to have increased threefold during peak periods, despite the elimination of drug-dealing activities. Women and older people, in particular, were found to use the park more than they had before. In all, a broader spectrum of users and activities made the park a livelier and better-used place than it had been (Figure 9.4).

Evaluation

Stage 1: Background analysis

This is a case whose development was influenced to an important degree by the time and place at which it occurred. The zoning regulations enacted in New York City in 1961 established as an important public-policy goal the creation of accessible public spaces. In return for providing spaces near their buildings where neighbors, workers, shoppers, tourists, and others could find refuge from the crowded, noisy city, real-estate developers received concessions worth millions of dollars. Because of the history of this floor-area-bonus program, public use of these urban plazas was the principal focus of those concerned and ultimately of Whyte's work at PPS. Whyte's longtime involvement in local issues of public use of open spaces in New York City helped to shape his response to the specific request by the chairman of the Planning Commission, Donald Elliott.

The local history of Exxon Minipark itself also played a role in the development of plans for its redesign. The fact that some of the original design elements that seemed to have contributed to the park's disappointing level of popularity also seemed to have attracted a core group of drug dealers and users as its principal clientele played a part in setting the agenda for the redesign project.

Stage 2: Behavioral goals

In developing their recommendations for the redesign of Exxon Minipark, Whyte and his colleagues were guided mainly by the goal of maximizing the use of that space by the large population of potential users, mainly for the reasons discussed earlier. Increasing the number of users, then, was the principal goal set for the redesign, and one can hardly imagine a clearer goal. Even the subsidiary goal of ridding the park of drug dealers and their customers (or at least of their obtrusive presence) was linked directly to attracting larger numbers of users. If more of the neighbors (office workers, for the most part) and passersby (shoppers and tourists) began to use the park, their presence presumably would discourage those who preferred to avoid notice of their activities and had been attracted to the park in the first place by its low level of use.

Stage 3: Environment–behavior relationships

The extensive and very detailed knowledge that Whyte and his PPS colleagues had acquired concerning the patterns of use of Manhattan's urban plazas and their environmental correlates came from a comparative study of 18 such spaces. The design employed in that research, a correlational study, falls fairly low on the methodologist's scale of establishing unambiguous causal relationships. Even though a large number of possible influences on usage rates were investigated directly, it is clear from the researchers' own analysis that other factors – such as the character of the surrounding neighborhood or district, the design of adjacent buildings, the nature of the user populations, and the differences in activities associated with them – that were identified as potential influences on levels of use were not addressed explicitly, either by assessment or exclusion.

Nonetheless, the reader finds little to question in the conclusions drawn from that research. Although it does not fall neatly under any of the established criteria for evaluating the validity of research findings, it seems clear that Whyte's understanding of the underlying issues involved shaped not only the research but also the interpretation of the results in a way that makes his conclusions utterly convincing. The case study of Greenacre Park, quite informal by modern social-science standards, illustrates that point as much as it adds independent support for the findings of the empirical comparative study (whose analysis makes little use of the data in any formal statistical sense). In sum, the conclusions drawn regarding the influences of the landscape and architectural characteristics of plaza design, such as seating, visibility from the street, and shelter from the weather, as well as management policies such as provision of food, entertainment, and permanent on-site staff, seem eminently reasonable, if not definitive, despite the absence of statistical controls for sampling error or methodological safeguards against alternative explanations for variations in usage rates among the 18 plazas studied. It would seem that the former (a standard statistical analysis of quantitative summaries of usage rates and physical characteristics) would have been relatively easy to arrange, whereas a strong quasi-experimental design addressed to the latter probably was not feasible under the circumstances.

On a more clearly positive note, the study was performed in the natural context of a large sample of existing plazas in everyday use, using observations of large numbers of users over significant periods of time in a mostly unobtrusive manner. That would seem to guarantee that the findings could be generalized safely to the target population of public plazas in New York City and perhaps beyond. Although the Greenacre Park case study used methods that were even less well controlled and more reactive (on-site observers and interviewers), it was used to corroborate, not to establish relationships between design and use.

Stage 4: Specific design plan elements

Several of the design and management elements that were found to character-ize successful plazas in the PPS study and were incorporated into the 1975 zoning-law amendments were later fed directly into the recommendations made for the Exxon Minipark redesign. They included movable seating, new trees and other plantings, permanent food kiosks, a stage where entertainment could be presented, and a managerial staff to oversee maintenance and moni-tor the needs and conduct of park users. The scheduling of the renovations was used to help accomplish the secondary purpose of discouraging drug dealers and users from continued use of the park. The decision to close the park completely for three months while renovations were made, rather than working around ongoing use of the park, was made with that goal in mind.

Stage 5: Overall design

The architects who created the final new design for Exxon Minipark chose the materials that would implement the recommendations made by PPS. Al-though they contributed a great deal to the look of the final product, the functional elements and arrangement of the space were determined almost exclusively by PPS. The renovation was motivated by an interest in achieving the specific goals for which PPS's earlier research had established specific facilitative design elements.

Stage 6: POE

Based on the evaluation they conducted, using the same data-collection methods as in their earlier research. PPS concluded that the new design for Exxon Minipark had succeeded unequivocally in increasing the use of the park and in replacing the previously thriving drug-related pursuits with more socially acceptable activities. In fact, it seems that the park became the type of beautiful, active, functional public space exemplified by Greenacre Park and Paley Plaza among the 18 pre-1975 plazas included in the original PPS study. Unfortunately, the POE study of the new Exxon Minipark provided little in the way of detail, statistical analysis, or internal-validity safeguards to support its conclusions. Its credibility rests on the underlying rationale, the past re-search from which it followed so directly and so logically, and the proven data-gathering methods with which it was conducted.

Stage 7: Future impact

Whyte's work has had great impact on the design of public plazas such as Exxon Minipark. Of course, the transformation of Exxon Minipark into a much more attractive and more intensively and broadly utilized public space in a very busy area of midtown Manhattan is an accomplishment that will in itself have a lasting impact on many people who live, work, and visit in New York City. Information about this successful application of the results of Whyte's research into the factors that influence the use of such spaces, as in an exhibit of EDR "success stories" organized by Wener (undated) and an article based on it (Wener, 1988), undoubtedly will influence the design and management of similar spaces elsewhere. It may also influence environmental-design research in a more general way by providing an example of a potentially powerful approach to that enterprise. Whyte began by comparing 18 public plazas that were already in operation in New York City. That research amounted to a POE study, on a grand and powerful quasi-experimental scale, that documented wide variations in their success and identified specific design elements that appeared to explain a significant portion of those variations. The results of that study were then used as a basis for recommendations about the redesign of Exxon Minipark. Finally, an evaluation of that project validated both the specific design solution implemented there and, indirectly, the conclusions drawn from the original comparative study. Such a powerful iterative or cumulative approach to design, using POE results from previous designs as guides for subsequent ones, deserves to be publicized as widely as possible in the hope of encouraging its increased use.

Whyte's original study has also been used to establish general guidelines for the design of urban plazas. In the books *The Social Life of Small Urban Spaces* (1980) and *Managing Downtown Public Spaces* (PPS, 1984) Whyte has made available systematic, detailed, and seemingly feasible recommendations based on his research. As a measure of its popularity and possible influence, *The Social Life of Small Urban Spaces* is still in print at this writing, 11 years after its initial publication. Whyte has also publicized his views regularly in the popular press (e.g., Whyte, 1972), as have others (e.g., Levine, 1984).

But perhaps the greatest impact of Whyte's work on plaza design has come as a result of the 1975 amendments to the 1961 New York City zoning law that first established a floor-area bonus for developers who provide public space. In the years since Whyte's detailed recommendations were enacted almost directly into law, many plazas of inestimable value (during a boom period of construction in the stratospheric real-estate market of midtown Manhattan) built under the floor-area-bonus program have been shaped by those regulations. Even the designs for plazas outside that bonus program (including Exxon Minipark) have been influenced by those guidelines. And by all odds those plazas are more beautiful, more hospitable and enjoyable, and more widely used spaces today than they otherwise would have been.

There seems little doubt that the success of Whyte's work in influencing plaza design stemmed largely from the manner in which he and his colleagues framed the issues. From the outset, Whyte emphasized the frequency of plaza use as a design criterion. The clarity and impact of that image of the design problem were reflected in accounts in the local press at the time the zoning amendments based on Whyte's work were considered and passed by the New York City Board of Estimate. The term "liveliness" was used again and again in press reports to summarize the goal of public-plaza design sought by Whyte and other supporters of the amendments (e.g., Fowler, 1975).

Whyte's presentation of the design features relevant to the frequency of plaza use was equally clear and captivating. The findings of the original comparative study could be summarized in three words: sittability, transition, and food. Even when, later on, many more details were added from the case study of Greenacre Park, they were not presented in the form of a long list of abstract causal relationships. Rather, Greenacre itself was presented as a concrete, coherent model whose essential features – multiple levels, attractive plantings, shelter, and a focal point of moving water – could simply be copied to assure the success of new plaza designs.

This easily understood presentation of the two elements of the programming problem – behavioral objectives and design solution – probably is attributable to the same approach to studying public plazas that seems so problematic on methodological grounds. The simplified and atheoretical approach that Whyte took in trying to understand how public plazas worked (perhaps reflective of his background as a writer rather than an academic) seems to have made a great deal more sense as a foundation for utilizing the newfound knowledge in the political and design arenas than as a model for theory builders or critics of research methods. Those two considerations – application and science – seem likely to conflict often in the process of developing environment–behavior knowledge and using it in specific design projects. It is surely possible to strike a better balance between the two than was achieved in Whyte's work, paying greater attention to scientific method and theory, but a more impressive final outcome would be an ambitious goal indeed.

Finally, an evaluation of the overall success of the application of Whyte's work is still awaited. The POE study of the Exxon Minipark project stands alone. Projects completed under the 1975 specifications for the floor-area-bonus program have not been evaluated formally, much less "meta-analyzed" in the aggregate. Formal evaluation probably should have been included as one of those specifications, but it was not. Only in that way can we be certain that the promise many have foreseen in Whyte's work, according to an editorial writer for *The New York Times* (Anonymous, 1975), "the promise of plazas filled with services and pleasures instead of sterile concrete," has been fulfilled.

174   *Community planning*

References

Anonymous (1975). Planning by compromise (editorial). *The New York Times*, May 31, p. 26.

Burden, A. (1977). *Greenacre Park: A study by Project for Public Spaces, Inc.* New York: Project for Public Spaces, Inc.

Fowler, G. (1975). Zoning law seeks live open spaces. *The New York Times*, May 22, p. 45.

Levine, C. (1984). Making city spaces lovable places. *Psychology Today, 18*(6), 56–63.

Project for Public Spaces, Inc. (1978). *Exxon Minipark: A redesign and management proposal.* New York: author.

Project for Public Spaces, Inc. (1984). *Managing downtown public spaces.* Chicago: Planners Press.

Wener, R. (1988). Doing it right: Examples of successful application of environment–behavior research. *Journal of Architectural and Planning Research, 5*, 284–303.

Wener, R. (undated). *Environment–behavior research "success stories."* New York: Polytechnic Institute.

Whyte, W. H. (1972). Please, just a nice place to sit. *The New York Times Magazine*, December 3, pp. 20, 22, 30, 32.

Whyte, W. H. (1980). *The social life of small urban spaces.* Washington, DC: The Conservation Foundation.

10
LIVABLE STREETS

Location: Berkeley, California
Participant: Donald Appleyard (research and design)

Vehicular traffic is becoming an ever more intrusive fact of modern urban life. In the United States, at least, it is difficult to think of any major urban area that has no serious traffic problems. No urban area has a system of mass transit that is efficient enough or attractive enough to discourage significant numbers of citizens from using their own automobiles to commute from outlying areas to work or shop or entertain themselves in the central city. Traffic from one city location to another and delivery-truck traffic are added to the commuter traffic to compound the problem.

For many public officials, and for many citizens, the problem is one of moving the resulting volume of traffic quickly and safely through city streets. Planners use a variety of mechanisms to help ease the burden. Traffic covering relatively long distances can be speeded up by establishing patterns of one-way streets, widening thoroughfares, raising speed limits, and coordinating traffic signals. Cars can be banned from parking along these high-volume, high-speed streets during peak traffic hours, and impediments like double-parking and jaywalking can be reduced by stricter police enforcement. Donald Appleyard (1981), inspired by many earlier researchers and planners, recognized that heavy traffic poses a nuisance and a hazard for people other than the drivers who create it. He became convinced that those who live along streets that carry heavy traffic volumes are placed at considerable risk. In fact, Appleyard believed that some of the planners' traditional solutions to the problem of moving traffic through the city might exacerbate the problems of those whose homes are located on the streets that carry the traffic. He saw that increasing the volume and speed of traffic on residential streets increased the burden on those who lived there.

The problems that concerned Appleyard were documented in research carried out in San Francisco by him and his colleagues. Like so much of the research conducted by those concerned with the impact of the environment on people's lives, this work is rich with observations that go beyond mere numerical description of environmental conditions and behaviors. In fact, it is a good example of the way in which such data, and the correspondingly rich understanding of the impact of specific environmental settings that they provide, facilitate applications of research findings to solutions of practical environmental problems. For reasons that will be developed throughout this chapter, Appleyard has not been able to turn his findings directly into concrete proposals for alterations in the street plans of any specific city. However, he has shown clearly how his ideas and those of others can be applied in solving problems caused by traffic, and he has described and evaluated numerous instances in which they have been. He has also analyzed the process by which such ideas are tested in the political arena, in a way that promises to facilitate the implementation of theory and research about environment–behavior relationships in the future.

The pilot study

The impact of traffic on the lives of San Francisco residents began to be uncovered in an intensive survey of the residents of three of the city's streets, carried out in 1969. The three streets were selected because they were similar in appearance but carried three different levels of traffic volume. The "light" street carried an average of 2,000 vehicles per day, the "medium" street 8,700, and the "heavy" street 15,750 (Figure 10.1).

Representatives of about 30% of the households on each street block were interviewed for approximately one hour. In addition, observations were made of pedestrian activity and traffic activity. Many differences emerged concerning the living environments, attitudes, and behaviors of the residents of the three streets.

First, there was evidence that the residents were well aware of the extent to which street traffic intruded into their lives. Residents of the heavy street were most likely, and residents of the light street least likely, to identify traffic as a hazard in their lives and to be aware of the noise, fumes, and dirt produced by it. Instruments documented the higher noise level on the heavy street, and observations there revealed more windows closed on the street sides of buildings and pedestrians having greater difficulty in crossing the street.

Second, there were different patterns of social interaction on the three streets. Residents of the light street reported having three times as many friends and twice as many acquaintances in their neighborhoods as did residents of the heavy street. Residents of the light street, especially children and the elderly, also reported making greater use of the street as a place for activities than did their counterparts on the heavy street.

Third, there were differences in the images residents held of their streets. The light street was seen more often as an extension of the residents' homes, and residents of the light street had more complex images of the street, which included individual houses and other details. Residents of the heavy street more often felt that their homes were contained entirely within the walls of their dwellings, and their image of the street was of a steady stream of traffic bounded by undifferentiated walls of buildings. In addition, residents of the light street felt that they had more privacy and took more pride in their street.

Finally, there were differences in the populations residing on the three

Figure 10.1. Depiction of light, medium, and heavy streets (top to bottom) compared in the San Francisco pilot study. Source: Appleyard (1981, p. 19); reproduced with permission of the University of California Press.

streets that may have resulted from the differences in traffic volume and their various impacts. Residents of the light street had lived there longer, had more children, were more likely to own their homes, and paid less for shelter than did residents of the heavy street.

The findings suggested that traffic might play a large and important role in the lives of San Francisco residents, because 60% of San Francisco's heavily traveled arterial streets are lined with residences. Heavy traffic may cause distress, disrupt social interaction and recreation, restrict mobility, degrade the quality of the home as a refuge from the outside world, and influence people's choices of places of residence. And to the extent that other cities are similar to San Francisco in their residents' exposure to traffic and in their responses to it, these impacts may be widespread.

However, Appleyard felt that the study was too limited to permit such definite conclusions, even about San Francisco. Not only was the pilot study limited to just three streets, but also there were differences among the residents in regard to number of children and length of residence (is that why residents of the light street had more friends nearby?), income and extent of homeownership (is that why residents of the light street took more pride in their homes?), and level of traffic to which they were exposed. Therefore, although San Francisco city officials used the findings in planning a program of traffic control, Appleyard used them to design a much more careful, more detailed, and more extensive follow-up study.

The plan for the follow-up study

The follow-up study of traffic impact on San Francisco streets was expanded to 21 streets in four categories (Figure 10.2). Six *light streets* had traffic volumes per day that ranged from 210 to 1,894, with five under 700. Traffic on most of the light streets traveled in two lanes, one in each direction, at 20–25 miles per hour. These streets ranged in width from 24 to 38 feet, with five of them being 28 feet wide or less. On average, there were 3.1 pedestrian accidents per 1,000 feet of street per year on light streets.

Five *medium streets* carried from 5,475 to 9,923 vehicles per day. Traffic moved in two or four lanes, in two directions, at about 30 miles per hour. These streets ranged from 38 to 62 feet in width. Medium streets saw an average of 13.0 pedestrian accidents per 1,000 feet per year.

Seven *heavy streets* were selected. Traffic volume on these streets varied from 12,771 to 18,683 vehicles per day. Traffic speed was generally 30–35 miles per hour. Most of these streets had four lanes, and their widths varied from 24 to 48 feet. Heavy streets were narrower than medium streets, and yet they carried more traffic because many were one-way, speed limits were generally higher, and some had synchronized traffic signals. Pedestrian accidents averaged 13.8 per 1,000 feet per year on heavy streets.

Three *very heavy streets* carried 23,974 to 52,275 vehicles per day, at 35–40 miles per hour. The lightest of the very heavy streets was four lanes and 36 feet wide. The other two were six lanes wide. The heaviest was 96 feet wide, including a divider, and would be referred to technically as an expressway at grade (street level), although it was lined with single-family homes. On the very heavy streets, there were 24.1 pedestrian accidents per 1,000 feet per year, on average.

Figure 10.2. Light, medium, heavy, and very heavy (top to bottom) streets, San Francisco, from the follow-up study. Source: Appleyard (1981, pp. 42–43); reproduced with permission of the University of California Press.

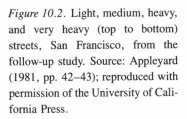

Most of these 21 streets were selected in groups of two or three parallel streets that differed widely in traffic volume. The streets within these groups shared the same neighborhood or district conditions and often were similar in regard to the architectural style of their buildings. They varied in the levels of traffic they carried because of a variety of factors. Some had been selected because they had been part of a plan to concentrate traffic on certain streets.

They had been widened or made one-way, or their speed limits had been raised, or the traffic signals synchronized, or some combination of these measures had been taken to move traffic more smoothly. In other cases, increased volumes of traffic had resulted because of the streets' connections with freeways, or their roles as part of a state highway through the city, or their locations near a large university or hospital, or some similar reason.

Appleyard's scheme for selecting streets for the study was intended to make the four groups, from light to very heavy, as similar as possible in all respects except traffic volume. This attempt to match the four groups of streets had only limited success, for very good reasons, as we will see shortly. In any case, differences among the groups of streets in regard to resident characteristics and other features will be considered later, along with the impact of traffic volume.

As in the pilot study, most of the information collected in the expanded follow-up came from intensive interviews with samples of residents from the streets being studied. Most of the results reported were based on respondents' answers to multiple-choice questions about the frequency and importance of various events in their lives. This picture was embellished lavishly with quotations from residents' free descriptions of their streets and their lives, as well as with sketches they drew and annotated. Observations made on the streets directly by the investigators completed the picture.

Living on the streets of San Francisco

The mass of data collected from interviews, sketches, and observations was organized into categories based on a model developed from the findings of the pilot study. We will be concentrating on the interviews, which were organized around that category system. Before we get to the results, let us take a look at the principal categories we will be considering and describe their contents briefly. These, then, are the five principal ways in which the impact of traffic volume was assessed in the interviews (other data were used primarily to corroborate and enlarge upon the interview results):

1. Street images: Respondents were asked to mention the first four or five things that came to mind when they thought of their streets.
2. Annoyances: On a list provided by the interviewer, respondents were asked to check off conditions that were annoying to them.
3. Street activities: Respondents were given a list of activities that might take place on their streets. They were asked to indicate how often each activity occurred: "frequently," "occasionally," or "never."
4. Traffic interference: The interviewer presented a list of seven activities that commonly take place inside and outside the home. Respondents were asked

whether street traffic bothered them "often" or "sometimes" during each of these activities.

5. Adaptations to traffic and/or noise: The interviewer presented a list of behaviors in which one might engage for the purpose of coping with the problems caused by traffic. Respondents were asked to check off those adaptive behaviors in which they had engaged.

The results of that study are quite voluminous. I have taken the liberty of summarizing some of the most consistent findings in Table 10.1. On the one hand, this is a small fraction of what Appleyard found; on the other, not all of what he found showed such consistent and reasonable differences among the four street types. We will be guided by this table in our examination of Appleyard's findings, but not bound by it.

Street images

Although a street's general appearance or level of attractiveness was the feature most likely to be mentioned spontaneously by its residents, excessive traffic ran a close second. And, as seems reasonable, the percentage of respondents who mentioned excessive traffic as a feature of their streets rose steadily and precipitously from light to medium to heavy and very heavy streets. Problems associated with traffic were also mentioned prominently. These by-products included dirt, noise, pollution, danger, and driving and parking problems. In most cases, these, too, were mentioned more often by residents of more heavily traveled streets. It probably would be an exaggeration to say that San Franciscans are preoccupied with traffic, even those who live on heavy streets. But the traffic passing by their homes and the problems it creates certainly form a major part of the images they hold of their streets, even for those who live on light streets. In fact, in some ways residents of light streets saw more danger in traffic than did residents of heavier streets. The occasional unexpected speeding car or motorcycle using a light street as a shortcut to avoid heavy traffic on neighboring streets, or as a rare opportunity to indulge a penchant for fast driving in an otherwise congested city, combined with children's use of the quiet street as a play area, created a very dangerous and frightening situation for many residents of light streets.

In addition, traffic seems to have quite a broad influence on residents' images of their streets, extending beyond noise, pollution, and the danger of accidents to perceptions of the general appearance of the street, including maintenance and decorations such as flowers, and even the friendliness of neighbors.

Not only is traffic an inescapable fact of life in a prosaic sense, it seems, but it clearly enters the consciousness of San Francisco residents to a significant

Table 10.1. *Impacts of traffic volume on street residents*

Variables	Responses by street type (%)			
	Light	Medium	Heavy	Very heavy
Street images				
Excessive traffic	13	31	51	52
People friendly	43	44	32	21
Quiet, not busy	39	18	17	6
Noisy	10	13	23	21
Traffic noise, pollution	7	7	13	19
Traffic danger	3	7	18	16
Annoyances				
Danger for children	54	77	80	77
Traffic noise, vibration	42	66	66	74
Air pollution	32	58	65	66
Trucks	30	56	56	76
Danger of being hit	22	42	44	51
Waiting too long	8	26	37	47
Street activities ("never" occur)				
People talking	11	8	7	22
Gardening	17	30	25	63
Car washing	12	11	16	25
Playing with toys	35	39	34	61
Sitting outside	39	38	39	61
Ball games, Frisbee, etc.	45	69	71	78

Traffic interference ("often" and "sometimes")

TV watching	18	44	40	60
Sleeping	25	45	42	41
Talking in house	16	36	36	44
Working in house	10	21	25	29
Eating	10	16	25	26
Children playing outside	34	35	51	58
Adaptations to traffic and/or noise				
Keep windows shut	17	42	49	59
Live more in back of house	13	36	39	29
Forbid children to play on street	16	14	28	34
Tell children not to cross certain streets	17	10	28	34
Go out on street less often	5	17	26	26
Accompany children to school	8	5	14	13

Source: Adapted from Appleyard (1981), Tables A3, A5, A9, A12, and A13.

degree. The sketches drawn by residents of heavy streets were dominated by the cars and other vehicles rushing past their homes.

Annoyances

Residents of all streets except light streets put traffic at the top of their list of things that bother them most – ahead of crime, dilapidation of their streets, lack of access to stores and other services, and problems with their neighbors. Traffic presented a host of problems, including the danger posed to children, difficulties in crossing streets and backing out of driveways, environmental pollution from fumes, noise and vibration, and the special annoyances of vehicles like trucks, buses, and motorcycles. Heavier streets not only carried more traffic overall but also were more likely to carry truck traffic and buses (none of the light streets and all of the very heavy streets served as bus routes). The dominance of traffic and its by-products as sources of annoyance across the entire sample of respondents is even more noteworthy in light of two related facts uncovered in the interviews. First, a fairly sizable minority of the residents of heavy and very heavy streets appeared to prefer busy streets to the quiet residential streets that were favored by most residents of San Francisco. In some cases this seems to have been a longstanding attitude of the people involved, and in others a recognition that busy streets provide certain benefits, such as convenient access to stores and transportation or an opportunity to purchase homes that would be too expensive elsewhere. Despite the presence of such individuals in the sample, traffic was perceived to be a problem by most respondents, and by more of those on heavier streets.

In addition, there was some evidence suggesting that problems with traffic cause some residents of heavy streets, especially young families with children, to migrate to streets with less traffic. People also adapt to heavy traffic in other ways, including staying away from it as much as possible, but we will discuss that in detail later on. Despite these accommodations, those who remain on heavy streets seem quite dissatisfied with their choices. This may be because those who selected houses or apartments on heavy streets paid more attention to the structure itself than to its surroundings. Or they may have made their choices in the evenings or on weekends, when traffic was lighter. Or they may be reacting to a worsening of the traffic problem, which is the most likely experience for all but the residents of the heaviest streets. Unmet expectations constitute an important factor in the dissatisfaction that many feel about the level of traffic on their streets.

Street activities

There was a great deal of evidence in the interviews that heavy traffic placed severe restrictions on the activities that residents were able to engage in outside their homes. According to the residents' reports, heavy traffic restricts social activity, or neighboring. People who live on streets with heavy traffic are less likely to know their neighbors, especially those who live across the street. These comparisons are hampered somewhat by the fact that residents of medium streets are more likely to rent than to own their homes, and they tend to have lived on their streets for shorter periods of time. But in general it seems that traffic makes it less likely that a street will be a friendly place.

On the heaviest streets, it can be difficult to hold a conversation over the traffic noise when one meets a neighbor on the street. The noise, fumes, and vibrations also make activities like sitting outside, gardening, and car washing more dangerous or difficult. This limits the opportunities for incidental contacts among neighbors that might foster friendships. Thus, the individual's freedom to engage in outdoor activities is limited by heavy traffic and its by-products, and the development of relationships among neighbors is hindered in the process. The consequent lack of social support may result in a number of third-level effects on the physical and emotional well-being of residents (including a lack of protection from crime and lack of support in times of personal stress) that are attributable indirectly to traffic.

Traffic interference

Interviews revealed quite clearly that residents' homes failed to protect them sufficiently from the impacts of heavy traffic. Residents reported that a wide variety of common and necessary activities within their homes suffered from the interference of traffic noise, fumes, and vibration. These activities included watching television, sleeping, talking, working, and eating. In addition, residents reported that traffic interfered with their children's opportunities to play outside. Further, the data indicate that the proportion of street residents affected in each of these ways increases with the traffic volume.

It seems safe to say that all four groups of residents studied by Appleyard, regardless of the levels of traffic on their streets, had their normal day-to-day routines disrupted by traffic and its by-products. This must have been particularly frustrating for those driven indoors by the noise, fumes, and dirt they encountered outside, especially in a mild climate like that of San Francisco, which places relatively few limitations on outdoor activity.

Adaptive responses

Still other indications of the ways in which traffic on residential streets can constrain residents' actions come from reports of attempts to cope with the unpleasant impacts of traffic. Significant numbers of residents reported keeping their windows shut and shifting their activities toward the rear of the home to lessen the noxious and disruptive effects of traffic. Significant numbers were also forced to take extraordinary precautions to protect their children from the dangers of traffic. They forbade their children to play on the street, told them never to cross certain streets, and even accompanied them to school. Residents also reported that they restricted their own movements, staying inside in order to avoid the traffic-dominated environment outside. And, as we have seen throughout, all of these indications of traffic impacts were strongest on the streets with the heaviest flows of traffic. And, again, they appeared over and above the choices people were able to make in selecting their homes in the first place or in migrating to a more desirable location later on.

Vulnerable groups

There seems little reason to doubt that traffic assumes a role of considerable proportions in the lives of those who live along city streets. It dominates their images of their environments, influences their activities outdoors and inside their homes, and causes considerable anxiety over the welfare of their children. These impacts, significant for every group, are greatest on streets where traffic volumes are highest.

If this were not bad enough, Appleyard's study also showed that two groups of citizens were affected in all these ways to an even greater extent than were other segments of the population: the very young and the very old. Children's experiences with traffic can be inferred from their parents' reports. Families with children felt the assault of traffic on environmental quality and safety especially strongly. The restrictions they felt compelled to impose on their children's activities, the loss of an important place for their children to play and to learn, and the constant fear for their children's safety, must have detracted significantly from their enjoyment of their homes and their lives. And despite their precautions, traffic must have caused many of them tragic loss and grief. In 1976, according to the National Highway Traffic Safety Administration, over 51,000 children under the age of 15 were injured in traffic accidents in this country, and 2,080 were killed. One-fifth of all deaths of children between the ages of 5 and 14 resulted from traffic accidents. And, of course, the overall accident rates on San Francisco's residential streets are known to rise with traffic volume.

The elderly are also placed at great risk by heavy traffic. They have difficulty in crossing busy streets. Traffic signals often change before an elderly person can cross a wide street. In 1976, according to government figures, 10,000 Americans over the age of 65 were injured in traffic accidents, and 2,010 were killed. Surprisingly, interviews of elderly residents showed them to feel less bothered by traffic than any other age group. There are many possible reasons for this. They may have better adapted their lives to endure the traffic because they have had longer to do so. They also may engage in fewer activities that bring them into conflict with traffic, such as travel to work or for entertainment. And they are less likely to have young children to protect or to worry about.

It is not clear that either the elderly or the very young feel as threatened by traffic as they really are. One group may know too much about life, and the other too little. But each suffers inordinately from traffic and its by-products.

Making streets more livable

In the introduction to *Livable Streets,* Appleyard set two goals for the book. The first was to find out what it is like to live on streets with different kinds of traffic. We have already seen some of the fruits of that exploration. The second goal was to find ways in which streets can be made safer and more livable. The need for such remedies has been documented already. The search for them is the subject to which we turn now.

Appleyard's research, along with the work of others, can be used as a basis for designing traffic-management systems to alleviate the problems that city residents have with traffic. However, it is not the case, to this point at least, that such research has been applied directly to solve such problems. In some cases, the actions of government agencies have been shaped by this research. In other cases, planners and citizen groups have instigated attempts to control traffic quite independently of researchers, and the results from their efforts can sometimes be used to evaluate the accuracy of researchers' conclusions. To some degree, often a considerable one, efforts to improve the lives of residents of city streets have proceeded independently of efforts to understand the effects of traffic.

The disjunction between research and applications in this area and the reasons for it make the story an interesting one to tell. But evaluations of outcomes of interventions in the traffic patterns of urban areas are complicated greatly in the process. For one thing, we almost always lack the neat before–after comparisons that can be designed into interventions when researchers participate directly. Even worse, those who implement traffic-management policies often are not greatly concerned with precise, unbiased evaluations of their handiwork. Or their evaluations may ignore issues of great interest to researchers and theorists, who may have to rely on secondary evaluations, piecing together the data collected by planners with those they are able to collect themselves.

The cases

Appleyard described in detail eight cases in which serious attempts had been made to lessen the destructive impact of traffic on residential streets. These cases were evenly divided between (1) London and its surrounding area in England and (2) the San Francisco Bay area in the United States. They were almost evenly divided between the work of professional planners carrying out their ongoing responsibilities as government employees and the efforts of groups of citizens who had organized to promote improvements in their communities.

But they all shared one basic form: In each case there was an effort to reduce traffic on lightly traveled residential streets by diverting it to more heavily traveled streets. The ultimate goal was to restrict residential streets to essential traffic: residents coming and going, visitors, and deliveries. Auto traffic from one part of the city to another would travel only on arterial streets, along with trucks and buses. In some cases the plans specified different levels of arterials, carrying traffic different distances at different speeds. But in each case an attempt was made to exclude through traffic from neighborhood streets.

Through traffic can be routed away from quiet residential streets onto major arterials by means of signs and physical barriers. If a neighborhood can be structured to consist of an interior network of quieter residential streets bounded by busier arterial streets, as many already are, then traffic diversion can be accomplished in large part by restricting access to the interior streets from the major perimeter streets, thus disrupting any through-traffic paths through the neighborhood. "Exit-only" signs can be placed at the arterial ends of interior streets. Interior streets can also be closed by devices known as diverters, which can be simple barriers (Figure 10.3) or more elaborate mini-parks. These streets can be marked with signs such as "Not a through street" at their arterial ends. Culs-de-sac can be created in this way, where only local traffic will be found. In neighborhoods with gridiron street plans, diverters can serve to discourage the practice of driving through the neighborhood to avoid busy perimeter streets (called rat-running in England). Frequent stop signs on long interior streets can have a weaker form of the same effect.

Through traffic can be discouraged in more subtle ways as well. "Chokers," concrete forms extending out from the curb at street corners, typically as far as one car width, can make turns into a street more difficult, especially for trucks.

"Townscaping" streets, with plantings (sometimes on chokers), benches, brick paving, diagonal parking, and the like, can emphasize the residential character of a street and thus make through traffic, especially speedy through traffic, seem inappropriate. Through traffic can also be discouraged, or at least slowed, on residential streets by posting extremely low speed limits, by building humps and "rumble strips" into the streets, and by placing diverters at intersections (Figure 10.4).

In conjunction with the diversion of traffic from interior residential streets, provisions have sometimes been made to soften the impact of the resulting increases in traffic on arterial streets. Speed limits can be raised, streets widened, traffic signals synchronized, left turns limited, and bus lanes estab-

Figure 10.3. Traffic diverters erected as part of the Berkeley, California, livable-streets project, with sign added by residents. Sources: Top, Appleyard (1981, p. 222); reproduced with permission of the University of California Press. Bottom, photo by author, 1990.

lished, among other measures, to lessen traffic congestion. At the same time, those who live on arterial streets can be helped to deal with the increases in traffic. Trees can be planted as buffers, new buildings can be sited at right angles to the street, and the level of the street can be lowered to reduce the impact. Residents can also be compensated by providing grants or loans to finance the addition of insulation or storm windows to their homes. Efforts can be made to relocate families with small children on quieter streets, or even to replace as much as possible of the residential use of the arterial streets with commercial and industrial uses. Improvements in public transportation systems can also help to reduce the burden of the diverted traffic on residents of arterial streets.

Evaluating the outcomes of efforts to make residential streets more livable

Figure 10.4. A traffic diverter slows traffic at Berkeley intersection, 1990. Photo by author.

is extremely complicated. As has been mentioned already, those who implement traffic-management plans often make little effort to conduct formal evaluations. When they do, they usually restrict themselves to more objective measures such as changes in traffic volume, speed, and composition. In the absence of direct measures of residents' perceptions and experiences, one is left to infer the impacts of traffic measures on residents. As we have seen, this is a risky thing to do, given the effects of residents' needs, preferences, and expectations on their responses to traffic.

When such inferences are drawn, or when researchers collect their own interview or questionnaire data from residents, as Appleyard has done in a number of cases, it generally turns out that traffic diversion improves the lives of the residents of neighborhood streets, where traffic loads are eased, but adds to the burden of residents of heavier arterial streets, which gain even more traffic volume. The balance is tipped somewhat in the direction of overall benefit to residents by the fact that more people live on interior streets than on perimeter streets, and so the gain on interior streets is greater than the loss on perimeter streets, where traffic conditions typically are poor in the first place. It could be tipped even further in that direction if efforts toward compensation and improvement of public transportation more often kept up with the easier and cheaper efforts toward traffic diversion.

The politics of the street

Another complicating factor is the varied composition of the population that is affected by traffic-diversion schemes such as those we have been considering. Families with small children and most other residents of light neighborhood streets are likely to approve of such efforts. But motorists who regularly drive across town may not. In fact, in Berkeley, California, where one of the most comprehensive plans of this sort was instituted, largely as the result of citizens' efforts, motorists organized in opposition and eventually forced the issue to a referendum (in which it was upheld). Some individuals reacted even more strongly against the Berkeley traffic-diversion plan, destroying diverters and disobeying signs that had been erected to limit their access to neighborhood streets or to alter their driving routes through the city.

In addition to neighborhood residents, residents of arterial streets, and impatient motorists, many other groups have a stake in traffic-management policies. Merchants located along busy arterial streets may fear that increased traffic congestion will keep customers and deliveries away from their shops. Merchants in neighborhood shopping centers may see a threat to the flow of potential customers. Those responsible for police and fire protection and ambulance service may see plans that restrict through traffic in neighborhoods as a hindrance to the efficient performance of their duties, particularly in regard to increasing the response times during emergencies. Residents of poorer neighborhoods may feel, with some justification, that traffic reduction and its associated improvements are likely to draw more people into their neighborhoods, thus driving property values up and driving them and their families out (a process called gentrification). In short, a traffic-management plan must be evaluated in terms of who is helped, who is hurt, and the balance between the two – not simply in terms of efficient traffic flow.

Evaluation

Stage 1: Background analysis

Although Appleyard's analysis of the effects of heavy traffic volume on residential streets was based on research conducted in San Francisco, it did not address to any significant degree conditions peculiar to that city. It would seem to apply equally to any large city in which, as in San Francisco, traffic on residential streets causes problems for the people who live along them. In fact, most of the applications of that analysis in projects intended to protect neighborhood streets from traffic have been carried out elsewhere than San Francisco.

Stage 2: Behavioral goals

The goals for those traffic-diversion projects were derived directly from the findings of Appleyard's research. They include the prevention or reversal of the many negative effects of traffic on residential streets. Increased safety, greater activity outside the home, and more frequent incidental contacts leading to closer relationships with neighbors are among those goals. They also include freedom from disruption of activities inside the home, freer use of those areas of the home near the street, and the option of opening windows without the penalties of noise and fumes.

Stage 3: Environment–behavior relationships

The research from which those goals were derived provided extensive and seemingly clear-cut evidence of highly salient negative impacts of heavy traffic volume on residential streets. However, whereas the images and activities reported by residents clearly differed among streets carrying different levels of traffic, the reasons for those differences are not quite so clear.

As part of their large-scale follow-up study of the effects of traffic volume, Appleyard and Lintell (1972) compared the resident populations of the four types of streets: from light to very heavy. They found that residents of light-traffic streets were more affluent and less likely to belong to ethnic minorities, had more elderly people and children in their households, were more likely to own their own single-family homes, and had lived on their streets longer, as compared with the residents of the other three types of streets. Residents of medium-traffic streets were most likely, of all the groups, to be unmarried and to be renters. The incomes on streets with very heavy traffic were the lowest of any of the four groups, and there were other differences as well.

The observed differences among resident populations indicate that Appleyard did not succeed in his attempt to equate the four street types for factors other than traffic volume. Therefore, it would seem to be necessary to qualify his conclusions about the effects of traffic volume. For example, if residents of light streets are more likely to see the street as an extension of their homes, it might be because they have more children in their families, or because traffic interferes with street activities less, or for some combination of those reasons. The less friendly atmosphere on medium streets may reflect the greater numbers of transient renters there, and their poorer appearance may be due to the neglect of absentee landlords, in addition to or as an alternative to being the result of traffic volume per se. And so on.

It is difficult to see, however, how a selection problem could be avoided in such a study. It seems inevitable that traffic volume would influence choice of residence. A light street is clearly a more appropriate choice for families with small children, for example. And because, unable to assign residents randomly, researchers are limited to quasi-experimental comparisons of existing street populations, such ambiguities of causal inference seem inescapable. Perhaps more complex statistical analyses might be undertaken in which resident characteristics could be used to adjust comparisons on other variables. But if the results of research on the effects of traffic volume are ever used as the basis for intervention, the residents on any target street probably will have the same distinctive characteristics relative to other streets that were observed by Appleyard and Lintell. In other words, although it may be impossible to determine their separate causal contributions, the combination of traffic volume and resident characteristics probably is inseparable in nature, so that any intervention would need to consider their joint effects.

Stage 4: Plan elements

The traffic-diversion projects based on the research evidence collected by Appleyard have been, of necessity, accomplished through very simple means. Transportation routes established by planners cannot be undone without seriously jeopardizing traffic flow or undertaking massive changes in a city's transportation infrastructure. Thus, these projects have been mainly efforts of neighborhood citizens' groups to reduce traffic on lightly traveled residential streets. That has been accomplished primarily by limiting vehicular access to the neighborhood. Typically, barriers are installed where neighborhood streets intersect with busy perimeter streets. In Berkeley, for example, several large concrete planters were spaced across some streets, along with signs alerting motorists that those streets could not be entered from that direction. Access to such streets was thus limited to their intersections with quieter interior neighborhood streets. In some cases, despite the diverters and signs, a small opening was left in each street for residents of the street to drive out at the "closed" end, onto the busy arterial street. In addition to those changes in traffic patterns, diverters (e.g., clusters of planters) were placed in the middle of intersections in the interior of the neighborhood to slow traffic and deter through traffic further.

Stage 5: Overall plan

In each of these projects, the overall plan consisted of creating a new traffic pattern that would protect quiet neighborhood streets by specifying locations for whatever types of traffic diverters were to be employed. In Berkeley, for example, the neighborhood perimeter was made less permeable by closing off access from busy arterial streets at all but a limited number of points. Those points were entrances to secondary streets that carried traffic into the neighborhood and provided access to the open ends of most of the neighborhood's residential blocks. On the secondary streets, where multiple-block trips through the neighborhood were still possible in some cases, diverters in intersections slowed traffic and presumably discouraged motorists from adopting those routes as habitual alternatives to arterial streets outside the neighborhood for trips across town.

Stage 6: POE

Unfortunately, no formal evaluation was carried out in Berkeley or in any of the other project venues identified by Appleyard to determine whether or not the plans that had been adopted had had the intended effects. Lacking empirical evidence that traffic flow or residents' perceptions and actions were changed for the better, one can only rely on common sense, on the evidence of generic relationships between traffic volume and residents' perceptions and actions, and on anecdotal reports of the success of applications based on that research to support the wider use of such interventions. That is all the more unfortunate because Appleyard and Lintell developed data-collection methods for their research that could be adapted easily for use in POE studies.

Stage 7: Future impact

Traffic-diversion projects such as those described by Appleyard are perfectly straightforward and technically and economically feasible, once community support has been won for their goals and for specific means of achieving them. Unfortunately, the actual applications were plagued by complications, misunderstandings, and complexities caused by the reactions of local government officials and community groups. As a result, those plans were difficult to carry out, and their effects difficult to evaluate. For that reason, Appleyard became as interested in the process by which the problems that traffic causes people can be identified and solved as in technical traffic-control issues. His analysis, in the form of advice to planners, which he labeled the Participatory Planning Process, consists of six steps, summarized briefly as follows:

1. Analyze the problems and needs: It is necessary to supplement objective traffic measures with an assessment of residents' perceptions of traffic impacts. At the same time, one must recognize that people adapt to traffic and may be willing to tolerate disturbing conditions when they need not.
2. Generate alternative solutions: Decisions must be made about the form of an intervention – whether it should be applied in a single street or an entire city; whether it should consist of a simple traffic barrier or more elaborate improvements to accomplish the same purpose; and which groups of people, street types, and specific traffic problems should be addressed.
3. Communicate the alternatives: It is important to reach large numbers of the people concerned and give them understandable descriptions of what might be done and what results might be expected. Those who are not reached or who do not understand may become stubborn opponents of the plan.
4. Evaluate the alternatives and make a choice: The likely effects of alternative policies need to be estimated and compared in light of existing knowledge. For example, heavy-traffic streets are likely to suffer less from diverted

traffic (from other streets) because the people who live there expect less and have fewer children.

5. Implement the chosen plan: It is preferable to choose a trial period, one that is short enough for residents to foresee redress of their grievances and yet long enough for a fair evaluation of the plan. The changes that are made should not, however, be skimpy or incomplete, or the plan will not be given a fair chance.

6. Evaluate and modify the plan: Any problems that are identified in a thorough evaluation should be discussed with the affected parties. Modifications should be negotiated between the parties and the planners, as they are needed. Serious problems that are evident early on should be attacked immediately, or the entire trial may be jeopardized.

In many ways, the most tangible outcome realized from Appleyard's research and the applications and (informal) evaluations that have taken place is the book *Livable Streets*. It is intended to be used as a handbook by those who are responsible for, or want to contribute to, the protection of city residents from harmful effects of traffic on their streets. In fact, an earlier version of the book (Appleyard, Gerson, & Lintell, 1976), published by the U.S. Department of Transportation, was a best-seller among planners and gave rise to several traffic-diversion projects around the San Francisco Bay area (Appleyard's home base) that were described in *Livable Streets* and were used to update the analysis in that book. In all, *Livable Streets* presents case histories of almost 30 traffic-management projects from all over the United States and Europe, and even from Japan, to augment the empirical research Appleyard conducted in San Francisco in arriving at an overall understanding of the harmful effects of traffic and the available means for ameliorating them.

Those books and another volume published by the U.S. Department of Transportation (Appleyard & Smith, 1980) have provided guidelines for other traffic-diversion projects, along with reports of Appleyard's research (which received an award from *Progressive Architecture* in 1979) and similar ideas. For example, planners in the Netherlands have created the residential street, or *Woonerf,* where vehicular traffic is limited to residents, and the cars share the space with children at play and other activities that Americans tend to associate with private yards and parks (see Moudon, 1987, for more on this and other examples). Santa Cruz architect Jeff Oberdorfer (1982) has coordinated a large "livable streets" project in that California city. He made use not only of Appleyard's technical traffic-control recommendations but also of the Participatory Planning Process framework in building community support for the project.

Although it is not possible to do justice here to Appleyard's enlightening and entertaining history of the research, theory, and planning about traffic impacts on behavior, two additional points that he made deserve to be repeated. First, traffic-management plans almost never reduce traffic. They merely redistribute it. Significant traffic reduction would require the substitution of public transit for private vehicles, a lengthy, costly, and perhaps even unrealistic solution for pressing traffic problems. However, the life of a community can be improved without a net reduction in traffic volume.

A related issue is that of equity. A redistribution of traffic impacts raises important questions about doing the most good for the most people – questions that can be answered only in the political arena. That makes the application of knowledge about traffic–behavior relationships a difficult and dangerous enterprise. The fact that even the best plans, effective implementations of the best research and theory, will inevitably hurt some people – residents of arterial streets onto which more traffic will be diverted, residents of poor neighborhoods where improvements will encourage gentrification, motorists who drive on even busier crosstown streets, and others – makes for complicated planning and evaluation problems. In that sense, this is probably a very realistic example of the involvement of social science in the public-policy arena.

Donald Appleyard's contribution to planning for traffic in urban residential neighborhoods is especially impressive for the balance it strikes among social-scientific analysis, technical-planning expertise, and concern for community welfare. For that reason, it provides an important model for environmental-design research, one that has influenced the work of many design and planning professionals who stress user participation along with scientific analysis and design expertise in their work. It is so unfortunate that Donald Appleyard's premature death prevented him from continuing his pioneering career and from seeing the full realization of the considerable body of work he had already produced.

References

Appleyard, D. (1981). *Livable streets*. Berkeley: University of California Press.

Appleyard, D., Gerson, H. S., & Lintell, M. (1976). *Livable urban streets: Managing auto traffic in residential neighborhoods*. Washington, DC: U.S. Department of Transportation.

Appleyard, D., & Lintell, M. (1972). The environmental quality of city streets: The residents' viewpoint. *Journal of the American Institute of Planners, 38*, 84–101.

Appleyard, D., & Smith, D. T. (1980). *Improving the residential street environment*. Washington, DC: U.S. Department of Transportation.

Moudon, A. V. (Ed.) (1987). *Public streets for public use*. New York: Van Nostrand Reinhold.

Oberdorfer, J. (1982, September). Livable streets in Santa Cruz. *Place*, p. 211.

11
DEFENSIBLE-SPACE
MODIFICATIONS AT CLASON
POINT GARDENS

Location: New York, New York
Participants: Oscar Newman and colleagues, Institute for Community
Design Analysis, New York City

More than half a million people, mostly minority families consisting of a mother and several children, are residents of public housing in New York City. They live in more than 100 "projects," or collections of buildings, that contain more than 150,000 individual apartments in all. Those projects come in all shapes, sizes, and locations. Some were made large, and others small. Some are composed of tall buildings of 20 stories or more, and others are two-story walk-ups. Some were placed in isolated locations, and others right in the middle of existing neighborhoods.

Are these various forms of public housing anything more than different designers' and government officials' responses to the aesthetic preferences, budget constraints, and available space of their clients? Oscar Newman's research suggests that they are. While at New York University, the architect and planner discovered that the rates of serious crimes varied among public-housing projects of different sizes, heights, and locations. But Newman did more than discover relationships between the architectural designs of public-housing projects and the incidence of crime. He went on to integrate his research findings into an insightful and influential theory that explained not only his findings but also a great many other facets of urban life. He also saw important implications of his work for improvements in the design of public housing. And he followed through to the practical implementation of his ideas and, even further, to the evaluation of the consequences of that implementation. In the end, he was able to corroborate his theory and to demonstrate the efficacy of the designs it spawned.

The research

Newman began with a study based on the voluminous records kept by the New York City Housing Authority police – virtually every complaint, no matter how minor, of an incident taking place within the housing projects, and

197

the exact location of each one. The total number of felonies in each project reported to the Housing Authority police, and the numbers of separate crimes that were reflected in those totals – robberies (muggings), assaults, burglaries, rapes, murders, and drug offenses – were first converted to rates per 1,000 project residents to make it possible to compare projects of different sizes. Then the rates per 1,000 were used to test hypotheses about the relationships between crimes and the sizes of the projects' populations and the heights of the projects' buildings.

The study compared the crime rates (per 1,000 residents) between the smaller projects of 1,000 units (apartments) or fewer and the larger projects of more than 1,000 units. The sample of 100 projects was also broken down into those made up of shorter buildings (six stories or fewer) and those made up of taller buildings (seven stories or more). The most striking result of that analysis was the appearance of a dramatic difference in crime rates between high-rise and low-rise projects.

Regardless of size, high-rise projects were the sites of many more crimes per 1,000 residents. But this difference was much greater in the larger projects, where the high-rise examples showed a dramatically high rate of reported felonies compared with any of the other categories of projects. A further analysis was conducted in which the total sample of projects was subdivided more finely into five categories on the basis of the heights of their buildings. Those figures showed a steady increase in crime rates from the shortest buildings to the tallest. The total number of felonies per 1,000 residents rose from an average of 8.8 for three-story buildings to an average of 20.2 for buildings of 16 stories or more. The rates for muggings that took place inside buildings rose even more dramatically, from 2.6 per 1,000 in six-story or lower buildings to 11.5 per 1,000 in buildings having 19 or more floors.

Newman was able to provide even more striking evidence of the contrast in crime rates between high-rise and low-rise housing projects, although that evidence is somewhat unconventional by the usual social-science standards of massed data and statistical comparisons across large numbers of cases. It was based on a direct comparison between two housing projects, one low-rise, called Brownsville, and one high-rise, called Van Dyke, which are located literally across the street from one another in the New York City borough of Brooklyn (Figure 11.1). Not only are these two projects located side by side, so that they share the poverty of the surrounding neighborhood and any other local conditions that might influence their crime rates, but also they are remarkably similar in many other respects. Their resident populations are quite similar: in number, racial composition, economic circumstances, and family size and composition. They are also similar in their physical characteristics (besides location and size): the number of acres they cover, their age, the size of the apartments they contain, the amount of space per resident

Figure 11.1. The Van Dyke and Brownsville projects, with very different crime rates, directly across the street from one another. Source: Newman (1972, p. 39); reproduced with permission of Macmillan Publishing Co.

inside the buildings, and the density of their resident populations over their entire areas.

But there was that one striking physical difference between them: Most of the families living in Van Dyke lived in buildings 13 or 14 stories high (although there were also some three-story buildings), whereas most of the families in Brownsville lived in six-story buildings (with some three-story wings). And the crime rates in Brownsville and Van Dyke were just as strikingly different; there were 1.5 times as many incidents reported overall in Van Dyke, the high-rise project. Broken down further, there were more than 1.5 times as many crimes and almost four times as many robberies (muggings) in Van Dyke as in its low-rise neighbor, Brownsville, just across the street. In addition, maintenance records kept by the Housing Authority showed that Van Dyke, although a few years newer, and no larger overall, required almost 1.5 repairs to be made for every one at Brownsville.

So the overall pattern in 100 housing projects containing 150,000 housing units and over half a million people seems fairly clear. More crimes were committed in high-rise projects, especially those that are large. The comparison between Van Dyke and Brownsville puts the problem in bold relief. One is forced to the conclusion that the choice of a high-rise design for public housing leads to greatly increased levels of crime suffered by the residents. Serious crimes occur more often, relative to the number of residents, in buildings that are seven or more stories tall than in buildings that are only six stories tall or shorter. It seems that architectural design and crime are seedy partners in the public-housing projects of the "Big Apple."

The theory

What is there about high-rise projects, especially large ones, that accounts for the increased dangers their residents face? How does the height of a building affect the actions of residents or criminals, or provide an arena for their confrontations, to produce the crime statistics we have been discussing? It was the solution of that puzzle, out of the pieces of observation and the pattern of the research findings comparing different project configurations, to which Newman turned next. Out of that analysis came the theory of *defensible space*.

According to Newman's theory, the key factor in determining the vulnerability of a housing project to criminal activity is whether or not the residents themselves act in ways that discourage crime. To start, residents can watch for potential criminals and crime on the project grounds and around building entrances, corridors, and stairwells. If they see someone suspicious or see a crime in progress, they can call police, or yell out, or get involved even more directly. By their active surveillance and intervention, residents can make their project a more difficult place for criminals to ply their trade. Newman took this basic idea from urban planner Jane Jacobs (1961) and developed it much further.

The connection between residents' behavior to deter crime and the physical design of a housing project is a key to Newman's theory. He believes that residents will attempt to protect their homes and the areas around them if the physical design encourages them to do so. There are several ways in which it can. One is to minimize the amount of public space, the space that anyone, resident or outsider, may use. The exterior project grounds can be divided by fences, or even curbing or landscaping devices such as shrubs or changes in material or texture, into smaller parcels. Most of these, in turn, can be assigned to specific buildings or even to individual apartments. The rest can be clearly dedicated to specific activities, such as small children's play, or to paths through the project. This kind of arrangement makes it clear to residents that substantial portions of the grounds belong to them and that strangers are supposed to stay in clearly marked areas while inside the project. All of this is easier in low-rise projects than in high-rise, because there is more outside space near individual apartments to begin with. It is also easier in small projects, where residents are more likely to know who is a neighbor and who is a stranger. Low-rise and small projects also have fewer interior public spaces that residents need to worry about as possible locations for crime. For example, a project designed as townhouses has no public entrances or corridors or elevators or stairwells at all. Each apartment opens directly onto the grounds, which can be assigned mostly as yards to the individual apartments. The physical design of a project can also make it easier for concerned residents to keep track of what is going on outside their homes. A suspicious stranger is more likely to be seen if kitchen windows overlook the paths through the project than if bedroom windows do. Lighting along the paths makes it easier to see what is going on at night. Building entrances that can be seen from nearby apartments and that are open to view from the project grounds and paths, so that people coming home can see what is waiting for them, make it more difficult for a criminal to lie in ambush. The elevators in housing projects, public spaces that are totally screened from surveillance, are the sites of 31% of all the robberies that take place in the projects.

The design of a project can also enable police patrols, passing motorists, and pedestrians on nearby sidewalks to help project residents control crime. Projects can be located in existing neighborhoods, rather than in isolated locations among warehouses, factories, and expressways or railroad tracks. Buildings can be located on project grounds so that their entrances and lobbies face adjacent streets, rather than inner courtyards. Such designs add naturally to the surveillance with which potential criminals will have to contend, thus discouraging crime further.

If these seem like obvious strategies, it should be noted that they contradict some strong preferences on the part of architects of public housing. Architects prefer designs that maximize the amount of ground-level open space available to residents for unrestricted social and recreational use. This objective, which some trace to the ideas of the Swiss architect of the early twentieth century, Le Corbusier, is often accomplished by housing the required number of residents in fewer, taller buildings. Moreover, designers often seek to maximize the usefulness of the open space by concentrating it in as large a unit as possible. In a common design, known as the "superblock," the site is unified by closing existing city streets. The tall apartment buildings ring the project site, leaving a large, open public space in the middle, including parking facilities that make it convenient to locate building entrances facing inward.

Unfortunately, though some expect this configuration to create an aesthetically pleasing site and to permit more varied activities by residents in its parklike green space, it more often provides a haven for criminal activity. It makes more of the space public, and thus beyond the control of residents. It moves more of that public space away from the buildings, where residents' windows would provide opportunities for surveillance, thus making it safer for a criminal to carry out a mugging or drug sale or other crime. Apartments on higher floors are as removed effectively from surveillance opportunities as those far away along the ground. Moreover, the ring of tall buildings shields the open space from passersby at the project's boundaries, when a site of such dimensions can be located in an existing neighborhood at all. When it cannot, the combination of design and location reinforces the stigmatizing effects of public-housing communities. The damage to residents' identities contributes to their feelings of helplessness and lack of control, and to criminals' perceptions of their vulnerability.

There are also more subtle aspects of building design that impact on criminal activity, according to Newman. In large buildings, especially, fire codes and other regulations require multiple entrances and exits. When there are several ways in and out of a building, routes that may terminate at doors on different sides of the building, it is more difficult to keep track of who is coming and going, and more difficult to catch a criminal who might be trying to escape after a mugging or some other crime. One of the ways in which multiple entrances and exits have been provided, presumably to conserve space and cut costs, makes criminal activity particularly difficult to control. It is known as "scissors stairs." Two sets of stairs run side by side, in different directions, in a single shaft that also contains the elevators. On each floor there are entrances to the two stairways, nearby one another on opposite sides of the elevator doors, although the stairways themselves are separated from one another for fire protection. If a criminal were to mug someone in the building, he or she could confuse pursuers by moving back and forth between the two scissors stairways, or between the stairways and the adjacent elevators. That would make it difficult to know the criminal's location at any given time or to predict the point at which he or she would exit. This may be one reason that those who commit crimes inside project buildings are only half as likely to be caught as those who commit crimes on project grounds. Separating the stairways and elevators would make it more difficult for the criminal to escape, and it would make the building a less attractive target for the potential criminal.

The number of apartments that open onto a single corridor is also a factor in project residents' ability to defend their community against criminals. Many buildings are made up of units called double-loaded corridors. Typically, the wings of such a building extend out from a central core that contains the lobby, elevators, and stairways. Each floor of each wing consists of a long corridor with a bank of apartments on each side. In such an arrangement, the number of residents who use the corridor to get to and from their apartments is quite large. This makes it difficult for residents to become acquainted with all those who are legitimate users of the corridor and to know when someone they see in the corridor does not belong there. That, in turn, makes the criminals' job easier. They are less readily suspected by their prey, especially if they have broken some of the light bulbs in the windowless corridor. An easier arrangement to defend is one where corridors serve fewer apartments. Entrances to several apartments may open on a small lobby in front of a single elevator. Instead of a large elevator tower shared by many shafts, with long banks of doors on every floor, separate shafts within small columns of apartments would make public-access spaces easier to defend against crime because of surveillance and recognition on the part of building residents. Even long, single-loaded corridors that can be lighted by windows or open galleries opposite the apartment doors are relatively safe.

All of these elements – entrances, paths, and other public areas obscured from surveillance, failure of neighbors to recognize one another, size of corridors, multiplicity and ambiguity of building entrances and exits, and separation of public spaces from the protection of nearby buildings and their residents' surveillance – contribute to crime, according to Newman's conception of defensible space. And these elements have something else in common: They are all much more likely to be found in high-rise than in low-rise projects. Therefore, they provide a potential explanation for the heightened vulnerability of high-rise projects to crime that was documented in Newman's research. Because they possess these design elements, and because so many more of their residents are isolated from their projects' principal public spaces on the ground, tall buildings make it more difficult for residents to keep track of those who are using a project's public spaces and what those people are doing.

But even tall buildings need not have all of the undesirable features that make life difficult for residents and easy for criminals. Newman's research findings and his theory provide a blueprint for the design of safer public housing that could be applied to tall buildings, if not as easily as to lower ones. Designs that create defensible public spaces are possible if designers are aware of the implications of these findings and act accordingly. Perhaps even more exciting is the possibility that existing public-housing projects could be modified in ways that would make their public spaces easier to defend. As we will see next, Newman has explored this possibility, and quite successfully.

The implementation

Most social scientists are accustomed to testing their theories through research. However, the most impressive evidence for the validity of Newman's theory of defensible space has come from its successful use to plan and execute modifications of existing public-housing projects. One of the most impressive examples of the theory's implementation involves a New York City housing project known as Clason Point Gardens.

Clason Point Gardens is one of the projects Newman studied in his research. It is decidedly a low-rise design, consisting of two-story buildings containing row houses and walk-up flats. With only 400 units and an area of 21 acres, it is a relatively small and low-density example of New York City's public-housing projects. In all, Clason Point Gardens is not typical of New York City projects, and it is certainly not a representative example of those project designs that are difficult to defend against criminal activity, such as

high-rise buildings with double-loaded corridors arranged in superblock configurations. But it is similar to many housing projects across this country, and
like most of them, it leaves a great deal to be desired in its vulnerability to
crime.

We do not know all the reasons for Newman's choice of Clason Point
Gardens as a place to test the practical implications of his theory, but he has
pointed out that in two very important respects all public-housing projects,
including Clason Point Gardens, have a great deal in common. First, most
residents of public housing lack the experience of being property owners. This
makes it unlikely that they will take a proprietary interest in their apartments
or the surrounding public areas of the project's buildings and grounds. They
are reluctant to try to control the activities of neighbors or strangers; they feel
dependent on the authorities to solve their problems. Public-housing management often reinforces this dependence through rules that severely limit residents' freedom to modify, decorate, or even use their homes as they would
like. Second, the stigma of living in public housing, the lack of individuality,
and the unattractive appearance of most public housing tend to cause residents
to take little pride in their homes and tend to cause outsiders to view the
projects as open to them without the consent of the residents, leaving them
vulnerable to crime and vandalism. Newman attributes these common problems – the residents' reticence, and outsiders' readiness for exploitation – in
part, at least, to the way most public-housing projects are designed. Because
these were the two major problems addressed by his redesign of Clason Point
Gardens, we may learn something that is generally useful from this specific
test of Newman's theory.

The ultimate goals of the modifications that were made at Clason Point
Gardens were to reduce the residents' fear of crime and to reduce the incidence of crime, along with reductions in vandalism and other minor problems. In order to accomplish those goals, Newman sought to change the
perceptions and behaviors of the projects' residents. He wanted to intensify
tenants' surveillance of the project grounds and to make tenants feel more
responsible for controlling the actions of neighbors and visitors. Those behaviors would depend on residents perceiving that they had special rights to the
areas near their homes and that those areas and their homes were worth
defending. Newman also sought to change the perceptions and behaviors of
outsiders. If he could increase the level of resident activity on project
grounds, and reduce the stigma associated with living in the project, potential
criminals would be made to feel less sanguine about loitering there, or engag-
ing in criminal activity, or vandalizing project property. In short, residents
would feel less helpless about crime and vandalism, and criminals would feel
less secure about carrying on those activities on the project grounds.

In order to effect these changes, Newman created a number of physical
modifications at Clason Point Gardens, each tied to specific target perceptions

and behaviors and, ultimately, to the goals of resident confidence and safety. First, significant portions of the public grounds of the project, almost 80% in all, were newly defined as private yards for the tenants' homes, circumscribed by installing fences and curbs. High iron fences enclosed the rear yards, which adjoined neighboring city streets and sidewalks, in clusters of 12 to 40 units. These rear yards were accessible only from the tenants' homes. The front yards, inside the grounds ringed by the project buildings, were separated from the public paths through the project by low curbs that delineated small lawns that were planted in front of the homes. This reassignment of space from the ambiguous public areas of the project to the private use of individual tenants and groups of tenants was intended to encourage tenants to exercise control over the activities that occurred on much of the project's grounds. It was also intended to deter the use of those same grounds by those who might threaten or actually harm the residents.

A second major aspect of the modifications concerned the areas of the project grounds that were to remain public. First, the former maze of paths through the project was reduced to a single route, well defined by a new and distinctive pattern of paving bricks. This new path ran past the front yards of the project buildings, to maximize opportunities for natural surveillance by the tenants. New seating and planting structures were located at nodes on the path, to encourage tenants to use the space and, at the same time, to discourage others from misusing it. New lighting extended the tenants' opportunities for surveillance, and their use of the path and its new conveniences, into the nighttime hours. (See Figure 11.2 for views of the original and modified rear yards, and Figure 11.3 for the original and modified front yards and paths.)

The remaining public area of Clason Point Gardens included a large green space that previously had been used as a hangout by teenage residents and as a meeting place by neighborhood drug dealers and their customers. It was regarded by most tenants as the most dangerous area of the project. This area was provided with new lighting and a general facelift. In addition, it was subdivided into three areas: a conversation area for adults, with new seating; a meeting place for teenagers, landscaped with large rocks and rough timbers; and a play area for younger children, with new playground equipment and seating for their attending parents. Greater use of this area by residents was expected to discourage loitering by individuals who might pose a danger to them. In addition, the design was intended to eliminate conflict among the activities of different age groups of residents. And the new lighting made the whole area safer at night, by encouraging tenant use, which in turn would discourage the illicit activities that had attracted dangerous outsiders to the project.

A final modification consisted of superficial physical changes in the buildings that were intended to produce more fundamental changes in residents' and outsiders' behaviors. The drab, uniform concrete façades of the buildings

Figure 11.2. Clason Point Gardens' backyards before (top) and after (bottom) defensible-space modifications. Source: Newman (1972, pp. 164, 175); reproduced with permission of Macmillan Publishing Co.

were resurfaced. The new façades gave the appearance of brick, and tenants were allowed a choice of colors for their own homes. It was hoped that by upgrading and individualizing the appearances of tenants' homes, some of the stigma of living in public housing would be removed. Making the project homes more closely resemble the private homes in the surrounding neighborhood was expected to increase tenants' concern for the maintenance and protection of their homes and to alter outsiders' views that the project was a safe haven or easy mark for criminal activities.

In all, Newman proposed and effected several relatively minor changes in

Figure 11.3. Clason Point Gardens' front yards and paths before (top) and after (bottom) modifications. Source: Newman, (1972, pp. 165, 254); reproduced with permission of Macmillan Publishing Co.

the physical design of Clason Point Gardens for the purposes of encouraging greater protection of the project grounds by residents and discouraging disruptive activities by outsiders and by some of the project's younger residents. New paving and lighting were installed to channel and illuminate pedestrian traffic through the project so that it would be easier for tenants to exercise surveillance from their front windows and yards. Landscaping and resurfacing of buildings were carried out to eliminate unused public areas that would otherwise pose a danger and to give tenants more pride in their homes. A large, ambiguous open space was converted to specific recreational uses, to increase tenant activity there and to make it more difficult for loiterers or criminals to stay on the project grounds. All of these changes were intended to give Clason Point Gardens and its residents a new vitality and sense of pride that would deter outsiders from abusing either one.

The outcome

The effects of the modifications that were carried out at Clason Point Gardens were evaluated in a variety of ways. Informal observations indicated that tenants took new pride in their homes. They planted and tended lawns. They added picket fences around their new front yards. They divided the common rear yards with their own fences into individual plots, where they planted shrubbery and flowers. By any standard, and especially in light of their means, they maintained their "property" well. They even cleaned up the public areas adjacent to their homes and disposed of their own trash when maintenance workers went on strike to protest the modifications, which they saw as threatening their jobs because of elimination of so much of the public areas for which the maintenance workers were responsible. In fact, half the maintenance staff was eventually reassigned to other projects because of the reduced work load at Clason Point Gardens.

Surveys of residents were conducted before and after the modifications were made. They showed a marked decrease in residents' fear of crime in the project. A majority of residents even said that they felt (many for the first time) that it was safe to walk the project grounds at night. And the percentage of residents who felt that they had a right to question strangers on the project grounds almost doubled, rising from 27% to 50%.

Not only did the residents of Clason Point Gardens feel that they could defend their homes, but also there is evidence that they may have done so and that potential criminals may have recognized the changes in their attitudes and behaviors. According to the statistics kept by Housing Authority police, there was a large reduction in crime on the project grounds. The overall crime rate, including minor offenses, was reduced by more than half, from 6.91 incidents per 1,000 residents per month before the modifications were made to 3.16 after they were completed. The rates of serious crimes (burglaries, robberies, and assaults) declined an average of 61.5%. Felonies committed during the evening and nighttime hours also fell by more than half.

In short, the modifications at Clason Point Gardens seemed to have precisely the effects Newman expected they would. They engendered in the residents a more active proprietary interest in their homes and the surrounding public spaces. They made the residents' lives safer from crime and other disruptions and, no less important, made the residents feel safe, even while walking to and from their homes after dark. It seems that those relatively minor physical modifications caused the residents to defend their homes against crime and, in fact, made their homes more defensible.

Broadening the focus

Newman's work has progressed much further in recent years. His research has continued and has led him to make modifications in what has come to be known as *defensible-space theory*. Others have tested the theory empirically and modified it. The theory has been applied much more widely, in combination with complementary ideas from other sources, in the arena of public housing and beyond – in private-housing settings, schools, and business districts. These developments have been so numerous and widespread that they can be reviewed only selectively and briefly here.

Extending the theory

Following the initial publication of defensible-space theory in 1972, Newman moved the focus of his work from public housing in New York City to private residential streets in St. Louis. Around the turn of the century, some of the wealthier citizens of St. Louis had built new homes at the edge of the city. In a novel arrangement, they retained ownership of the streets themselves, and they often limited traffic through their streets by closing them at one end. Around midcentury, residents of other, more modest homes in St. Louis tried to stabilize their declining neighborhoods and reduce crime by reclaiming legal ownership of their streets from the city. The success they experienced inspired Newman to adapt some of the principles of private streets to the design of public and private housing elsewhere and to incorporate them into defensible-space theory. One of these is the principle of limited access. Applied to public housing and other multiple-family dwellings, this means a design that limits the number of families sharing a common entry and the common public space for informal interaction and recreation. Following this principle, existing projects could be modified by using landscaping to cluster buildings together, or by dividing long corridors to create smaller groupings of apartments. In private housing, streets could be closed, creating functional culs-de-sac. In both settings, the recognition of neighbors and proprietary interest in public space around the home would increase. Increased informal control over crime presumably would follow.

The second principle derived from the study of private streets that was incorporated in the current version of defensible-space theory is the segregation of residents of a housing setting by age and life-style. This controversial idea is based on Newman's contention that in order to be safe, a housing setting must be designed to accommodate the life-styles of its residents. Teenagers frighten, and sometimes prey on, the elderly. Working couples who have no children are home too little to watch out for criminals. Young children cannot be supervised adequately in a high-rise building. And so on. Therefore, different types of structures and configurations of interior and exterior public spaces are needed for different groups. Specifically, the elderly are at home frequently enough to control crime in high-rise buildings that provide space for interaction and recreation, working singles and couples without children are often away from home and do well in high-rises with limited public space and control over access by a doorman or security staff, and families with children require low-rise housing with individual yards and public spaces that serve small numbers of households and can be seen well from surrounding homes. These arrangements, which Newman argues may actually permit increased integration by race and income level, can maximize control over outsiders and crime.

Another major attempt to improve defensible-space theory has been made by Taylor and his colleagues (Taylor, Gottfredson, & Brower, 1980). With the avowed purpose of better explaining the behavioral links between housing's physical features and its level of crime and fear, they developed an expanded, or second-generation, theory of defensible space. It provided needed detail about the mechanisms by which residents' informal interactions could deter crime. It took explicit notice of residents' degree of acquaintance with their neighbors and identification with their neighborhood. The concept of territoriality was also given an expanded role. Residents' proprietary attitudes were hypothesized to result in behaviors such as property maintenance and the creation of barriers to intrusion – real ones, such as fences, and symbolic ones, such as flower beds. These outcomes of territorial motives were hypothesized to serve as cues for potential intruders, whose recognition of residents' intentions to protect their property would discourage plans to victimize them.

Defensible-space theory has also been influential in stimulating other theoretical approaches to reducing crime by appropriate environmental design. Gardiner and Brill (see Rouse & Rubenstein, 1978), especially, have emphasized surveillance opportunities, access control, and social cohesion within a community as keys to crime prevention. They have designed crime-prevention programs for existing settings in which improved lighting, organization of community groups, and the use of security hardware play prominent roles.

Adding to the evidence

Supportive evidence for defensible-space theory, in its original form and its later variations, has been accumulating for over a decade. Newman (1981) found that residential blocks in St. Louis that had been converted to private streets experienced lower levels of crime and fear and increased stability. He has also completed a study similar to the original analysis of crime in New York City public housing, but expanded greatly in many respects (Newman & Franck, 1982). In federally assisted, moderate-income housing projects in Newark, San Francisco, and St. Louis, he found that building size, defined as the number of housing units sharing an entry, influenced both crime and fear of crime. The more units per entry, increasing from row houses to walk-ups to high-rises, the greater the rate of personal crimes and the greater the fear of crime found among residents. Consistent with Newman's and Taylor's expanded versions of defensible-space theory, this relationship was shown to be mediated by residents' use of and control over the space outside their apartments. In projects where each entry was shared by relatively large numbers of housing units, residents used and controlled public space less.

Taylor and his colleagues (Taylor, Gottfredson, & Brower, 1984) found that in private residential blocks in Baltimore, crime-deterrent resident behaviors, crime rates, and fear were related to physical features associated with defensible space. Defensible-space features such as fences and decorative plantings reduced crime directly and by encouraging social cohesion among neighbors. In a separate study (Brower, Dockett, & Taylor, 1983), evidence was found that residents of these neighborhoods perceived defensible-space features as symbols of proprietary attitudes and territorial motives, as potential criminals apparently did also.

Brown and Altman (1983) found that private homes in Salt Lake City were more likely to be burglarized if they lacked defensible-space features. Burglarized houses were less likely to be personalized by their owners' names or addresses (or by any sign) were less likely to have fences or locked gates, had fewer objects in view that indicated the presence of or use by occupants (such as toys or lawn sprinklers), and were less visible from the street and from neighboring houses than were nonburglarized houses on blocks where no burglaries had occurred.

Molumby (1976) found that property crimes in a university apartment complex were also predictable from the defensible-space features of its various units. Apartments located on busy perimeter streets, those that were less visible from the street, and those with poor visual contact with their surrounding grounds were more likely to be victimized. Greenburg, Rohe, and Williams (1982) found that a contrast in the same defensible-space features, access control and surveillability, was associated with differential crime rates in pairs of adjacent Atlanta neighborhoods.

There have been many more studies that have tested defensible-space theory empirically during the past decade. Reviews of the evidence by Murray et al. (1980) and by Taylor et al. (1980) indicate that the theory has been supported, for the most part. Departures from Newman's original conceptualization have been more in the nature of extensions and refinements than contradictions.

Applying the theory more widely

At about the same time as the successful program at Clason Point Gardens, Newman planned and carried out a modification of a high-rise public-housing project in New York City called Bronxdale Houses (Newman, 1972). A closed-circuit television system was installed to permit residents to monitor the most dangerous public areas in their buildings, the lobbies and elevators, on their home television sets. No measurable reduction in crime was produced, in part because of managerial and equipment problems and a lack of responsiveness on the part of the security personnel that discouraged residents from participating. Although these circumstances probably make it unfair to characterize this as a failure of defensible-space theory, Newman also noted that project residents showed little enthusiasm for the program and speculated that the cumulative effects of poor design and victimization might be to blame.

Since Newman's earliest efforts at Clason Point Gardens and Bronxdale Houses, several large-scale demonstration projects have been carried out based on defensible-space theory – in its original or modified form alone, or in combination with other theories. One of the most successful projects was carried out in a center-city neighborhood in Hartford, Connecticut, known as Asylum Hill (Fowler, McCalla, & Mangione, 1979; Fowler, 1981). A declining neighborhood consisting mostly of older houses converted to apartments, Asylum Hill was suffering from high rates of burglary and street crime. Analyzed from the point of view of defensible-space theory, it seemed that high levels of vehicular and pedestrian traffic to and from downtown office buildings had discouraged residents from perceiving the streets as a neighborhood for which they should share responsibility, had made recognition of strangers difficult, and had brought potential criminals into the neighborhood. Physical modifications to the neighborhood consisted primarily of closing some street entrances and narrowing others to restrict vehicular traffic. In addition, a permanent police team was assigned to the neighborhood, and efforts were made to promote neighborhood organizations that would work with police to reduce crime. An evaluation of the Hartford project found that one year later there were signs of positive effects on rates of burglary and street crimes and on fear among residents. Residents used the streets more and reported greater confidence in their ability to recognize strangers and more frequent cooperation with their neighbors to watch each others' homes. Although it is not possible to attribute all of these positive outcomes to the application of defensible-space theory, the evaluation team believed that the physical modifications to the neighborhood, based largely on Newman's analysis of private streets in St. Louis, had been essential to achieving those results (Fowler et al., 1979, p. vii).

During the 1970s, three demonstration projects were based on a comprehensive theory of crime prevention that included defensible-space theory as a principal component. These projects were conducted by Westinghouse Corporation, with federal funding (Westinghouse National Issues Center, 1977). One was carried out in a residential neighborhood in Minneapolis, a second in a neighborhood shopping area in Portland, Oregon, and the third in four high schools in Broward County, Florida. All followed a complex strategy based on defensible-space, community-organization, and law-enforcement improvements known as Crime Prevention Through Environmental Design (CPTED). Each was planned specifically for the crime problems and site to be addressed. The results were mixed, as were the successes in actually implementing the plans for the three sites. The Portland project was the most successful, achieving reductions in crime and fear despite limited implementation (Wallis & Ford, 1980a). Benefits were still in evidence four years after the project was completed (Kushmuk & Whittemore, 1981). More modest success was achieved in Broward County in reducing crime and fear at the four high schools involved. The residential project in Minneapolis had little effect. An additional outcome of the Westinghouse CPTED program was a manual for planners that would allow the theory to be applied to any site (Wallis & Ford, 1980b).

Additional applications have been developed by Newman, based on more recent versions of defensible-space theory. In *Community of Interest* (1981) he reported on modifications of low- and moderate-income public-housing projects in Oklahoma City and Jersey City. Unfortunately, it is impossible to evaluate the success of those programs based on the information he provided. In the same book, Newman described two alternate plans for modifying an existing moderate-income project in Seattle and plans for two new projects in Newark and in New York City. All three of those proposals were based on segregation of the elderly and families with children in separate and different building types on a single site. Finally, Newman has also published a series of manuals for those who wish to apply defensible-space theory elsewhere (1973a,b, 1975), although his books could easily serve the same purpose.

Evaluation

Stage 1: Background analysis

Oscar Newman's interest in the relationships between the designs of public-housing projects and the crime rates in them began while he was serving as a consultant to the New York City Housing Authority. His research began in their projects. But as his understanding of the issues grew, Newman's focus broadened to address more general aspects of architectural design, and he gradually developed a more general theory linking architectural design with human motives and actions that mediate decisions to resist and to commit crimes. The resulting theory of defensible space is general enough to be applied without much regard for local conditions, and its applications seem to have been successful in a wide variety of social, geographic, and architectural contexts.

In each application, however, the analysis of design features and configurations that are likely to deter crime must be tailored to the population and the types of structures involved. As was pointed out earlier, the life-styles of the residents play an important role in determining which housing-design arrangements will be successful. And different design devices may be required in massed public housing than on a street of individual private houses, as well as in a poor neighborhood compared with a wealthy one, and so on.

Stage 2: Behavioral goals

The principal goal of Newman's work was to reduce crime, especially violent crimes against people. As defensible-space theory emerged, through Newman's work and that of the many others who contributed to its development, the specific behaviors of residents and reactions by potential criminals that were believed to bring about a reduction in crime were gradually elaborated. For residents, the most important were efforts at surveillance of and control over the public spaces near their homes, based on identification of the boundaries between private and public spaces and on proprietary attitudes that would motivate them to watch for and act to deter incipient criminal activity. Potential criminals would be discouraged if they perceived environmental cues that their activities were likely to be detected by concerned, vigilant, protective residents. Thus, these motives, attitudes, and actions on the part of the residents and the criminals stalking them were the targets of Newman's design for the renovation of Clason Point Gardens, as they are for defensible-space design projects in general.

Stage 3: Environment–behavior relationships

The identification of environmental features that would be likely to elicit resident behaviors and criminal reactions tending to discourage crime, defensible-space features, began with Newman's research in New York City's public-housing projects. Unfortunately, the design of that correlational or preexperimental study did not rule out in a positive way alternative explanations for differences in crime rates across projects, such as differences in economic or social conditions or population characteristics among the neighborhoods where the projects were located. In fact, some critics have argued that the internal validity of Newman's initial findings was so poor as to destroy confidence in the theory, despite the impressive internal consistency of the configuration of architectural elements found to be related to crime rates in that study and the subsequent Brownsville–Van Dyke comparison, which showed similar relationships in the apparent absence of any differences in local conditions. Hillier (1973), in particular, dismissed the theory because of what he claimed to be evidence overlooked by Newman that the low-rise Van Dyke project had a more advantaged population, which might have accounted for its low crime rate compared with the high-rise Brownsville project across the street. Although a close inspection of the data reveals that Hillier was wrong – there simply were large numbers of Van Dyke residents for whom income data were missing, but other socioeconomic data indicated that those missing data probably were comparable to the data for Brownsville residents – the threats to the internal validity of Newman's initial findings must be considered serious.

However, the design modifications at Clason Point Gardens and in other defensible-space projects were based at least as much on defensible-space *theory* as on the empirical findings of Newman's research. And that theory has grown far beyond the boundaries of those early data. It has incorporated Newman's (1981) rather informal analysis of the success of street privatization in St. Louis, as well as the results of research by Newman and Franck (1982) and Taylor et al. (1980) that addressed directly the patterns of social behavior that mediate relationships between architectural features and crime-related outcomes, using powerful multiple-regression and path-analytic statistical techniques.

Along the way, the basic framework of defensible-space theory has accommodated many new elements suggested by empirical research, as well as continuing analyses of existing housing settings. Newman's focus shifted from project size and building height to the number of buildings sharing an entry and interior circulation area as a key determinant of the effective size of a project. His earlier endorsement of low-rise buildings on smaller sites has been enlarged to include clustering of buildings and segregation of residents of incompatible ages and life-styles in separate buildings on a single site. Feasible modifications have been designed for private residential and other settings, as well as public-housing projects.

Although much of this theory development postdates the Clason Point Gardens project, Newman's reliance on a larger vision, supported but not constrained by his early empirical findings, can be seen in his work there. Although building height was the single most influential architectural factor in the variability of crime rates across all projects, Newman's overall conceptualization of defensible space as a configuration of elements that together would have an impact on the likelihood of motivated surveillance by project residents made it possible to plan a crime-reduction design strategy for Clason Point Gardens despite the fact that all of its buildings were of two-story design.

Stage 4: Design elements

The plan for Clason Point Gardens emphasized four main design changes, all of them based on clear defensible-space images. Most of the open spaces immediately surrounding residents' homes would be attached to specific buildings as individual front lawns and fenced common rear yards, to eliminate a good deal of the public areas in which residents might find it difficult to take a proprietary interest. Paths would be reconstructed to better define public areas and would be lighted to facilitate surveillance after dark. Public areas, including paths and recreation areas, would be improved to increase residents' use of them, thereby increasing incidental surveillance opportunities. And the façades of residents' homes would be individualized and made more attractive to encourage proprietary feelings.

Stage 5: Overall design

In the case of Clason Point Gardens, the alterations in public-space allocations and amenities and in building appearance described earlier constituted the entire renovation design. The same could be said for the new electronic security arrangements at the Bronxdale high-rise project. In most of the crime-prevention projects outside of public-housing settings, such as those where planners used traffic-diversion schemes to make urban neighborhoods safer, the physical alterations to create more defensible spaces often were accompanied by organizational changes such as the mobilization of neighborhood residents and decentralization of police operations. In those latter cases, the expanding scope of defensible-space theory is evident. Behavioral mediators of architectural-design effects, the proximate causes of much of any reduction in crime that may take place, became increasingly important to the theory as it incorporated data from more methodologically sophisticated research and concepts from other environment–behavior theories. Rather than simply change the environmental features and expect crime-deterrent behaviors to follow, efforts to encourage those behaviors directly were included in latter-day CPTED plans.

Stage 6: POE

Newman's evaluation of the effects of the design changes implemented at Clason Point Gardens provided extensive evidence of multiple benefits, reflected in such indices as lowered crime rates, reductions in residents' fear of crime, and residents' increased efforts to maintain and improve their homes and, especially, the newly reassigned outdoor spaces surrounding them.

The POE conducted at Clason Point Gardens followed a familiar approach, comparing a variety of measures before and after implementation of a new design. In the absence of any comparison with other projects or a more comprehensive analysis of long series of measures, it is difficult to know whether or not other factors that could affect crime rates may have been introduced at that same time. However, in the absence of any rival hypothesis that carries, by virtue of supportive research evidence and the apparent success of other applications, the considerable weight of defensible-space theory, it seems plausible to attribute at least a significant portion of the changes in criminals' and residents' behaviors at Clason Point Gardens to the defensible-space modifications introduced there.

Stage 7: Future impact

According to the available evidence, the Clason Point Gardens project and the other defensible-space projects carried out by Newman's group, by Westinghouse, and by others have had a considerable positive impact on the lives of thousands of Americans that continues to this day. Defensible-space theory and the design guidelines based on it have been applied as widely (in terms of the size and variety of the settings and user populations involved) as any behaviorally based design or planning improvement idea. One practitioner in South Florida, Randy Atlas (1991), even helps police to cope with drug dealers' strategic use of nondefensible space to elude surveillance. Given its broad exposure, through Newman's books for commercial publishers (Newman, 1972, 1981), as well as the publications sponsored by various federal law-enforcement agencies (Newman, 1973a,b, 1975; Wallis & Ford, 1980a,b), it is difficult to gauge exactly how great an impact defensible-space theory has had on the design of housing and other settings, as well as on crime-prevention policy decisions. Whenever an idea has been disseminated as widely as this one, information about its influence on design projects and policy is brought to public notice in only a small proportion of cases.

Newman's work has also engaged the interest of environment–behavior scientists working on relevant basic environment–behavior relationships. In particular, analyses of territoriality by Taylor et al. (1980, 1984) have attempted to explicate the behavioral mechanism underlying crime-deterrent behaviors by residents of various housing settings. And Altman's (1975) distinction among primary, secondary, and public territories gives greater coherence to explanations for variations in crime-deterrent behaviors associated with spatial boundaries in residential settings.

Scientists like Taylor and Altman have been critical of defensible-space theory for its failure to incorporate more basic research and analysis like their own. Other researchers, working primarily in the field of criminology, have claimed that there is a substantial body of research findings that contradict Newman's theory (e.g., Mayhew et al., 1980; Baldwin, 1975; Mawby, 1977; Sturman, 1980). With fair consistency, those studies have found that crimes (including vandalism, assault, and robbery) that occur in public places, such as buses, telephone booths, and streets in shopping and entertainment districts, are unrelated to opportunities for surveillance by passersby, nearby residents, or those who work in and around those locations.

Those latter critics can be answered quite simply: The sites in which their studies were carried out were not spatially related to people's homes. Therefore, according to defensible-space theory, at any rate, there is no reason to have expected the people present at such sites to have adopted proprietary attitudes toward any of them, or to have attempted to protect them, or to have exerted control over the behaviors that took place in them. Although surveillance is a key feature of defensible-space theory, it is just one feature of a complex theory. Newman never claimed that any place that could be better seen would necessarily be better protected. Only when the observers can claim special rights in a given place will they defend it against intruders and enforce norms for the behaviors of those who use it. Perhaps these misdirected criticisms are best taken as an indication of the need for a more explicit account of the behavioral mechanisms underlying the deterrent effect of defensible space that Taylor, Altman, and others have pointed out.

Although the theory of defensible space has been criticized for its failure to specify adequately the underlying behavioral mechanisms, and particularly for its lack of articulation with established theories that address relevant behaviors, as well as for its failure to account for some existing data, it is bolstered against those criticisms by the large and varied archive of demonstration projects in which the application of defensible-space principles has been shown to reduce crime rates. The results from Clason Point Gardens and Asylum Hill are particularly impressive. The replication of positive findings in different types of settings in different places at different times argues against coincidental changes in economic or political conditions, or other extraneous factors influencing crime rates, as plausible rival explanations, even though the research designs used in the individual POEs do not rule them out. And the diversity of populations and settings, and the use of nonreactive data-collection techniques that leave undisturbed those whose behaviors are being assessed, would seem to leave the external validity of the evidence beyond reasonable doubt. In the end, it is the scope and effectiveness of these interventions, no doubt attributable in large part to Newman's background as an architect, with an overriding concern for the practicality of ideas, that speak loudest for the value of defensible-space theory to the design and planning fields.

Even if one is persuaded, on balance, of the validity and utility of Newman's analysis, it should be pointed out that efforts to deter crime through defensible-space design principles fail to deal with the problem of crime displacement. Successful creation of defensible spaces may merely drive criminals to other sites and different victims. Some criminologists (Repetto, 1976; Phillips, 1980) believe that the potential for displacement is limited, but it seems clear that crime prevention through environmental design is directed primarily toward protecting a specific site. It is not a strategy for dealing with the root causes of crime, merely some of the factors that create opportunities for crime.

Still, whatever its limitations, Newman's work has had widespread influence. The concept of defensible space has become part of the vernacular of students of environment–behavior relationships, as well as designers. Most of the recent research to explore the relationships between the designs of environmental settings and their vulnerabilities to crime, as well as such basic environment–behavior mechanisms as territoriality, has been influenced to some extent by Newman's work. And in public housing and private neighborhoods, as well as in stores and schools in cities across this country, people are living in places that are safer for the work begun by Newman and carried on with the help of many others.

References

Altman, I. (1975). *The environment and social behavior*. Monterey, CA: Brooks/Cole.

Atlas, R. (1991, March). Defensible space: Obstruction of law enforcement through environmental design. *Security Management*.

Baldwin, J. (1975). Urban criminality and the "problem" estate. *Local Government Studies, 1,* 12–20.

Brower, S., Dockett, K., & Taylor, R. D. (1983). Residents' perceptions of territorial features and perceived local threat. *Environment and Behavior, 15,* 419–437.

Brown, B. B., & Altman, I. (1983). Territoriality, defensible space and residential burglary: An environmental analysis. *Journal of Environmental Psychology, 3,* 203–220.

Fowler, F. J., Jr. (1981). Evaluating a complex crime control experiment. In L. Bickman (Ed.), *Applied social psychology annual* (Vol. 2, pp. 165–187). Beverly Hills, CA: Sage.

Fowler, F. J., Jr., McCalla, M. E., & Mangione, T. W. (1979). *Reducing residential crime and fear: The Hartford neighborhood crime prevention program. Executive summary*. Washington, DC: National Institute of Law Enforcement and Criminal Justice.

Greenberg, S. W., Rohe, W. M., & Williams, J. R. (1982). Safety in urban neighborhoods. *Population and Environment, 5,* 141–165.

Hillier, W. (1973, November). In defense of space. *RIBA Journal*, pp. 539–544.

Jacobs, J. (1961). *The death and life of great American cities*. New York: Vintage Books.

Kushmuk, J., & Whittemore, S. L. (1981). *Re-evaluation of crime prevention through environmental design in Portland, Oregon – Executive Summary*. Portland, OR: Portland Office of Justice, Planning and Evaluation.

Mawby, R. I. (1977). Kiosk vandalism. *British Journal of Criminology, 17,* 30–46.

Mayhew, P., Clarke, R. V. G., Hough, J. M., & Winchester, S. W. C. (1980). Natural surveillance and vandalism to telephone kiosks. In R. V. G. Clarke & P. Mayhew (Eds.), *Designing out crime* (pp. 67–74). London: Her Majesty's Stationery Office.

Molumby, T. (1976). Patterns of crime in a university housing project. *American Behavioral Scientist, 20,* 247–259.

Murray, C., Motoyama, T., Rouse, W. V., & Rubenstein, H. (1980). *Link between crime and the built environment – the current state of knowledge,* Vol. 1. Washington, DC: U.S. Government Printing Office.

Newman, O. (1972). *Defensible space.* New York: Macmillan.

Newman, O. (1973a). *Architectural design for crime prevention.* Washington, DC: U.S. Government Printing Office.

Newman, O. (1973b). *Design guide for improving residential security.* Washington, DC: U.S. Government Printing Office.

Newman, O. (1975). *Design guidelines for creating defensible space.* Washington, DC: U.S. Government Printing Office.

Newman, O. (1981). *Community of interest.* Garden City, NY: Anchor Books.

Newman, O., & Franck, K. (1982). The effects of building size on crime and fear of crime. *Population and Environment, 5,* 203–220.

Phillips, P. D. (1980). Characteristics and typology of the journey to crime. In D. E. Georges-Abeyie & K. D. Harries (Eds.), *Crime: A spatial perspective* (pp. 167–180). New York: Columbia University Press.

Repetto, T. A. (1976). Crime prevention and the displacement phenomenon. *Crime and Delinquency, 22,* 166–177.

Rouse, W. V., & Rubenstein, H. (1978). *Crime in public housing: A review of major issues and selected crime reduction strategies. Volume I: A report.* Washington, DC: U.S. Government Printing Office.

Sturman, A. (1980). Damage on bases: The effects of supervision. In R. V. G. Clarke & P. Mayhew (Eds.), *Designing out crime* (pp. 31–38). London: Her Majesty's Stationery Office.

Taylor, R. B., Gottfredson, S. D., & Brower, S. (1980). The defensibility of defensible space: A critical review and a synthetic framework for future research. In T. Hirshi & M. Gottfredson (Eds.), *Understanding crime* (pp. 53–71). Beverly Hills, CA: Sage.

Taylor, R. B., Gottfredson, S. D., & Brower, S. (1984). Block crime and fear: Defensible space, local social ties, and territorial functioning. *Journal of Research in Crime and Delinquency, 21,* 303–331.

Wallis, A., & Ford, D. (Eds.) (1980a). *Crime prevention through environmental design: The commercial demonstration in Portland, Oregon. Executive Summary.* Washington, DC: National Institute of Justice.

Wallis, A., & Ford, D. (1980b). *Crime prevention through environmental design.* Columbia, MD: Westinghouse National Issues Center.

Westinghouse National Issues Center (1977). *CPTED annotated bibliography.* Arlington, VA: author.

12

CIUDAD MODELA DE LA UNIVERSIDAD CATOLICA (MACUL), CHILE

Location: Santiago, Chile
Participants: Joseph J. Valadez and Esmee Bellalta (design and research)

In 1969, when contemplating a gradual move from the center of Santiago to a suburban site, the Catholic University of Chile commissioned a plan for a new suburban residential community for many of its employees. The far-reaching goal was a community in which employees at all levels, from administration and faculty to clerical and maintenance personnel, would live together. Even the blatant realities of differing incomes and family sizes would be reflected only minimally in three different styles of single-family houses and two styles of multiple-family dwellings that were to be built side by side in the "Ciudad Modela de la Universidad Catolica," nicknamed Macul after the hilly region nearby.

The heightened consciousness about social issues reflected in the objectives for Macul was matched by a sensitivity to the importance of environmental design and a commitment to a research-based approach to it. The staff that was assembled to plan Macul included not only architects but also an EDR team composed of a Chilean landscape architect, Esmee Bellalta, and an American sociologist, Joseph Valadez, who had together taught a course in urban ecology at the university. Bellalta and Valadez worked to develop a plan for a substantial part of the Macul community that was intended to make use of environmental-design features that past research had shown to foster community development, to draw together the disparate elements of the new community, while at the same time investigating further in Macul the relationship between environmental design and community development. That plan itself drew together a number of disparate elements, "islands of theory" as Valadez has referred to them: the use of the plaza as a design element, thus adapting a traditional cultural form to help unify the residents; sociological and psychological research on the effects of housing design on friendship formation in neighborhoods; social-psychological research on the motivating effects of participation in environmental design on acceptance and involvement on the part of the users of the setting; and Donald Campbell's (1969)

221

concept of "reform as experiment" to use the community as a living laboratory where theories could be tested empirically.

In the end, the plan developed by Bellalta and Valadez helped to shape the living environments of the families in Macul and provided an empirical test of their theory that validated a number of their underlying assumptions and demonstrated important methodological innovations as well (Valadez & Bellalta, 1984; Valadez, 1982/83).

The theory behind the behavior-based design for Macul

The design and research plans for Macul had their origins in studies of the development of relationships among neighbors. Social psychologists in the United States and urban sociologists in England had carried out studies of actual communities in which the layout of the physical environment – the distances between dwellings and the orientations of dwellings to one another – has been shown to be an important determinant of friendship choices and the level of interaction among neighbors.

One of the earliest of those studies was conducted by Festinger, Schachter, and Back (1950). They studied the development of friendships among married World War II veterans who had become students at Massachusetts Institute of Technology (MIT) and had moved into two university-owned housing projects as complete strangers to one another. Based mostly on interviews with the students' wives, it was found in both projects – one (Westgate) consisting mostly of one-story duplex houses arranged around grassy courts, and the other (Westgate West) consisting of 10-unit two-story apartment buildings – that the families' best friends came most often from among their closest neighbors. The distance from doorway to doorway was a strong predictor of friendship choices. In addition, there were seemingly trivial locational features that made some families more popular than others with their neighbors. In the duplex courts of Westgate, a small number of houses faced away from the others, toward surrounding streets. Their occupants were named far less often as friends by other residents of their courts. In Westgate West, the apartment project, residents of apartments near the outdoor stairways and gang mailboxes in each building were more popular than the other residents.

Festinger and associates interpreted their findings in a way that has influenced most other researchers in this field. They argued that the architectural layout forced some residents into repeated contacts with one another and that these "passive contacts" led to the formation of friendships. They also went beyond the empirical description of a simple architectural determinism to interpret its consequences on the basis of qualitative observations about life in Westgate and Westgate West. They credited the overall enhancement of group formation due to both the physical design of the projects and the homogeneity and common interests of their resident populations with making two important contributions to the quality of life there. First, they observed a high level of satisfaction with the housing itself, despite the fact that it was shoddily built and subject to leaky roofs, drafty conditions in winter, and muddy yards. Second, residents showed a high level of community participation, especially in Westgate West, where a strong tenants' organization was formed by residents initially concerned about possible problems with fire protection. For these reasons, Festinger and associates became convinced that group formation should be encouraged by intentionally designing residential communities with architectural and planning features that would force passive contacts among neighbors, which would lead to individual friendships and, through them, to community development.

Merton (1951) conducted a similar study at almost the same time, in a housing development in New Jersey to which he gave the pseudonym Craftown. Seven hundred families lived in owner-occupied multiple-family housing in Craftown. The friendships that were formed within the community were strongly influenced, as at MIT, by the distances between people's homes and the layout of homes in the community. For example, for each resident, approximately 2.5% of the total population of the community lived in that resident's own building, in the buildings immediately next door, or in the buildings directly across the street. By contrast, residents identified 54% of their close friends among those closest neighbors. Among friendships between across-the-street neighbors, a finding emerged that was reminiscent of some of the observations of Festinger and associates about dwelling and street layout. For some reason, perhaps a desire for visual relief or complexity, some of the buildings in Craftown had been built facing directly on the street, with their front entrances opening on the street, whereas others had been built at right angles to the street, with front entrances opening onto a private court. Of the 82 across-the-street friendships reported, 74% were between residents whose front entrances both opened directly on the street and directly faced each other. Of the rest, 22% were between pairs in which just one building faced directly on the street, and only 4% were between pairs whose doorways were both off the street.

Although his findings were quite similar to those of Festinger and associates, Merton made an even stronger plea that knowledge about architectural and planning influences on friendship formation be used in housing design. He pointed out the increasing prevalence of planned housing developments in both the public and private sectors. Compared with "crescive" housing development, in which homes are added to neighborhoods one or a few at a time without any overall coordination, planned communities can permit the use of social-science knowledge about the effects of housing policy on the lives of individual families, as well as on community development, in the planning process. In addition, Merton pointed out that his findings had identified important design and planning variables whose influences were outside the awareness of the residents of Craftown. This highlights the importance of remote observational data, in addition to surveys of prospective residents who might take such influential factors as building and neighborhood layout for granted.

Further corroboration of the effects of dwelling location on friendship formation comes from a study by Caplow and Forman (1950). In University Village, a housing project for married veteran students with children at the University of Minnesota, 25 duplex buildings were separated into groups of five by lanes or paths running between them and connecting surrounding streets. Friendship choices among the families were higher among the 10 residents in each lane than between them and neighbors from the nearest contiguous lane, even though the families that shared each duplex building lived in different lanes. This is a dramatic example where physical distance was far less important than functional distance, which apparently concentrated passive social contacts among residents who used the same lane to enter and leave the project.

Influenced by these social-psychological studies carried out in the United States in the late 1940s, several urban sociologists subsequently investigated similar hypotheses in planned communities that arose as part of the effort to rebuild Britain after the destruction of so much of its housing during World War II. For example, Kuper (1953) replicated the earlier findings of functional distance among residents in a more heterogeneous community of single-family homes. In addition to extending the validity of those findings beyond homogeneous resident populations, he took into account residents' attitudes toward close relationships with their neighbors, rather than assuming a universal preference. Significantly, he found that families that favored a reserved rather than sociable relationship with neighbors actually disliked architectural features such as facing side entrances that forced passive social contacts between them and their neighbors.

In a later study, Carey and Mapes (1972) found that individual family characteristics such as age, wife's work status, and children were the most important determinants of friendship formation in heterogeneous housing developments in the private sector. However, despite the lack of a clear contrast in the area of architectural and planning features, they did find that similar families were more likely to become friends when their homes were near one another and oriented toward one another in a way that facilitated contact (e.g., on a cul-de-sac). Michelson (1977), in a large-scale study of housing choice and satisfaction in Toronto, Canada, also found that family characteristics were of great importance in understanding residents' behaviors.

Bellalta and Valadez used this body of research findings as the basis for their contribution to the design of Macul. They worked on the assumption that friendships within a community are desirable for their effects on satisfaction of individual residents, as well as on community development, and that a heterogeneous population such as that planned for Macul might be less likely to pursue such relationships spontaneously. They utilized a local architectural form, the "plazoleta," as a mechanism to encourage friendship-building contacts among neighbors. In the Chilean culture, this small plaza, or common space around which a small number of houses are located was far more familiar than the cul-de-sac of American or British residential developments. Further, the design of each plazoleta was left unfinished, for the owners to design, in order to foster contact among neighbors. It was a ready "excuse" for friendships to form and community development to occur. One little-known finding of the seminal study by Festinger and associates was that community development in the student-housing projects for married veterans at MIT was much more extensive in Westgate West, which had not been finished when it was first occupied, thus posing problems that residents needed to solve cooperatively, than in Westgate, whose residents had no such problems. Finally, the plan for Macul included three different plazoleta types that varied in privacy or the extent to which the owners were given a separate group identity by the physical setting. That made it possible to study whether or not the plazoleta would function in Macul in the same way as the courts of Westgate, the buildings of Westgate West, the facing front doors in Craftown, or the lanes in University Village, to help create social groups among the residents, rather than merely assuming that those earlier findings from other cultures and other resident populations could appropriately be generalized to Macul.

The physical plan for Macul

The model city of Macul was designed for almost 1,600 families. Several types of housing were provided. There were single-family houses of a variety of sizes and designs, with private gardens approximately 23 feet square, and there were one-, two-, and three-story multiple-family or apartment complexes. There were also open spaces for recreation, as well as schools and commercial facilities.

Valadez and Bellalta's work focused on 240 single-family dwellings that were clustered in groups of eight around 30 communal open spaces or plazoletas that measured approximately 75 feet square. Most of those houses were of an L-shaped design, with their private gardens occupying the remaining corner of their rectangular lots, separated from the plazoleta and adjacent houses and gardens by wooden privacy fences.

All of the plazoletas were identical in most respects. Each was owned jointly by the owners of the adjoining houses. The surface was covered with sufficient topsoil to permit planting. The only amenities supplied at the time of initial construction were three saplings in large planters and a low, movable wall that described an arc of 270° in the center of the plaza.

The 30 plazoletas did differ, however, in one significant respect. That was the degree of access that non–plaza residents were afforded by the location and design of the plazoleta and the houses of its owners. None was entirely enclosed by the adjoining houses, and the relationship of plazoleta to the surrounding larger community took three different forms (with minor variations in each). See Figure 12.1 for schematic diagrams of the basic plazoleta and the three plazoleta configurations.

The most private or isolated plazoletas each had one entrance beyond the direct access provided from each of the owners' houses. The only gap in the enclosure of the plazoleta by the adjoining houses and their private gardens was this single separate entrance located at the end of an alley that ran between nearby apartments that separated the plazoleta from a nearby street. There were 14 of these one-entrance plazas in Macul.

Seven of the remaining plazas had two separate entrances in addition to direct access from each owner's house. One entrance was at the end of a passage between adjacent apartments. The second was at the end of a street that provided access within the large block or sector where the plaza was located. This internal street within the sector had sidewalks that carried pedestrian traffic among the clusters of neighborhood houses. Thus, the two-entrance plazoleta design made it possible to use the plaza as an element in a walking path through the neighborhood, between the arterial streets that defined blocks or sectors. This design, therefore, provided greater potential access to the plaza by nonresidents, or less isolation from the surrounding neighborhood.

Nine of the 30 plazoletas were even less isolated. One or two sides of these plazas (seven and two of each, respectively) bordered arterial streets running through the neighborhood.These open-sided plazas were located alongside major auto and pedestrian routes, open to visual and physical access by nonresidents and routinely made available to large numbers of passersby.

Plazoletas and community development

The clustering of 240 residences in Macul around 30 plazoletas was significant on a number of levels. First, it gave part of the new community a traditional form that provided continuity with the local culture and history. The design of Spanish-American towns around plazas is a widespread and long-standing custom.

Second, it provided residents of the plaza clusters additional outdoor space, which is valued highly in Santiago. Because of climate and custom, families spend a good deal of their leisure time outdoors. Spontaneous visits among families are common, and outdoor garden spaces are the preferred locations for entertaining visitors.

But the form of the plazoletas was an even more significant element in the

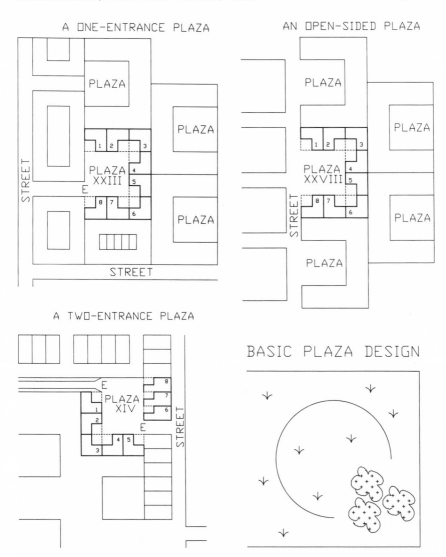

Figure 12.1. The generic plazoleta design, and the three plazoleta configurations. The one-entrance plazoleta is the most private, with access from the eight owners' houses and one additional dead-end entrance from an adjacent street or walkway. The two-entrance design connects two outside entrances, thus completing a potential path through the neighborhood and reducing the owners' privacy in its use. The open-sided plazoleta adjoins a neighborhood street, and is the most public of the three designs. Diagrams by Tamra Leible for author.

plans for Macul. First, they were purposely left in a rather primitive or undeveloped state. The intention of the designers, particularly those with a strong interest in the behavioral implications of the design, was to facilitate the social integration of the community by providing communal spaces whose optimal utilization would depend on the cooperative efforts of their users. It was left up to the owners to plan and implement improvements in the physical facility, based on their needs and preferences for its use. Whereas all residents of Macul shared a common affiliation with Catholic University, at the same time they were all newcomers to Macul, coming from disparate socioeconomic backgrounds. Valadez and Bellalta saw the creation of a need to cooperate in the completion of the plazoletas as a mechanism to encourage community development.

At the same time, the variation in plaza form provided the basis for a rigorous evaluation of the intended role of the plazoletas in community development. Borrowing Donald Campbell's (1969) concept that social reforms should be treated as experiments, Valadez and Bellalta used the three variations in plaza design – one-entrance, two-entrance, and open-sided (one or two sides) – as a basis for testing the hypothesis that leaving to residents the task of completing the design and construction of their common outdoor space would facilitate community development. If this were true, they reasoned, it should be possible to find evidence of differences in the rates and types of development across the three types of plazas, as a function of their relative degrees of isolation or privacy or accessibility to residents outside the group of owners of adjoining houses and the plaza itself. They believed that more privacy in the plazoleta should facilitate the cooperation needed among neighbors, thus increasing the rate of development. It should also lead to the use of designs that would emphasize use of the plazoleta by the owners themselves. Thus, Valadez and Bellalta incorporated the design feature of open space that would be owned in common by those who lived around it and would be left unfinished for its owners to design and build, with the expectation that this physical feature would favorably influence the course of community development. And they did so in a way that created a basis for testing their specific application of the more general effects of participation on social integration.

The quasi-experiment in Macul

The policies that were established for Catholic University personnel to purchase homes in Macul gave Valadez and Bellalta confidence that they would be justified in attributing differences in the rates and forms of plaza development to the degree of external access. Borrowing another concept from Donald Campbell (Campbell & Stanley, 1963), they characterized their investigation as a quasi-experiment. That implied that the groups of residents whose developments of their plazas were to be compared would be sufficiently similar to one another to make the results of that comparison a valid test of the hypothesis.

Each family chose the type and location of its home from a plan without any knowledge of who had chosen or would choose the adjoining properties. There seemed to Valadez and Bellalta to be no reason to believe that families' choices would be related to their preconceptions about nonresidents' accessibility to the plaza where their homes would be located, at least not in any way that would result in systematic differences between the groups of residents of houses adjoining one-entrance, two-entrance, and open-sided plazas. In addition, houses of different sizes were mixed together within the plazoleta-based clusters, greatly reducing the likelihood that different plazoleta types would be developed by groups of owners from different backgrounds.

It would also be possible to use measures of the development of each family's private garden to check on the possibility that there had been initial differences among groups of residents associated with the different types of plazas. Finally, demographic data about the families that were to be collected in interviews could be used to rule out or analyze the effects of such differences.

The data for this quasi-experiment were to be provided mainly by periodic photographic records of the development of the 30 plazoletas and the private gardens of their owners. These photographs were to be rated by landscape architects for the degree and type of development that were evident, compared with the original state of the plaza. Their ratings could then be used to make comparisons among plaza types and between plazas and gardens and to examine relationships with resident characteristics.

The relationship between spatial form and community development in Macul

The outcome of the design experiment in Macul was evaluated on the basis of ratings of the degree and type of development in each plaza, the ratings being made from color slides taken approximately one, two, and three years after construction, by Esmee Bellalta, the landscape architect who helped plan the project. The designs developed by residents were assigned to one of three categories. "Garden plazas" resembled private gardens in their style and usage. They were informal and were devoted mainly to growing flowers and vegetables. "Formal gardens" resembled public plazas in their use of more exotic plants, statuary, and seating for visitors. The third category consisted of miscellaneous designs or mixtures of the garden and formal designs. The ratings were made by eight landscape architects in the United States who were unaware of the plan for Macul or the hypotheses being tested. The interrater reliabilities calculated from their ratings indicated significant agreement for both types of ratings, but considerably greater agreement on degree of development ($.72$, $p < .001$) than on type of development ($.44$, $p < .01$). The discrepancy may reflect the fact that one of the three categories for type of development was essentially a miscellaneous or indeterminate category.

There was evidence that the plazas were developed by their owners during the period of the study. The correlation between date of assessment and degree of development was $.32$ ($p < .05$) for all 30 plazoletas. However, this modest relationship for the entire sample of plazas obscured differences in the progress of development among the three plaza types. The linear increase in development over time was highly significant ($r = .69$, $p < .01$) in the one-entrance plazas, but there was essentially no such trend in either the two-entrance or open-sided plazas (correlations of $-.12$ and $.09$, respectively; neither significantly different from zero).

There was also evidence of a relationship between the design of a plaza and the type of development chosen by its owners. Of the 14 one-entrance plazas, 8 were found to have developed in one of the two definable types: garden and formal civic. Of those, a clear majority of six were garden plazas. Among the seven two-entrance plazas, four followed the two clear types. Three of those were formal civic, and the remaining one was garden. Among the nine open-sided plazas, two were developed as garden plazas, and three as formal civic, with the remaining ones being of neither distinctive type. Although these patterns are not strikingly clear (a χ^2 analysis applied retrospectively to the data showed no significant deviation from a random distribution in the plaza-design–development-type matrix, probably in large part because of the fact that 40% of the total fell into the miscellaneous category), Valadez and Bellalta concluded that one-entrance plazas, because of their high degree of privacy from intrusions by outsiders, were more likely to be developed as garden plazas. Their owners would plant common local species of plants, and even grow vegetables, without much regard for how much outsiders might admire the results. Two-entrance plazas were more likely than one-entrance plazas to be developed as formal civic plazas. The fact that people from the surrounding neighborhood would occasionally take advantage of the design to use the plaza as part of a footpath from one place to another may have led the plaza's owners to choose more exotic and more impressive species of plants and to provide benches and other furniture that outsiders could admire or even use to rest during their walks.

Despite the fact that the quantity and clarity of their research data seem to pale beside the theoretical and practical significance of their project, Valadez and Bellalta were able to claim objective evidence for the efficacy of the plazoleta design and at the same time to add modestly to the body of evidence and theory on which it was based. They did provide evidence that the plazoleta was a basis for community development among the residents of Macul. The plazoleta seems to have functioned as a device that encouraged social contact among neighbors and, through its unfinished character, to have further encouraged cooperative goal-directed effort on their part. In addition, the extent to which those functions were realized depended to some extent on the degree of privacy afforded by the place of the plazoleta in the larger community plan. The most private design – the one-entrance plaza – seemed to facilitate the cooperative effort among co-owners referred to by Valadez as community development and to encourage that development along a course dictated more by the needs of the developers or owners than by concern for others' reactions, in the form of the garden plaza.

This evidence, modest as it may seem by the usual standards of social-science research, still serves to corroborate past findings and to substantiate their value in environmental design and planning. The plazoleta seems to have influenced contacts and the development of relationships among neighbors in much the same way as the courts of Westgate, the cul-de-sac of British residential developments, and the across-the-street orientation of buildings in Craftown. In addition, the inference that community development in Westgate West had been spurred by the unfinished state of the environment received some corroboration from the success of the unfinished design of plazoletas in Macul, as reflected in the evidence of development by their co-owners. Not only is the evidence that one-entrance plazas were the only group to show significant development over time and that owners of those plazas were most likely to develop them as garden plazas consistent with the theoretical arguments favored by Bellalta and Valadez, but also the direct comparisons of different levels of privacy for degree and type of development constitute, with Kuper's work in England, a rare evaluation of the specific design features associated with the development of relationships among neighbors.

Evaluation

Stage 1: Background analysis

Valadez and Bellalta's analysis of the local conditions in Macul was important to the development of their plans for the project in several ways. The most obvious example was their recognition that the plazoleta was an indigenous form that would be appropriate for the role of fostering contacts among neighbors in Macul, a role that had been played by the cul-de-sac and the other European and North American designs that had been studied in previous research. The use of the plazoleta was consistent with the preference for communal use of public spaces in Latin America, attributable to the Spanish influence there. Whereas people in other cultures often seek privacy for themselves, for their family unit, or for other immediate social groups in parks, restaurants, and other public places, Hispanic culture values interactions among larger groups that tend to be accommodated in larger, accessible spaces such as the plazoleta. In addition, the recognition of local customs that favored outdoor dining and entertaining made clear the importance of providing residents with private gardens in addition to the communal plazoletas.

Thus, although the general principle of incorporating a layout that would promote incidental social contacts among neighbors was adopted from earlier research conducted elsewhere, it was adapted to the special needs of the people of Macul, based on analysis of their Hispanic cultural heritage and of the local customs in Santiago's particular geographic/climatic setting.

Stage 2: Behavioral goals

The ultimate goal of Valadez and Bellalta's plans for Macul was to enhance community development. In the case of Macul, that required the social integration of people from disparate backgrounds who shared a common affiliation with the Catholic University. To bring about that end, they sought to promote cooperative contacts among groups of immediate neighbors by providing them with a public space that they would own in common and whose utilization would depend on their joint decisions and efforts. Although "neighboring" is no less a simple, unambiguous response than is crime reduction or a lowering of crowding stress, its measurement in terms of the degree and type of plaza development seemed somewhat indirect by comparison with the behaviors used as indicators of those latter constructs. Those measures caused some problems for Valadez and Bellalta, although they were advantageous in other respects.

Stage 3: Environment–behavior relationships

The relationship between functional proximity among neighbors (a combination of the distances and orientations between their homes) and the development of friendships among them had been well established in quasi-experimental studies conducted in a variety of settings, from American college campuses to British "new towns." Although individual studies may have failed to rule out alternative explanations, such as differences among the resident groups in the locations compared within a particular community, the size and consistency of the total data base provided by those studies leave little doubt about the causal role of location in neighboring and friendship formation. It seems quite clear that neighbors whose homes are located such that they are likely to have frequent unintended contacts with one another are more likely to interact voluntarily and become friends than are those who face different locational relationships.

Furthermore, the data on which those comparisons have been based (mutual reports of interaction and identification of friends by residents of a community) seem unlikely to have been influenced by respondents' perceptions of the researchers' intent. Without specific knowledge of the researchers' hypotheses about the effects of particular locational features within their community, residents would be hard-pressed to provide hypothesis-confirming data, even if they were motivated to do so.

Finally, the diversity of settings and populations among which those studies were conducted makes the relationships they uncovered seem relatively robust across variations in housing type (from student apartments to private homes on culs-de-sac), geography (from the banks of the Charles River to the suburbs of London), and resident characteristics (from college students to middle-class families).

However, it should be pointed out that Valadez and Bellalta's goals for the residents of Macul went beyond the kind of friendship formation studied in that earlier research. Because of the nature of the community and perhaps because of their own values, Valadez and Bellalta sought to promote community development on a larger scale, among the group of eight families surrounding each of the plazoletas, or even beyond, in the community as a whole.

Of course, Valadez and Bellalta relied secondarily on other "islands" of empirically supported theory as well. Those included the well-established influence of participation on social change, a principle that dates back to the social psychologist Kurt Lewin (1958) and that has been shown to be valid in his research as well as in recent applications to the design process (cf. Sanoff, 1990). They also included Campbell's (1969) model for carrying out incremental social change in a way that can facilitate systematic evaluation of its effects.

In sum, Valadez and Bellalta built upon established, mainstream social science in formulating their plans for Macul. Their approach maintained ties to well-established theories that incorporated extensive, consistent, and reliable empirical findings. It also emphasized the use of those theories in a way that would repay their contributions in the form of new data to continue their development.

Stage 4: Plan elements

It is not clear how much influence Valadez and Bellalta were able to exert on the actual configuration of spaces in the one neighborhood or sector they studied in Macul. The decisions to cluster houses in groups of eight around plazoletas, and the variations in plazoleta design that were associated with their relationships to surrounding streets, probably were made by architects and planners without consulting Valadez and Bellalta. However, they did contribute the decision to provide the plazoletas in an unfinished form that was amenable to completion by the residents themselves. And that may have been the most important element of all from their point of view – that of encouraging community development.

Valadez and Bellalta also contributed the valuable conceptual scheme that differentiated among the plaza types in a way that made it possible to evaluate the causes of community development in Macul. By recognizing the functional implications for community development of the variations in plaza design, by grouping them in three categories that were ordered on the basis of their openness to those beyond the immediate circle of owners, they were able to set the stage for a more systematic and useful analysis of the owners' responses.

Stage 5: Overall plan

The sector of Macul in which Valadez and Bellalta conducted their planning experiment constituted less than one-sixth of the entire community, represented only one of several housing types used in Macul, and included none of the community's larger public areas. Even within that one sector, the plazoleta and its relationship to the houses surrounding it composed just one element of the overall design. The arrangement of connecting streets and the relationships among plazoleta clusters were taken as givens by Valadez and Bellalta as the background for their work. Their role in developing the overall plan for Macul was relatively minor in scope and was carried out in virtual isolation from other planning decisions. It probably should not be surprising that the type of social experiment they carried out would occupy a peripheral role in the overall plan for a project such as Macul, where decisions had to be made about costs, transportation, utilities, and so many other basic problems.

Stage 6: POE

The evaluation of the role of the plazoleta in community development in Macul, along with a comparison among the three plazoleta designs, was an integral part of the Valadez and Bellalta project. The finding that the plazas were developed over time by their owners suggests that they succeeded in fostering cooperative effort or community development. The finding that the one-entrance plazas, the most private of the designs, were developed faster and further and more often in the form of private gardens, whereas owners of two-entrance plazas more often developed more formal public spaces, provides more support for Valadez and Bellalta's hypotheses. However, both findings must be evaluated in the light of a number of methodological issues.

Valadez and Bellalta described their POE study as quasi-experimental, comparing three nonrandomly constituted groups of plazas and owners. Unfortunately, the impossibility of obtaining prior measures of plaza develop-

(no development was possible prior to the study) rendered it a preexperimental or correlational study that left open questions about the initial comparability of the three groups of residents. Although residents chose the locations of their homes from a map, without any knowledge of their future neighbors, it must have been obvious to them at that time that the sites of the plazoletas would vary considerably in the degree of privacy they would afford from passersby and traffic. It is possible, therefore, that those who chose to live closer to major traffic arteries, around open-sided plazas, had different attitudes toward neighboring or had fewer children in their families than those who chose more private locations around one-entrance plazas. Earlier findings that homeowners' sociable or reserved attitudes toward neighboring (Kuper, 1953) and family structure (Carey & Mapes, 1972) mediate locational effects on friendship formation suggest that owners of houses around different plaza types may have been differently predisposed toward community development. However, the effects of such differences, if they existed, are unclear. If the more reserved people chose to live around the more private one-entrance plazas, it would seem that they would have been less likely to join in cooperative development plans with neighbors – the opposite of what actually occurred. On the other hand, families with more children may also have chosen the more private locations, but been more eager to join their neighbors in developing their plazoleta. In short, the possibility of a selection bias exists, but it is not clear that it would invalidate Valadez and Bellalta's findings.

Other factors also complicate inferences about cause and effect in this POE study, although the likelihood of the potential bias is less clear in these cases. First, political unrest in Chile at the time of this project caused a disruption in the construction schedule for Macul. If occupancy rates were uneven across the three types of plazoletas, development may have been favored in one or more. Second, if the same political events caused financial difficulties for some of the homeowners in the section of Macul studied by Valadez and Bellalta, they may have been forced to rent their homes rather than live there themselves. If this was more common in some locations than in others, the different rates of development may reflect the different actions of homeowners and renters, rather than simply the effects of plazoleta design.

Other than those questions about the comparability of groups of residents, raised by rather typical problems in large-scale projects such as Macul that researchers can do little about, the classification scheme for types of plaza designs that resulted in such a large miscellaneous category made statistical analysis of the results difficult and should have been improved while the study was in progress. The use of sequential photographs of plazas as sources of data had the advantage of being unobtrusive, not subject to response biases on the part of residents, but it may have contributed to ambiguity about the outcome.

In sum, the results of Valadez and Bellalta's outcome research in Macul are favorable to the project and to their theoretical hypotheses if taken at face value. Difficulties in doing that are attributable in large part to the researchers' lack of control over the arrangements that produced the comparisons they needed to make.

Stage 7: Future impact

Other than a workshop at the 1982 Environmental Design Research Association conference at the University of Maryland (Valadez & Bellalta, 1982), at which, unfortunately, Valadez was the only project participant able to attend, and two somewhat obscure journal articles (Valadez, 1982/83; Valadez & Bellalta, 1984), little information about Macul has been made public. Beyond the residents of that community who participated in the project (a not inconsiderable number of people), its impact has been quite limited to date.

It is to be hoped that this report will bring several potentially important lessons from Macul to a wider audience, particularly to those interested in the use of design and planning to foster development of a sense of community in the absence of traditional mechanisms such as leadership by long-term residents, established institutions, and common backgrounds and interests among community members. One such lesson is that it is possible to make use of existing social-science data and theory from a variety of sources in the development of design and planning solutions. In this case, knowledge about the relationship between the locational features of homes and the social ties that develop among their residents, the role of participation in the acceptance of social change, and the use of "experimental" approaches to implementation of social policy prompted Valadez and Bellalta to leave plazoletas unfinished and to arrange, in their plans for Macul, to compare outcomes in different plazoleta designs.

A second important lesson to be learned from Macul is that it is possible to import general theories of environment–behavior relationships into a culture that is far different from those in which the theories were developed. Although siting homes so that residents will share a lane or a cul-de-sac may be an effective means of fostering incidental social contacts and eventual community development among neighbors in America or Britain, planning for a community in Chile required consideration of the local culture and climate. Nonetheless, it was possible to create analogous environmental arrangements, the plazoletas in Macul, that actually took advantage of local customs to make the general principles work well there.

Additionally, the case of Macul points out the need to reconsider the types of amenities that will be provided for residents of new communities, or perhaps even established ones. It may be more desirable to provide smaller-scale facilities shared among fewer residents who live directly around them (and to leave much of the work of completing those facilities to the neighboring residents themselves) than to provide parks or other facilities of impressive scale and professional construction, most of whose users will feel no attachment to the place or to the people they meet there.

Finally, Valadez and Bellalta's work provides a salient example of the use of Campbell's experimental approach to design, planning, and other "social reforms." Despite the difficulties of carrying out research as part of the process of reform, exemplified by Valadez and Bellalta's experiences in Macul, more knowledge about the effectiveness of design and planning solutions for a particular project, and about the validity of environment–behavior theories in general, is gained from such an approach than from blindly trusting foresight or casual inference. Macul is a valuable reminder that it is easier to find out where one is going by looking than by understanding.

References

Campbell, D. T. (1969). Reforms as experiments. *American Psychologist, 24,* 409–429.

Campbell, D. T., & Stanley, J. C. (1963). *Experimental and quasi-experimental designs for research.* Chicago: Rand McNally.

Caplow, T., & Forman, R. (1950). Neighborhood interaction in a homogeneous community. *American Sociological Review, 15,* 357–366.

Carey, L., & Mapes, R. (1972). *The sociology of planning.* London: Batsford.

Festinger, L. A., Schachter, S., & Back, K. (1950). *Social pressures in informal groups.* New York: Harper & Row.

Kuper, L. (1953). *Living in towns.* London: Cressett Press.

Lewin, K. (1958). Group decision and social change. In E. E. Maccoby & E. L. Hartley (Eds.), *Readings in social psychology* (3rd ed.). New York: Holt, Rinehart & Winston.

Merton, R. K. (1951). The social psychology of housing. In W. Dennis et al. (Eds.), *Current trends in social psychology* (pp. 163–217). Pittsburgh: University of Pittsburgh Press.

Michelson, W. (1977). *Environmental choice, human behavior, and residential satisfaction.* Oxford: Oxford University Press.

Sanoff, H. (1990). *Participatory design.* Raleigh, NC: Author.

Valadez, J. J. (1982/83). Habitat as experiment: Theory as practice. *Urban Ecology, 7,* 281–305.

Valadez, J. J., & Bellalta, E. (1982). *Macul: Completing the designed environment.* Workshop presented at the 13th international conference of the Environmental Design Research Association, College Park, MD.

Valadez, J. J., & Bellalta, E. (1984). Macul: Influences of tasks on the development of social and physical spaces. *Human Organization, 43,* 146–154.

PART IV
ENVIRONMENTAL
MANAGEMENT

What to look for

The three cases discussed in part IV differ somewhat from the others in this volume. They are similar to the others in that they describe efforts to make systematic use of information about human behavior to improve the way environmental settings work. But these projects focused on preventing behaviors that would threaten to degrade the environment – unnecessary consumption of energy for home heating and cooling (chapter 13), construction of high-rise buildings that would clash with existing architecture or create shadows or wind currents that would cause discomfort for people in nearby streets and open spaces (chapter 14), and residential, commercial, and industrial developments that would destroy valuable scenic resources (chapter 15) – rather than on improving the designs of elements in the environment.

Whereas the other cases in this volume are concerned, for the most part, with enhancement of additions to the built environment, these three are concerned with protection for the natural environment through limitations on the use of and alterations of the built environment. Energy conservation (chapter 13) ultimately reduces the need for exploitation of coal, oil, and other natural resources whose extraction can scar the environment and whose use can entail the discharge of polluting by-products of the energy industries. Strategic controls on high-rise development (chapter 14) can avert unnecessary degradation of the architectural character and microclimate of a city. And controls on development along a scenic river (chapter 15) can help to preserve the appearance of a region whose beauty is important to large numbers of recreational users and residents, as well as to the tourist industry.

Two of these projects have affected the environment on a large scale, although their ultimate impacts are still in doubt. The new zoning controls in San Francisco (chapter 14), albeit somewhat fragile, covered the city's downtown area, including the shopping and hotel districts, as well as some of its most significant public open spaces – Union Square, Portsmouth Square, St. Mary's Square, the Chinese Playground, and many more. The Lower Wisconsin State Riverway Act (chapter 15) established seemingly strict and enforceable controls over almost a hundred miles of river valley, including heavily used areas with well-known tourist attractions and some quite undeveloped, solitary stretches. By contrast, each of the energy-conservation projects de-

240   *Environmental management*

scribed in chapter 13 was fairly small, covering a single apartment or townhouse complex. And each was relatively short-lived, as compared with either San Francisco's 1985 Downtown Plan (which is in danger of being softened by future planning decisions) or the act creating the Lower Wisconsin State Riverway (which seems unlikely to be compromised in the foreseeable future).

Neither the San Francisco project (chapter 14) nor the Lower Wisconsin State Riverway project (chapter 15) was greatly influenced by existing social-science theory. Both cases were driven mainly by practical considerations, including political ones, although Chenoweth and Niemann's work on the Lower Wisconsin State Riverway drew in a general way on the methods of previous environmental-appraisal research. Again, the energy-conservation projects (chapter 13) were different in that they were based on and reflected directly on mainstream psychological theories of learning.

Finally, the three cases in part IV cover a broad range in regard to the spread of their influence. The energy-conservation projects (chapter 13) have spawned other demonstrations, but have had little practical impact on energy conservation. This is ironic in light of the trustworthiness of the underlying theories and the reliability of their effects in practice, but understandable in light of the politics involved. The Lower Wisconsin State Riverway project (chapter 15) seems to have great potential for influencing the courses and outcomes of similar planning processes elsewhere, although it is so recent that there has as yet been no opportunity to gauge its impact. The impact of the 1985 Downtown Plan for San Francisco (chapter 14) has already been widely felt, in raising issues about the urban natural environment elsewhere, in influencing the general approach to zoning in other cities to be more site-specific, and in spreading the use of powerful simulation technologies to evaluate the futures promised by alternative planning solutions.

Again, there is considerable room for analysis by the reader, and more analysis by the author is to be found in chapter 16.

13
PROMOTING ENERGY CONSERVATION

Locations: Various
Principals: Many researchers

The conservation of those natural resources that serve as energy sources or are used to produce energy in the form of electricity has far-reaching ramifications. It is important to those who seek to preserve the natural environment in an unspoiled state (where that is still possible) because it reduces the need for resource extraction by strip mining, offshore drilling, and other destructive means, as well as the need to exploit energy sources such as high-sulfur coal and nuclear power that pose serious risks to environmental quality. Conservation is just as important to those who fear that depletion of those resources and the resulting escalation of their costs would harm the nation's economy and lower our standard of living. It is also important to corporations that produce energy or consume large quantities of it in their production processes, and to individuals who work for those corporations or who simply use energy to run their automobiles and their homes each day. And it is especially important in the United States, where we are responsible for roughly one-third of all the energy use on this planet, and where, since the Arab oil embargo of 1974, the accident at Three Mile Island in 1980, and the conflict in the Middle East in 1990, the possibility of energy shortages has loomed especially large.

Unfortunately for those who see energy conservation as a pressing need, it is still less important to many people than are economic growth, material comfort, and individual freedom of action. And the prevailing view among government policymakers, reinforced by the lobbying efforts of the energy industry, is that energy use is a purely economic matter, to be resolved by free market forces that will eventually bring supply and demand into balance. Nevertheless, dozens of behavioral scientists have made energy conservation an important focus of their research during recent decades. They have taken the view that there are important behavioral determinants of energy use that lie outside the bounds of economic theory and that must be understood and controlled if greater energy conservation is to be achieved.

Those researchers have worked to explicate the relationships between psychological and social forces, on the one hand, and energy consumption and conservation behavior, on the other. Their work has explored many diverse influences on energy use, including attitudes and communication processes, incentives, and feedback about outcomes. Perhaps most interesting, it has

Table 13.1. *Approaches to encouraging conservation behavior*

A. Attitude change
  1. Promoting pro-conservation attitudes through persuasive communication
  2. Evoking attitude-consistent conservation behavior
     a. Increasing attention to conservation actions
     b. Making attitudes more salient to behavior choices
     c. Linking attitudes more closely to actions
B. Behavior modification
  3. Inducing conservation with material incentives
     a. Providing financial incentives
     b. Providing convenience and comfort as incentives
  4. Inducing conservation with social incentives
     a. Providing recognition and approval as incentives
     b. Inducing public commitment
     c. Creating group discussion
  5. Providing models of conservation
  6. Facilitating the implementation of conservation intentions
     a. Providing information about appropriate actions
     b. Increasing the accessibility of conservation alternatives
     c. Minimizing negative consequences of conservation behavior
C. Behavior maintenance
  7. Providing information about the effectiveness of conservation efforts
     a. Feedback provided by others
     b. Feedback through self-monitoring of behavior

Source: Cook and Berrenberg (1981).

extended to the evaluation of alternative means of encouraging conservation through behavioral changes that can result in the reduction of energy use. And many of the cases where behaviorally based means of reducing energy use or increasing conservation behavior have been evaluated may also be viewed as applications of environment–behavior research. In those cases, basic theories about human behavior have been used to design interventions that actually have succeeded in promoting conservation, if only for a short time and on a limited scale in many of the cases.

Viewed another way, those studies have tested and proved the utility of interventions that might be applied in different places where pro-conservation policies are being implemented. Therefore, such studies would seem appropriate subjects for this chapter. However, rather than describe one such case in far greater detail than may be warranted by its scope or impact, this chapter will review briefly many of the existing cases and describe three of them more fully. It will emphasize residential energy conservation, particularly the use of energy for home heating and cooling, because that has been, thus far, the most common focus of such work.

The discussion will be organized around a framework devised for this particular body of work by Cook and Berrenberg (1981), as presented in Table 13.1. It classifies the approaches to encouraging conservation into three types. The first includes attempts to persuade people to adopt more favorable attitudes toward conservation, on the assumption that more favorable attitudes will be followed by greater efforts toward conservation, or to increase the impact of existing pro-conservation attitudes by making them more salient at the time decisions about conservation are being made. The second includes attempts to modify people's energy use directly, by providing financial or social incentives for reductions in energy use, or by providing information, instruction, or material resources that will make it more likely that people will expect favorable consequences and will follow through on their intentions to conserve. Finally, the third category consists of ways of providing people with feedback or evidence about their consumption of energy and about the efficacy of their conservation behaviors. Each of these approaches will be considered in turn, with a brief review of some of the evidence that can be adduced to support it, followed by a detailed description of one exemplary study of its type.

Persuasion

Many studies of the effects of persuasion toward more favorable conservation attitudes have followed the model of the classic Yale studies of persuasive communication conducted by Hovland and his colleagues over 30 years ago. They have attempted to exploit the reliable findings from those studies that attempts at persuasion are more likely to succeed when the target perceives the source of the message to be a credible one, both expert or knowledgeable about the subject at hand and trustworthy or motivated by other than selfish concerns (especially when the source is concerned for the welfare of the target).

Many would be skeptical about the prospects for changing attitudes toward conservation and subsequent conservation behaviors in this manner, for two reasons. First, according to Aronson and Stern (1984), the targets of such attempts at persuasion are likely to be skeptical about the source of pro-conservation messages because they have been subjected in the past to a great deal of incorrect (contradicted by better information later on) and inconsistent information. Second, such information is most likely to come from the government or from energy producers, the only parties likely to attempt to induce conservation outside the research context, both of which lack credibility in the eyes of many energy users because they are perceived to place selfish organizational motives ahead of the welfare of energy users (Aronson & Stern, 1984).

Nevertheless, studies have shown that persuasive messages consisting of information about energy waste and inefficiency and recommendations for conservation measures can serve as effective interventions. Craig and McCann (1978) sent 1,000 electric-utility customers information with their bills that contained a plea for conservation, specific suggestions about how to reduce their air-conditioning costs, and business-reply postcards they could use to get more information about energy conservation. When such information appeared to have been sent by the chairman of the New York State Public Service Commission, it produced a significantly greater reduction in electricity consumption and a higher rate of postcard return than when it was attributed to the manager of consumer affairs for the local utility. Hutton (1982) reported some evaluations of media campaigns, sponsored by the U.S. Department of Energy, to promote conservation. One particularly effective program, based on a telephone survey of those exposed to it in New England and a comparison sample in nearby upper New York State, combined a mailing (consisting of a booklet listing low-cost and no-cost energy-saving techniques and a device that could be installed in a shower head to restrict water flow and reduce water-heating costs) with paid advertising in a variety of media and free public-service announcements. And Winett, Love, and Kidd (1982b) found that home visits by trained energy specialists that combined written information with personal instruction in lowering hot-water-heater settings and using fans at night in place of air-conditioning resulted in lower electricity consumption, especially on warmer days, as compared with baseline consumption rates or rates in control households that were not visited but simply received fans along with the others.

Ester and Winett (1982) have made the point that the use of persuasion or information campaigns has the great advantage of being able to reach large numbers of energy consumers at relatively low cost. They suggest that for that reason it is important to continue to study such techniques to determine which are most effective. The existing research, including that reviewed earlier, suggests that such an approach has some potential.

The second approach to encouraging conservation through pro-conservation attitudes is designed to make more effective use of existing favorable attitudes. Although Cook and Berrenberg described three possible means for evoking such "attitude-consistent conservation behavior," prior research has been concentrated in one area, and in the work of one group of investigators, led by Michael Pallak (e.g., Pallak & Cummings, 1976). They conducted studies of fairly large scale (both in the numbers of participants involved and in the durations of the studies) regarding the effects of making pro-conservation attitudes more salient to those who already hold them at the time that they are making decisions or choosing among alternative behaviors relevant to energy use. They designed their studies of the effects of public commitment to conservation behaviors based on the assumption that residents of the college community of Iowa City, Iowa, would mostly be favorable toward conservation (of course, some would expect widespread support for energy conservation because energy savings mean financial gain to everyone, although economists disagree whether or not the size of that gain is sufficient to foster conservation behavior by itself). Thus, the problem for someone designing a policy to increase energy conservation in such a community would be to find a way to encourage residents to act on their desire to conserve.

Pallak and his colleagues chose to test a means for doing that based on classic social-psychological research, some of which had been conducted by Pallak himself. That research and the theory that underlies it constitute one approach to understanding why people's actions are sometimes, if not often, inconsistent with their attitudes – in the present case, for example, why people may report that they are in favor of energy conservation, and yet not act as though they were (not engage in conservation behaviors themselves to the degree that their professed attitudes would lead one to expect). In brief, the position developed in that work and taken by Pallak and his colleagues in the study to be discussed here is that attitudes and behaviors may diverge because attitudes often are expressed in situations where many of the other factors that join with them to influence the relevant behaviors are absent. By the same token, behaviors related to those attitudes are often performed in situations where one's relevant attitudes are much less salient than other factors that can exert an influence on one's behavior.

In the case of energy conservation, the difference between the situation in which a favorable attitude might be expressed and the situation in which conservation behaviors might be elected – the problem of salience of pro-conservation attitudes – is one in which the likely consequences seem fairly clear. One might express support for energy conservation in an interview, or on a questionnaire, or in an informal discussion with friends or colleagues at a time and place where there is no demand or perhaps even no opportunity to engage in conservation behaviors. When such a demand or opportunity does present itself, as one passes the thermostat on the way to a favorite chair with the newspaper after dinner, many factors that influence one's response other than the relevant attitudes may be more salient than the latter. One might feel a slight chill in the air in winter or a hint of oppressive heat and humidity in summer. Or one might be preoccupied with a personal or career problem, or a conversation that is going on at the time, or the thought of getting back to a good book or on to a favorite television program.

If it seems a formidable task to overcome such barriers to acting on pro-conservation attitudes, or to forge a stronger link between such attitudes and behaviors related to them, the work of Pallak and his colleagues shows that such is not the case. In both their studies, one concerned with the consumption of natural gas for home heating that was conducted during the winter of 1973–1974, and another concerned with the consumption of electricity for home cooling (air-conditioning) that was conducted during the summer of

1974, they used a simple procedure derived from the earlier attitude-change research. That earlier research showed that when people were induced to make a public commitment to some personal attitude, as compared with expressing the same attitude privately, they were more likely to be influenced by a subsequent communication advocating a more extreme position further along in the same direction as their existing attitude, more likely to resist a subsequent communication attacking their existing attitude (less likely to be influenced by it), and, most important for the present discussion, more likely to comply with a subsequent request for actions consistent with their attitude.

In both the heating and air-conditioning studies, then, Pallak and colleagues followed the same rather simple procedure. The local utilities were first convinced to give the researchers access to monthly billing records, where the rates of energy consumption, natural gas or electricity, for individual homes could be obtained. Then individual households in Iowa City, selected randomly from city blocks, were contacted by telephone to arrange interviews at which they would be asked to participate in an energy conservation study and to sign release forms giving the researchers permission to see their utility bills.

Over 200 households were contacted in all. Over 95% of those agreed to the interview, and of those interviewed over 98% agreed to participate in the studies. The participants in each study were assigned randomly to one of three groups. Two of the groups were invited to try to conserve energy for a period of one month after the interview. They were told that the purpose of the study was to demonstrate to the larger community that individual homeowners' actions could make a difference in the effort to conserve energy (those studies were conducted at a time of rising energy prices and rising concerns over the nation's vulnerability to disruption of the supply of imported oil and to shortages in domestic energy supplies). To that end, the results of the participants' efforts were to be publicized locally at the conclusion of the study. The subjects in one group were told that their anonymity would be guaranteed when the results were made public (the private-commitment group). Those in the second group were told that all participants' names would be made public when the results were reported (the public-commitment group). In that way, the researchers sought to vary the participants' commitments to conservation behavior consistent with their pro-conservation attitudes. It was predicted that those who agreed to participate believing that their names as well as their collective performance would be made public would be more committed to following through on their attitudes and would reduce their energy consumption more. Subjects in a third group selected for the study were interviewed at the end of the one-month conservation period. They were asked simply to give permission for access to their utility bills as part of a study of energy conservation, not to change their behavior in any way (in any case, it was their prior behavior that was of concern). Those who agreed served as a control group against which energy consumption by both the private- and public-commitment groups could be compared.

One month after their interviews, the participants in the private- and public-commitment groups were informed that the study was over and that the project had been a success (in vague terms, that the participants had succeeded in reducing their natural-gas or electricity consumption). However, the researchers continued to track their consumption, as well as that of the controls, for a total period of 12 months, at least for the 90% or so who continued to live at the same addresses during that period. Thus, the effects of public commitment could be evaluated for a realistic period of energy use and for its effects beyond the period during which contact was maintained with the agent that actually elicited the commitment.

In the heating study, the results showed a greater reduction in consumption of natural gas among the public-commitment group during the initial month of the study, as compared with their level of consumption during the previous (baseline) month. Actually, all groups increased their levels of consumption during the month following baseline measures because the weather was getting colder as the winter season came on. However, the public-commitment group increased its consumption significantly less than did the other two. The advantage of public commitment in eliciting attitude-consistent conservation behavior held up over the 12-month comparison as well. The public-commitment group used less natural gas over that period, entirely because of their conservation during the coldest six months – the heating season. No differences were found between the private-commitment and control groups.

In the air-conditioning study, participants were divided into those with central air-conditioning and those with window air-conditioning for purposes of increasing the precision of the analysis. The results in both cases were similar to those in the heating study. Both those with central and those with window air-conditioning increased their use of electricity less during the month following their interviews (as the weather got hotter) if they had made a public commitment to conservation. This difference held up uniformly across the 12-month duration of the study for those with central air-conditioning, as well as for the hot summer months for those with window air-conditioning. Again, the private-commitment group and control group were indistinguishable from one another.

The results of these studies provide clear confirmation of the hypothesis that a public commitment to pro-conservation attitudes can lead to greater compliance with a request for conservation behavior consistent with such attitudes. Despite the fact that no effort was made to select the participants in these studies for extreme pro-conservation attitudes (although the results suggest that the researchers' assumption that, in general, members of the community would favor conservation was well founded), public commitment to conservation was found to reduce energy consumption overall. Given the overwhelming success in obtaining cooperation from randomly sampled prospective participants and the facility with which public commitment could be induced in the course of a 20-minute interview, along with the observed effects, the feasibility of using this behavioral mechanism for encouraging conservation behavior seems well supported by the research program carried out by Pallak and colleagues.

Behavior modification

Theory and research directed toward understanding the environmental (read situational) factors that determine which response an organism will select from the large number of alternatives available to it to solve a problem lie at the heart of the discipline of psychology. This is usually referred to as the study of learning, although it is concerned less with how new responses are added to an organism's repertoire than with how responses are chosen from the repertoire in the face of some environmental demand.

Not only has the study of learning been a central concern in the study of human behavior, but also it has proved to be an extremely useful basis for the development of practical means of modifying behavior, including the behavior of people. In particular, the study of how behavior is shaped by the consequences it produces has been a fruitful area for theory, research, and applications. Beginning with Thorndike's statement of the "law of effect," through Skinner's development of the construct of reinforcement, to the more cognitive focus on expectancies in the present day, this problem has played a central role in the development of psychological theory. It has also played a central role in the development of behavioral technologies that have been used in a wide variety of applications, including psychotherapy, education, penology, and industry.

Collectively, these applications of the psychology of learning are known as behavior modification. In most cases, they employ some form of incentive that is made available to the target individuals for the performance of actions that have been defined as appropriate for a particular situation. A schoolchild may receive the approval of a teacher in the form of a smile and approving words ("Very good," for example), or a gold star on a test paper, for performing a class assignment well. A patient in a mental hospital may receive a token that can be exchanged for candy, or time in the television lounge, or a walk on the hospital grounds, for doing a good job of self-grooming or housekeeping or for good table manners. Or a worker may receive a monetary bonus or points toward an individual or group award for working efficiently or safely over a period of time.

These same principles of reinforcement, as they are known to many, have been applied in attempts to increase energy-conservation behaviors. Although conservation brings rewards automatically in some situations, as when a homeowner saves heating oil by setting the thermostat to maintain a lower indoor temperature in winter, there are other cases where tangible rewards do not automatically follow conservation. Tenants in apartment buildings where utilities are provided from central sources and the cost is divided equally among the tenants, students living in dormitories on a college campus where heat and electricity are provided to the entire campus from a central source, and others do not directly pay the costs of the energy they use or realize direct savings when they conserve.

In the latter situations, individual and group incentives have been applied in experimental demonstrations, and in many cases they have been shown to be effective. Kohlenberg, Phillips, and Proctor (1976) used an orthodox operant-conditioning procedure with just three families to show that monetary incentives were effective in reducing peaking (high consumption of electricity for brief periods), as compared with information appeals or feedback regarding electricity use. McClelland and Cook (1980) found that group monetary incentives offered to residents of master-metered clusters of apartments in a University of Colorado housing complex were effective in reducing the consumption of natural gas (the effect was reliable, though not great). Newsom and Makranczy (1977–78) tested a similar "contest" procedure, as well as one in which a single prize was raffled off among the residents of each group. Both reinforcement procedures were effective in lowering electricity consumption in master-metered university dormitories, and their effects continued, although to a lesser degree, after the incentives were withdrawn. Walker (1979) offered cash rewards to residents of master-metered apartments in a university housing complex for compliance with a list of conservation measures designed to reduce electricity consumption by air-conditioners. With compliance being checked by spot visits to apartments, it was found that the residents included in the test complied more frequently than they had before rewards were available and complied better than did residents of similar apartments to whom the rewards had not been offered. Winett et al. (1978) found that high monetary rebates combined with conservation information and weekly written feedback were effective in promoting electricity conservation during the air-conditioning season in a volunteer sample of Texas households, as compared with lower rebates plus feedback and information, or feedback or information alone.

As Cook and Berrenberg (1981) pointed out, there are ways of modifying energy-conservation behavior other than the application of tangible or even social incentives. Even with incentives available and a desire to conserve energy, people may not be able to follow through on their intentions to conserve. In the case of residential energy conservation, for example, they may not know which actions will be most effective in reducing energy use. Should they turn the thermostat down to save heating costs (or up in the case of air-conditioning), or invest in insulation for their homes, or buy a more efficient heating or cooling system? They may be skeptical of actions suggested in advertising by utilities, manufacturers, or even government, as discussed earlier. They also may lack the financial resources to follow through on their intentions. The investments required for retrofitting homes with more efficient technology may be beyond their means. Or they may fear that in undertaking such major projects they will be cheated by contractors or vendors.

Programs that provide homeowners with credible information about conservation alternatives, or that facilitate the financing for retrofitting homes, or that recommend or guarantee the work of reputable contractors who can do the job have been shown to increase the likelihood that homeowners will take advantage of opportunities to conserve and to save on their energy costs. The studies by Craig and McCann (1978), Hutton (1982), and Winett et al. (1982b) described earlier provide corroboration for that argument.

Another approach to increasing consumers' capabilities to engage in energy-conservation behavior is illustrated by the work of Winett et al. (1978, 1979, 1982a). In separate studies of energy use for home heating and cooling, they used a technique based on the work of learning theorist and researcher Albert Bandura (1977). Bandura's social-learning theory stresses the role of models in shaping our behaviors. We learn what to do in many situations by observing others' responses to the same problems we face ourselves. Not only may we see a model do something we would not have thought of doing ourselves, but also the model's actions may inform us that a response we had considered using would have been appropriate in the situation in which we had been uncertain about it, or we may gain the opportunity to observe the consequences of the model's actions and thus develop firmer expectations about the consequences of our own actions.

Winett and his colleagues tested the hypothesis that homeowners who were motivated to reduce their consumption of energy for home heating or cooling would be more successful in doing so if they had the opportunity to observe models of effective conservation behaviors. Their studies were conducted in Blacksburg and nearby Salem, Virginia. Although they were similar in many respects, those two studies of heating in winter and cooling in summer were sufficiently different to warrant separate treatment here.

The winter study, in Blacksburg, was conducted in two all-electric townhouse complexes occupied for the most part by young single men or women living as roommates who rented their town houses and paid their own electricity bills. The housing units compared were similar in all relevant respects. The researchers canvassed the complexes door-to-door to solicit volunteers who would participate in a study of energy conservation that would require attendance at one preliminary group meeting and periodic completion of brief questionnaires, who intended to remain in their town houses for the duration of the study, who would not be put at risk by lower indoor temperature, and who were willing to have their outdoor electricity meters read periodically by a research assistant. Fifty-eight percent of those contacted volunteered to participate. Eighty-three households in all were assigned randomly to five comparison groups, with the groups stratified on the basis of the volunteers' self-reports of their thermostat settings during the heating season. In addition, 30 households that were not willing to participate in the study but were willing to have their meters read were chosen for comparison with the volunteer control group, to determine whether or not the volunteers for the study were systematically different in their energy use from the complexes' population as a whole (more predisposed to conserve, for example).

At a preliminary meeting, held on one of the complex sites, participants were told about the objectives of the study and were allowed to ask questions. They were also given a schedule that they could follow to lower their thermostat settings gradually and to lower them even further when their town houses were unoccupied or while they were asleep. Both the gradual permanent reduction and the temporary reductions in indoor temperature while absent or asleep (setbacks) were tailored to the pre-study settings reported by participants when they were first recruited for the study. Participants were also given a list of items of clothing and their insulation (clo) values, which they would need to fill out a checklist that was to be administered at intervals throughout the study, along with questionnaires asking how comfortable and how warm they felt, what activities they engaged in at home, and how well they felt. At these meetings, all participants signed a pledge that they would try to reduce their consumption of electricity by 15%.

In addition to reading the participants' electricity meters and questioning them about their comfort and behavior, the researchers installed a hygrothermograph in each of the town houses. Those instruments kept continuous records of temperature and humidity. The records were collected weekly by research assistants, along with the questionnaires that were to be filled out at three specific times during each week. At that time, the instruments were reset, and new questionnaires were delivered. All of these arrangements were explained to participants at the preliminary meetings. At those meetings, each group in the study was also exposed to a special set of information that constituted the conditions whose effects on their conservation performance were to be evaluated. Of course, each group met separately.

Two groups of participants were shown a videotape in which a young couple discussed with an interviewer how electricity consumption could be reduced during the heating season. The interview, which had been videotaped in a town house identical with the ones in which participants lived, outlined the case for energy conservation and described specific practices that could be applied in the home. This tape was labeled the "discussion" tape. One of the two groups that watched it was selected to receive feedback during the study regarding their efforts at conservation. Each day they each received a written report of the amount of electricity they had used during the previous 24 hours. When they were told in the preliminary meeting that they would be receiving this information, it was described as an aid to reducing their consumption of electricity.

Two other groups of participants were shown a videotape in which the same young couple in the same setting demonstrated energy-conservation behavior, as well as contrasting wasteful and ineffective practices, in a series of vignettes. In addition to showing conservation behaviors, this "modeling" tape, rather than simply describing or identifying them, showed the couple expressing a commitment to conservation and expressing their satisfaction with the positive consequences of their successful conservation behavior. One of these groups was also selected to receive feedback during the study.

In addition to the four groups described already – discussion tape with and without feedback, and modeling tape with and without feedback – a fifth group, the control group, was pledged to attempt to conserve and was informed about the procedures of the study, but saw neither tape and received no feedback. The study lasted 15 weeks in all. During the three weeks following recruitment of the participants (including the nonvolunteers), baseline meter readings were taken. Then the group meetings were held, and for the following five weeks (the intervention phase) the meters were read, hygrothermograph recordings were made, feedback was given, and questionnaire responses were collected. After the intervention phase, participants were informed that the study was over, the hygrothermographs were removed, and feedback and questionnaire administration ended. However, the researchers continued to read the participants' electricity meters weekly for the following seven weeks, known as the follow-up phase of the study.

The results of that study are summarized in Table 13.2. They are presented as average percentage increases or decreases compared with the baseline period. During the intervention phase, there were statistically significant and substantial energy savings associated with exposure to the modeling tape, although the discussion tape in conjunction with feedback about electricity consumption produced similar savings. This was true equally for overall electricity use and electricity use for heating only (estimated by comparing levels of consumption between the heating and nonheating seasons for comparable housing units). However, during the follow-up phase (when reductions seemed quite large compared with baseline consumption, because outdoor temperatures were rising late in the winter) it was found that exposure to modeled conservation behavior made an especially positive contribution to participants' efforts to conserve. Not only did it produce a lasting effect (over the 15 weeks of the study, at any rate), but also its effectiveness increased relative to the levels for the other conditions evaluated.

The effects that those various means for increasing conservation had on actual consumption of electricity are made even more meaningful by an

Table 13.2. *Winter study: changes in electricity consumption compared with baseline period*

Usage category	Group	Intervention phase	Follow-up phase
Overall electricity use	Control	+4%	−25%
	Discussion tape	−1%	−35%
	Discussion tape plus feedback	−13%	−33%
	Modeling tape	−11%	−41%
	Modeling tape plus feedback	−14%	−41%
Electricity use for heating	Control	+6%	−46%
	Discussion tape	−3%	−64%
	Discussion tape plus feedback	−23%	−60%
	Modeling tape	−23%	−75%
	Modeling tape plus feedback	−23%	−74%

examination of other results from this study. Although indoor temperatures were lower in the homes of all intervention groups than in the homes of the controls (who were, by the way, no different from their nonvolunteer counterparts), the participants reported continuing to wear similar clothing (similar in insulation value) as they gradually reduced the temperatures in their homes and began to use setbacks when away or when asleep, and they reported no changes in perceived warmth or in personal comfort. Thus, energy savings were achieved without discernible changes in life-style or comfort.

The summer study, in Salem, was conducted at two all-electric apartment complexes that were centrally air-conditioned. The housing units compared were again similar in all relevant respects. For the most part, they were occupied by married couples or by families with children, with above-average incomes. All were renters and paid their own utility bills. Participants were recruited as in the winter study in Blacksburg, except that in Salem only 45% agreed to participate. Again, nonvolunteers who agreed to have their meters read by the researchers were used to check on the representativeness of the volunteer participants.

Again, information was distributed, instructions were given, and the conditions to be evaluated were created (through appropriate videotapes, instructions, etc.) at preliminary on-site meetings that were held for the groups of participants after baseline meter readings had been collected for three weeks. Of course, participants were instructed to raise their thermostat settings gradually and to use setbacks to an even higher setting when away or when asleep.

Four groups totaling 54 households in all were created by random assignment. Two groups were shown a tape in which ways of conserving electricity by modifying air-conditioning use were modeled by a young couple in an

Table 13.3. *Summer study: changes in electricity consumption compared with baseline period*

Usage category	Group	Intervention phase	Follow-up phase
Overall electricity use	Control	−2%	−11%
	Feedback	−19%	−29%
	Modeling tape	−12%	−28%
	Modeling tape plus feedback	−22%	−37%
Electricity use for cooling	Control	−5%	−24%
	Feedback	−42%	−65%
	Modeling tape	−26%	−63%
	Modeling tape plus feedback	−49%	−82%

apartment identical with their own. The models stressed the goals of savings and efficiency, rather than conservation, exemplified a strong commitment to reducing their energy consumption, and expressed satisfaction with their success in doing so. One of the two groups that were shown the "modeling" tape also received feedback. A third group received feedback, but otherwise got only the information and instructions given to all four groups, the fourth group being the controls.

The intervention phase of the summer study, during which hygrothermograph recordings were collected, questionnaires were administered, and feedback was given, lasted four weeks. Then, after direct contact between participants and researchers ended, follow-up meter readings were made for an additional three-week period. The conservation results of the summer study are shown in Table 13.3. Modeling was effective in reducing electricity consumption, particularly for cooling, and added an obvious increment of savings when combined with effective feedback. As in the winter study, the relative effectiveness of the modeling tape increased in the follow-up phase, as compared with the intervention period. Again, the savings, compared with the baseline period, reflect a change toward cooler weather toward the end of the study.

The supplemental findings in the summer study are even more interesting than the comparable findings in the winter study. No significant changes in temperature or humidity were found to accompany or explain the reductions in consumption that were observed. Participants substituted less costly fans and free natural cooling for some of their air-conditioning use. According to their reports, the clothing worn by participants, their comfort, and the perceived temperatures of their homes all remained virtually unchanged while they used their air conditioners less and reduced their electricity consumption considerably.

Taken together, these two studies by Winett and colleagues demonstrate how a brief and inexpensive instructional device can facilitate the learning and performance of conservation behaviors among individuals who are willing to try to conserve. Although those in the control groups had the same financial incentives and information about how to pursue them, as well as researchers looking over their shoulders to check on their progress, their efforts were quite ineffective, especially when compared with the efforts of those who were exposed to knowledgeable, committed, attractive, successful models (something that seems from these studies quite easy to arrange). Moreover, those who begin to pursue conservation diligently may benefit from the ensuing knowledge that their daily lives and the levels of comfort within their homes have changed very little, if at all, in the process.

The effectiveness of modeling was also shown in a study by Aronson and O'Leary (1983) that, though it lacked the scope of Winett's research, made its point in dramatic fashion. Male students at the University of California at Santa Cruz who used the fieldhouse shower room saw signs on the walls that asked them to conserve water by turning their showers off while they soaped up. Observation revealed that only 6% complied. When a much larger sign was placed in the middle of the shower room itself, 19% complied. But when students entering the shower room saw another student complying with the request (a confederate of the researchers soaping his wet body with his shower turned off), 49% followed suit. And when two models were provided, 67% imitated their compliance.

Feedback

One of the most stubborn obstacles to energy conservation is that energy use, especially in the home, is hidden from the user. Homeowners who rely on electricity and natural gas for cooling and heating, in particular, receive monthly bills that arrive long after the billing period has ended. Their bills reflect varied uses of the energy source in question – space heating and water heating and possibly cooking as well in the case of natural gas, or possibly all of those plus lighting, kitchen appliances, television and stereo, and even more in the case of electricity. Under those circumstances, it can be quite difficult for individual homeowners to evaluate their success at efforts to conserve energy by altering thermostat settings.

Attempts to conserve energy by retrofitting one's home involve similar problems. Any conservation behavior may be followed by changes in weather (as the heating or cooling season intensifies or subsides) or changes in energy costs that in combination with long billing cycles and delayed bills can confuse the homeowner about any savings that may actually be attributable to conservation behaviors, in addition to confusion about the specific actions or level of effort required to bring about reduced consumption and the savings that accompany it. Thus, even when there is motivation to conserve and information about effective strategies to use, one may fail to act appropriately or to feel satisfaction with one's efforts in the absence of timely, clear information about their consequences.

Psychologists who study learning emphasize the need for feedback to guide efforts toward a goal. And many studies have shown that feedback can contribute to a homeowner's success in achieving the goal of energy conservation. In some cases, the actual amount of consumption has been reported to the homeowner: kilowatt-hours of electricity, cubic feet of natural gas used, and so on. In other cases, more complex calculations have been used to provide the homeowner with a comparative index, usually reporting current usage as a percentage of usage before conservation efforts began, adjusted for outside temperature. Both kinds of feedback have been shown to be effective, although there has also been evidence that when feedback is presented in ways that are not sufficiently understandable or believable, it fails to make a positive contribution to conservation.

For example, McClelland and Cook (1979/80) installed measuring devices in a randomly chosen group of 25 of 101 energy-efficient all-electric homes in Carrboro, North Carolina. Residents in those 25 houses were informed continuously of the rates of electricity consumption in their homes, displayed as cents per hour. Those households used 12% less electricity overall than the others, a reliable difference that persisted in each of the 11 months the study continued. Moreover, the fact that greater savings were observed during milder months made it seem that the principal effects of feedback were on electricity uses other than heating and cooling.

Winett et al.(1979) gave daily written feedback about electricity consumption, including symbolic smiles or frowns and gold stars, depending on the amount used, to residents of town houses and detached houses in Greenbelt, Maryland (suburban Washington, D.C.), during the summer of 1977. There were reductions in electricity use generally, but they were reliable only for the higher-use consumers who lived in larger, detached houses with central air-conditioning.

A study by Becker and Seligman (1978) will be considered in detail because it shows how feedback can be applied to a very specific conservation problem in a way that is, at the same time, extremely effective and economical of time and effort. The study was carried out in a sample of three-bedroom townhouses, chosen at random from a complex, that were identical in floor plan and construction, all located in the interior of a row, and all equipped with identical air-conditioning systems. Participants were solicited by telephone. The persons contacted were asked to participate in a test of a new device designed to aid in energy conservation. At the time of that initial contact, they were told that the researchers were in the process of building a list of willing participants, although they were not yet certain how many of the devices would be available for use in the test.

Forty households volunteered, and they were divided randomly into four groups of 10. The conditions under which each group would participate in the study were established during a second telephone call. Two groups were told that the devices to be tested would be installed in their homes. The other two groups were told that there were not enough devices available to offer one to each of them. One group in each of those pairs was told that with their permission the researchers would provide feedback three times each week regarding their consumption of electricity compared with their own prior rates of use, adjusted for the outside temperature. All participants were informed about the need to conserve energy and about specific conservation measures to reduce the use of air-conditioning to cool their homes. They were advised to keep shades, windows, and doors closed to prevent solar heating, and to open doors and windows and use fans when the outside temperature was low enough to provide natural cooling.

The device that was installed in 20 of the town houses consisted of a small bulb under a blue Plexiglas cover that was mounted near a wall telephone, where it was visible from the kitchen and adjacent family room of the town house. This bulb was wired between the control switch for the air-conditioning system and a thermometer mounted outdoors. It was wired in such a way that when the outside temperature fell below 68°F and the air conditioner was running, the bulb would flash intermittently until the air conditioner was turned off.

Feedback was provided on a chart that was marked three times each week by a research assistant after reading the family's electricity meter. It was placed in a plastic pocket attached to the outside of a glass patio door so that it was visible from inside the town house. The chart showed a continuous record, as the individual points were added and connected, of the percentage of electricity consumption that was being conserved (below a baseline shown on the chart) or wasted (above the baseline).

The signaling device and feedback procedure were maintained for one month. Of the 12 readings made of the participants' electricity meters during that time, 6 readings followed periods during which the outside temperature had fallen below 68°F and, therefore, during which the signaling device had operated and provided those participants who had the devices in their homes with an opportunity to save energy by turning their air conditioners off and opening windows and doors and using fans to draw in the outside air, which was cooler than that being provided by their electrical cooling systems at the time. During those six periods, the participants who had the signaling devices in their homes used 15.7% less electricity overall than those who did not have the devices. The provision of the feedback chart had no effect on electricity consumption. Families receiving feedback alone used as much electricity as those having no feedback or signal, and those receiving feedback and having the signal used no less than those with the signal alone. Thus, a very simple device had a powerful effect on energy use in the specific situation for which it was designed. People who wanted to conserve and knew how were informed quickly and clearly when their behavior was out of line with their goal, and apparently they were able to make an effective correction.

Evaluation

Stage 1: Background analysis

None of the energy-conservation projects described in this chapter took much account of the particular setting in which it was carried out. Based as they were on very general theoretical analyses of such fundamental psychological processes as persuasion, modeling, and feedback, none addressed the local culture or history of the people or places involved. Of course, it was necessary to know such local conditions as the layout of a specific townhouse to determine the location for a warning system to reduce unnecessary air-conditioning use, or the characteristics of the tenants in an apartment complex in order to be able to choose appropriate models for a videotaped demonstration of conservation practices and outcomes. But even in those cases it could not be said that background analysis contributed significantly to the researchers' understanding of the basic problem they were trying to solve.

Stage 2: Behavioral goals

In all of those cases, the ultimate goal of reducing energy consumption for home heating or cooling was quite clear. In most cases, that outcome could be measured directly and precisely by gaining access to participants' utility meters or monthly bills. The only difficulties that arose concerned adjustments for changes in outdoor temperature over the several months during which the effects of each intervention were evaluated. However, compared with most design and planning projects, these were exemplary for the clarity with which desired outcomes were both specified and assessed.

Stage 3: Environment–behavior relationships

Each of the three interventions on which this chapter focuses was based on a specific theory of behavior change. Pallak and his colleagues based their work on the analysis by Hovland and the Yale group of the role of public commitment in fostering attitude-consistent behavior. Winett and his colleagues drew on Bandura's (1977) social-learning theory and its analysis of the ways modeling can change behavior. And Becker and Seligman used classic analyses of operant conditioning that stress the role of feedback in maintaining goal-directed behavior.

Each of these theories is a well-established part of the psychological analysis of behavior, each specifying one mechanism of behavior control. Each is based on a long line of empirical research conducted principally in the form of laboratory experiments. Although individual experiments may raise issues about the artificiality of the settings in which they were conducted, and about generalizing from observations of the behaviors of college students, children, or even pigeons to the typical participants in an energy-conservation program, the consistency of their findings, the scientific stature of the theories that summarize and explain them, and the broad range of successful applications to behaviors in schools, factories, and elsewhere argue strongly for their value as bases for interventions such as those carried out in the cases under consideration here.

Stage 4: Intervention elements

In each of the three energy-conservation intervention programs described in detail in this chapter, the theoretical position underlying the efforts to change the participants' behaviors was represented quite clearly and appropriately by one or more very specific elements. When participants agreed to have the results of their conservation efforts made public, or viewed a videotape in which people who appeared similar to themselves demonstrated effective conservation techniques, or had installed in their kitchens a signal light that informed them when they could turn off their air-conditioning in favor of using outdoor air to cool their homes, the underlying theory of behavior change was implemented quite directly.

Stage 5: Overall intervention

In most of these cases, the specific theory-based intervention elements that were evaluated were embedded in a larger treatment. In order to set up meaningful comparisons that would help to make clear the role of each of those elements in the behaviors of participants, a package of information about the need for conservation, specific measures that might be taken to reduce energy consumption, and outcomes that could be expected as a result of taking them was generally administered to all participants. In addition, permission was requested for access to records of participants' energy use. Then alternative versions of the targeted intervention element were added. For example, Pallak's group compared public commitment with private commitment as well as with no commitment at all. Winett and colleagues included non-modeling videotapes and feedback about energy consumption in their project. Only Becker and Seligman made a simple (feedback–no feedback) comparison, but even in that case all participants received information about measures for reducing air-conditioning use. Of course, the complex variations of these interventions were introduced to facilitate inferences about the causes of resulting behaviors from the measures of their effects.

Stage 6: POE

These interventions were planned from the outset in the form of research studies. As discussed earlier, each intervention was shaped in part by methodological considerations. Comparison groups of participants were created so as to sharpen the evaluation of the effects of the intervention in terms of the underlying theoretical rationale. Fortunately, the nature of these projects made it possible for Winett and Becker and Seligman to restrict their samples to occupants of identical dwellings within a single housing complex and for all the researchers to assign participants at random to the various forms of intervention they wished to compare. It also made it possible to use precise, clear measures of the participants' energy consumption (in the study by Winett and colleagues, the reliability of that measure was found to be perfect, a rare event in social-science research). And even though these studies lasted up to several months, the groups being compared lived in small communities where they all shared such extraneous experiences as seasonal changes in temperature, changing energy prices, and exposure to media conservation campaigns. Furthermore, the context in which the interventions were evaluated not only was common to all groups being compared but also provided a rich, realistic background against which to gauge the outcome.

As a result of all of these factors, each evaluation took on the form of a powerful experimental study. There was little difficulty in attributing the differences in energy consumption among groups of participants to differences in the forms of the behavioral interventions they received. And even though they were volunteers, there is some reason to believe that they were representative of their respective populations. Pallak's group compared volunteers who received no special intervention (controls) with nonvolunteers who merely agreed to have their utility meters read, and they found no difference in energy consumption. However, the participants were generally favorably predisposed to conserving energy from the outset, casting some doubt on the advisability of generalizing the findings to the population as a whole.

In brief, the level of control these researchers were able to exercise over the form and distribution of the interventions they created to encourage energy conservation, while working within the natural context for that behavior, made it possible for them to carry out evaluation studies that addressed successfully virtually all of the methodological challenges they faced. In this respect, these cases contrast markedly with most of the examples of environmental-design research that are considered in this volume, and most others as well. They are, collectively, an object lesson in the degree to which the adequacy of research methods depends on the nature of the research question and the context in which it is addressed, rather than simply the faithful application of correct methodological principles.

Stage 7: Future impact

These cases are also different from most of the others in this volume in the fact that they involved little in the way of change in the physical settings in which they took place. The follow-up data from the evaluations of these efforts to change the behaviors of these setting users suggest, however, that these reductions in energy consumption might be expected to continue as long as these participants remain in their homes, unless the effects should dissipate during the long temporal gaps between heating or cooling seasons.

The actual spread of these particular interventions to other housing complexes is difficult to estimate. The results of these demonstration projects have been published in books and journal articles, but primarily within academic circles. This may be attributable in part to a lack of effort on the part of the researchers to inform the general public or even environmental groups. However, it probably is due more to the declining interest in energy conservation that followed the return to stable energy prices and supplies during the 1980s, encouraged by a government policy that persuaded energy consumers that conservation was less important than unguarded optimism about business growth. Even mainstream energy-conservation strategies, such as improved home insulation and increased fuel efficiency for automobiles, seem to receive less attention today than they did at the time of these studies, when concern about energy conservation seems to have reached its height.

Whatever their actual impact, it seems clear that the interventions used in these studies have great potential, far greater than has been estimated by some experts. According to a study by Neels (1982), the potential for reducing residential energy consumption through behavioral change is limited to 5%, compared with 20–50% from the design of more energy-efficient housing, and 5–10% from retrofitting existing housing with improved insulation, new doors and windows, and more efficient heating and cooling appliances. The cases described in this chapter have demonstrated that carefully designed behavioral interventions that provide motivated consumers with more than encouragement and advice can bring greater reductions in energy consumption, in the range of 10–20%. Moreover, the interventions evaluated in these cases were all first attempts to apply their respective theories to the problem. Each of them undoubtedly could be improved through further study, and combinations of them, such as effective feedback with public commitment, or modeling with more effective feedback, probably could produce better results than any one alone. And, of course, low-cost or no-cost approaches such as those used in these projects (public commitment to conservation; attractive, instructive, and successful models for conservation behavior; effective feedback) that require consumers merely to adjust thermostats or open windows clearly are more feasible for many homeowners and renters than are the high-cost alternatives of moving to new, energy-efficient housing or undertaking extensive retrofitting of their existing homes.

These cases also provide more examples of the value of utilizing an experimental, incremental approach to improving environmental design, planning, or, in this case, management. Through iterative refinement of effective individual devices, as well as combinations of them, by comparing alternative interventions in actual use as these cases did, it should be possible eventually to provide interested parties (government agencies, private utilities, environmentalists, and consumers) with proven tools for residential energy conservation. Some, based on principles such as commitment and modeling, might even prove useful in spurring those who are already motivated to conserve to undertake more costly measures, such as increasing the insulation in their homes.

Finally, these cases may provide encouragement for those who would apply basic theories of human behavior, such as psychological learning theories or decision theories, to improve environmental management. These projects demonstrate that such theories, though based largely on data from laboratory experiments using research subjects seemingly far different from targeted environmental user groups, can provide a basis for effective intervention. At the same time, evidence of the effectiveness of such interventions, such as that provided in the cases described here, can add to our confidence in basic behavioral science as an underpinning for the study of environment–behavior relationships in the "real world."

References

Aronson, E., & O'Leary, N. (1983). The relative effectiveness of models and prompts on energy conservation: A field experiment in a shower room. *Journal of Environmental Systems, 12,* 219–224.

Aronson, E., & Stern, P. (Eds.) (1984). *Energy use: The human dimension.* New York: Freeman.

Bandura, A. (1977). *Social learning theory.* Englewood Cliffs, NJ: Prentice-Hall.

Becker, L. J., & Seligman, C. (1978). Reducing air conditioning waste by signalling it is cool outside. *Personality and Social Psychology Bulletin, 4,* 412–415.

Cook, S. W., & Berrenberg, J. L. (1981). Approaches to encouraging conservation behavior: A review and conceptual framework. *Journal of Social Issues, 37*(2), 73–107.

Craig, C. S., & McCann, J. M. (1978). Assessing communication effects on energy conservation. *Journal of Consumer Research, 5,* 82–88.

Ester, P., & Winett, R. A. (1982). Toward more effective antecedent strategies for environmental programs. *Journal of Environmental Systems, 11,* 201–221.

Hutton, R. B. (1982). Advertising and the Department of Energy's campaign for energy conservation. *Journal of Advertising, 11*(2), 27–39.

Kohlenberg, R. J., Phillips, T., & Proctor, W. (1976). A behavioral analysis of peaking in residential electricity energy customers. *Journal of Applied Behavioral Analysis, 9,* 13–18.

McClelland, L., & Cook, S. W. (1979/80). Energy conservation effects of continuous in-home feedback in all-electric homes. *Journal of Environmental Systems, 9,* 169–173.

McClelland, L., & Cook, S. W. (1980). Promoting energy conservation in master-metered apartments through group financial incentives. *Journal of Applied Social Psychology, 10,* 20–31.

Neels, K. (1982). Reducing energy consumption in housing: An assessment of alternatives. *International Regional Science Review, 7,* 69–82.

Newsom, T. J., & Makranczy, V. J. (1977/78). Reducing electricity consumption of residents living in master-metered dormitory complexes. *Journal of Environmental Systems, 7,* 215–235.

Pallak, M. S., & Cummings, N. (1976). Commitment and voluntary energy conservation. *Personality and Social Psychology Bulletin, 2,* 27–31.

Stern, P. C., & Aronson, E. (1984). *Energy use: The human dimension.* New York: Freeman.

Walker, J. M. (1979). Energy demand behavior in a master-metered apartment complex: An experimental analysis. *Journal of Applied Psychology, 64,* 190–196.

Winett, R. A., Hatcher, J. W., Fort, R. R., Leckliter, J. N., Love, S. Q., Riley, A. W., & Fishback, J. F. (1982a). The effects of videotape modeling and daily feedback on residential electricity conservation, home temperature and humidity, perceived comfort, and clothing worn: Winter and summer. *Journal of Applied Behavioral Analysis, 15,* 381–402.

Winett, R. A., Kogel, J. H., Battalio, R. C., & Winkler, R. C. (1978). The effects of monetary rebates, feedback and information on residential energy conservation. *Journal of Applied Psychology, 63,* 73–80.

Winett, R. A., Love, S. Q., & Kidd, C. (1982b). Effectiveness of an energy specialist and extension agents in promoting summer energy conservation by home visits. *Journal of Environmental Systems, 12,* 61–70.

Winett, R. A., Neale, M. S., Williams, K. R., Yokley, J., & Kander, H. (1979). The effects of individual and group feedback on residential electricity consumption: Three replications. *Journal of Environmental Systems, 8,* 217–233.

14
THE 1985 DOWNTOWN PLAN

Location: San Francisco, California
Participants: Peter Bosselman and colleagues, Environmental
Simulation Laboratory, University of California,
Berkeley (research and planning)

The setting: San Francisco

Anyone who has had the good fortune to spend time in San Francisco knows something of the reason that so many songs have been written about that city and so many motion pictures and television programs have been filmed there. Perhaps above all, it is a visually striking place. In particular, the views from Telegraph Hill and Russian Hill and the other hills that overlook San Francisco Bay, and from the many steep streets that climb them, are often breathtaking. One can look across the rooftops down to the bay and the Golden Gate Bridge, and across to the hills of Marin County – on a clear day.

Besides its rare natural beauty, San Francisco is notable for what has been built there – and for what has not. Its residential streets are lined with seemingly endless rows of low, light-colored buildings, many of them Victorian houses with extensive ornamentation. Even the streets of the downtown shopping area and other areas that have high pedestrian traffic, such as Chinatown, North Beach, and the Tenderloin, are lined with buildings no more than five or six stories high. Except for parts of the financial district, there are none of the "canyons" created by high-rise buildings that characterize so much of Manhattan's pedestrian environment and significant portions of other major American cities as well.

San Francisco's low, light-colored buildings create an unusual street ambience for such a large city, one that some have characterized as having a delightfully human scale. They also serve as an important adjunct to the city's unique combination of topography and natural beauty. The relative absence of tall buildings minimizes interference with the beautiful views from the city's higher elevations. The low buildings follow the contours of the hills, becoming an important part of the view themselves. More sunlight reaches sidewalks and small parks and other public spaces, where shoppers, workers on their lunch breaks, and residents of the center-city area (many of whom are elderly, unemployed, or otherwise limited in their resources) benefit from the warmth and brightness it brings. The prevalence of light-colored buildings also adds to the beauty of the scenic views, and the buildings reflect sunlight into the streets and other public spaces.

Sunlight at street level is a particularly important commodity in San Francisco. For all of the accolades that have been given to "the city by the bay," its climate leaves something to be desired. Although winter weather in San Francisco is milder than that in much of the rest of the United States, there are few periods of really warm summer weather. The two warmest months of the year there are September and October, when the average high temperatures are only 68.8°F and 68.2°F. Moreover, the cool temperatures during the period from May to October, when residents and visitors expect to wear lighter clothing and to enjoy being outdoors, as beautiful as that is, are often accompanied by strong winds and fog off the bay, except for a few midday hours. During those cool, damp times, especially, any blocking of sunlight by buildings can detract significantly from the comfort of those who are outdoors and interfere with the enjoyment of their activities, and may discourage other people from going out at all. The same is true of turbulent wind effects that are sometimes caused by tall buildings, especially those of massive design and those much taller than surrounding structures.

The problem: high-rise development

The low profile and pastel coloring of San Francisco's architecture clearly mean a great deal to how the city looks (the availability of scenic views from its hills toward the bay and beyond, and the brightness and attractiveness of those views) and how the city feels (the availability of sunlight at street level provides relief from frequent cool temperatures, wind, and fog). They also make a significant contribution to the image that San Franciscans have of their city, as unique both in its beauty and in its freedom from the problems of urbanization that plague other large American cities. San Francisco's beauty is important not only as an attraction for tourists and filmmakers but also as a source of great pride and satisfaction for its residents.

But in the 1960s the city's architecture began to change. Rising land values in San Francisco, especially in its financial, shopping, and hotel districts, encouraged developers to begin to plan and to build high-rise buildings in those areas. In the late 1960s, twin curved apartment buildings were built side by side on the city's shoreline, near Fisherman's Wharf and other tourist attractions. The Fontana Towers, as they were called, were about 20 stories high, tall enough to block the views of the bay and Alcatraz Island for many residents of Russian Hill behind them, and for many people passing through that section of the city (Figure 14.1). They drew criticism from some quarters for that reason.

In 1967, the Alcoa Building was completed on Battery Street, between Clay and Washington. It stood 25 stories tall, and its exterior was covered by a slab-sided black skin, with external diagonal bracing structures. This was a building that blocked views, shaded streets, and clashed visually with the

Figure 14.1. The Fontana Towers apartment buildings, built on the waterfront at the foot of Russian Hill, blocking San Francisco Bay and Alcatraz Island from the view of many of the area's residents. Photo by author.

buildings around it. It is no wonder that it drew critical comments from many residents of the city, primarily for its height and atypical appearance. Such criticism was fanned by the completion of another tall, dark-colored building in the financial district at about the same time, the Bank of America headquarters located at California and Kearny. It stood 52 stories tall and was clad in dark red marble.

High-rise buildings and criticism of them came very late to San Francisco. In New York City, criticism of the "skyscraper" appeared in the first decade of the twentieth century. *New York Times* architectural columnist Paul Goldberger (1983) has described the reactions of New Yorkers to a series of buildings that reached successively far beyond the heights of their neighbors in lower Manhattan. Even though those earliest high-rise buildings in New York were admired for their style, the magnificent views they afforded occupants and visitors, and the progress they symbolized, they were at the same time criticized for shattering the scale of the city and stealing light from those in their shadows, to borrow Goldberger's words (1983, p. 3).

As whole blocks of tall buildings grew up in New York City, and as designs became less graceful, more massive, and consequently more disruptive, the criticism became more intense and spread across issues of aesthetics, fire safety, and light and ventilation in canyonized streets. Some early critics predicted that city streets would eventually require artificial light and ventilation. By 1916, a year after the completion of the 39-story (reduced from a proposed 62-story design blocked by opponents eight years earlier), full-built-out ("parallelopized"), and much-criticized Equitable Building at 120 Broadway, opposition to unfettered high-rise development in New York had grown strong enough to prod the city into adopting a zoning ordinance limiting the total floor area of any new building to 12 times the area of the site on which it would be built.

Today, analysts recognize an even longer and more comprehensive list of problems associated with high-rise development (e.g., Appleyard & Fishman, 1977). These include degradation of the adjoining physical environment through changes in the microclimate, caused by shading and deflection of air currents above street level down into the streets; the threat of falling objects, including parts of the buildings themselves; increased motor-vehicle and pedestrian traffic; litter and physical deterioration because of the larger numbers of building users; and interruption of views. They also include negative social impacts, such as the loss of privacy in nearby buildings, decreased neighborhood cohesion, and a loss of territorial control, with consequent increases in problems with crime (see the discussion of defensible space in chapter 11) and the oppressive symbolism of an impersonal, unfriendly city.

Although some of these problems were discussed in the early debates over high-rise development in San Francisco, the emphasis there was quite different, because the city was so different from New York and the other cities that had already experienced accelerated high-rise development. Foremost among the differences was the image San Franciscans held of their city. Kreimer (1973) has used media stories about the early debates over high-rise development in San Francisco to document that image and the role it played in arousing opposition to the "Manhattanization" of the city. She found that San Franciscans saw their city as unique in its beauty, because of its complementary relationship to its hilly, seaside natural setting. They also saw a unique value in the extent to which their city reflected its history, especially the tastes of the many individuals who had been responsible for determining the shapes of its older buildings and of the neighborhoods and other areas they formed. San Franciscans felt that their city had changed so little in its appearance, and in terms of the relationship between its appearance and its natural setting, because its development had not been guided by outsiders and narrow financial interests that might have erased its history (as had happened in other cities) and because it was relatively free from so many of the problems of other large cities, including those attributable to extensive high-rise development.

In light of those beliefs, it is not surprising that San Franciscans responded strongly to the prospect of increased high-rise development. To them, that would mean not only the likelihood of more shade and wind in a climate that could ill afford either, and more traffic and crime in a city whose relative lack of both distinguished it from other cities its size, but also the loss of the natural beauty and historical uniqueness they prized. Goldberger (1985) has written of San Francisco that "there is no city in America in which the skyscraper is more disliked than here."

The forces that supported high-rise development as a step toward progress and prosperity were faced with a large and active opposition voicing a broad set of concerns. In part, that was because high-rise development would pose a more serious and comprehensive set of problems for San Francisco than it had for other cities. San Francisco's climate, topography, and architectural context were quite different and seemingly much less compatible with high-rise development than were those of New York, Chicago, or Houston. In addition, and perhaps just as important, the debate over high-rise development and the accompanying planning process in San Francisco took place under quite different social and political conditions.

San Franciscans, unlike residents of other large American cities, had not grown accustomed to high-rise development on a large scale. The environmental movement of the 1960s had brought an increased concern with the preservation of environmental values and an increased awareness of their importance in people's lives, as compared with the views that had existed when high-rise development began in other large American cities. That heightened consciousness of environmental issues was particularly acute in San Francisco, where the Sierra Club had been founded by John Muir and others, and where it still makes its home today, in a relatively liberal political climate.

Furthermore, during the period of debate over the future course of high-rise development in San Francisco, new environmental-protection laws were being put into effect, such as the National Environmental Policy Act of 1969 (NEPA), which made it necessary for developers to address such concerns in their plans for high-rise buildings and which directed planners to hold developers accountable for them. This case is an especially good example of the way that sweeping legislation like NEPA extended protection of the environment to include its aesthetic, cultural, and other subjective qualities and to range far beyond the borders of national parks and wilderness preserves, to city streets, parks, and playgrounds, and even to the sidewalks outside our cities' office buildings and department stores. The grass-roots environmental movement became a party to the process of planning for high-rise development in San Francisco.

In 1969, the United States Steel Corporation (now known as USX) announced plans to build a new corporate headquarters building in San Francisco. That declaration catalyzed a growing opposition to high-rise development in the city, among its citizens and their supporters elsewhere. Although it is doubtful that anyone knew it at the time, the company's plans and the local political struggle they brought about would lead eventually to the development of a comprehensive plan to regulate high-rise development in San Francisco. Furthermore, the debate in San Francisco would trigger renewed concerns nationwide about the effects of high-rise development on the urban environment. And the resolution reached in San Francisco, which was more far-reaching and comprehensive than any previous planning policies for high-rise development, would become a model for planners' responses to similar concerns in other cities. Finally, the process of developing plans for high-rise zoning in San Francisco provided fertile ground for the application of EDR methods that were being developed during that same period across the bay in Berkeley.

The U.S. Steel plans called for a building of 50 stories that would stand 550 feet tall. It was to be built on a platform extending 1,000 feet into San Francisco Bay. At that time, building heights were limited to 150 feet in the area where U.S. Steel planned to build. When the developer asked the San Francisco Board of Supervisors (the equivalent of a city council) for a variance that would allow the project to go forward as an exception to the existing zoning regulations, latent opposition to high-rise development in the city was galvanized to oppose the variance, to attempt to prevent the building from being built.

A local clothing manufacturer, Alvin Duskin, spearheaded the opposition to the U.S. Steel plan. He led a coalition that included architectural preservationists, environmentalists, and neighborhood groups that saw the building as a threat to the quality of their lives. The views of this anti-high-rise coalition were promoted by a popular local newspaper columnist, Herb Caen of the *San Francisco Chronicle,* who acted as their spokesperson. The group also paid for advertising to spread their message. In October 1970, Duskin ran a provocative advertisement in local newspapers in which a panoramic photograph of San Francisco in 1957 was shown above the same view of the city in 1969 (Figure 14.2). That comparison demonstrated very effectively how high-rise development in a modern architectural style was already changing the appearance of the city (and anticipated quite remarkably the systematic and extensive use of environmental simulation a decade later to help write new regulations for high-rise development).

The efforts of the opponents to the U.S. Steel proposal were countered by many groups: by the developer who had proposed the project; by local business people, who viewed opposition to the proposal as a threat to their own freedom of action; by local politicians, who saw in the opposition to the proposal a threat to the area's prospects for economic growth (including the mayor, Joseph Alioto); and by developers around the country, who feared the precedent that might be set by placing such constraints on their activities in the name of protecting the environment in such a comprehensive way.

STOP THEM FROM BURYING OUR CITY UNDER A SKYLINE OF TOMBSTONES

Both the above pictures are of downtown San Francisco. Same spot. Same time of day. Same weather conditions. The top one was twelve years ago. The bottom one, last year. San Francisco was once light, hilly, pastel, open. Inviting. In only twelve years it has taken on the forbidding look of every other American city. Forty more skyscrapers are due in the next five years. They are as great a disaster for the city economically as they are esthetically. Ask a New York taxpayer.

What can you do to stop it?

Contact SAN FRANCISCO OPPOSITION, 520 Third Street (second floor) or telephone 397-9220.

Figure 14.2. The advertisement placed by anti-high-rise activist Alvin Duskin in the *San Francisco Chronicle* in October 1970. Source: Conway (1977, p. 83); reprinted with permission of Dowden, Hutchinson & Ross, publishers.

In the context of the long fight over the U.S. Steel building, a number of long-standing generic issues surrounding high-rise development surfaced in San Francisco. Ever since New York City had experienced the first skyscraper – as buildings were built that were much taller than those around them or, in some cases, than any of their predecessors – people had expressed reservations. As Paul Goldberger has pointed out (1979), it became clear early on that tall buildings, and especially those of great mass, built in rectangular shapes, uniform from top to bottom, could cause discomfort for people in their vicinity. They limited the views of residents or workers in nearby buildings, they cast shadows that darkened and cooled the surrounding street-level environment, they could cause uncomfortably windy conditions at street level as ambient winds struck their façades and were forced toward the ground at intensified speeds and in swirling patterns, and they could disrupt people's sense of human scale and order in the city.

Professionals involved in evaluating the U.S. Steel proposal and the environmental-impact statement were aware of these concerns. As a result, issues of microclimate and the effects of the building on sun and wind, and thus on the comfort of pedestrians in the area surrounding the building, joined the issues of aesthetics and scale raised by lay critics of the proposal. In the end, the U.S. Steel proposal was rejected, in a roundabout way. In February 1971, the San Francisco Board of Supervisors voted a 175-foot-height limit for new buildings in an area of the waterfront that included the U.S. Steel site. But the issues raised in this case lived on. For the next 15 years or so, a more generalized debate on those issues continued in San Francisco. While new high-rise buildings continued to be built, planners, elected officials, and citizens' groups searched for a comprehensive solution for the potential problems of high-rise development in the city. In that effort, they were aided by researchers at the University of California, across the bay in Berkeley, using an exciting new technology known as environmental simulation.

The role of environmental simulation

The public debate between those who had proposed the U.S. Steel building and those opposed to their plan eventually developed into a comprehensive consideration of the future of high-rise development in San Francisco. The initial focus of the Duskin-led coalition that opposed the plan was on the danger to the scenic and architectural beauty of the city. From there, the issues expanded to include a variety of well-known possible effects on the microclimate in the immediate vicinity of the building, especially loss of sunlight and increased wind speeds at street level and their effects on the thermal comfort on nearby sidewalks and in adjacent public open spaces. Concern spread from the issue of the proposed U.S. Steel building itself to the possibility that other high-rise buildings would be planned for sensitive sites within the city around which there were high levels of use of sidewalks, parks, playgrounds, and other public spaces that would be threatened with loss of sunlight and increased wind speeds at street level during critical hours of heavy use and seasons of greatest outdoor activity. There was also concern for areas in the city where the existing architecture was low, light-colored, and uniform, such that the prevailing character or image of the city would be threatened by high-rise development.

In the most general sense, the questions about high-rise development that were debated in San Francisco were similar to those that are raised whenever the suitability of a change in the use of an existing site is at issue. There was a need in San Francisco, as there always is, to determine exactly what effects the U.S. Steel building and other high-rise buildings would have on the cultural and aesthetic life of the city, on the physical comfort of those who use its sidewalks, playgrounds, and other public spaces, and, by implication at least, on the personal, commercial, and recreational activities that take place there. It is common practice when a new building (or roadway, or government policy) is proposed that we ask or demand that the designers and planners who are about to change our world give us a preview of its effects.

In many cases this is done exclusively through words – written reports, speeches, answers to questions at hearings and press conferences, and the like. When a change in the built environment is proposed, however, the preview usually is presented in visual form. Usually there are architectural drawings – floor plans and elevations, for example – and often scale models of the proposed building or park or whatever. In many cases, especially when the project is large and costly, these representations are quite detailed and realistic. However, even the best of them beg the real question that faces designers and planners: the question of how the behaviors of those who use or merely encounter these new environmental forms will be affected by them – how, if at all, their feelings, movements, work, or play will be changed, shaped, improved, or impaired as a result of the implementation of the eventual design or plan.

For the past 20 years or so there has been a concerted effort on the part of some in the field of environmental-design research – in a genuine collaboration between behavioral scientists and designers – to systematize, evaluate critically, and improve the means available to designers, planners, and others involved in the process of environmental-design decision making to preview the effects of the environmental changes they help to bring about. Collectively, those means are known as environmental simulation.

Environmental simulation probably has been used in environmental design, in one form or another, since one of our primitive ancestors took a pointed stick and drew on the ground the floor plan for the use of a new cave. To this day, Sheppard (1982) has found, it still most often takes the form of drawings – the floor plans and elevations that architects typically show their clients. Some projects, especially larger ones, warrant the use of more costly, three-dimensional scale models. In an effort to achieve greater realism, environmental-design researchers have worked to develop more realistic simulations that can incorporate the movements and multiplicity of perspectives that characterize actual encounters with real environmental settings. But their real contribution has come in devising means of assessing potential users' reactions to a simulation of an existing place or a proposed design or, even better, to several different places or alternative designs. These assessment methods make it possible to predict users' reactions to the settings themselves and, perhaps more important or at least more basic, to determine the validity of simulations in evoking responses similar to those evoked by the real places they simulate, for the purpose of research or to advance a particular design project. A good deal of the work on environmental simulation has taken place at the University of California, Berkeley, in the Institute for Urban and Regional Development.

In all, a wide variety of environmental-simulation techniques have been used and evaluated. McKechnie (1977) has suggested that they can best be described by their positions on two dimensions. The first ranges from perceptual to conceptual. Perceptual simulations are realistic. They look like the places they simulate. They include realistic drawings and models, photographs of places or models, and films or videotapes made in those places or models. Conceptual simulations convey information about places without actual physical resemblance. These are schematic representations such as floor plans and other abstract drawings, made either by people or through computer software. McKechnie's second dimension of simulations ranges from static to dynamic. Static simulations provide just one view or perspective of the place, such as in a drawing or photograph. Dynamic simulations provide a series of views or a continuous tour of a place (real or modeled). This type is exemplified best by films and videotapes made as a camera is moved through a large-scale environmental setting or a model of one. There are other varieties of simulations that might also be considered dynamic, though somewhat less so, such as a series of photographs showing sequential or at least different views of a setting, models that can be viewed from a variety of perspectives, and full-scale mock-ups that people can explore.

There have been several systematic attempts to evaluate the validity of these environmental-simulation techniques by comparing people's responses to existing settings and to simulations of them. Such studies have recently been comprehensively reviewed by Craik and Feimer (1987) and Bosselman and Craik (1987). Summarized briefly, the existing evidence suggests that even relatively simple simulations, such as color slides, can be extremely effective in evoking responses similar to the responses evoked by the actual settings they are meant to simulate. The most extensive and most encouraging validity studies have been carried out to evaluate the innovative forms of environmental simulation that are used at the Environmental Simulation Laboratory (ESL) at the University of California, Berkeley.

Those "modelscope" simulations utilize a three-dimensional model of an environmental setting – an existing setting for the purposes of many research studies, including those to test the validity of the simulation, or a proposed new or modified setting for the purposes of previewing the effects of a proposed design (see chapter 4 for an example). A miniaturized camera probe, suspended from overhead supports, is "driven" through or around the model by a computer-controlled transport system. It is possible to simulate a variety of different speeds, such as walking or automobile travel. It is also possible to simulate a variety of different perspectives: from the eye level of a pedestrian, an automobile passenger, or a helicopter passenger. The system can provide a live television picture of the camera's tour through the model and a permanent record on videotape or film.

The result is an extremely realistic facsimile of the experience of traveling through the modeled environmental setting in person or watching a film that was made in the setting itself. That personal impression, gained from viewing a film of a simulated nine-mile-long, 25-minute auto tour of an eight-square-mile area of Marin County, California (near San Francisco), was verified in the most extensive validation study carried out to date for any environmental-simulation technique.

Four randomly constructed groups of environmental-design professionals and planners were shown the Marin County area, which contained a variety of natural and built settings, in four different ways. One group was taken on an actual automobile tour. A second group watched a color film made by a camera in the front passenger seat of an automobile that had been driven over the same route. A third group watched a color film made in a model of the same Marin County area using the modelscope technique described earlier. A fourth group watched a black-and-white modelscope videotape of the model.

After the "showings," all participants completed an extensive battery of measures of their cognitive, perceptual, and evaluative impressions of the area they had seen, as well as a battery of personality and environmental-attitude measures. Summarized briefly, it was found that the responses to the color film made by the ESL modelscope were virtually indistinguishable from the responses of those who had taken actual automobile tours (Craik & Feimer, 1987). In fact, the participants' personality traits and attitudes affected their responses to the experimental measures considerably more than did the form in which they were exposed to the environmental setting (Feimer, 1984).

The modelscope technique and other innovative environmental-simulation methods used at the Berkeley ESL made an important contribution to resolution of the high-rise-development debate in San Francisco. In fact, the ESL, founded around 1970 by the late landscape architect Donald Appleyard and the environmental (and personality) psychologist Kenneth Craik, and directed since Appleyard's death by Peter Bosselman, partly as a result of their involvement in the high-rise zoning case, serves today as an ongoing adjunct to the work of the San Francisco Department of City Planning, in addition to its role as occasional consultant to many other cities on high-rise development and a wide variety of other design and planning issues.

The modelscope simulation technique was used during the process of developing high-rise zoning regulations in San Francisco to give policymakers previews of the effects that high-rise buildings would have on street scale, on the mix of uses, and on the openness of the streets to sky and sunlight (Bosselman & Craik, 1987, figures 5–8, p. 179). A representative scale model of a downtown street was used to illustrate the consequences of alternative planning controls. Varied sizes and types of high-rise buildings were added successively to the model in place of the existing buildings, at locations where planners judged that such development was most likely to occur. Modelscope films showing the various forms of the model were used in an effort to educate policymakers and the public about the choices implied by alternative zoning controls. The films were shown in meetings of planners and planning commission members and to the public as part of a community-affairs program on a local television station.

The modelscope simulation technique was also used to show the changes that had taken place in the San Francisco skyline between the 1930s and the 1970s. This film of a large-scale model of the city, showing a longer-range perspective above street level, addressed the same issue that Duskin raised in his newspaper advertisement showing photographs of the downtown area taken in 1957 and 1969. However, it is believed that the simulation film provides a more detailed record, continuous and realistic (dynamic), to describe how prior high-rise development had changed the visual character of the city.

These two modelscope applications reflect the most common uses of environmental simulation to preview and evaluate prospective changes in the visual character of places by comparing existing forms with a range of possible alternatives. Thus, most efforts to improve simulation techniques have been directed toward producing sequential visual experiences. However, the issues that carried the greatest weight in the long debate over high-rise zoning controls in San Francisco were the possible decreases in solar access on sidewalks and in plazas and other public spaces and the possible increases in wind speeds or swirling at street level that high-rise buildings might produce.

The Berkeley researchers, led by Peter Bosselman, used simulation techniques to evaluate the risks of such negative effects on the microclimate in the city's downtown and hotel districts (Bosselman, Flores, & O'Hare, 1983; Bosselman et al., 1984). Using the same modifiable models as in the modelscope simulations, they were able to target important sites where there was heavy use: sidewalks for shoppers and public open spaces for residents of densely populated center-city areas with large numbers of vulnerable users (children, the elderly, and poor people). They used simulation techniques that are rarely seen in environmental-design research – techniques designed to assess potential users' evaluative responses to alternative designs.

In a wind tunnel, existing structures were compared with new structures of various heights, and comparisons were made between massive straight-sided designs and designs whose sides were stepped back or tapered so that the floor areas of upper stories would be smaller than those of lower stories. In general, smaller height discrepancies between a new building and the surrounding structures, as well as less massive, stepped-back designs, were found to be associated with smaller undesirable changes in prevailing wind conditions.

An even more important focus of the Berkeley simulation research program on the effects of high-rise development was the availability of sunlight in streets and in the variety of important open spaces that might be shadowed by tall buildings. These simulations of solar access also compared existing buildings with hypothetical new buildings at likely development sites that would vary in height and in the way in which they would be stepped back from the existing street wall. These simulations resulted not only in predictions for varied development scenarios but also in the development of a more general test to which any proposed building design could be put.

The simulation of high-rise buildings' effects on solar access was accomplished in two different ways, one for sidewalks and another for public open spaces. Each began with a photograph taken by a still camera fitted with a fish-eye lens that gave an optically distorted but useful 360° view. The camera could be placed in the middle of an existing street or in any location in an existing public open space that needed to be protected. The resulting photograph would show the profiles of the surrounding buildings (see Figure 14.3 for an example). Then lines representing the paths traveled by the sun across the sky at different times of the year during the hours of daylight could be superimposed on the photograph. The interest in this case was in the summer months, during the afternoon hours, when outdoor activities in San Francisco are most in need of sunlight at street level.

In the case of streets, photomontage techniques were then used to simulate the addition of high-rise buildings at likely development sites, at varying heights and of alternative designs. The resulting photographic simulations permitted determinations of exactly how much sunlight would be lost during the time period in question under each of the development scenarios considered. Using this technique, it is immediately apparent when a hypothetical new building will block sunlight; alternatively, one can easily see the maximum height of a new building on a specified site that will avoid shadowing on the sunny side of the street.

For public open spaces, the original fish-eye photograph was used in conjunction with computer software to construct a representation of the maximum building height (at each of a number of systematically chosen distances from the point in question) above which new construction would block sunlight on

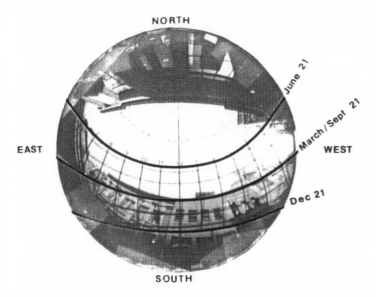

Figure 14.3. Fish-eye photo with sun-path overlays that can be used to set a maximum height limit for buildings on the south side of the street, to prevent shadowing of the opposite sidewalk during midday hours from March to September. Source: Bosselman, Flores, and O'Hare (1983, p. 28); reproduced with permission of the Institute for Urban and Regional Development, University of California, Berkeley.

dates and during hours of heavy use, when a loss of sunlight would materially reduce the thermal comfort of the people there. These diagrams are known as solar fans (see Figure 14.4 for an example). If a proposed new building is to be located on one of these sites, the maximum allowable height can be determined at both the point nearest the protected open space and the point farthest from it. The top of the new building will have to fit that contour, using a stepped-back design, or stay below it to avoid shadowing that space.

Both the photomontage technique for streets and the solar-fan adaptation for public open spaces can be used to provide permanent guidelines for high-rise construction at any particular location. Any proposal for a new building at a specific site along a street or near a public open space can be evaluated quickly for its effect on necessary sunlight at street level. In effect, by setting a limit on the amount of loss of solar access that is acceptable at the sidewalk on the sunny side of a street or in a specific location within a public open space, where sunlight is available on summer afternoons and where use at those times is heavy, the simulation results can be used to determine whether or not a building proposal is acceptable, or to guide the designer of a building in adjusting its height and/or the way in which its upper floors are stepped back from its base in order to avoid unacceptable shadowing effects.

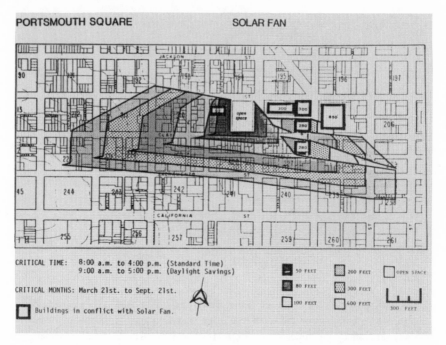

Figure 14.4. The solar fan for Portsmouth Square, showing height limits for surrounding building sites that would prevent shadowing of heavily used areas of the park during critical periods of use. Source: Bosselman, Flores, and O'Hare (1983, p. 33); reproduced with permission of the Institute for Urban and Regional Development, University of California, Berkeley.

In the case of the proposed U.S. Steel building, it would have been possible to use all of these simulation techniques together in a straightforward way to preview the changes that would have taken place in the appearance of the surrounding streetscape and in wind conditions and sunlight at street level in specific locations surrounding the building site. Or it would have been possible to use that same information as a basis for altering the design of the building (e.g., reducing its height, tapering its top, or stepping back its upper stories) to reduce any negative impacts on appearance (the height of a tall building is far less obvious if only the lower floors, up to the level of surrounding buildings, are flush with the street wall), wind, or sunlight.

But by the time these techniques became available, the interest among planners and the public in San Francisco had broadened far beyond that single building, reaching to the question of how to regulate all future development in the main shopping and hotel areas north of Market Street in such a way as to achieve an acceptable balance between economic interests in development and interests in preserving the prevailing appearance of existing streets and districts, in addition to minimizing losses in thermal comfort due to increases in wind and decreases in sunlight at street level in those heavily used locations at those times of the year and of the day when such conditions would materially lessen the comfort and hinder the activities of users.

The goal, in short, had become a comprehensive set of zoning regulations for high-rise development that would protect the urban environment as much as possible in light of the city's economic needs.

Landmark high-rise zoning regulations for San Francisco, based on environmental-design research

In 1971, the political coalition opposed to unrestricted high-rise development in San Francisco, spurred on by the Board of Supervisors' rejection of the proposal for the U.S. Steel building, led an unsuccessful effort to pass a ballot referendum that would have limited new construction in San Francisco to a maximum height of six stories. Two more referenda, one in 1972 for a 14-story limit and one in 1979 for 20 stories and a limitation on total plan area, also failed. Between 1971 and 1981, 65 new high-rise office buildings were built in the city, containing a total of 30 million square feet of floor space.

The 1983 election ballot in San Francisco contained yet another referendum proposing limitations on high-rise construction in the city: Proposition K. Based in large part on the work done at the Berkeley ESL by Bosselman and colleagues, it contained more precise recommendations for varying high-rise controls, targeted to preserving sunlight and avoiding uncomfortable winds in heavily used outdoor public spaces, by both limiting the height and controlling the design of new buildings in specified areas of the city. By a vote of 50.6% to 49.4%, so close that the result could not be announced until the following day, the proposition passed.

The passage of Proposition K was not the end of the struggle for high-rise zoning controls in San Francisco, however. For the next year and a half the San Francisco Board of Supervisors worked to develop a comprehensive plan that would provide specific regulations to implement the general provisions of Proposition K, as well as other needed zoning changes for the downtown area. Like the language of the successful referendum proposal, their deliberations were shaped by the simulation research at Berkeley that provided essential information about means for preventing undesirable effects of high-rise development on the appearance and comfort of surrounding city areas.

On July 3, 1986, at 1:00 a.m., after an eight-hour final debate, the San Francisco Board of Supervisors passed an amendment to the city planning code for a three-quarter square-mile area north of Market Street in downtown San Francisco. Known as the 1985 Downtown Plan (San Francisco Department of City Planning, 1985), these new zoning regulations reflected directly the simulation-based analyses carried out during the preceding several years by

Bosselman and his colleagues at Berkeley. Their provisions with respect to high-rise development in the 470-acre downtown zone were intended to slow its growth, to shift growth to the industrial area south of Market Street, where use of public open spaces was judged to be less vital to the city and its residents, and to minimize the negative impacts of high-rise buildings on the surrounding environment and on users of nearby public spaces in the targeted zone.

Specifically, the 1985 Downtown Plan set various maximum building heights, from 50 feet to 550 feet (the previous limit had been a uniform 700 feet), that followed from the results of simulation analyses of the impacts on visual quality and thermal comfort at specific locations throughout the zone. The new zoning regulations also limited the design alternatives for architects of new buildings. Requirements for stepped-back or tapered designs (to minimize undesirable changes in the appearance of the street wall, to protect sunlit sidewalks and public open spaces from undesirable shadowing during the times of the year and hours of the day when their use would otherwise be degraded or discouraged, and to avoid creating uncomfortable downdraft winds at street level) were passed, along with limitations on maximum square footage or floor area based on the size of the site, to ensure against massive, slab-sided designs. In addition, 251 historic buildings in the zone were protected absolutely against redevelopment, and 200 others were protected to a lesser degree. Liberal provisions were included for transferring air rights from historic buildings and other buildings in the restricted zone to other areas of the city; the aim was to discourage even many developments that otherwise would have been acceptable, thus further precluding development where its negative impact on the appearance and the local culture of San Francisco would have been greatest. Finally, an overall limit of 950,000 square feet of new development was set for the zone over each of the first three years (approximately equal to the floor area of the famous TransAmerica building).

There are many who have expressed the opinion that the 1985 Downtown Plan seriously compromised the intent of the framers of Proposition K. For one thing, buildings that had been proposed prior to the adoption of the plan were given "grandfather" exemptions from the new regulations. In addition, it is still possible for developers to seek variances from the zoning regulations. After all, the U.S. Steel proposal of 1969 was in violation of the building-height regulations in effect at that time, and the political struggle that followed was over the developer's request for a variance.

However, it seems that the plan can be applauded on two accounts. If it stays in place, undoubtedly it will afford some degree of protection from future degradation of the visual quality and microclimate in the downtown area north of Market Street. In addition, its provisions, based on knowledge gained from environmental simulation, limit building heights and designs in ways and at locations where the greatest protection for the environment and the greatest consideration for the people who use those areas can be gained with the least unnecessary restrictions on the economic growth of the city, the economic freedom of developers and other citizens, and the artistic freedom of designers. They may be inadequate, as some critics have charged, but these new high-rise controls are revolutionary in their scope and in the precision with which they seek benefits and prescribe restrictions accordingly.

Evaluation

Stage 1: Background analysis

In this case, detailed knowledge of San Francisco's history and culture, as well as its geographic and climatic characteristics, was critically important to the successful development of high-rise zoning laws for the city's downtown. San Franciscans, who have been known to refer to their city as the "Paris of the West," feared Manhattanization, although residents of Chicago might be more likely to claim bragging rights as the inventors of the skyscraper. In San Francisco, unregulated high-rise development threatened the hilly city's famed scenic views and the scarce sunny, warm summer hours on its streets and in its parks, whereas in Manhattan, where there are few scenic views to protect, shade is at a higher premium than sun during New York's hot, hazy summer days. In order to gain a sense of why high-rise development was a problem and of how that problem could be approached, it was necessary for Bosselman and the others involved in that analysis to know the city well and to be aware of its citizens' feelings about it.

Stage 2: Management goals

There were several clear goals for the development of new high-rise zoning controls for San Francisco. One was to preserve the architectural character or visual image that was unique among major American cities: streets of uniform, low, pastel-colored buildings of traditional design. Another was to avoid interference with the scenic views from the uniformly tiered buildings and the streets on the city's many hills: views of the streets and houses below, of the bay, with its islands and bridges, and of the hills beyond. A third was to protect people in the city's streets and public open spaces from the shadows and wind currents that high-rise buildings of the wrong design in the wrong locations could create, particularly during the precious hours of midday sunshine during the city's predominantly cool, foggy, damp summer season.

Stage 3: Environment–behavior relationships

The research that was conducted at the ESL at Berkeley, by Bosselman and his colleagues in the Institute for Urban and Regional Development, was in most respects quite unlike that on which most of the projects in this volume were based. Only one aspect of that research directly involved prospective users' responses to alternative solutions to the problems being addressed. And that aspect – the simulation of alternative scenarios for high-rise development along downtown streets in order to depict their effects on the visual image of San Francisco, or on people's appraisal of it – did not involve systematic collection or analysis of data. Rather, the simulations were used to educate policymakers, particularly the city's Board of Supervisors, and concerned citizens about the need for limitations on the amount and type of high-rise development. The simulations showed what would result if there were large increases in the numbers of high-rise buildings at likely development sites, particularly buildings of modern, slab-sided design rising flush with the street wall; that was contrasted with the possibility of less dense concentrations of tapered or stepped-back buildings that would preserve the existing uniform five- or six-story street wall, which obviously would do less damage to the image of the city, and that helped convince viewers of the need for appropriate new controls.

Precise calculations were made for maximum allowable building heights at all locations so that new buildings would not cast shadows in downtown streets and open spaces, using photomontage techniques (for streets) and solar-fan techniques (for open spaces), along with meteorological data. Knowledge of the sun's path during the critical hours on summer days made it possible to set criteria on a street-by-street, park-by-park basis in such a precise way that necessary setbacks from the street wall could be determined for every floor of a proposed new building above the existing street wall, at any site that posed a shadowing problem.

Finally, wind-tunnel tests for specific building sites were used to identify those locations where, given the prevailing winds and the nature of the surrounding buildings, slab-sided buildings would cause problems with downdrafts. In those cases, the same tests could be used to identify tapered designs whose use would eliminate the problem.

In all of these cases, particularly the latter two, the methodological questions that plague more conventional behavioral research aimed at uncovering the behavioral consequences of alternative design or plan elements are vitiated for the most part. There is no agonizing causal inference to be made. There is little doubt that the simulations used in this project succeeded in previewing realistically the changes in appearance, solar access, and wind conditions that a prospective high-rise development would actually bring about, or that the height and design limitations indicated or actually tested would prevent those unwanted outcomes. Nor does there seem to be much question that these techniques could be adapted for use in other cities that might decide to set similar goals for high-rise development.

Stage 4: Plan elements

As described earlier, the final 1985 Downtown Plan identifies maximum building heights and more specific design limitations for every building site in the area it covers. The limits on height are set to prevent loss of sunlight at street level during midday hours on summer days. In some cases, that necessitates precise setbacks on a floor-by-floor basis. This can be seen quite clearly in the design of a building across Market Street from United Nations Plaza at the edge of the city's Civic Center (Figure 14.5). The profile of that stepped-back building follows the solar fan for the plaza so as to avoid any loss of sunlight on those summer days when the fog lifts and the shoppers, office workers, and homeless people who use the plaza are fortunate enough to be able to bask in the sunshine.

Along streets where the existing buildings compose a uniform five- or six-story street wall, new high-rise buildings must be designed to preserve that appearance, through the use of appropriate setbacks for floors above that level. And at locations where downdrafts could be a problem for those on the nearby streets, only buildings of tapered designs that have been shown to pose no such threat can be erected.

Stage 5: Overall plan

The elements described earlier that were addressed to problems of visual image, solar access, and wind currents, based on the Berkeley simulation studies, were parts of the much more comprehensive 1985 Downtown Plan. However, they were, fortunately, highly consistent both with one another (i.e., tapered building designs can be used to preserve the appearance of the existing street wall, to follow the contours of solar access, and to avoid wind downdrafts) and with other elements addressed to traffic and other zoning issues. Thus, whereas they did not constitute the entire plan, they were not seriously compromised in the process of being fit into it.

Stage 6: POE

There has been no formal evaluation of the impact of the 1985 Downtown Plan on any of the management goals discussed in this chapter. Although it might seem that it could be taken for granted that new buildings conforming to the height and design limitations established in the plan would present fewer problems of clashing architectural styles on San Francisco streets and fewer problems with shadowing and wind in those streets and in the 200 or so parks, playgrounds, and squares in the affected area than would the taller and boxier buildings that otherwise might be built, it is not clear how many such substitu-

Figure 14.5. Three views of a building across Market Street to the southeast of San Francisco's United Nations Plaza, whose stepped-back design avoids interference with solar access on the often damp and windswept plaza. Photos by author.

tions have been or will be made. There are clear examples to be seen of new buildings whose sizes and shapes obviously were constrained by the new zoning regulations. In fact, at least one guidebook makes a point of identifying several of them for interested visitors (Wurman, 1987). However, many high-rise projects were exempted from the new zoning controls because their formal proposals had been filed before the new controls were enacted. The new law also contains a provision by which exceptions can be granted, and some believe that this could seriously undermine the protections that the law seems to afford.

In addition, one of the issues raised earlier concerning the impact of high-rise development in San Francisco seems to have been overlooked. The simulations of the impacts of new high-rise buildings did not address concerns about preserving either specific views from existing buildings and streets or the hilly appearance of the city as a whole. Although a computer-simulation technique developed by Winter (K. Craik, personal communication, 1980) for assessing the quality of the view from a building in terms of real-estate values could have provided the Berkeley group one method, apparently it was not used to preview the impact of new high-rise development and was not incorporated into the new zoning regulations in the way that simulations of street-wall appearance, solar access, and wind effects were. The issue of changes in the city's "hillscapes" seems not to have been addressed at all in the EDR process, despite the fact that the photomontage and modelscope simulation techniques would seem perfectly capable of dealing with those problems. It seems fairly clear, moreover, that controls designed to deal with architectural style, solar access, and wind problems would not necessarily protect views or contours. A tall building might be located where it would not block sunlight from any street or open space, be tapered to prevent downdrafts at street level, and be set back above the street wall to avoid a clash with the existing architecture, and yet still block the views of neighbors and passersby and disrupt the even contour of a hillside. Thus, one would not expect a salutary result should anyone ever carry out an evaluation of the impact of the new high-rise controls on degradation of scenic views and hillside contours.

Stage 7: Future impact

The impact on San Francisco itself of Bosselman and colleagues' contributions to the 1985 Downtown Plan can be seen only in individual buildings, not evaluated as a whole from the information that is currently available. We do know that there has been a good deal of construction that falls outside the plan: building projects approved prior to its enactment into law. It seems likely that developers, aided by the economic pressures of recent years, will succeed in having additional projects exempted from at least some of the provisions of the plan to which the research discussed in this chapter contributed. And continuing efforts by developers threaten further to force changes in the controls before they have had a chance to exert their intended impact on the city. The law has even been attacked by critics who decry the limitations it places on the artistic freedom of architects (Goldberger, 1987). This case certainly provides a clear example of how, in the real world, environmental-

Figure 14.6. Belden Street, a downtown alley whose outdoor café seating draws lunchtime crowds. Left: looking south toward Bush Street, where new high-rise development is limited to preserve sunlight at street level at midday during the summer. Right: looking north toward Pine Street, where extensive high-rise development does not interfere with solar access in the popular lunchtime spot. Photos by author.

design researchers work in a complex, whirlwind mix of economic, political, and design pressures that can obscure the effects of even their best work.

Yet the potential value of the new controls is evident in the existing conditions in the city. In Belden Street, where cafés serve lunch outdoors to office workers on pleasant summer days, the preservation of the low street wall to the south will prevent loss of midday sunlight, and the tall buildings to the north present no problem (Figure 14.6). And in Portsmouth Square, a favorite haunt of elderly citizens of Chinatown, continued solar access will be guaranteed if high-rise development is properly controlled on the crucial southwest edge (Figure 14.7); the looming presence of the famed TransAmerica (pyramid) building on the opposite side poses no threat. Even some private interests have learned about the importance of preserving solar access. The Levi Strauss Company headquarters building at the foot of Telegraph Hill was designed to follow the natural contour, with a stepped-back design that allows sunlight on the adjacent private plaza for the lunchtime pleasure of employees and others (Figure 14.8).

At the same time, environmentalists and architecture preservationists in

Figure 14.7. Portsmouth Square, an important outdoor space in crowded Chinatown, looking south toward Lum Street, whose low street wall allows ample sunlight to reach the heavily used park surface and is preserved through the new high-rise zoning regulations of the 1985 Downtown Plan. Photo by author.

San Francisco are still working to ward off the various problems that have been attributed to high-rise development, despite the view of pessimists who believe that it is already too late. A popular guidebook (Fodor, 1982) makes reference to the high-rise development issue, and a poster that resembles Duskin's 1970 newspaper ad, with a sequence of four historical views of downtown San Francisco purportedly showing the declining beauty of the area from 1915 to 1986, is on sale at local bookstores and galleries.

Whatever the long-term impacts in San Francisco, one bright practical note from this project is the spread of the influence exerted by the Berkeley researchers and the advocates of environmental protection in San Francisco. The high-rise zoning regulations enacted to implement the 1985 Downtown Plan have received widespread attention across the United States and abroad. The debate in San Francisco and the resulting planning and legislative decisions apparently have raised the general level of awareness of the negative impacts of urban high-rise development on the aesthetic and climatic quality of a city's natural environment. They also have publicized the use of sophisticated new environmental-simulation techniques, such as the Berkeley ESL modelscope to forecast such impacts and to help devise ways of avoiding them. And they have introduced the concept of building-by-building zoning controls to try to prevent environmental degradation in precisely targeted

Figure 14.8. The Levi Strauss headquarters building at the foot of Telegraph Hill, whose stepped-back design avoids shadowing on its own popular adjacent plaza. Photo by author.

locations and avoid unnecessarily general restrictions on the freedom of developers, as well as the perception, at least, that efforts at environmental protection posed arbitrary threats to economic prosperity that together may have delayed passage of the enabling referendum, Proposition K, in San Francisco and may have even more serious effects elsewhere.

In New York City, the putative source of Manhattanization, plans for the redevelopment of the valuable Coliseum site at Columbus Circle (its functions having been transferred to the new Javits Convention Center to the southwest) have been held up by controversy surrounding proposals for very tall buildings that would cast shadows into heavily used areas of Central Park across the street, according to a cover story in *New York* magazine (Taylor, 1987). In the most urban and skyscraper-dominated of American settings, the Municipal Art Society, an influential watchdog organization for architecture and planning issues, sponsored a lecture on the environmental impacts of concentrated development at the Coliseum site (*New York,* 1987). Proposals for high-rise buildings have raised similar concerns in many other locations as well, including such unlikely ones as Burlington, Vermont (Gold, 1988), and Nairobi, Kenya (Perlez, 1990).

The simulation research of the Berkeley group in connection with high-rise zoning in San Francisco has earned them invitations to apply those techniques elsewhere. Bosselman has produced dynamic simulations of the alternative redevelopment plans for the Times Square area in New York City to address issues of alterations in the distinctive architectural character of the area (yes, there are some preservationists concerned about Times Square's giant billboards and "stimulating" street life). And his work there has been credited with preventing the inadvertent blocking of prominent views of at least one landmark building nearby (Gottlieb, 1985).

Recent changes in high-rise zoning controls in Los Angeles and other cities have copied the fine-grained approach pioneered in San Francisco, based on the work of the Berkeley researchers. The regulations adopted there make specific prescriptions for specific sites for the protection of specific resources, in preference to the more traditional approach of setting uniform height limits for entire districts of a city regardless of the variations among its individual sites and their uses.

It appears, in sum, that there is good reason to hope that this EDR project will provide lasting benefits for San Francisco and suggest solutions to similar problems of high-rise development elsewhere. Although the precise combination of history, architecture, topography, climate, and values in San Francisco will not exist anywhere else, this project may well serve to help raise the consciousness of planners and concerned citizens everywhere regarding the need to balance the economic benefits of high-rise development with protection of the natural environment in cities, in addition to informing them of the availability of effective means for achieving that end. It may turn out that benign high-rise development is not possible, but thus far it still seems a goal worth pursuing.

References

Appleyard, D., & Fishman, L. (1977). High-rise buildings versus San Francisco: Measuring visual and symbolic impacts. In D. F. Conway (Ed.), *Human response to tall buildings* (pp. 81–100). Stroudsburg, PA: Dowden, Hutchinson & Ross.

Bosselman, P., & Craik, K. H. (1987). Perceptual simulations of environments. In R. B. Bechtel, R. W. Marans, & W. Michelson (Eds.), *Methods in environmental and behavioral research* (pp. 162–190). New York: Van Nostrand Reinhold.

Bosselman, P., Flores, J., & O'Hare, T. (1983). *Sun and light for downtown San Francisco.* Berkeley, CA: Environmental Simulation Laboratory, Institute for Urban and Regional Development, College of Environmental Design, University of California.

Bosselman, P., et al. (1984). *Sun, wind, and comfort: A study of open spaces and sidewalks in four downtown areas.* Berkeley, CA: Institute for Urban and Regional Development, College of Environmental Design, University of California.

Conway, D. J. (Ed). (1977). *Human response to tall buildings.* Stroudsburg, PA: Dowden, Hutchinson & Ross.

Craik, K. H., & Feimer, N. (1987). Environmental assessment. In D. Stokols & I. Altman (Eds.), *Handbook of environmental psychology* (Vol. 2, pp. 891–918). New York: Wiley.

Feimer, N. R. (1984). Environmental perception: The effects of media, evaluative context and observer sample. *Journal of Environmental Psychology, 4,* 61–80.

Fodor (1982). *Fodor's San Francisco.* New York: David McKay.

Gold, A. R. (1988). Montpelier journal: A rising debate over a plan to raise the skyline. *The New York Times* (national edition), August 1, 10.

Goldberger, P. (1979). *The city observed: A guide to the architecture of Manhattan.* New York: Vintage.

Goldberger, P. (1983). *The skyscraper.* New York: Knopf.

Goldberger, P. (1985). San Francisco tries to tame the skyscraper. *The New York Times,* July 28, 24H, 27H.

Goldberger, P. (1987). When planning can be too much of a good thing. *The New York Times,* December 6.

Gottlieb, M. (1985). Glimpsing the future before it's set in stone. *The New York Times,* September 8, 6E.

Kreimer, A. (1973). Building the imagery of San Francisco: An analysis of controversy over high-rise development, 1970–71. In W. F. E. Preiser (Ed.), *Environmental design research* (Vol. 2, pp. 221–231). Stroudsburg, PA: Dowden, Hutchinson & Ross.

McKechnie, G. E. (1977). Simulation techniques in environmental psychology. In D. Stokols (Ed.), *Perspectives on environment and behavior: Theory, research and applications* (pp. 169–190). New York: Plenum.

New York (1987). 20(42), October 26.

Perlez, J. (1990). Kenya decides to reduce planned 60-story tower. *The New York Times* (national edition), February 12, A4.

San Francisco Department of City Planning (1985). *Downtown Plan.* San Francisco: author.

Sheppard, S. R. J. (1982). Predictive landscape portrayals: A selective research review. *Landscape Journal, 1,* 9–14.

Taylor, J. (1987). The shadow: The uproar over the Coliseum project. *New York,* October 5, 40–48.

Wurman, R. S. (1987). *San Francisco access.* New York: Access Press.

15
THE LOWER WISCONSIN
STATE RIVERWAY

Location: Lower Wisconsin River, from Prairie du Sac Dam to
confluence with Mississippi River at Prairie du Chien
Principals: Richard E. Chenoweth and Bernard J. Niemann, Jr.,
School of Natural Resources, University of Wisconsin
(researchers, advocates, and planners)

In the late 1970s the U.S. Department of the Interior conducted a study to
determine if a 92-mile section of the Lower Wisconsin River, from a dam at
Prairie du Sac (Figure 15.1) to the Mississippi (Figure 15.2), could qualify for
inclusion in the National Wild and Scenic Rivers Program. Concerned about
the reactions of local landowners and public officials to the prospect of the
federally mandated controls over development that would come with its designation as a wild and scenic river, the Wisconsin Department of Natural Resources (WDNR) began work on an alternative plan for controlling development along the river. It would establish the "Lower Wisconsin River State
Forest," with state controls to protect fisheries, game for hunting, and timber,
among other natural resources.

Word of the WDNR's activities reached Rick Chenoweth and Bernard
Niemann at the School of Natural Resources at the University of Wisconsin a
few blocks away. They were concerned that two important issues for the
future of the Lower Wisconsin River would be ignored by the fish biologists,
game managers, and foresters doing the planning at WDNR. One was the
scenic beauty of the river and the surrounding wooded bluffs and hillsides, a
resource that was not so salient to the natural-science-based staffers at WDNR
as fish, game, and timber. A second, related issue concerned the social
carrying capacity of the river, or the problems that increasing levels of use
would pose for those who enjoyed boating, fishing, hunting and trapping,
camping, hiking, swimming, or just looking at the natural beauty along the
river. Fortunately, Chenoweth and Niemann were aware of a unique legal
history and governmental structure in Wisconsin that promised support for
efforts to protect those scenic resources.

A 1952 Wisconsin State Supreme Court decision in *Muench* v. *Public
Service Commission* established that Wisconsin citizens had the right to enjoy
the scenic beauty along all of the state's navigable waters under the public-
trust doctrine. The court ruled in favor of the plaintiff in a lawsuit brought

Figure 15.1. The dam near Prairie du Sac, Wisconsin, that marks the upstream (northeastern) boundary of the Lower Wisconsin State Riverway. Photo by author.

against a public utility that planned to construct a dam that would threaten the scenic beauty of a Wisconsin river, the Namekagon, later designated a federal wild and scenic river. Armed with knowledge of those facts, and a prior relationship in which they had acted as consultants on issues of protecting scenic beauty, Chenoweth and Niemann approached officials in the Public Intervenor's office, a branch of the Wisconsin Department of Justice that had been established to protect Wisconsin citizens' rights to the benefits of the state's natural environment. They pointed out that preliminary plans for the "Lower Wisconsin River State Forest" failed to make adequate provision for protection of scenic resources along the river. In response, they were given a grant to do research to determine what scenic resources were at stake, how important they were to various groups concerned about the river, and how much agreement existed among river users regarding scenic resources and means of protecting them.

The research that was carried out with that funding from the Department of Justice and other sources eventually contributed to a radical change in the plans of another state agency, the WDNR. Protection of scenic resources rose from a largely ignored issue to become the central focus of the final plan. Radical steps were taken to establish that protection, where virtually no steps had been likely before.

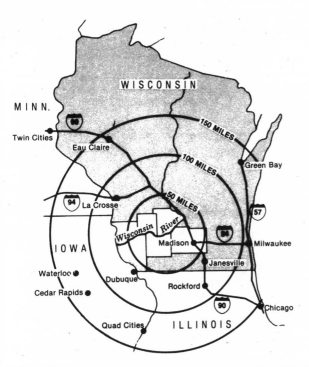

Figure 15.2. A map showing the location of the section of the Lower Wisconsin River protected by the Lower Wisconsin State Riverway Act of 1989. Source: Wisconsin Department of Natural Resources (1988, p. 7); reproduced with permission of the WDNR.

The research into scenic beauty along the Lower Wisconsin River

Research questions and methods of data collection

The major goal of Chenoweth and Niemann's research was to ensure that proper consideration be given to aesthetic landscape issues during the development of a master plan and environmental-impact statement for the river project and during the related public-review process. To do that, they knew that they would have to be prepared to deal with arguments that landscape beauty is in the eye of the beholder, that each individual has a unique view of what is beautiful in the natural environment, and that whereas natural beauty may be important to some groups of citizens concerned about the river, such as canoeists, hikers, and campers, it may be relatively unimportant to hunters or local landowners or other groups more concerned about the availability of game, timber management, economic development, and other nonaesthetic issues. To achieve that goal, they posed a list of specific questions for research (Chenoweth, 1985):

1. How important to river users was enjoyment of scenic beauty in the Lower Wisconsin River Valley (LWRV), compared with other activities?
2. What landscape features were perceived to make the greatest contribution to scenic beauty in the LWRV, and to what extent did river users agree on those features?
3. How well were the landscape features that were perceived to be important for scenic beauty being protected under existing statutes or administrative policies at the various governmental levels?
4. Based on knowledge of the important landscape features, along with other important natural resources, where should the boundaries of the proposed river project be located?
5. What groups or governmental levels were best equipped to manage the scenic resources of the LWRV?
6. How did local officials evaluate the likely effectiveness and political feasibility of alternative methods for protecting the scenic resources of the LWRV?
7. How acceptable would effective protective measures be to the local landowners?
8. How important did the public perceive the enjoyment of scenic beauty to be when compared with the economic costs of protective measures?

To answer those questions, Chenoweth and Niemann used two data-gathering techniques. Extensive survey questionnaires were prepared for recreational river users (canoeists, fishermen, etc.), owners of land along the river (riparians), public officials in towns and counties along the river, and hunters and trappers. The items for those surveys were generated from the published research literature on leisure pursuits, the researchers' personal knowledge of the river, and suggestions from staffers in the WDNR, whose input was solicited in part to promote acceptance of the survey findings by assuring their relevance to WDNR concerns. Instructions that accompanied the survey questionnaires stressed the importance of public input into the policy discussion that was under way to develop plans for the future of the river. In addition to the surveys, a sample of river users were asked to photograph landscape features that added to or detracted from their enjoyment of scenic beauty during their trips along the river.

The River User Survey, which was never discussed in print (more about that later) was distributed to 688 individuals as they ended their trips at 27 access points along the river on weekdays and on weekends during the summers of 1980 and 1981. They were asked about themselves, their past use of the river, their activities on the river during their current trip and the importance of each, their observations of activity and conditions on the river, the conditions that influenced their enjoyment of the river, including possible problems, the expenses incurred on their trip, and their opinions about possible river planning policies and legal-governmental mechanisms for administering them.

The Landowner Survey (Chenoweth & Niemann, 1984a) was mailed to a representative sample of 174 individuals who owned property that could be seen from the river. With the help of a follow-up mailing, 128 (74%) responded. Survey questions asked about landowners' use of their property, what they liked about owning land in the LWRV, their recreational activities, problems they saw in the river valley, landscape features that contributed to the scenic beauty of the area, their receptivity to possible regulation of development, including specific hypothetical regulations, their preference among protection strategies, and their overall preference for the type of area the LWRV should be.

The Public Officials Survey (Chenoweth & Niemann, 1984b) was mailed to a representative sample of 285 town, county, and state (e.g., WDNR) political and planning officials whose responsibilities included policies affecting the LWRV; 218 (76%) responded. They were asked for their perceptions of public sentiment and the sentiments of specific groups regarding the future of the LWRV and possible controls on development, their views of problems in their areas, their plans and preferences for using zoning to regulate development and specific landowner activities, and their evaluations of the appropriateness of various governmental agencies and levels for managing the scenic resources in the LWRV.

Copies of the Hunters and Trappers Survey (Chenoweth & Niemann, 1984c) were mailed to 671 individuals whose cars were observed to be parked at locations that indicated that they were engaged in hunting or trapping. With the help of the WDNR, their addresses were obtained through their license-plate numbers; 570 responses (85%) were received, but 148 (22% of the entire group) respondents indicated that they had not been hunting or trapping, leaving 423 (63% of the original group and 81% of those eligible) usable questionnaires. They were asked about their past and current hunting and trapping activities, their views on the effects of a variety of potential development and protection strategies, and the reasons for their choices of areas to hunt or trap. Specific questions were addressed to upland game hunters, waterfowl hunters, deer hunters (bow and gun), and trappers.

In connection with the distribution of the River User Survey, 50 river users were each asked to take a camera provided by the researchers on their day trips along the river. They agreed to take 12 photographs of features that "detract from or add to your experience of scenic beauty while on the river." The participants in this visitor-employed photography (VEP) study were informed in the printed instruction booklet that they could select features "very near you or as far away as you can see, . . . people or activities, natural features or man-made features, wildlife, whole views or specific objects."

The booklet also contained a page on which they were asked to write a brief description of the central feature in each photograph, how much it added to or detracted from their experience of scenic beauty ($+3$ to -3), and how great its scenic beauty (on a 10-point scale with end-points labeled extremely low and extremely high). The choices of subjects to be photographed and the ratings were to be made without consulting other members of the individual's travel party. The camera and booklet were collected by a research assistant as the respondent left the river.

Research results and their implications for planning for the future of the LWRV

The results of the survey and VEP research provided strong evidence that all user groups considered scenic beauty to be an important factor in their activities on and enjoyment of the river and that the wooded bluffs and hillsides visible from the river contributed more than any other landscape feature to the scenic beauty of the area.

Each of the three user groups surveyed ranked 25 factors that contributed to their enjoyment of the river. Those traveling on the river (River User Survey respondents) ranked scenic beauty second only to canoeing as a factor in their enjoyment of their trip. Hunters ranked scenic beauty fourth in importance; the availability of game ranked first. Riparians ranked scenic beauty as the most important reason that they enjoyed owning land along the river.

The questionnaire surveys all contained fold-out maps of the entire LWRV area. Respondents were asked to circle the areas that they considered most beautiful and to list the landscape features that led them to make the choices they did. There was clear evidence that views of wooded bluffs and hillsides, both at the river's edge and in the distance, were considered the LWRV's most important scenic resources. Almost every respondent in every group circled those areas containing bluffs and hillsides and identified those features as their reasons for doing so (Figure 15.3).

The survey of local public officials and a review of applicable laws and regulations revealed that no mechanisms existed for protecting the bluffs and hillsides from development that could potentially reduce or even destroy their value as scenic resources. Given the evidence that those features were most responsible for the perceived scenic beauty of the river valley and that scenic beauty was one of the most significant factors in the enjoyment of the river for each of the user groups surveyed, it seemed clear that the wooded bluffs and hillsides that were visible from the river needed to be included within the boundaries of the proposed project.

The survey data indicated that, overall, respondents believed that the WDNR was best qualified to manage the scenic beauty of the river valley. Although smaller numbers preferred local governments, and a substantial

Figure 15.3. A section of the wooded bluffs along the Lower Wisconsin River that is protected as a scenic resource under the LWSR act. Photo by B. Wolfgang Hoffman.

number of landowners felt that they themselves should have primary responsibility for determining what would happen on their land, the largest group of respondents seemed to agree that the privately owned bluffs and hillsides along the river were important resources for all users and for all citizens of Wisconsin, along with the river itself, and needed to be protected under the management of a statewide agency.

These views were echoed in respondents' preferences among specific measures that might be taken to protect the bluffs and hillsides. Most chose public or governmental methods – zoning controls, purchase of land or purchase of easements (rights to the scenic resources on the land) – in preference to voluntary cooperation by landowners. However, the public officials surveyed were skeptical about the political feasibility of such measures. Fewer than half believed that it would be possible to get such controls over private lands instituted as public policy.

Only a minority of the riparian landowners themselves agreed that it was appropriate for them to be required by law to protect the beauty of their property as seen by others, despite the fact that they agreed that the scenic beauty of their property was an important asset to themselves and to other users of the river that needed to be protected. However, a significant minority did support a variety of hypothetical regulations that would place restrictions on construction on their land and on alterations in the existing vegetation and stands of timber. When these proposals included mechanisms for compensating landowners for economic losses due to such restrictions, support among landowners rose to almost 50%.

The survey and VEP data also provided evidence that the levels of recreational activities in the LWRV posed a threat to the enjoyment of boaters and fishermen, hunters and trappers, landowners, and other user groups – a threat that was felt by samples of individuals from those groups as well as by state and local public officials concerned with the future of the area. In planners' terms, there was a strong consensual concern that the social carrying capacity of the river was being or might soon be exceeded.

All of the survey instruments contained a list of potential problems in the LWRV and asked the respondents to estimate the severity of each at the time they responded and the severity five years earlier, as well as to make projections five years into the future, assuming no governmental intervention. Significant percentages of all of the groups surveyed perceived troubling magnitudes of the problems caused by high levels of recreational activity – problems that directly threatened the natural resources on which the quality of their experiences in the LWRV depended, including scenic beauty, privacy, and peace and quiet, as well as habitat for fish and game and conditions for good fishing and hunting. The problems included litter, vandalism, trespassing, noise, and intrusive and destructive use of four-wheel-drive vehicles. And all of those problems were perceived as having increased in severity, as compared with five years earlier, and as likely to continue increasing into the future.

Consistent with the survey data, VEP participants photographed litter and structures located incongruously in scenic areas to illustrate sights that detracted from their enjoyment of their outings on the river.

Following up on these concerns, respondents were asked to evaluate alternative methods for dealing with problems created by development and overuse. Specific measures, such as limiting the numbers of boaters or hunters, or using restrictive zoning to prevent subdivisions from being built in undeveloped areas, drew significant support, but also significant opposition that seemed to reflect a general reluctance to interfere with individuals' rights to pursue their chosen activities. However, a different form of measuring opinions about future controls over development elicited greater consensus.

Respondents were asked to choose among the following general management strategies for the LWRV:

1. a *primitive undeveloped* recreation area, with no new facilities or development visible from the river
2. an *undeveloped* recreation area, with limited facilities and with protection of the shoreline beauty
3. a *developed* recreation area, with expanded facilities

4. a *tourist attraction*, with development visible from the river, such as bluff-top motels and campgrounds

5. a *laissez-faire approach* that would leave the area to develop as it would

In all groups (public officials estimated the opinions of their local constituents), majorities favored an undeveloped area, a view that implied acceptance of the need for controls, including limiting the provision of facilities for recreational users (boat landings, campgrounds, etc.) and restrictions on development that would threaten scenic beauty. In fact, only the public officials favored the undeveloped over the primitive undeveloped strategy, perhaps underestimating their constituents' concern about the problems caused by increasing levels of recreational use and increased development.

Finally, the researchers used the results of a previous study by Boyle and Bishop (1984) to estimate the economic value of the scenic beauty in the LWRV. Based on users' estimates of the fees they would be willing to pay for using the river, limited to the use of the upper third of the river during the summer months, that study estimated such value at $311,000 per year at the time.

The impact of Chenoweth and Niemann's research and analysis on plans for the LWRV

Chenoweth and Niemann's research results had a major impact on the plans of the WDNR before anyone had actually seen them. When word came that data had been collected concerning the perception and importance of scenic beauty in the project area, the agency abandoned a first draft of a management plan for the "Lower Wisconsin River State Forest" that had been written by a WDNR official with the consultation of agency experts on fish biology, wildlife management, timber management, water quality, and other natural-science-based resources in the river valley. That plan would have virtually ignored the questions of scenic resources and social carrying capacity, as Chenoweth and Niemann had expected.

It was decided that a new plan would be drawn up by a task force of agency personnel, on which Chenoweth and Niemann would serve as nonvoting participants, and that a Citizens' Advisory Committee representing user groups and local landowners and officials, and including Chenoweth, would be formed to provide public input into the new plan.

As described to me by Rick Chenoweth in conversation, the research data continued to influence the new plan, which would rename the project the "Lower Wisconsin State Riverway," in an unusual manner. In contrast with the more traditional approach, in which researchers write reports of their findings and send them to influential policymakers, most of the important data were never put into written reports at all. The key data showing how important scenic beauty was to the enjoyment of the river by all of the groups of users that were surveyed, and showing that the wooded bluffs and hillsides visible from the river were the most important landscape features contributing to the natural beauty of the area, were brought to meetings of the task force and committee by the researchers in the form of computer printouts. When skepticism was expressed by other participants regarding the possibility that the wide variety of people using the river might agree on what they saw as beautiful, or if it was asserted that different user groups would assign radically different priorities to scenic beauty among the whole list of resources they valued in the river valley, or if anyone questioned the idea that local landowners or local citizens in general would ever accept government controls over activities on private lands that did not directly affect the water or wildlife on the river, the researchers would simply thumb through their printouts to find the relevant statistical analysis and quote the percentages of scale ratings or choices among alternatives, obtained from large, representative samples of the particular group of concerned citizens involved. It is Chenoweth's belief that had the same research results been delivered to the WDNR in the form of written reports, they might have been ignored in favor of the preexisting biases they directly contradicted. Instead, their informal presentation at meetings convinced the task-force members and citizen participants alike that the plan for the river had to give high priority to protecting the wooded hills and bluffs from development that would detract from the scenic beauty of the river and the enjoyment of all of its users.

The final plan gave its highest priority to the protection of scenic beauty along the river. It identified the wooded hills and bluffs that were visible from the river as the key targets of that protection. The plan also stressed the importance of limiting growth in the use of the river by restraining the number, size, and convenience of new recreational facilities, especially in areas of the LWRV where use levels were still low enough to allow access to the solitary experience of unspoiled nature.

The plan for the Lower Wisconsin State Riverway evolved over a period of approximately 10 years. The first "in-house" version of the plan (later abandoned) had been prepared in the late 1970s. A "concept plan" for protecting the natural resources of the LWRV was first made public in 1985 (WDNR, 1985). Although copies of that document are no longer available, references to it in other reports suggest that both scenic-resources protection and carrying capacity had emerged as significant concerns in WDNR planning by that time. In 1987, the agency published a draft environmental-impact statement (EIS) for the "Lower Wisconsin River State Forest" (WDNR, 1987) that set scenic-beauty protection as its primary objective, crediting Chenoweth and Niemann's research in a statement that "concerns about the future recreational and the aesthetic quality of the river corridor were further validated by several

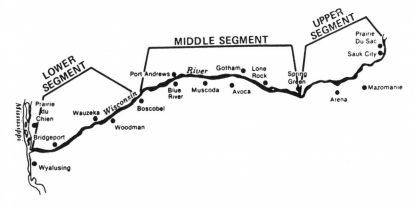

Figure 15.4. A map showing the segmentation of the Lower Wisconsin River that allows varied development controls under the LWSR act. Source: Wisconsin Department of Natural Resources (1988, p. 23); reproduced with permission of the WDNR.

University of Wisconsin Extension surveys of recreation users, local landowners and local public officials" (WDNR, 1987, p. 3). The draft EIS also recognized the limited social carrying capacity of the river and suggested a management plan based on the concept of segmentation. It would encourage facility development and management policies that would extend the existing pattern of most concentrated use in the upper or easternmost part of the river, with much less intensive use, especially for group activities such as camping and fishing, in the middle part and especially the lower or westernmost section of the river (Figure 15.4).

Perhaps the most significant feature of the draft EIS was its establishment of a new boundary for the "State Forest." Protection was to extend beyond the shoreline of the river to the bluffs and hillsides that had been identified in Chenoweth and Niemann's research as the landscape features that contributed most to scenic beauty. An appendix to the report describing the recommendations of the Citizens' Advisory Committee (CAC), which was established by the WDNR in response to the issues raised by that research on scenic beauty and carrying capacity, and whose 35 members included Rick Chenoweth, suggests the reason for this approach. The CAC recommended that scenic-beauty protection be extended to areas of the landscape based not on their positions on a map but on their visibility from the river.

However, though the draft EIS adopted the policy of extending the project boundary to include the "viewshed" of the river (to protect scenic beauty along with fish and game) and to include the concept of segmentation (to concentrate new facilities in the most developed areas and protect the most natural or primitive areas from increased levels of use), it proposed management policies whose capacity to achieve those objectives was questionable. The bluffs and hillsides whose development would pose the greatest threat to scenic resources were to be protected by local zoning ordinances put into place with technical assistance from the state and advice from a citizens' group. Although that procedure would have been faster and less costly than purchasing private lands or easements for private lands that provided scenic views for river users, it would have depended on local officials to pursue the establishment of new regulations and to administer penalties for violations against the interests of influential constituents. Some of the landowners' representatives on the CAC strongly opposed any abridgement of private landowner rights, preferring voluntary cooperation.

In addition, the draft EIS proposed increasing recreational facilities on the river, albeit for "non-intensive uses." While accepting the concept of segmentation, in response to public concerns about the threat to enjoyment of the river posed by high levels of use, the WDNR apparently responded to the concerns of landowners, public officials, and tourist-industry representatives about the possible negative economic impacts of restrictions on development by suggesting limitations on the locations and sizes of new facilities, but, within those limitations, continuing their expansion.

The movement toward greater protection for scenic beauty and greater restraint in expanding facilities for recreational users continued with the final EIS for the Lower Wisconsin State Riverway (WDNR, 1988). First, the final EIS firmly established scenic-beauty protection beyond the river's shoreline, to include wooded hillsides visible from the river that might be as much as a mile away and not contiguous with any riparian property. It added 4,450 acres to the Scenic Management Area of the proposed project, bringing its total acreage to over 33,000 out of a project total of 77,300. The emphasis on protection of scenic beauty had evolved to become truly the most important priority of the plan. Where fish, game, endangered species, historic and archeological sites, and other resources were all to be protected, scenic beauty stood out from all of those concerns. The final EIS identified the greatest need for action in managing the riverway this way: "Long-term development pressures that, if ignored would threaten the outstanding scenic and natural qualities of the river corridor. . . . The concern is that *unplanned* development will alter the rural and natural aesthetic quality of the river corridor that is important to residents and visitors alike" (WDNR, 1988, pp. 3–4). Similarly, the stated first objective of the plan was to "protect, maintain and enhance the generally natural and undeveloped scenic beauty of 92.3 miles of river corridor, including islands, immediate shoreline, and important bluffs and hillsides visible from the river" (p. 19).

The final EIS recommended much stronger means for scenic-beauty protection. It added 11,025 acres to the lands to be acquired by the state in the riverway project. These were prominent bluff lands near the river that had originally been targeted for zoning-only protection. It also described four zoning options for the rest of the Scenic Management Area, along with the advantages and disadvantages of each. The descriptions made it clear that only state-mandated zoning, planned and enforced at the state level, could ensure adequate protection. The report also suggested more secure protection for the most "highly developable" bluffs, in the form of scenic easements purchased from landowners by the state. The arguments presented were clearly consistent with the opinions of river users, riparian landowners, and public officials as expressed in the Chenoweth and Niemann surveys a few years earlier, as well as subsequent input from the CAC.

In addition to the written report, the final EIS included maps of the proposed riverway that showed the various management areas, including natural resources, nature preserves, endangered-species habitats, and state-park and intensive-use areas (boat landings, campgrounds, picnic areas, etc.). The Scenic Management Area included both acquisition (land and easement purchases) and nonacquisition (zoning) lands. One interesting feature of the map showing the sites to be protected for their scenic beauty is that many of them are not contiguous with other protected lands, because their height above the river makes them visible and in need of protection even though land parcels between them and the river are not visible and thus were not slated for protection (Figure 15.5).

The final EIS also strengthened the plan's endorsement of the segmentation concept and related management policies. An appendix to the report describes strong support for policies to protect the river from increased use, support from both the CAC and Friends of the Lower Wisconsin River, a citizen advocacy group. Despite opposition from some landowners and tourist-industry representatives, the final EIS stressed the need for *reducing* recreational-facility development: "In light of the public's expressed desire for less facility development at the river access sites, the revised plan proposes that the standard access site facilities be more spartan" (WDNR, 1988, p. iii). In addition, WDNR withdrew from the plan a specific proposal to develop a 100-unit auto-accessible campground and suggested that any future plans for such a facility be restricted to a location that was not directly on the river.

After further public comment on the Lower Wisconsin State Riverway (LWSR) plan, in response to the final EIS, the plan was approved by the state's Natural Resources Board and governor. The 1989–90 state legislature then passed a new law specifying the formal mechanisms by which the objectives of the plan were to be achieved. It called for strong measures to protect the scenic beauty of the river valley, consistent with the public input collected in Chenoweth and Niemann's research and elicited by the CAC throughout WDNR's planning process of successive plan drafts and public comments, including public meetings throughout the river valley. In the language of the law itself, it was an act to revise the statutes related to "regulating develop-

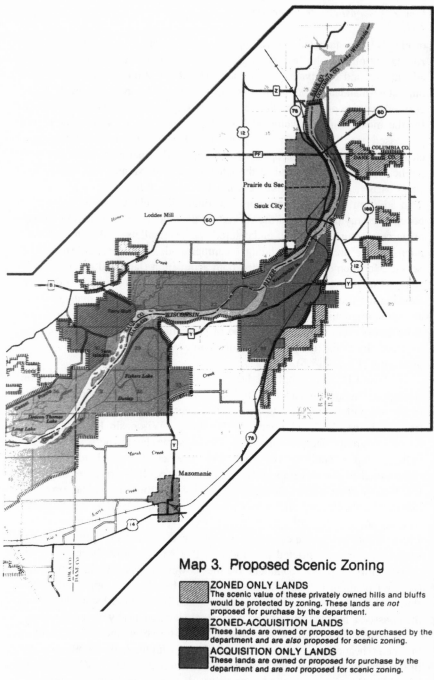

Map 3. Proposed Scenic Zoning

ZONED ONLY LANDS
The scenic value of these privately owned hills and bluffs would be protected by zoning. These lands are *not* proposed for purchase by the department.

ZONED-ACQUISITION LANDS
These lands are owned or proposed to be purchased by the department and are *also* proposed for scenic zoning.

ACQUISITION ONLY LANDS
These lands are owned or proposed for purchase by the department and are *not* proposed for scenic zoning.

Figure 15.5. Section of the EIS map showing scenic-beauty protection controls under the LWSR act, including zoning protection for noncontiguous hillsides. Source: Wisconsin Department of Natural Resources (1988, map 3); reproduced with permission of the WDNR.

ment and use of land along the lower Wisconsin river, creating a lower Wisconsin state riverway board, granting rule-making authority, providing penalties, and making an appropriation." Thus, the legislature chose to put management of the river into the hands of a statewide Lower Wisconsin Riverway Board that would set standards, require permits for activities that impinged on the scenic beauty or other natural resources of the protected corridor, and enforce the restrictions specified in those permits. The governor would appoint nine members to overlapping terms on the board, to be paid $50 per day and reimbursed for expenses. Six members were to represent the six counties directly affected by the project, and three were to represent groups of recreational users and reside outside the six-county area. The board would issue permits for activities on private lands that would have an impact on scenic beauty, such as erecting, modifying, or repairing any building, walkway, stairway, bridge, pier, or utility facility that would be visible from the river. Any new construction or repair would have to be "visually inconspicuous," defined as "difficult to be seen and not readily noticeable from any point on the river during the time when the leaves are on the deciduous trees." In order to qualify for a permit, any construction plan would have to include screening vegetation (e.g., trees could not be pruned to give a better view of the river if that would make the structure visible); in addition, the height of any structure could not exceed that of the surrounding vegetation, the colors used would have to blend into the natural environment, glass or other reflective materials could not be used where they would create glare visible from the river, the structure would have to be located behind or below the top of a bluff and on a fairly level site, and so on.

Although exceptions were provided for farm buildings (farmhouses and barns could be painted in their traditional white and red colors), for municipalities' structures, and in cases of extreme hardship, this legally mandated system of permits and board review ensured strict control over any development that might lower the scenic quality of bluffs and hillsides visible from the river.

In addition, the Wisconsin Department of Transportation was required to "minimize the visual impact of [its] activity and any resulting highway or structure . . . to the extent that it is economically and technically feasible." Any land currently held by the Natural Resources Board could be sold only if a scenic easement were retained. Any high-voltage transmission lines built in the area would have to be designed to minimize their impact on scenic beauty. Permit income would be used, along with state appropriations, to purchase land and easements for scenic-beauty protection as funds permitted. These activities would be carried out by WDNR in cooperation with local governments and individual landowners.

Although no specific mechanisms for instituting management by segmentation was included in the legislation, several measures to mitigate the effects of increasing activity levels were. These included laws mandating the use of waterproof refuse containers on boats, banning the use of glass containers (except on private lands, by owners or tenants), and banning the operation of motor vehicles, including all-terrain vehicles, off the roads.

The Lower Wisconsin Riverway Board was empowered by the law to give warning notices, level fines, and institute legal actions in the event of non-compliance with permit regulations. In turn, the board's performance would be reviewed every two years.

In summary, Chenoweth and Niemann's survey and VEP studies in 1980 and 1981 had a profound impact on the direction of planning for the area that is now established as the LWSR. The specific protections for scenic beauty that are now legally in place and the WDNR commitment to limiting rather than promoting recreational activity on the river, particularly in the lower or westernmost two-thirds of it, as well as the great impact of public comment from a wide spectrum of Wisconsin citizens in shaping the final form of the project, can be traced directly to their work.

Evaluation

Stage 1: Background analysis

In one sense, knowledge about the uses of the LWRV and its scenic resources and the views of users and relevant government officials about needed controls and acceptable ways of implementing them did not precede Niemann and Chenoweth's work. Rather, it was the objective of that work. In effect, the approach taken in this case was that effective means of protecting scenic resources in the LWRV could be drawn directly from an understanding of existing conditions, both in nature and in local political institutions.

However, Chenoweth and Niemann were already familiar with the river and its problems. Their prior knowledge shaped their research, including the choices of questions for surveys of river users' opinions. And they became involved in the planning for the LWSR in part because of their familiarity with the local history of that issue in Wisconsin, and more specifically because of their relationship to the Wisconsin Department of Justice's Public Intervenor's office. The legal precedent for protecting the public's interest in scenic resources on private riparian lands and the prior experience of using empirical research to define that interest were crucial factors leading to the search for knowledge in this particular case.

Stage 2: Management goals

In the same vein, goals for the implementation of the research results were first set in such a way that they could accommodate the perceptions and values of the various interest groups that deserved to have input into the planning process. Chenoweth and Niemann's objectives can be summarized as three more general goals. One goal was to protect what users valued most about the river valley and to determine the specific assets that would need to be protected in order to honor those values. If scenic beauty were valued highly, it would be necessary to determine precisely which landscape features contributed most to that beauty for users of the river valley. Another goal was to evaluate existing mechanisms for protecting whatever resources were identified as deserving of protection. Any weaknesses in those controls would need to be remedied by the plan for the region. Finally, it was important to identify the preferences of all interested parties among specific mechanisms that could provide the needed controls if the plan for the river valley were to be viable politically.

Later, armed with the results of their research, Chenoweth and Niemann were able to set more specific goals for the LWSR plan. One was protection of the scenic beauty of the river valley, particularly the wooded bluffs and hillsides that appeared to be its key components. Another was the use of zoning controls to constrain development that would threaten the beauty of views from the river, as well as management policies that would limit increases in the use of the river beyond its social carrying capacity. A third was administration of those controls and policies by a statewide authority that could resist pressures from local landowners and development interests where necessary.

Stage 3: Environment–behavior relationships

The surveys that Niemann and Chenoweth conducted among river users, local landowners, and local government officials, along with the results of their VEP study, provided a clear basis for identifying scenic beauty as a valuable asset for all groups (one that needed to be protected from dangerous forms of development) and for identifying the wooded bluffs and hillsides along the river as the key landscape features in all parties' perceptions of scenic beauty, in addition to documenting the lack of effective controls over development that were needed to protect crucial scenic resources, the perception that the current level of river use was so high as to endanger those resources, and the surprisingly high levels of public support for effective nonvoluntary controls statewide, even if landowners' freedom of action on their own property was limited in the process.

Because their research was intended to estimate users' perceptions and opinions, not to test hypotheses about the causes of them, the methodological issues it raises are quite limited. The key methodological concerns in evaluating this research have to do with its generalizability or external validity. First, it seems that the samples surveyed were generally chosen quite carefully to be representative of the user groups most concerned about the future of the river and its surroundings, and they were large enough to provide fairly precise estimates of the prevailing sentiment in those groups. However, the sample selected to represent concerned public officials contained a large number of WDNR staff members. Although they may not have been overrepresented relative to their role in management policies for the river, it should be recognized that the support expressed for WDNR as the best possible administrator for the development controls may have come largely from staff members in that agency.

The instructions provided to survey respondents stressed that their responses would serve as input for the process in which decisions were being made about future development in the river valley. This seems a reasonable way to encourage honest representations of personal opinion. However, respect for natural beauty is highly valued in the society as a whole, and people may feel reluctant to express a lack of concern about it, even if they actually value their own comfort or finances more (e.g., landowners and public officials who may have a personal stake in the profits that can be made from development).

The fact that all of the groups were clearly identified by their prior activities as concerned about the future of the area increases confidence in the likelihood that their survey responses were honest. Confidence in the representativeness of the samples and in the respondents' motivation to make their voices heard on the issues is bolstered by the high return rates for the three mail surveys: 74% for the landowners, 76% for the public officials, and 81% for the hunters and trappers (ignoring those respondents who indicated that they had been in the area for other reasons on the days when their license-plate numbers had been taken) in response to the initial request and one follow-up mailing – a very high return rate for a mail survey.

The issue of reactivity, however, is somewhat more troublesome in connection with the VEP study. When asked to photograph and evaluate scenes that added to or detracted from their enjoyment of the river, canoeists and fishermen may have felt some pressure to display an aesthetic sense that would conform to the perceived societal norm or even to the researchers' expectations. Bluffs and hillsides may have been photographed as positive exemplars, and litter as negative ones, because they seemed to be the landscape features that should be appreciated or found repellent during a trip down the river, not because looking at them ordinarily occupied much of the subjects' time or contributed much to the positive or negative feelings they experienced.

The involvement of Chenoweth and Niemann in research to identify scenic resources was attributable in large part to the peculiar legal history of scenic protection in Wisconsin. This may mean that such an approach is less likely to be accepted elsewhere, and the results of their studies in the LWRV may not reflect the values of recreational river users elsewhere. However, the fact that the research was dedicated to producing answers that could provide a basis for a development plan for the LWRV appropriate for those who use it makes the issue of generalizability of their results seem less important.

Stage 4: Plan elements

Following up on the earlier statement of goals, there were three major elements that Chenoweth and Niemann's work contributed to the final plan for the LWSR that was enacted into law. First, the determination that scenic beauty was important to river users and that wooded bluffs and hillsides were critically important elements in that beauty led to the establishment of boundaries for the riverway that were based on visibility from the river, rather than on the river's banks or other "natural" boundaries. That led to the inclusion of noncontiguous parcels of land, some the property of nonriparian landowners, because they belonged to the "viewshed" of the river. Second, the fact that existing controls on development were found to be inadequate and that current levels of use were threateningly high led to the inclusion of new controls on construction and resource harvesting, as well as river use, based on the concept of segmentation that created higher levels of protection, including fewer public amenities, along the lower, lesser-developed sections of the river. Finally, the documented consensus that legally mandated, statewide controls were necessary and feasible (sufficiently acceptable to the various groups involved) led to the establishment of a permit-granting board with the power of prior review of development proposals, with legal sanctions to stop or punish developers who failed to conform to the requirements of the law.

Stage 5: Overall plan

Under the impetus of effective advocacy by Niemann and Chenoweth, within the WDNR's CAC, and through sympathetic coverage in the news media, protection for scenic resources emerged as the centerpiece of the final plan for the LWSR. Although it does not seem that protection for other resources would seriously threaten the effectiveness of development controls to protect scenic beauty, the priority given to the latter issue eliminated that potential problem completely. In this unusual case, the EDR advocates proved more than a match for competing interests, even such powerful ones as the entrenched WDNR scientists, local landowners and their local government officials, and the tourist industry.

Stage 6: POE

Although the law establishing the LWSR contains a provision for periodic review of the effectiveness of the LWSR board in keeping development within the prescribed limits, it does not mandate a formal, systematic, empirical evaluation of its impact. At this writing, even the informal review specified in the law has not come due, but Rick Chenoweth is seeking support from WDNR to establish a formal evaluation process. He is currently testing the feasibility of using aerial photography to monitor recreational use of the project area, and mail and on-site surveys to track the attitudes of users. His long-range plans are to conduct longitudinal research that will reveal any changes that take place in use patterns or in the environment itself. Although such data would not permit clear-cut comparisons between the plan adopted and the alternatives that were rejected, they could provide some gauge of the effectiveness of the plan itself. As is discussed later, such data could also allow the use of new techniques that might be applied more widely to evaluate changes in scenic beauty.

Stage 7: Future impact

There seems ample reason to be optimistic that Chenoweth and Niemann's work will have the direct effect of protecting the scenic beauty of 77,300 acres of the LWRV and its viewshed. That vast area attracts over half a million person-days of recreational use each year, along one of this country's few unspoiled stretches of river located conveniently near large metropolitan areas (in this case, Milwaukee and Chicago). The continuing value of that work makes the generation of a site-specific data base seem, even by itself, to be eminently worth the cost and effort invested in it. Nonetheless, there is the promise of additional benefits as well.

   First, the methods used by Chenoweth and Niemann could be adapted easily, it would seem, to analyses of other scenic corridors: along a river, canal, highway, or railroad right-of-way, almost anywhere. In another setting, with a different population of users, the value of scenic resources and the landscape features that would be most important in determining scenic beauty might well differ from what was found in the LWRV, but they still could be assessed using the methods applied in this case.

   Although the methods used by Chenoweth and Niemann have been available for some time, this project demonstrates their value in a way that may encourage wider use. This is especially true of visitor-employed photography. Though long known as a method for identifying landscape features that contribute to the perception of scenic beauty (Cherem, 1972), it had not been widely used and never before with the dramatic impact achieved in this case. In this study, examples of photographs taken by river users, together with bar graphs showing the numbers of users who had photographed similar scenes and the ratings they had given them, were mounted on posters and taken to public meetings where citizen input was being sought for the planning process. According to Chenoweth, this graphic representation of the VEP results was very effective in countering claims from special-interest groups or skeptics that scenic beauty was too personal or too mysterious to be used as a basis for planning. Even beyond the LWSR project, Chenoweth (1984) has publicized the VEP method and described its research and practical potential.

In recent years, a powerful new tool has been developed for landscape-architecture research such as that conducted for the LWSR project. It is known as image-capture technology (Orland, 1988): Visual images from film or videotape are converted into digital records that can be manipulated using one of several computer software packages. Elements can be added or deleted, magnified or reduced, moved, or changed in color or in other ways. As Chenoweth (1991) has pointed out, this new technology will make it possible to implement, enforce, and monitor the LWSR policies with unmatched precision. For example, permits granted by the Lower Wisconsin Riverway Board could include visual images of the proposed construction or modification superimposed on the existing landscape as viewed from the river. In this form, a permit would be considerably clearer than a verbal description, drawing, or diagram regarding whether or not the change in the landscape would be visually inconspicuous, as required by the LWSR act. Later, a photograph of the completed work could be used to determine if it was in compliance with the permit.

Image-capture technology could also be used in the future in environmental-impact statements, in assessing monetary penalties for violations of scenic-beauty zoning restrictions, and in developing management plans such the LWSR plan. Communication in all phases of planning for scenic-beauty protection could be enhanced by the use of visual "documents" in place of words to describe the visual resource. Although other forms of simulation are available (see chapter 14), image-capture technology has the advantage of being so fast and so portable that it could even be used in discussions of alternative proposals at public meetings. And where scenic views are at issue, the static nature of image-capture simulations poses no serious problem.

The research plans proposed and implemented by Chenoweth and Niemann and the ways in which they worked to influence the outcome of the planning process provide a useful blueprint for anyone faced with similar cases in the future. In particular, this project highlights the role of environmental-design researchers as advocates for better design, planning, and environmental management. The impact of Chenoweth and Niemann's research findings on the outcome of the LWSR planning process derived as much (or even more) from the strategies for their use as from the quantity or quality of the data themselves.

There are, however, a few points where constructive suggestions may be in order. Methodological issues of sampling and reactive opinion measurement were discussed earlier. In addition, it might be pointed out that the research approach adopted in this case was more atheoretical than necessary. Although the choices of survey targets and instruments surely were guided by a highly developed understanding of the nature of scenic beauty, strategies for protecting it, and related public-policy issues, they were not guided by or structured as a test of any existing or proposed theory of environment–behavior relationships. Perhaps in the future the practical concerns for the protection of scenic resources in endangered settings such as the LWRV can be merged with theories of the determinants of aesthetic responses (e.g., Berlyne, 1974) and responses to natural beauty (e.g., Kaplan, 1975) to promote a deeper understanding of issues and even better solutions to problems.

Chenoweth (personal communication, 1991) has expressed strong doubt that such an approach would work. With respect to the development of survey instruments, in particular, he believes that "items generated directly from such theories would have been considered highly obtuse and the results regarded as academic poppycock by the public, the media and [WDNR]." Although his accomplishments in this case lend great weight to his opinion, others may still see value in trying to use and advance theory while vigorously pursuing important practical goals. One might hope for the same kind of synergistic gains from apposing practice with theory as were realized in this case from the combined efforts of an environmental psychologist (Chenoweth) and a landscape architect (Niemann).

References

Berlyne, D. E. (1974). The new experimental aesthetics. In D. E. Berlyne (Ed.), *Studies in the new experimental aesthetics* (pp. 1–25). Washington, DC: Hemisphere.

Boyle, K. J., & Bishop, R. C. (1984). *Lower Wisconsin River recreation: Economic impacts and scenic values.* Agricultural Economics Staff Paper No. 216. University of Wisconsin–Madison.

Chenoweth, R. (1984). Visitor employed photography: A potential tool for landscape architecture. *Landscape Journal, 3*(2), 136–143.

Chenoweth, R. (1985). Beauty and the beast: Aesthetic policy for the Lower Wisconsin Riverway. In J. Popadic (Ed.), *Proceedings of the 1984 National Recreational Rivers Symposium* (pp. 156–165). Baton Rouge: Louisiana State University.

Chenoweth, R. E. (1991). Seeing the future: Aesthetic policy implications of visualization technology. *Journal of the Urban and Regional Information Systems Association, 3*(1), 6–13.

Chenoweth, R. E., & Niemann, B. J., Jr. (1984a, March). *Lower Wisconsin River Valley landowner survey: Results and interpretations.* Madison: School of Natural Resources, University of Wisconsin.

Chenoweth, R. E., & Niemann, B. J., Jr. (1984b, March). *Lower Wisconsin River Valley public official survey: Results and interpretations.* Madison: School of Natural Resources, University of Wisconsin.

Chenoweth, R. E., & Niemann, B. J., Jr. (1984c, August). *The opinions and preferences of hunters and trappers in the Lower Wisconsin River Valley.* Madison: School of Natural Resources, University of Wisconsin.

Cherem, G. (1972). Looking through the eyes of the public, or public images as social indicators of aesthetic opportunity. In P. J. Brown (Ed.), *Proceedings, aesthetics opportunity colloquium.* Logan, UT: Utah State University.

Kaplan, S. (1975). An informal model for the prediction of preference. In E. H. Zube, R. O. Brush, & J. A. Fabos (Eds.), *Landscape assessment: Values, perceptions, and resources* (pp. 92–101). Stroudsburg, PA: Dowden, Hutchinson & Ross.

Orland, B. (1988). Video imaging: A powerful tool for visualization and analysis. *Landscape Architecture, 78*(4), 78–88.

Wisconsin Department of Natural Resources (1985, September). *Lower Wisconsin River conceptual actions plan.* Madison, WI: author.

Wisconsin Department of Natural Resources (1987, July). *Draft environmental impact statement: Proposed Lower Wisconsin River state forest.* Madison, WI: author.

Wisconsin Department of Natural Resources. (1988, August). *Final environmental impact statement: Proposed Lower Wisconsin State Riverway.* Madison, WI: author.

PART V
CONCLUSION

16
EPILOGUE: THE PAST, PRESENT, AND FUTURE OF ENVIRONMENTAL-DESIGN RESEARCH

This chapter is intended to review briefly the history of environmental-design research, to catalog the resources that are currently available to support that research, and to attempt to predict the future of that enterprise. The history of environmental-design research is reviewed in two parts, first through an overview of the cases treated in this volume, and then in a brief summary of other significant EDR projects that were not chosen for inclusion. The current resources for the practice of environmental-design research that are described include the pattern or model that has been provided by past work and is reviewed in the first section of this chapter, the expertise of the EDR practitioners who produced that work, training programs for EDR professionals that often also serve as centers for research and practice, and the published archive of work in environmental-design research. Finally, a discussion of the future prospects for environmental-design research concludes with some suggestions for maximizing the considerable potential of the enterprise.

The past: completed EDR projects

Lessons from the cases in this volume: setting a good example for environmental-design research

Although the original goal of this book was to document and evaluate individual cases of environmental-design research, it has become clear that the value of that work to our field can be greatly enhanced by bringing together those important contributions in some sort of synthetic analysis. In this section, the framework on which evaluations of individual cases were based is used to show how all of these cases, taken together, illustrate how EDR problems might best be addressed to maximize the immediate and long-term benefits of the designs and plans that are realized from the process.

An overview Table 16.1 summarizes the pattern used throughout this volume for evaluating individual cases. After a brief overview of the seven stages in the EDR process that make up that pattern, the stages will be reviewed more

317

318   *Conclusion*

Table 16.1. *A model of the EDR process*[a]

1. Background: establishing project parameters
   (a) the setting; local context (history, geography, climate, etc.)
   (b) activities (user characteristics, tasks, etc.)
2. Program: goals for the design/plan: behavioral goals; needs and preferences of users (among structural, financial, aesthetic, and other goals)
3. Environment–behavior relationships: environmental features believed to support behavioral goals
   (a) existing theory and research literature
   (b) setting-specific research (surveys of potential users, comparisons of simulated design alternatives or alternative plan outcomes)
4. Design/plan based on environment–behavior relationships: materials, layout, size, etc.
5. Implementation: construction, enactment, etc.
6. Postoccupancy evaluation: evaluating design/plan effectiveness vs. program/goals (post-only, pre–post, or quasi-experimental comparisons)
7. Contributions to future designs/plans
   (a) feedback to the environment–behavior knowledge base (strengthening or weakening theoretical or empirical generalizations on which design/plan was based)
   (b) contributions to the development of methods for environment–behavior research
   (c) information for modification of original design
   (d) guidelines for future designs
   (e) next "generation" of design
   (f) institutional changes (e.g., policy mandating POE)

[a]It is recognized that this model has been simplified greatly by focusing exclusively on user behavior, omitting structural, aesthetic, financial, and other considerations.

fully, using cases from this volume to illustrate the most important aspects of each stage.

The research that has gone into the preparation of this volume has reinforced my view that successful environmental-design research is likely to begin with a thorough analysis and understanding of the setting for which the design or plan is intended. It is important to take account of the local context, including its history and climate. As Sommer (1974) has written, and as these cases bear out, a design concept "will be expressed differently according to geography, climate, and the nature of the surrounding community" (p. 49). It is also important to understand the activities that the design or plan is intended to support, activities that will constitute a joint product of the specific individuals who will use the setting and the tasks they will perform there. Based on analysis of the setting, specific behavioral goals must be set for the design or plan. Although a behavioral goal is just one of several types of goals that must be considered, including structural, financial, aesthetic, and others (it is to be understood that this is also true of subsequent steps in the design or planning process), nonetheless this discussion will focus exclusively on behavioral issues.

Those target behaviors serve as the starting point in the search for environmental features that might support or facilitate them. Those features might be inferred from environment–behavior relationships that are specified in existing theory or research, or they might be sought in new research that is specific to the setting and the design problem being considered, such as a survey of potential user groups or comparisons among prospective users' responses to alternative designs or plans.

Then the design or plan elements that are identified as likely to enhance the target behaviors must be incorporated into a complete design or plan that specifies materials, layout, sizes of spaces, and relationships among those elements. This may require the resolution of serious conflicts between behavior-related goals and the interests of other parties to the design or planning process. As we have seen, eventual achievement of behavioral goals may depend on effective advocacy by environmental-design researchers.

Implementation of a design or plan is rarely as straightforward a matter as a description of it implies. Construction from a design, or implementation of a plan, involves complex negotiations that may have a profound effect on the degree to which the goals of the design or plan are realized. Inaccuracies in initial cost estimates often are at the root of such difficulties.

In order to determine if the design or plan elements were selected through valid inferences from the available environment–behavior knowledge base, a POE study is required. The value of the POE will be enhanced if all available opportunities to make more powerful quasi-experimental comparisons, over time or in contrasting settings, are exploited to the fullest.

Finally, the results of the POE may modify the current state of knowledge about environment–behavior relationships, contribute to the available arsenal of research methods, influence subsequent designs or plans for related settings, and influence the process through which design or planning decisions are made. Many examples of such contributions are given throughout this volume.

Stage 1: Background analysis Several of the cases included in this volume illustrate the importance of understanding the particular setting to which environmental-design research is being addressed. Consider the case of San Francisco's 1985 Downtown Plan (chapter 14): Without knowledge of the architectural and social history of the city and its topographic and climatic conditions, which were all quite atypical of large American cities experiencing significant high-rise development, the success of Bosselman and colleagues' research would have been highly unlikely. Neither appropriate goals nor appropriate planning approaches to them could have been developed otherwise. The same is true of Valadez and Bellalta's plan for fostering community development in Macul (chapter 12), although the cultural background of the residents and the climate-related, outdoors-oriented local lifestyle in Santiago were the key background issues in that case. And the alternative living arrangements compared at Belchertown State School (chapter 5) were shaped by the normalization principle that carried the day in the litigation out of which the project arose.

These are some of the most prominent examples of cases in which background analysis played a significant role. But even in cases where it seems that universal laws of behavior can be applied – as in the application of defensible-space theory based on mechanisms of territoriality (chapter 11) and the application of principles of reinforcement through provision of feedback about energy consumption (chapter 13) – one might wonder if analysis of the background of the particular setting involved might not produce even better results.

Stage 2: Setting behavioral goals In his analysis of the EDR process, John Zeisel (1981) referred to the setting of goals for the behavioral outcomes of a design or plan as "imaging." By that, he meant grasping the broad environment–behavior issues that determine how well the setting fulfills the needs of its users.

The cases in this volume include several examples of the ways in which an effective image can help steer the design or planning process to a successful conclusion. The modular/direct-supervision approach to jail design (chapter 3) seems clearly to be based on a good grasp of the basic interpersonal processes involved – privacy and communication in particular. Effective designs for living space for the developmentally disabled residents of Belchertown State School (chapter 5) were also based on the recognition that privacy is a key element in normal social interactions. "Sociopetal space" (chapter 8) is a concept that summarizes quite effectively the ways in which spatial arrangements shape social interactions. And defensible-space theory (chapter 11), though based on a number of simple relationships between individual architectural features such as mass and building height, captures an essential aspect of a community's relationship to its territory that can be extended to analyses of different design and planning elements in new settings.

All of those cases provide strong support for the importance of an understanding of basic environment–behavior relationships to the success of environmental-design research. Of course, they are all concerned with settings in which relationships among users are important. For other types of problems, such as designing wayfinding systems for a hospital (chapter 4), planning effective traffic controls for city streets (chapter 10), or devising effective means of controlling high-rise development (chapter 14), such well-established theoretical social-science analyses may not be available or even necessary. In those cases, an understanding of the underlying technical system may be more important.

Stage 3: Establishing environment–behavior relationships Establishing a knowledge base for a design or planning intervention is arguably the key link in the EDR process. Setting goals is of little use without it, nor is a design or plan likely to achieve those goals without it. The cases in this volume illustrate two quite different but potentially effective alternative approaches to the task. One is to tie into basic theories that explain relevant environment–behavior relationships. It is exemplified by the interaction-inducing designs for mental-hospital wards based on the analysis of sociopetal-space arrangements introduced by Osmond and later explicated by Sommer (chapter 8). Newman's use of the concept of territoriality in his theory of defensible space and its application to prevent crime through environmental design (chapter 11) and Baum and Valins's use of the concept of privacy in their analysis of crowding stress in college dormitories and design changes to reduce it (chapter 7) are other excellent examples.

Another approach is the atheoretical study of settings similar to the setting at issue in a particular design or planning project, in order to identify design or plan features that are associated with desired behaviors. The use of Wener's evaluations of modular/direct-supervision Metropolitan Correctional Centers in the design of the Contra Costa County Main Detention Facility (chapter 3) illustrates this approach. So do Whyte's study of the architectural correlates of intensive use of New York City's public plazas (chapter 9) and Appleyard's study of the effects of varying levels of traffic volume on residential streets in San Francisco (chapter 10).

Of particular interest in the latter approach is the use of environmental simulation to compare alternative designs for their potential in realizing the behavioral goals for a project. Carpman and colleagues' use of the model-scope simulation technique to compare alternative locations for parking-garage entrances at the new University of Michigan Hospital (chapter 4) and Bosselman and colleagues' use of the same technique, at the Berkeley laboratory where it was developed, to compare alternative design controls on high-rise buildings in downtown San Francisco for their effects on the architectural character of existing streetscapes (chapter 14) highlight the great potential of sophisticated simulation to evaluate in advance alternative design or planning solutions whose effects could otherwise be estimated only from comparisons with the most similar existing settings. Full-scale mock-ups of design alternatives, such as those tested at Belchertown State School (chapter 5), fulfill similar functions for the smaller-scale settings where they are feasible.

Stage 4: Creating design/plan elements As Zeisel (1981) has pointed out, environment–behavior knowledge relevant to the behavioral goals for a project must be translated into specific designs that can actually be built, or planning or management policies that can be implemented. It is at this point in the EDR process that it becomes clear how important technical expertise in design or planning is to the success of the EDR enterprise as a whole, as much as understanding behavioral issues or conducting useful social-science research – and how difficult it can be for experts to communicate and cooperate across disciplinary boundaries.

The design for modules in direct-supervision jails (chapter 3), the grouping of houses with their private gardens around common plazoletas in Macul (chapter 12), the creation of sociopetal-space arrangements combining central activity areas surrounded by seating and leaning surfaces on a mental-hospital ward (chapter 8), and many other design and planning solutions devised for the projects described in this volume illustrate the importance of design creativity in environmental-design research.

Several of the projects also illustrate the value of devising alternative designs that can be compared. Although some of these cases show that a designer or planner can use environment–behavior knowledge to produce a single solution that proves effective for the target setting, it stands to reason that a process that generates multiple solutions and compares them for effectiveness using proven social-science methods generally will produce a better outcome. The Belchertown State School study (chapter 5) is a good case in point. The design alternative that followed the guiding concept of normalization most literally proved to be only second-best to a design that apparently achieved the key underlying goal of privacy most successfully. The three plazoleta designs in Macul (chapter 12) were found to be differentially effective in promoting community development. And generally successful designs for modular/direct-supervision jails were able to be improved through comparisons across successive iterations (chapter 3).

Stage 5: The role of EDR-based elements in the overall design EDR research requires a combination of talents for research design, technology, and design. But success in understanding or discovering environment–behavior relationships and translating the resulting knowledge into feasible design solutions, or planning or management policies, still does not assure that one's work will be represented in the final design or plan. The cases in this volume make this point in two ways. First there are the cases in which, because of conflicts with other interests in the decision-making process, the EDR work was omitted from the final design or plan. In the case of the University of Michigan Hospital (chapter 4), the evidence concerning intelligible labels for signs directing patients and visitors to various medical specialties was ignored in favor of more "professional" medical jargon, and the demonstrably superior elevator symbols for floors below grade could not be used because of space limitations on the elevator display – both likely to decrease the ease of wayfinding. Evidence of effective and practical means for encouraging conservation of energy in household heating and cooling (chapter 13) has had little impact in a social and political atmosphere that encourages short-term personal comfort and promotes the use of familiar technology, to the exclusion of long-term concerns about the environment and the economy.

However, there is a more hopeful and useful message to be found among these cases. When environmental-design researchers take on the additional role of advocates for user-appropriate design and planning, they can broaden and deepen the impact of their work considerably. Chenoweth and Niemann not only verified the importance of scenic beauty to users of the Lower Wisconsin River Valley and identified the landscape features on which those judgments of scenic beauty were based (chapter 15) but also were instrumental in making the preservation of scenic beauty a high priority in the final plan for the Lower Wisconsin State Riverway. By their strategic use of their research results, based on an astute understanding of the decision-making process, they were able to overcome apathy and resistance, to the point that politically sensitive controls were placed on the activities of private landowners, including some whose property was not even contiguous with the river. Other examples of effective advocacy include the initiative by Janet Carpman and the staff of the Patient and Visitor Participation Program to pursue patients' and visitors' concerns on a level beyond the routine problems assigned to them by the higher echelons of the Replacement Hospital Program (chapter 4), as well as the research and design team for the Seattle FAA building (chapter 6), who strongly promoted user participation and consultation based on the general mandate they received from the General Services Administration.

In all of these positive examples, environmental-design researchers acted as surrogates for the eventual users of the settings for which their designs and plans were intended. By taking on users' concerns in addition to their clients' mandates, they were able to go beyond producing useful data and feasible interventions, thus ensuring that those products of their work would have real impact on the places and people at stake.

Stage 6: POE Most of the projects described in this volume were subjected to systematic empirical evaluations to determine if the designs and plans they produced had the effects intended. The varied methods used in those evaluation studies illustrate the choices available to environmental-design researchers and demonstrate the need to choose wisely because of the considerable consequences of those choices for the value of the resulting gains in knowledge about the effectiveness of the interventions being assessed and the validity of the underlying theory or research findings.

In many cases, environmental-design researchers either are constrained or feel they are constrained to rely on simple pre–post comparisons of the behaviors of setting users. Unfortunately, the results of such comparisons can be difficult to interpret. If the users seem to be better off after a design or plan has been implemented, is it because the design or plan "worked" as the theory or research findings on which it was based had indicated it would? Or is it because the users of the setting expected that it would, or simply because they appreciated the efforts made on their behalf? Or because those administering the activities in that setting saw the period of change as a good time to introduce other reforms (make a clean sweep of the old) that actually made the difference? Or because of some coincidental change in economic conditions or the law or the weather? Unfortunately, the possibilities for such confusions are almost endless.

That is the reason that several of the POE studies conducted in connection with projects described in this volume provide such valuable lessons for the field. In those studies, more powerful research designs could be used to rule out alternative explanations for the findings of benefits from the designs or plans being evaluated.

Several of those cases constituted demonstrations of the designs or plans, with evaluation being one of the major goals of each project, and the intervention being either temporary or on a small scale. Such was the case in the Belchertown State School (chapter 5) and Jones Dormitory (chapter 7) projects, each of which utilized a quasi-experimental approach in which alternative designs were compared among nonequivalent groups of users. In the case of the energy-conservation demonstrations described in chapter 13 it was possible to use experimental random assignment to create equivalent groups of users and dwellings for comparison.

More powerful quasi-experimental research designs have also been used in full-scale, permanent interventions, such as the Seattle FAA building project (chapter 6), where outcomes were compared with those for another new FAA facility outside Los Angeles, and in Macul (chapter 12), where theoretically contrasting planning alternatives (plazoleta designs) were compared among nonequivalent groups of residents. The outcomes of the modular/direct-supervision design used in the Contra Costa County jail were amenable to comparison to a limited degree with those at a Detroit facility (chapter 3). In the case of the sociopetal-space renovation at the Cleveland State Hospital (chapter 8), the existing hospital policy of assigning new patients randomly to admissions wards made possible an even more powerful experimental comparison.

Although it is clear that quasi-experimental evaluation studies (much less experimental evaluation studies) are not always possible, their considerable methodological advantages argue strongly for their use. Perhaps with more knowledge of those advantages and more (and more varied) models of their use, such as those discussed earlier, EDR practitioners will in the future make greater efforts to employ such research designs where possible. And with their efforts, perhaps even more and better models will be developed – a growing arsenal of solutions to the difficult problems of establishing useful comparisons in POE studies.

Stage 7: Future impact The cases in this volume describe a number of alternative paths for spreading the benefits of environmental-design research beyond the boundaries of a single project. Several of the cases, from all three categories, but all based on dedicated research in the target setting or very similar settings, have provided a model for intervention in other projects carried out in similar settings. The modular/direct-supervision design for the Contra Costa County jail (chapter 3) is an outstanding example of this direct type of impact, having influenced the design of many jails around the country through its well-documented and well-known success. The successful defensible-space modifications at Clason Point Gardens (chapter 11), along with Newman's other work, have led to defensible-space projects in many types of settings across the country. Similarly, the site-specific approach to control over high-rise development pioneered by Bosselman and colleagues for San Francisco (chapter 14) has been adopted in other cities. To a lesser degree, Appleyard's livable-streets projects (chapter 10) and Whyte and colleagues' blueprint for public-plaza design in New York City (chapter 9) have had similar influences. And Chenoweth and Niemann's work on the plan for the Lower Wisconsin State Riverway (chapter 15) seems to have the potential to do the same, given time. In each of these cases, environmental-design researchers have succeeded in creating a model that can be applied easily to other settings with similar parameters.

In other cases, all tied closely to social-science theory, broad impact has been achieved by spreading influential conceptualizations of environment–behavior relationships that have shaped designers' basic views or images of the settings in which they work. Sociopetal space (chapter 8) is a prominent example of such a conceptualization; it has been influential in designers' approaches to spatial arrangements in psychiatric hospitals and other facilities where social interaction is an important behavioral issue. Defensible space (chapter 11) is another prominent example, shaping designers' and planners' views of the influence of larger spatial relationships on territorial behavior and crime. And Valadez and Ballalta's work in Macul (chapter 12) extends the basic concept of propinquity, fostering community development through neighborhood plans that encourage unintended social contacts among neighbors, first introduced by Festinger, Schachter, and Back (1950).

Finally, several of the cases have spawned guidebooks for design: for patient and visitor facilities in hospitals, in Carpman, Grant, and Simmons's *Design That Cares* (1986); for correctional facilities, in Farbstein's *Corrections Planning Handbooks* (1981); and in Newman's *Defensible Space* (1972) and *Community of Interest* (1981), among others.

There are, thus, several effective ways of making environmental-design research go further than service in a single project. Design and planning researchers need to consider the value of creating an adaptable procedure, of tying their work to established theoretical concepts that can serve as schemata for others, and of creating explicit guidelines based on their work. Each of these would seem to provide a path that others can follow.

The rest of the iceberg

It might be argued that the cases described in this volume overestimate the potential of environmental-design research. They were selected as outstanding examples for their directness of application of research and/or theory and for the magnitude of the impact of the behavioral-science contribution to the final design, plan, or policy and the users affected by it. The criteria for inclusion were adapted from criteria originally suggested by Wener (undated) that were even more stringent, requiring behavioral evaluation of the outcome and use of the results to inform subsequent "generations" of similar projects. In fact, it was difficult to find cases that could be documented to meet even the weakened version of Wener's criteria. The meager baker's dozen included in this volume were selected from only a slightly larger number of eligible cases.

However, it seems to me that rather than overestimating the true potential of environmental-design research, these "ideal" cases may actually do just the opposite. Whereas it might be argued that they demonstrate the ultimate potential of environmental-design research, there may be an even stronger argument for the potential of environmental-design research that can be made on the basis of the research conducted for this volume of case studies. In that research, I was discouraged at times by the difficulty of finding suitable examples. But I also learned that ideal cases, such as those described in this volume, can lead one to seriously underestimate in several ways the contributions that environmental-design research has made to environmental design, planning, and policymaking and to the ubiquitous settings they help to produce. The outcomes of environmental-design research extend far beyond the cases described in this volume, to other cases that are similar but could not be documented adequately to fit the format of this volume or were not chosen because they were judged to be less useful examples for the purposes of this volume. Those outcomes also extend to several products of environmental-design research other than the completed settings, plans, or policies to which this volume is addressed.

One of the difficulties encountered in doing the research for this volume was the problem of access to information about environmental-design research. That information is scattered among many sources, including many that are not in the public domain. The format into which cases had to fit for this volume required more detail than was available for some cases that seemed otherwise to be appropriate. Those included two housing facilities for the elderly, the New York State Veterans' Home at Oxford, whose design was influenced by research conducted in the outdated facility it replaced (Snyder & Ostrander, 1974; Nahemow, undated), and Captain Eldridge House, a congregate housing facility in Hyannis, Massachusetts, based on research into the privacy needs of elderly residents by Zeisel and Korobkin (*Progressive Architecture*, 1981), and a facility for multiple sclerosis patients utilizing research by Gifford and Martin (1991). They also included a series of dormitory projects at Indiana State University in Terre Haute, by the team of psychologist Lawrence Wheeler and architect Ewing Miller (Miller, 1968, 1972), in which the results of the evaluation of each project were used to design the next. There was also an extensive series of research-based design projects at Bellevue Hospital in New York City that involved a wide variety of spaces, including the main entrance (a wayfinding project) and visitor lounges, carried out by Richard Olsen and several of his colleagues in environmental psychology at City University of New York (Olsen & Pershing, 1981; Olsen, Pershing, & Winkel, 1984). M. Powell Lawton used behavioral research in developing designs for the Philadelphia Geriatric Center (Lawton, Liebowitz, & Charon, 1970). Brolin and Zeisel (1968) used the results of research into cultural differences in patterns of home use to design multifamily housing for Puerto Rican families. Reizenstein and her colleagues used behavioral research to design offices for social workers in a Cambridge, Massachusetts, hospital (Reizenstein, Spencer, & McBride, 1976), as did Weinstein and Pinciotti (1988) for a school playground.

There are large numbers of cases in which user participation in the process of generating and selecting among design alternatives has served as the principal mode of environment–behavior input. These include a public-library project by Deasy (1970), a medical-hospital project by Becker and Poe (1980), a public-playground project by Francis (1982), and a park project by Kaplan (1980). In addition, architect Henry Sanoff of North Carolina State University has used the participation method of design extensively and has collected examples of his and others' work in that area, ranging from housing to transit planning, in a recent book (Sanoff, 1990).

In addition to their use in energy conservation, behavior-modification techniques based on psychological learning theories have been used extensively by Geller and his colleagues to develop policies for litter control (e.g., Geller, Witmer, & Orebaugh, 1976) and by Everett and his colleagues to plan strategies for increasing mass-transit use (e.g., Everett, Hayward, & Myers, 1974). And efforts to use behavioral research to protect scenic resources have included the use of a newspaper public-opinion survey in planning a strategy for dealing with extensive erosion at Niagara Falls (American Falls International Board, 1974).

There are many examples of projects where environment–behavior research and theory have had less direct influences. These "quasi cases" include plans for coastal development in the Virgin Islands, based in part on perceived scenic-beauty measurements by Zube and his colleagues (Virgin Islands Planning Office, 1977a,b; Zube & McLaughlin, 1978), and plans for development in the scenic Connecticut River Valley utilizing similar research by the same group (Zube, Pitt, & Anderson, 1975). Concern for preservation of scenic resources also influenced the design of an elevated section of the Blue Ridge Parkway at Grandfather Mountain, North Carolina (Jakovich, undated), the design for an interstate-highway bridge near Cross Lake, Louisiana (Atkins & Blair, 1983), and plans for the management of large tracts of public land in the West, influenced by research on perceptions of scenic beauty by Daniel (Daniel, Zube, & Driver, 1979). Donald Appleyard's well-known research on wayfinding in cities (extending the work of his mentor Lynch on imagability) influenced plans to accommodate the rapid population expansion in Ciudad Guayana, Venezuela (Appleyard, 1970).

There are many examples of published design and planning guidelines that reflect the results of environment–behavior theory and research. Appleyard and Carp (1974) formulated guidelines for planning station locations for the BART rapid-transit line based on their survey research. Guidelines based on behavioral research have been published for designing radiation-treatment facilities (Conway, Zeisel, & Welch, 1977), housing for the elderly (Howell, 1980; Welch, Parker, & Zeisel, 1984; Zeisel, Epp, & Demos, 1978, 1984), child-care facilities (Moore, Cohen, & McGinty, 1979a; Weinstein & David, 1990; Moore et al., 1979c), facilities for handicapped children (Moore et al., 1979b; Moore, 1980), correctional facilities (Farbstein, 1986), banks (Wise & Wise, 1984), outdoor play areas for children (Moore, 1990), residential facilities for Alzheimer's patients (Calkins, 1988; Cohen & Weisman, 1990), theaters (Beckley & Myers, 1981), and shelters for battered women (Refuerzo & Verderber, 1990). Behavior-based guidelines have also been produced for the reduction of school vandalism (Zeisel, 1976), the design of barrier-free buildings (Adaptive Environments Center, Inc., and Welch & Epp, no date), and the design of space stations (Clearwater & Coss, in press).

Environmental-design researchers have made numerous contributions to the design process in the form of POEs. Evaluations of housing for the elderly have been reported by Carp (1966), Lipman (1968), and Orzeck, Marsh, and Weisman (1983). Reizenstein and McBride (1978) and MacEachron (1983) have conducted POEs of institutions for retarded persons. Evaluations of government-subsidized housing have been published by Cooper (1971), Zeisel and Griffin (1975), Wiedemann et al. (1989), and Kantrowitz and Nordhaus (1980). Bitgood et al. (1987) and O'Reilly, Shettel-Neuber, and Vining (1978) have evaluated responses to museum exhibits. The Research and Design Institute (1974) conducted a POE of a renovated dormitory at the

University of Rhode Island, and King (1980) evaluated a new student-union building at California State University, Los Angeles. POEs have been carried out at facilities for the handicapped, including a rehabilitation center (Burton, 1980) and a residential institution (Landesman-Dwyer, 1984). Farbstein et al. (1988) evaluated post offices, Barkow, Scalzitti, and Piipponen (1983) a concert hall, Zube et al. (1975) national-parks visitors' centers, Rutledge (1975) a public plaza adjacent to a Chicago bank building, Keller (1978) a large-scale housing development, and Marans and Spreckelmeyer (1981) a federal office building in Ann Arbor. In addition, several volumes of POE guidelines and case studies have been published (Preiser, Rabinowitz, & White, 1991; Reizenstein & Zimring, 1980; Preiser, 1989), in addition to the many individual evaluation studies conducted in connection with the cases described in this volume and those reported in this chapter.

Lasting contributions have also been made in shaping policies that have institutionalized the use of environmental-design research. Although it is impossible to know the extent, illustrations can be given. The American Corrections Association guidelines for accrediting correctional facilities re-flect the knowledge gained through POEs of direct-supervision jails like the federal MCCs and CCCMDF, and the General Services Administration, which builds, procures, and manages office space for government agencies in almost inconceivable amounts, requires empirical evaluation (POE) in its building contracts and leases as a matter of policy, no doubt influenced by the large number of independent POEs of federal facilities that have proved valuable in the past. Shibley (1985) has identified the U.S. Army Corps of Engineers and the New Zealand Ministry of Works and Development as organizations that have incorporated POE into their construction policies. In this connection, Ventre (1986) has suggested building standards as an addi-tional avenue for institutionalizing environment–behavior knowledge in de-sign practice.

There is also, of course, a vast literature of research and theory in a variety of design and social-science desciplines that does not qualify as environmental-design research per se because it is not tied to particular design or planning projects. Rather, it describes environment–behavior relationships that may suggest design or planning alternatives via what Seidel (1985) has labeled conceptual application (i.e., background knowledge that is relevant to the problem at hand). The R/UDAT program of the American Institute of Architects brings social scientists with such knowledge together with de-signers to stimulate this kind of conceptual application (Sommer, 1990).

Finally, EDR practitioners have developed research tools that promise to make a lasting contribution by facilitating such work in the future. Prominent examples include Farbstein and Wener's standardized instrument for evaluat-ing correctional institutions (Farbstein, Wener, & Gomez, 1979), realistic video simulation techniques pioneered by Appleyard and Craik (1974) at the Berkeley Environmental Simulation Laboratory (see chapters 4 and 14), and more recent digital-image-capturing simulations techniques (Orland, 1986).

It is important to note that the cases, EDR studies, guidelines, POEs, and research tools reviewed here do not by any means represent an exhaustive list of the past contributions of environmental-design research. It has become quite clear in the course of the research for this volume that those contributions are scattered far and wide, among professional journals, university research-center publications, conference proceedings, textbooks, professional books, government documents, and, least accessible of all, the private professional practices of designers and their behavioral-scientist consultants. There is no unified accessible data base from which to assemble this information. One can only estimate the extent of the EDR enterprise. In fact, as environmental-design research becomes integrated more fully into design and planning processes, it is becoming more difficult to identify, as compared with the time when it was so unusual that participants, usually academics, made a point of publishing it as a lesson for the uninitiated. Although this is an example of co-optation in a positive sense, it does make new cases more difficult to find and evaluate.

The present: an armamentarium of resources for the practice of environmental-design research

A pattern for the practice of environmental-design research

The past efforts of environmental-design researchers, as partially reviewed earlier, have left several important legacies to the field today. First, they have set a pattern for incorporating environment–behavior knowledge into the design and planning process. That pattern, discussed in detail earlier in this chapter, is not conceived here as a blueprint that EDR practitioners must follow, nor as one that will ensure their success, but rather as a systematic summary of past work in the field that may prove useful to the current practitioner.

Expertise in the hands of experienced EDR practitioners

Another legacy of past environmental-design research is an established corps of practitioners. There are private firms and individuals with considerable experience in a wide variety of design and planning activities and settings, as well as university-based research and consulting groups. It would be quite difficult to produce a complete, current list of those individuals and organizations. However, many of them are affiliated with the Environmental Design Research Association (EDRA), an international organization with headquarters in the United States. EDRA publishes a directory that is updated every few years; it lists member practitioners along with their addresses and special interests. Similar organizations in other parts of the world include the International Association for the Study of People and Their Physical Environments (IAPS), based in England, People and Physical Environment Research (PAPER), in Australia and New Zealand, and the Man–Environment Research Association (MERA), in Japan.

Graduate programs for training in environmental-design research

There are several graduate programs that strongly emphasize environmental-design research. These include programs in the design professions, principally in architecture and landscape architecture, as well as programs in the social and behavioral sciences, including environmental psychology and social ecology. EDRA is a good source for information about these programs.

These programs conduct research (several are included in the list of EDR practitioners affiliated with EDRA), train new researcher-practitioners, and help to publicize environmental-design research on their campuses, in their communities, and more broadly. Several have established publication series in order to disseminate reports of their work.

One potentially significant contribution of these programs is the creation of a new generation of environmental-design researchers who are able both to conduct research and to create designs or plans for actual projects. If application of environment–behavior knowledge is hindered by a "gap" between researchers and practitioners, as many have observed, one solution may be to develop a new type of professional whose capabilities will include both research and design or planning. Interestingly, several of the most successful projects described in this volume were the work of such individuals. Oscar Newman, Donald Appleyard, and William H. Whyte were all involved in both the research and design aspects of their work.

An archive of EDR projects

We also have the legacy of an extensive archive of published listings and descriptions of quite varied length and level of detail for EDR projects and bits and pieces thereof. The most concentrated sources of these include the following:

• The published proceedings of the 21 annual conferences (through 1990) of the Environmental Design Research Association (EDRA); a cumulative index to the first 18 conferences was recently published (Wener & Szigeti, 1988).
• The first comprehensive *Handbook of Environmental Psychology* was published by Wiley in 1987, edited by Stokols and Altman.

• Cambridge University Press has published close to a dozen volumes in its Environment and Behavior series, edited by Altman and Stokols. Several of those address directly EDR issues discussed in this volume (which is also part of that series).

• Plenum Press has published a series of books edited by Altman and Wohlwill (and others), under the heading Environment and Behavior studies, that had reached 11 volumes in 1990.

• EDRA publishes a quarterly newsletter, *Design Research News,* now in its 22nd volume (1991).

• Annual awards from *Progressive Architecture* and from the American Society of Landscape Architects (announced in *Landscape Architecture*) regularly honor EDR projects.

• EDRA sponsors a series of books under the general title *Environment, Behavior, and Design,* published by Plenum Press under the editorship of Zube and Moore. The third volume was published in 1991.

• Lists of research reports are available from most of the university-based research centers mentioned earlier in this chapter.

• Textbooks in environmental psychology have been published by Ittelson et al. (1974), Proshansky, Ittelson, and Rivlin (1976), Holahan (1982), Gifford (1987), and Bell et al. (1990).

• Dowden, Hutchinson & Ross of Stroudsburg, Pennsylvania, and Van Nostrand Reinhold of New York City have been among the most active publishers of books on environmental-design research.

• *Environment and Behavior,* the *Journal of Architectural and Planning Research,* the *Journal of Environmental Psychology,* and the journals of the American Planning Association and the American Institute of Architects frequently publish articles about environmental-design research.

In sum, at present there is reason to be confident that, in general, knowledge of environment–behavior relationships can productively inform design and planning decisions and that considerable expertise is available to carry out specific EDR projects in almost any type of setting, with considerable guidance from past efforts in most cases.

The future: prospects for environmental-design research

There seems little reason to fear that the reader will place too much confidence in prognostications about the future of environmental-design research. However, several participants have made useful observations in this regard, and I cannot resist adding my own.

There are many good reasons to predict a bright future for environmental-design research. Its value has been demonstrated clearly and repeatedly, as this volume attempts to document. Environmental-protection laws have created a need for verifiable means of predicting the outcomes of decisions about environmental design and planning, particularly the National Environmental Policy Act (NEPA) of 1969 and the individual states' adaptations of it that mandate the filing of environmental-impact statements during the design and planning stages of many construction projects. Many public and private organizations have accepted the need for evaluations of policies and programs in general, and thus decisions about environmental design and planning are more likely to be subjected to close and objective scrutiny. And increased economic pressures to conserve scarce resources have prompted more realistic appraisals of the costs of such projects, including estimation of the long-term costs of operating a setting, costs that have been estimated by Villeco and Brill (1981) to average 97% of the total costs over the life of a building project, with only the remaining 3% being attributable to the initial cost of construction.

There seem to be so many good reasons for increased use of environmental-design research by designers and planners that many have been expecting an explosive expansion in the field for some time. Several recent analyses suggest reasons that those expectations have not yet been fulfilled. According to those analyses, the problem may lie not within the field of environmental-design research itself – not with environment–behavior theory and research, or research methods, or the ability to translate knowledge into designs or plans – but in the field's relationships to the other parties involved in making decisions about design and planning: the design and planning professionals and their clients.

Concerns about the relationships between environmental-design researchers and designers and clients were a prominent theme of a special issue of *Environment and Behavior* devoted to the application of "E&B research" (Kantrowitz & Seidel, 1985). In that issue, Shibley (1985) stressed the importance of providing the information that is requested by the client, rather than information that the researcher believes to be important to the client. He suggested in that article that the success of environmental-design research be measured by the degree to which it is institutionalized or incorporated into the policies of the organization for which it is done. Kantrowitz (1985) argued that the utilization of environment–behavior research has been hindered by a lack of integration of the design and research processes and that increased utilization will depend on increased "understanding among client groups that E&B research can help solve client problems" (p. 43). Finally, Seidel (1985) suggested that successful utilization of environment–behavior knowledge awaits the implementation of new strategies for bringing information users and researchers together.

If one is persuaded that the future of environmental-design research should be measured by the degree to which it is integrated into or institutionalized in design and planning practice, and that its prospects in that regard are threatened more by organizational processes that keep designers or planners and researchers apart than by weaknesses in the EDR process itself, then one of the most promising developments in recent years may be these first serious attempts to understand the relationship between environmental-design researchers and their influential colleagues who make the decisions in the design or planning process.

Carpman's (1983) dissertation research, carried out in connection with her work on the University of Michigan Replacement Hospital Program (chapter 4), exemplifies one approach toward such understanding, utilizing empirical research to identify the factors that influence research utilization. Schneekloth (1987) has used established forms of organizational analysis to describe the process by which knowledge and application interact and to suggest means of improving the outcome of such interaction. This work, and other work like it, may mark the beginning of a new era of meta-environmental-design research. The future of the field may depend as much on the success of this new enterprise as on the quality of its continuing contributions to actual design and planning projects.

References

Adaptive Environments Center, Inc., and Welch & Epp Associates (no date). *Design for access: A guidebook for designing barrier free state and county buildings.* Boston, MA: authors.

American Falls International Board (1974). *Preservation and enhancement of the American Falls at Niagara: Final report to the international joint commission.* Buffalo, NY: author.

Appleyard, D. (1970). *Planning a pluralist city: Conflicting realities in Ciudad Guayana.* Cambridge, MA: MIT Press.

Appleyard, D., & Carp, F. (1974). The BART residential impact study: An empirical study of environmental impact. In T. G. Dickert & K. R. Domeny (Eds.), *Environmental impact assessment: Guidelines and commentary.* Berkeley: University Extension, University of California.

Appleyard, D., & Craik, K. H. (1974). The Berkeley Environmental Simulation Project: Its use in environmental impact assessment. In T. G. Dickert & K. R. Domeny (Eds.), *Environmental impact assessment: Guidelines and commentary* (pp. 121–126). Berkeley: University Extension, University of California.

Atkins, J. T., & Blair, W. G. E. (1983). Visual impacts of highway alternatives. *Garten und Landschaft, 8,* 632–635.

Barkow, B., Scalzitti, B., & Piipponen, V. (1983). A building use study of Roy Thompson Hall, Toronto. Ottawa, Canada: National Research Council of Canada.

Becker, F. D., & Poe, D. B., Jr. (1980). The effects of user-generated modifications in a general hospital. *Journal of Nonverbal Behavior, 4,* 195–218.

Beckley, R. M., & Myers, S. M. (1981). *Theater facility impact study: Guidelines and strategies for theater facilities.* Milwaukee: University of Wisconsin–Milwaukee, School of Architecture and Urban Planning.

Bell, P. A., Fisher, J. D., Baum, A., & Greene, T. E. (1990). *Environmental psychology* (3rd ed.). Ft. Worth, TX: Holt, Rinehart & Winston.

Bitgood, S., Pierce, M., Nichols, G., & Patterson, D. (1987). Formative evaluation of a cave exhibit. *Curator, 30*(1), 31–39.

Brolin, B. C., & Zeisel, J. (1968). Mass housing: Social research and design. *Ekistics, 158,* 51–55.

Burton, D. J. (1980). User evaluation of a rehabilitation center for the elderly and handicapped programmed and renovated to optimize performance in meeting user needs. In R. Stough & A. Wandersman (Eds.), *Optimizing environments: Research, practice and policy* (pp. 39–58). Washington, DC: Environmental Design Research Association.

Calkins, M. P. (1988). *Design for dementia: Planning environments for the elderly and the confused.* Owings Mills, MD: National Health Publishing.

Carp, F. (1966). *A future for the aged: Victoria Plaza and its residents.* Austin: University of Texas Press.

Carpman, J. R. (1983). *Influencing design decisions: An analysis of the impact of the Patient and Visitor Participation Project on the University of Michigan Replacement Hospital Program.* Unpublished doctoral dissertation, University of Michigan, Ann Arbor.

Carpman, J. R., Grant, M. A., & Simmons, D. A. (1986). *Design that cares.* Chicago: American Hospital Association.

Clearwater, Y. A., & Coss, R. G. (in press). Functional aesthetics to enhance well-being in isolated and confined settings. In A. A. Harrison, Y. A. Clearwater, & P. McKay (Eds.), *From Antarctica to outer space: Life in isolation and confinement.* New York: Springer-Verlag.

Cohen, U., & Weisman, G. (1990). *Holding on to home: Designing environments for people with dementia.* Baltimore, MD: John Hopkins University Press.

Conway, D., Zeisel, J., & Welch, P. (1977). *Radiation therapy centers: Behavioral and social guidelines for design.* Washington, DC: National Institutes of Health.

Cooper, C. (1971, December). St. Francis Square: Attitudes of its residents. *American Institute of Architects Journal, 56,* 22–27.

Daniel, T. C., Zube, E. H., & Driver, B. L. (1979). *Assessing amenity resource values.* Ft. Collins, CO: Rocky Mountain Forest and Range Experiment Station.

Deasy, C. M. (1970). When architects consult people. *Psychology Today, 3,* 54–57, 79.

Everett, P. B., Hayward, S. C., & Meyers, A. W. (1974). The effects of a token reinforcement procedure on bus ridership. *Journal of Applied Behavioral Analysis, 7,* 1–10.

Farbstein, J. (1981). *Corrections planning handbooks.* Sacramento: California Board of Corrections.

Farbstein, J. (1986). *Correctional facility planning and design.* New York: Van Nostrand Reinhold.

Farbstein, J., Kantrowitz, M., Schermer, B., & Hughes-Caley, J. (1988). *Postoccupancy evaluation and organizational development: The experience of the United States Postal Service.* Presented at the 10th conference of the International Association for the Study of Man and His Physical Surroundings.

Farbstein, J., Wener, R., & Gomez, P. (1979). *Evaluation of correctional environments: Needs assessment survey.* San Luis Obispo, CA: Jay Farbstein & Associates.

Festinger, L., Schachter, S., & Back, K. (1950). *Social pressures in informal groups.* New York: Harper & Row.

Francis, M. (1982). Designing landscapes with community participation and behavioral research. *Landscape Architectural Forum, 32,* 14–21.

Geller, E. S., Witmer, J. F., & Orebaugh, A. L. (1976). Instructions as a determinant of paper-disposal behaviors. *Environment and Behavior, 8,* 417–439.

Gifford, R. (1987). *Environmental psychology: Principles and practice.* Newton, MA: Allyn & Bacon.

Gifford, R., & Martin, M. (1991). A multiple sclerosis center program and post-occupancy evaluation. In W. F. E. Preiser, H. Z. Rabinowitz, & E. T. White (Eds.), *Post occupancy evaluation.* New York: Van Nostrand Reinhold.

Holahan, C. J. (1982). *Environmental psychology.* New York: Random House.

Howell, S. (1980). *Designing for aging: Patterns of use.* Cambridge, MA: MIT Press.

Ittelson, W. H., Proshansky, H. M., Rivlin, L. G., & Winkel, G. H. (1974). *An introduction to environmental psychology.* New York: Holt, Rinehart & Winston.

Jakovich, G. S. (undated). *Design and construction of the Linn Cove Viaduct.* Arlington, VA: Federal Highway Administration.

Kantrowitz, M. (1985). Has environment and behavior research "made a difference"? *Environment and Behavior, 17,* 25–46.

Kantrowitz, M., & Nordhaus, R. (1980). The impact of post-occupancy evaluation research: A case study. *Environment and Behavior, 12,* 508–519.

Kantrowitz, M., & Seidel, A. D. (Eds.) (1985). Applications of E&B research. *Environment and Behavior, 17* (Whole No. 1).

Kaplan, R. (1980). Citizen participation in the design and evaluation of a park. *Environment and Behavior, 12,* 494–507.

Keller, S. (1978). Design and the quality of life in a new community. In J. M. Yinger & S. J. Cutler (Eds.), *Major social issues: An interdisciplinary view* (pp. 277–289). New York: Free Press.

King, E. D. (1980). *Post-occupancy evaluation of the California State University, Los Angeles, student union.* Unpublished M.A. thesis, Claremont Graduate School, Claremont, CA.

Landesman-Dwyer, S. (1984). Residential environments and the social behavior of handicapped individuals. In M. Lewis (Ed.), *Beyond the dyad* (pp. 299–322). New York: Plenum.

Lawton, M. P., Liebowitz, B., & Charon, H. (1970). Physical structure and the behavior of senile patients following ward remodeling. *Aging in Human Development, 1,* 231–239.

Lipman, A. (1968). A socio-architectural view of life in three homes for old people. *Gerontologica Clinica, 10,* 88–101.

MacEachron, A. E. (1983). Institutional form and adaptive functioning of mentally retarded persons. *American Journal of Mental Deficiency, 88,* 2–12.

Marans, R. W., & Spreckelmeyer, K. F. (1981). *Evaluating built environments: A behavioral approach.* Ann Arbor: Institute for Social Research and Architectural Research Laboratory, University of Michigan.

Miller, E. H. (1968). Put a behavioral scientist on the design team. *College and University Business, 44*(2), 68–71.

Miller, E. H. (1972, February). The student quarters that teamwork created. *American Institute of Architects Journal,* pp. 56–58.

Moore, G. T. (1980). The application of research to the design of therapeutic play environments for exceptional children. In W. M. Cruickshank (Ed.), *Crossroads to learning.* Syracuse, NY: Syracuse University Press.

Moore, G. T., & Chawla, L. (1986). Neighborhood play environments: Design principles for latchkey children. *Children's Environments Quarterly, 3*(2), 13–23.

Moore, G. T., Cohen, U., & McGinty, T. (1979a). *Planning and design guidelines: Child care centers and outdoor play environments* (7 vols.). Milwaukee: University of Wisconsin–Milwaukee, Center for Architectural and Urban Planning Research.

Moore, G. T., Cohen, U., Oertel, J., & Van Ryzin, L. (1979b). *Designing environments for handicapped children.* New York: Educational Facilities Laboratories.

Moore, G. T., Lane, C. G., Hill, A. H., Cohen, U., & McGinty, T. (1979c). *Recommendations for child care centers.* Milwaukee: University of Wisconsin–Milwaukee, Center for Architectural and Urban Planning Research.

Moore, R. C. (1990). *Play for all guidelines: Planning, design and management of outdoor setting for all children.* Berkeley, CA: MIG Communications.

Nahemow, L. (undated). *New York State Veterans Home, Oxford, New York: I. Behavioral and research objectives.* Albany: State of New York: Department of Health.

Newman, O. (1972). *Defensible space.* New York: Macmillan.

Newman, O. (1981). *Community of interest.* New York: Doubleday.

Olsen, R. V., & Pershing, A. (1981). *Environmental evaluation of the interim entry to Bellevue Hospital.* Unpublished report, Environmental Psychology Department, Bellevue Hospital, New York.

Olsen, R. V., Pershing, A., & Winkel, G. (1984). *A patient and staff evaluation of the Scanmural lounges.* Unpublished research report, Environmental Design Program, Bellevue Hospital Center and Environmental Psychology Program, City University of New York.

O'Reilly, J., Shettel-Neuber, J., & Vining, J. (1978). The use of post occupancy evaluation in aviary: Implications for a continuing assessment program in museums. In A. Osterberg, C. Tierman, & R. Findlay (Eds.), *Design research interactions* (pp. 318–325). Washington, DC: Environmental Design Research Association.

Orland, B. (1986). Image advantage. *Landscape Architecture, 76*(1), 58–63.

Orzeck, M. J., Marsh, K. J., & Weisman, G. (1983). Post occupancy evaluation of a behaviorally designed nursing home. In P. Bart, A. Chen, & G. Francescato (Eds.), *Knowledge for design.* Washington, DC: Environmental Design Research Association.

Preiser, W. F. E. (Ed.) (1989). *Building evaluation.* New York: Plenum.

Preiser, W. F. E., Rabinowitz, H. Z., & White, E. T. (1991). *Post occupancy evaluation.* New York: Van Nostrand Reinhold.

Progressive Architecture (1981). Congregate living. *Progressive Architecture, 8,* 64–68.

Proshansky, H. M., Ittelson, W. H., & Rivlin, L. G. (Eds.) (1976). *Environmental psychology: People and their physical settings* (2nd ed.). New York: Holt, Rinehart & Winston.

Refuerzo, B. J., & Verderber, S. F. (1990). Dimensions of person–environment relationships in shelters for victims of domestic violence. *Journal of the Architectural and Planning Association, 7,* 33–52.

Reizenstein, J., & McBride, W. (1978). *Designing for mentally retarded people: A social-environmental evaluation of New England Villages, Inc.* Ann Arbor: Architectural Research Laboratory, University of Michigan.

Reizenstein, J., Spencer, K. R., & McBride, W. A. (1976). *Social research and design: Cambridge Hospital social services offices.* Cambridge, MA: Harvard University, Graduate School of Design.

Reizenstein, J., & Zimring, C. (Eds.) (1980). Evaluating occupied environments. *Environment and Behavior, 12*(Whole No. 4).

Research and Design Institute (1974). *Butterfield Hall: Evaluation of a renovated dormitory at the University of Rhode Island.* Providence, RI: author.

Rutledge, A. J. (1975). *First National Bank Plaza, Chicago, Illinois: A pilot study in post construction evaluation.* Urbana: Department of Landscape Architecture, University of Illinois.

Sanoff, H. (1990). *Participatory design: Theory and techniques.* Raleigh, NC: author.

Schneekloth, L. H. (1987). Advances in practice in environment, behavior, and design. In E. H. Zube & G. T. Moore (Eds.), *Advances in environment, behavior, and design* (Vol. 1, pp. 307–334). New York: Plenum.

Seidel, A. (1985). What is success in E&B utilization? *Environment and Behavior, 17,* 47–70.

Shibley, R. G. (1985). Building evaluation in the main stream. *Environment and Behavior, 17,* 7–24.

Snyder, L. H., & Ostrander, E. R. (1974). *Research basis for behavioral program: New York State Veterans' Homes at Oxford.* Ithaca, NY: Cornell University.

Sommer, R. (1974). *Tight spaces.* Englewood Cliffs, NJ: Prentice-Hall.

Sommer, R. (1990). Research on utilization: Did anyone use it? Where did we lose it? Keynote address at the 21st annual conference of the Environmental Design Research Association, University of Illinois at Urbana-Champaign.

Stokols, D., & Altman, I. (Eds.). (1987). *Handbook of environmental psychology* (2 vols.). New York: Wiley.

Ventre, F. T. (1986). Who's to know: A discussion of four papers on using knowledge in the regulatory process. In J. Wineman, R. Barnes, & C. Zimring (Eds.), *The cost of not knowing* (pp. 329–333). Washington, DC: Environmental Design Research Association.

Villeco, M., & Brill, M. (1981). *Environmental design/research: Concepts, methods, and values.* Washington, DC: National Endowment for the Arts.

Virgin Islands Planning Office (1977a). *Preliminary program, Virgin Islands coastal zone management.* Charlotte Amalie, St. Thomas: author.

Virgin Islands Planning Office (1977b). *Public attitude survey, technical supplement no. 2.* Charlotte Amalie, St. Thomas: author.

Weidemann, S., Anderson, J., Chin, Y., Perkins, N., Kirk, N., & Bain, B. (1989). *Resident evaluation: A basis for redevelopment.* Urbana: Housing Research and Development Program, University of Illinois.

Weinstein, C. S., & David, T. G. (Eds.) (1990). *Spaces for children: The built environment and child development.* New York: Plenum.

Weinstein, C. S., & Pinciotti, P. (1988). Changing a schoolyard: Intentions, design decisions, and behavioral outcomes. *Environment and Behavior, 20,* 345–371.

Welch, P., Parker, V., & Zeisel, J. (1984). *Independence through interdependence: Congregate living for older people.* Boston: Massachusetts Department of Elder Affairs.

Wener, R. (undated). *Environment–behavior research "success stories."* New York: Polytechnic Institute.

Wener, R., & Szigeti, F. (Eds.) (1988). *Cumulative index to the proceedings of the Environmental Design Research Association, Vols. 1–18, 1969–1987.* Oklahoma City: Environmental Design Research Association.

Wise, J. A., & Wise, B. K. (1984). *Bank interiors and bank robberies: A design approach to environmental security.* Seattle: James A. Wise and Associates.

Zeisel, J. (1976). *Stopping school property damage: Design and administrative guidelines to reduce school vandalism.* Arlington, VA: American Association of School Administrators.

Zeisel, J. (1981). *Inquiry by design.* Monterey, CA: Brooks/Cole.

Zeisel, J., Epp, G., & Demos, S. (1978). *Low-rise housing for older people: Behavioral criteria and design.* Washington, DC: U.S. Government Printing Office.

Zeisel, J., Epp, G., & Demos, S. (1984). *Mid-rise elevator housing for older people.* Washington, DC: U.S. Department of Housing and Urban Development.

Zeisel, J., & Griffin, M. (1975). *Charlesview housing: A diagnostic evaluation.* Cambridge, MA: Graduate School of Design, Harvard University.

Zube, E., Crystal, J., & Palmer, J. (1976). *Visitor Center design evaluation.* Amherst, MA: Institute for Man and Environment, University of Massachusetts.

Zube, E. H., & McLaughlin, M. (1978). Assessing perceived values of the coastal zone. *Coastal Zone, 1,* 360–371.

Zube, E. H., Pitt, D. G., & Anderson, T. (1975). Perception and prediction of scenic resource values of the Northeast. In E. H. Zube, R. Brush, & J. Fabos (Eds.), *Landscape assessment: Values, perceptions, and resources.* Stroudsburg, PA: Dowden, Hutchinson & Ross.

INDEX